Introducing quality assurance of education for democratic citizenship in schools

Comparative study of 10 countries

Edited by Hermann Josef Abs

Council of Europe Publishing

The opinions expressed in this work are the responsibility of the authors and do not necessarily reflect the official policy of the Council of Europe.

All rights reserved. No part of this publication may be translated, reproduced or transmitted, in any form or by any means, electronic (CD-Rom, Internet, etc.) or mechanical, including photocopying, recording or any information storage or retrieval system, without prior permission in writing from the Public Information and Publications Division, Directorate of Communication (F-67075 Strasbourg Cedex or publishing@coe.int).

STIFTUNG
ERINNERUNG, VERANTWORTUNG
UND ZUKUNFT

Cover design: Document and Publications Production Department,
Council of Europe
Layout: Jouve, Paris

Council of Europe Publishing
F-67075 Strasbourg Cedex
http://book.coe.int

ISBN 978-92-871-6522-0
© Council of Europe, February 2009

Printed at the Council of Europe

Contents

Preface by the Council of Europe 5

Preface by the Foundation "Remembrance, Responsibility and Future" 7

Acknowledgements 9

Chapter 1 – Aim, background and methodology of the study 11
Hermann Josef Abs

Chapter 2 – Country-specific reports

Member states of the Council of Europe

Czech Republic 25
Viola Horská

Estonia 61
Anu Toots

Germany 80
Tobias Diemer

Latvia 104
Irēna Žogla and Rudīte Andersone

Lithuania 133
Elvyra Acienė

Poland 158
Alicja Pacewicz

Russian Federation 190
Galina Kovalyova and Elena Rutkovskaia

Ukraine 215
Olena Pometun

Additional countries

Belarus 245
Galina Shaton

Israel 267
Yael Ofarim

Chapter 3 – The tool from the point of view of evaluation theory 299
Harm Kuper

Chapter 4 – Preconditions for tool implementation 315
Sarah Werth

Chapter 5 – Approaches to enhancing use of the tool 329
Hermann Josef Abs

List of authors 339

Preface by the Council of Europe

It is my great pleasure to introduce the readers to this book, which is devoted to the topical issue of quality assurance. The phenomenon that is described by this term is both new and old. Society has always looked into ways of ensuring, supporting and developing quality of education. What is somewhat different is that in the past the emphasis was often put on quality control based on externally imposed criteria and inspections. Today, there is a growing acceptance that this approach is not sufficient. Similar to the emerging trends in other areas, less punitive and more motivational approaches are promoted. Participatory self-evaluation is seen today by many as a more effective way of ensuring quality than external assessment. On the other hand, the two approaches can be mutually supportive and complimentary.

From the Council of Europe perspective, the concepts of democracy and human rights lie at the heart of quality assurance, because it implies that all school actors express their views and opinions about school life; such views and opinions are taken into account; decisions about future school development are taken jointly and everyone is involved in putting such decisions into practice. And this process is facilitated in a democratic, inclusive and respectful way.

Quality assurance in this sense requires time, resources and commitment, as well as support from relevant authorities. Practical guidelines and systematic training are also needed. The "Tool for Quality Assurance of Education for Democratic Citizenship in Schools" (2005) published jointly by UNESCO, the Council of Europe and the Centre for Educational Policy Studies (Ljubljana) aims to provide guidance for various actors. The present publication looks at whether and how the tool could be used in a particular context, based on examples from several countries. The tool is also being piloted in a number of countries and further supporting materials will be developed on the basis of this experience. The tool itself is part of a series of manuals produced as part of the "EDC/HRE Pack", which is being developed by the Council of Europe for various audiences on specific aspects of citizenship and human rights education. It includes a "tool on key issues of EDC/HRE for policy makers", a "tool on democratic governance of schools" and a "tool on teacher training for EDC/HRE".

In conclusion, I would like to thank the Foundation "Remembrance, Responsibility and Future" for their generous contribution to this project, and the German Institute for International Educational Research (DIPF) for the enthusiastic and thorough realisation of this very timely initiative. We hope that the present publication will serve as an inspiration for researchers, policy makers and education practitioners, and we wish you the best of success in promoting quality education for all.

César Bîrzea
Chairperson of the Steering Committee for Education

Preface by the Foundation "Remembrance, Responsibility and Future"

On behalf of the Foundation "Remembrance, Responsibility and Future" I would like to express my thanks to the Council of Europe for publishing this study, which was produced with the support of the foundation.

The Foundation "Remembrance, Responsibility and Future" was established in 2000 and entrusted with the task of disbursing payments to former forced labourers and other victims of National Socialist injustice. As of 2007, a total of €4.37 billion has been paid out to more than 1.66 million people in almost 100 countries. Following the completion of payments last year, the foundation's main task has been to support international projects that strengthen co-operation in a spirit of partnership between Germany and countries subjected to particular hardship under National Socialism. Support has been provided to almost 1 500 international projects in three activity areas: critical examination of history; working for democracy and human rights; and humanitarian commitment to the victims of National Socialism.

In its priority partner countries, the foundation has supported initiatives to promote education for democratic citizenship among young people. It has provided financial assistance for and published several studies, including three last year on the theme of civic education in Belarus, the Russian Federation and Ukraine. A further study on democratic education in Israel is to be published in 2008. In 2006, the foundation and the German Youth for Understanding Committee launched an international essay competition for school pupils on the theme of "democracy at school". The young authors who wrote the winning essays have been invited to Berlin to discuss their experiences with experts from the worlds of politics and science. We support the international academy of the German Society for Democratic Education in providing training for teachers, school heads and lecturers on school development on the basis of children's rights.

In 2005, the foundation established the programme Europeans for Peace – Looking Back and Moving Forward. This programme promotes international partnerships between schools or non-school institutions in Germany, central, eastern and South-Eastern Europe and Israel that implement history projects and/or take a critical look at democracy and human rights today. By encouraging the partnerships to share the knowledge and experience gained in their joint projects, the programme also supports democratic school development in the participating countries.

In April 2006, the German Institute for International Educational Research (DIPF) launched an initiative to implement the "Tool for Quality Assurance of Education for Democratic Citizenship in Schools". The tool was developed by the Council of Europe, UNESCO and the Centre for Educational Policy Studies (Ljubljana). The foundation is convinced of the value of the tool and its underlying principles and has therefore supported the initiative to examine how the tool can be implemented in 10 countries.

A team under the leadership of Dr Hermann Josef Abs at the DIPF quickly succeeded in finding experts to undertake the necessary reporting functions in each country. In November 2006, the draft reports were discussed in Frankfurt with the tool's developers and the authors of the country reports. Together with Ms Ólafsdóttir from the Council of Europe and Ms Tinio from UNESCO, the DIPF also presented the results of the reports in Sarajevo in September 2007 at the XIII Congress of the World Council of Comparative Education Societies (WCCES), which was held on the theme of "Living together: education and intercultural dialogue". The authors from Israel and Poland explained the opportunities for using the tool in their countries. Other experts, including Ulrike Wolff-Jontofsohn, Wolfgang Mitter and Harm Kuper, examined the results of the studies from a variety of different perspectives.

Thanks to the excellent work of the DIPF, the publication not only includes country reports but also a comparison of the specific evaluation systems in the given countries. The DIPF has also compiled an overview of the applicability and relevance of the tool from international perspectives and examined the quality assurance requirements in the field of education for democratic citizenship (EDC). The accuracy of the reports was also confirmed through the political feedback provided by the EDC co-ordinators in the participating countries. We would like to express our gratitude to the DIPF for implementing this project and for the fruitful co-operation between our organisations.

Our thanks also go to Ms Ólafsdóttir from the Council of Europe and Ms Tinio from UNESCO for supporting the project and publishing the results. Above all, we would like to express our gratitude to all the authors who examined the application of the tool in their countries. We very much hope that the education bodies and civil society actors in the various countries will take up the challenge and adapt and introduce the tool in the near future.

Dr Martin Salm

Acknowledgements

First of all we are indebted to the Council of Europe. The compilation of material within the context of the European Year of Citizenship through Education 2005 has been a precondition for all subsequent initiatives. We thank Dr Reinhild Otte, Chairperson of the Ad hoc Advisory Group on Education for Democratic Citizenship and Human Rights at the Council of Europe, who saw the need for an initiative and helped to develop it in close contact with the Foundation "Remembrance, Responsibility and Future".

Furthermore we are grateful for the inestimable support provided by the Department of School and Out-of-School Education within the Council of Europe. We owe special thanks in this regard to Ólöf Ólafsdóttir and Yulia Pererva: if they had not put their weight behind the initiative with regard to the general activities on education for democratic citizenship, we would not have dared to embark on the project. Moreover, we would also have been lost without their support for the political recognition of the research presented here. Additional counselling was provided by Linda Tinio from UNESCO, with respect to the World Programme for Human Rights Education.

The Foundation "Remembrance, Responsibility and Future" gave its support not only financially but also by making important contacts in the field and asking questions that contributed considerably to the development of the project. In this respect, we would especially like to thank Sonja Böhme and Dr Ralf Possekel.

We are additionally indebted to two authors of the "Tool for Quality Assurance of Education for Democratic Citizenship in Schools": Dr Janez Krek and Professor Dr Vedrana Spajić-Vrkaš discussed their ideas on the use of the tool with the authors of the country-specific reports.

A publication like this one does not purely rely on its authors: it would not have been feasible without the support of many other people who worked on various aspects. In particular, we would like to thank Amira Bieber, who worked as an assistant on the project at the German Institute for International Educational Research (DIPF), and who organised contracts and financing as well as managed the first project conference in Frankfurt-on-Main.

Moreover, we especially thank Stephan Malerius, Professor Dr Wolfgang Mitter, Dr Botho von Kopp, Dr Gerlind Schmidt, Dr Wendelin Sroka, and Dr Ulrike Wolff-Jontofsohn for reviewing the first drafts of the country reports.

DIPF also provided assistance via contributions made by student assistants, with our thanks in this regard going to Stephan Müller-Mathis, Annette Richter, Sarah Troxel and Alexander Wicker. We appreciate their engagement in many ways during different stages of the project.

Finally, we would like to thank Dr Simon Scott-Kemball and Dr Gwendolyn Schulte, who independently worked as language consultants on different parts of the project.

Chapter 1 – Aim, background and methodology of the study

Hermann Josef Abs

1. Context and purpose of the study

For over a decade the Council of Europe has been working on policies in the field of education for democratic citizenship (EDC). One result has been that the Committee of Ministers of the Council of Europe agreed on a recommendation stating that EDC is central to educational politics, and that it is a "factor for innovation in terms of organising and managing overall education systems, as well as curricula and teaching methods" (Recommendation Rec(2002)12). According to this recommendation, European governments acknowledged their responsibility for ensuring the cultural basis of democracy through education. However, politics is not so simple that supranational recommendations are immediately translated into policy in national states. This gap between agreed and realised policies has been termed a "compliance gap". One of the most logical reasons for non-compliance comes from a lack of awareness or competences. Therefore the Council of Europe concentrated on producing materials that could help raise awareness and develop competences. Key products resulting from this effort have been collected as an "EDC/HRE Pack" since 2005. This collection covers the areas of policy making, democratic governance of educational institutions, teacher training and quality assurance. The "Tool for Quality Assurance of Education for Democratic Citizenship in Schools" (Bîrzea et al., 2005), which is one of these materials, forms the reference document for this study.

This study analyses relevant conditions and possible activities with regard to implementing the tool in 10 national educational systems. As relevant conditions, the study considers the existing attempts to deliver educational quality within countries, together with the teacher training programmes that accompany these attempts. As possible activities, national adaptations of the tool, and various ways of working with different target groups, are also taken into account.

The following sections provide background information concerning the project. This will help the reader understand why the tool needs to be adapted in different circumstances. Section 2 presents points of reference that open theoretical perspectives on the work presented. Section 3 provides a rationale for the selection of participating countries and gives and describes the methodology used when conducting this study. Finally, Section 4 provides an overview of the remaining contents of this book.

2. Points of reference for the research presented in this book

Besides the tool itself, the study concept relies on some theoretical considerations deriving from comparative education, from school development research, from theories of evaluation, and from research on innovations. This section looks at each of these theoretical considerations in turn.

2.1. The "Tool for Quality Assurance of Education for Democratic Citizenship in Schools"

The tool is designed to answer the needs of all those who are responsible for developing EDC measures at school. It provides a conceptual background as well as exemplary materials showing how the quality of schooling with respect to education for democratic citizenship can be ensured.

The tool was developed as a result of analysing EDC experience in South-East European countries and by adapting mostly western European materials to this context. Thereby the principles, methods and instruments have been described, all of which are intended as a generic resource for users in any country. In order to make the tool manageable for people without previous knowledge of it, the first chapters explain its basic concepts. Thus there are first of all introductions to EDC, quality assurance, evaluation and school development planning before these concepts are all related to each other. At its core, the tool offers an evaluative framework for EDC in schools, providing a set of broader indicators in the sense of questions an evaluation has to answer (for example, "Are the design and practices of assessment within the school consistent with EDC?"). Each indicator is accompanied by a set of sub-themes (for example, fairness, transparency and improvement) coupled with concrete statements that can be taken as evaluation checkpoints (for example, "Teachers do not use assessment of knowledge and skills in specific subjects for enforcing discipline"). Different ways of collecting data and working with results in school development planning are also illustrated.

The tool is a free online resource and can be downloaded from the Council of Europe's website: www.coe.int/t/dg4/education/edc/Source/Pdf/Documents/2006_4_Tool4QA_EDC.pdf

Further information about the Council of Europe's work in the field of EDC is available at: www.coe.int/edc.

2.2. Comparative education research

As the study presented here deals with different educational systems, the research tradition of comparative education (Bray, 2007; Postlethwaite, 1995) can be used as a reference in order to reflect the given aims and alternatives in conducting the work. The objectives of comparative education can vary with respect to research interests. Hörner et al. (2007) distinguishes four classical purposes of comparative studies:

- ideographic purpose: this purpose is fulfilled by various types of educational systems. A study may be interested in identifying common structures and developments in different systems, or in distinguishing the principles that guide the actors in different settings just because there is scientific interest in the phenomenon;
- meliorist purpose: for this purpose the units of analysis are determined by the goal of finding a feature in one educational system that may be useful to improve another system. This approach is popular but nevertheless problematic, because of the entelechy of each system, which may result in the same feature working differently in one system than in another;
- evolutionist purpose: here researchers try to discover emerging developments within at least two compared systems. The emerging trends are then taken as a point of reference when analysing countries that have not yet shown any signs of these trends. However, there is an inherent danger in this approach in the often undisputed normative understanding of the new discovered trends;
- experimental purpose: in this approach the compared systems are viewed as participants in an experiment. Researchers are interested in learning about the different systems by the way they deal with a common intervention. Unlike a scientific experiment, however, there is no random assignment of interventions to the experiment or to the control group. Preconditions and implementation procedures differ.

This study is primarily linked to two of these purposes: ideographic and experimental. First of all, to some degree the different country reports follow an ideographic purpose: information about specific features within the educational systems of 10 countries is presented in a systematic way, and compared. However, this alone is insufficient, given that broader up-to-date descriptions of the educational systems within nine of the 10 participating countries can be found elsewhere (Hörner et al., 2007; Döbert, 2007; Giedraitienė, Kiliuvienė and Brauckmann, 2007; Hellwig, Lipenkowa, 2007; Hörner and Nowosad, 2007; Průcha, 2007; Rajangu, 2007; Schmidt, 2007; Sroka, 2007; Žogla, Andersone, Černova, 2007), along with two recent international comparisons on general EDC within Europe (Bîrzea, 2004; Eurydice, 2005). In addition to specialising in the relationship between quality assurance and EDC, this study therefore has a second, experimental purpose. It presents all countries in the comparison with new material, the "Tool for Quality Assurance of Education for Democratic Citizenship in Schools". Descriptions are not purely ideographic, but selected and given as preconditions for the implementation of the material, accompanied by the individual authors' ideas on how to support implementation given their country-specific context.

However, departing from most experimental studies, this study actually precedes the real experiment, which is the practical implementation of the tool. Indeed, a feasibility study can be looked at as a mental experiment. In this sense, we can interpret the authors of the 10 country reports as making different forecasts and showing different opportunities according to their country-specific context. This emphasises the fact that it is not only the situation within a country that shapes the content of reports, but also the standpoint of the individual authors.

2.3. School development research

The basic assumption in the field of school development is that schooling can make a difference to students' competences and attitudes in a way that is relevant for democracy. Theories of school development (Fend, 2008; Dalin and Kitson, 2005) distinguish between three main levels for initiating change within school practices:
- level of the school system;
- level of schools as organisations;
- level of different actors within schools.

At the system level, schooling is influenced by the legal setting, which defines the space for decision making for different political actors (national, federal, regional and school board actors). Further, policy makers influence the composition of students by limiting access and giving rights to entitlement to certain grades; they also influence the composition of the teaching body by defining the study routes that lead into the teaching profession, as well as selection procedures and remuneration. They can choose to give more or less financial autonomy to schools, and offer incentives (or punishments) for the (non)fulfilment of certain tasks. Further, policy makers decide on curriculum issues and on the mechanisms of distribution resources to schools or single tasks. Finally, policy is responsible for the character and liability of quality measures and for the legitimisation of the system to the public.

A second source for the varying potential of schools consists in the fact that they can act to different degrees as organisations. Being an organisation in the full sense of the word means having the right to create oneself as a social entity and to determine the end of that entity. Being an organisation implies the establishment of organisational goals and a structure of tasks, which enables co-operation and division of labour. To fulfil their tasks, organisations need certain resources at their disposal. Schools differ with regard to these criteria, and therefore their general scripts of organisational development need to be adapted. As the establishment of goals, distribution of resources, division of labour and co-operation of different subjects are all bound up with a multitude of interests, organisations rely on internal procedures when it comes to making decisions and controlling their implementation.

Finally, the individual members of a school are also actors for change or continuation. Individuals within a school can be divided into various groups. Three groups interact permanently: pupils, teachers and the school management. Further, groups interact but are not as involved in the core processes as the other three: parents, the community and educational authorities/supervisors. Schools differ with respect to the homogeneity of these groups, especially as groups and group members possess certain capacities that enable them to take part in educational processes. They all have limited resources, pursue their own interests, have ideals, and possess certain competences. This means that the educational processes of schooling are essentially built on differences and on the development of given capacities.

The countries in this study differ with respect to the weight given to these three levels in school development planning. However, contemporary thinking about the development of schooling in all systems is dominated by two competing yet also intertwined discourses: on accountability, and on autonomy.

The discourse on accountability tries to strengthen the function of schools by mechanisms of legitimisation and control. School is viewed as a highly reliable organisation that needs frequent monitoring by the educational authorities to guarantee that every member enjoys certain rights and fulfils his or her professional duties. School administrations follow the model of a professional bureaucracy, ensuring an equal distribution of resources, centrally planned initiatives for professional development and uniform procedures of student assessment.

The discourse on autonomy, on the other hand, seeks to strengthen the development of schools by methods of self-organisation. School is viewed as a unit of organisational learning. Development can be supported and asked for from the outside, but only the organisation itself can undertake it. Professionals are seen to be responsible for deciding how to distribute resources, what additional competences they need and how grading should be implemented. Autonomy is looked on as the precondition for meeting the individual needs of students and for adaptive education.

Any attempt to relate these two discourses to each other generates many questions, such as: Does a certain degree of autonomy invite corruption? Do rigorous accountability procedures and bureaucracy act as effective controls, or do they distract from pedagogical work and prohibit the development of self-responsibility? Is it possible to build up effective accountability systems that are so flexible that they do not harm adaptive approaches within single units of the system? Is there any evidence that professionals are sufficiently capable of deciding for themselves which further competences they need? How are the interests of different groups incorporated in an autonomous school? How is it possible to stimulate development within a context of autonomy?

As a general tendency, these questions are today often addressed by focusing accountability measures more on the results of schooling and allowing greater latitude as far as processes are concerned (for example, Döbert, Klieme and Sroka, 2004): these developments represent a trend within many educational systems. The idea is that schools legitimise their relative autonomy by accounting for the outcome of their work. However, in practice things are more difficult: complications ensue when new accountability procedures clash with old approaches. Further difficulties are created by a lack of professional competences when it comes to interpreting centralised tests and student results, or in terms of working towards achieving the newly established benchmarks. Finally, complications may also result from difficulties in the definition and determination of the outcomes to be measured, because in an output steering system, the scope and measurement procedure define the relevant goals.

The tool focuses on the level of a school as an organisation, and is inspired by the idea that quality within schooling is best developed by means of participatory self-evaluation. Schools as autonomous entities and the different actors within them are seen as being able to ensure an improvement in quality. However, as this is not the dominant approach in all 10 countries, it is necessary to adjust this approach on various grounds.

2.4. Theories of evaluation

The field of research on evaluation focuses on the advantages and disadvantages of various evaluation approaches. Evaluation must not only describe a phenomenon, but should also contextualise this description with respect to purpose (Scriven, 2003). Prototypical contextualisations of evaluations are within personnel or organisational development, domain-specific research, and financial or legal controlling. Evaluation approaches and methods on how to conduct evaluation vary according to their context (Sanders and Davidson, 2003).

Three guiding purposes for the selection of approaches and evaluation methods may be identified. First, a unit (school, class, teacher, student) may need a certain type of information in order to optimise its work. Second, knowledge that can be used as a general resource for planning interventions may be required. Third, donors or responsible administrations may need certain information to legitimise their investment. Following Chelimsky (1997; Abs and Klieme, 2005), three evaluation paradigms can be derived from these purposes: developmental, research and legitimisation.

Working within the developmental paradigm requires the participation of all stakeholders, who are expected to engage in development. Even the evaluation criteria have to be developed or at least discussed with the persons in question, who are expected to change their behaviour or adopt new shared working practices. Evaluations that follow this paradigm focus on objects that can be influenced by the stakeholders, as otherwise they could lead to frustration.

In sharp contrast, the research paradigm excludes stakeholders from taking decisions on the evaluation. Even participation in an evaluation may be regulated from outside. People are randomly selected to take part in a study as a control or a treatment group, meaning that they cannot decide whether or not they are confronted with the intervention. The results are not necessarily discussed with the participants, but related to scientific theories and other research findings.

In similar fashion the legitimisation paradigm excludes those who are the focus of evaluation from all decisions about the evaluation process, albeit for different reasons. Whereas in the research paradigm exclusion is justified by the need to avoid influencing the phenomenon being studied, in the legitimisation paradigm the people being evaluated are aware of the criteria they are being evaluated on. It is the purpose of this type of evaluation to make them comply with these criteria. Unlike the research paradigm, the whole setting is constructed to elicit social desirability. In this respect there is a link to the developmental paradigm. Both paradigms want to influence the field, but whereas the developmental paradigm wants to make people change themselves, the legitimisation paradigm imposes external necessities. Within the tool these paradigms are introduced under the notions of quality assurance and quality control, and are discussed from the perspective of democratic citizenship.

Answering the demands of practitioners, researches and professional societies for evaluation have developed standards for the planning and conduct of evaluations (for example, Stufflebeam, 2003). However, these standards are general statements and not specific to the purposes of evaluations, and may thus be used as broader guidelines but not as action plans.

2.5. Innovation research

Research on innovation deals with questions such as what can be changed and how change happens. Of special interest in our context are strategies that enhance change by providing system actors with new materials. The literature on innovation makes it clear that change is generally difficult to achieve and typically constrained by many factors (Marinova and Phillimore, 2003; Rogers, 2003; Sternberg, Pretz and Kaufman, 2003; Spillane, Reiser and Reimer, 2002; Weiss and Bucuvalas, 1980). Constraints are related to what is already there, to the process of adaptation and to the expected use of an innovation.

Thanks to learning psychology we have long known that the single most important factor for what a person is capable of learning is what he or she already knows (Ausubel, 1968). At a system level, it is also true to say that given institutional or organisational patterns are a central precondition for change. We suppose that everything that is already in place formerly had – or even still has – a function in the system.

Not all innovations directly require something that exists to be abolished, but in every case innovations require resources that are used to sustain the existing system. A belief in the adequacy of existing approaches in the field of quality assurance is a central precondition for debates on innovation. Or, put differently: system actors will only be motivated to adopt new patterns or to change their existing patterns if new approaches are sufficiently convincing from their perspective.

Innovations may affect the working procedures of a system or can impact on both procedures and aims. In the first case, system actors contextualise the innovation by a kind of "utility test" (Weiss and Bucuvalas, 1980), checking whether the new ways of working are more effective or more efficient than the old ones. When they are convinced of the usefulness of the innovation, change can take place. From the perspective of organisational development, this kind of innovation is often referred to as "single loop learning" (Argyris and Schön, 1978). In the second case, system actors have to contextualise the innovation beforehand with respect to the objectives of their system. They check whether the proposed shift in ideology is consistent as such and makes sense. Weiss and Bucuvalas (1980) call this checking a "truth test". If an innovation holds true within the ideological mindset of a system, it still has to pass a utility test, which makes the adoption of an innovation more complicated. Because an organisational change in terms of aims and procedures is required, Argyris and Schön (1978) talk of "double loop learning". One threat to this process is that change happens only at the level of officially declared objectives and not at the deeper level of working processes within a school. Another threat is that new working procedures are partially introduced, yet the need to rethink the whole system is overlooked. If so, this might affect the sustainability of the innovation.

Moreover, innovation research teaches us that it is not only the willingness and ability of the actors within one organisation that can be held accountable for change, but also their context. In our case, this means not only establishing the preconditions within schools, but also the different support and control systems that work around schools. These actors are central to the reception of an innovation in five ways. First, they have to agree on how to use the tool. Second, they must support change by recognising the new material. Third, they can integrate the tool into their practice. Fourth, they can sustain the implementation process by offering training on how to use the tool. And fifth, educational support and control agencies can make it obligatory for schools to use the tool or tool-related approaches.

3. Methodology of the study

This section provides a short description of the methodology of the study, offering a rationale for the selection of participating countries and experts, listing the guiding questions for country reports written by the experts, and finally describing the working processes behind the conducting of the study.

3.1. Selection of participation countries and country experts

As mentioned above, the authors of the tool are educational experts with experience in South-Eastern and western European countries. For a project supported by the Council of Europe, precisely how other European countries react to the tool is of particular interest. The final selection of participating countries was made by the financing body of the study, the Foundation "Remembrance, Responsibility and Future". This is reflected in the specific focus of the project: eight of the 10 countries (namely, Belarus, Estonia, Lithuania, Latvia, Poland, Russian Federation, Czech Republic and Ukraine) have a common experience in that they suffered from German occupation during the Third Reich, and were obliged to suffer forced labour of their people during that period. Because of the history of the Third Reich, the two additional countries selected were Israel and Germany.

Today, the political preconditions of these 10 countries vary greatly. Eight share the historical experience of at least forty years of communism (except Israel and the western half of modern Germany). Eight are full members of the Council of Europe (namely, all except Belarus and Israel). Six are members of the European Union (with the exception of Belarus, Israel, Russian Federation and Ukraine). Notwithstanding these historical differences, all selected countries are currently undergoing a process of educational reform, and have witnessed changes within the system of quality assurance in recent years. Moreover, all are members of UNESCO, which also promotes the tool within the framework of its human rights activities.

Within the participating countries, experts in the field have been systematically selected, with first a list being drawn up comprising experts from the fields of science, administration and civil foundations for every country. These lists were then internally ranked on the basis of publications, before inviting the best-ranked experts to participate in the project.

3.2. Guiding questions for country reports

To ensure comparable information, all country reports were obliged to follow the same set of questions. The questions aimed at assessing the relevance and usability of the tool in schools in the participating countries, and were developed on the basis of the points of reference stated in Section 2 of this introduction. They aim at exploring the preconditions for adopting the tool within each country in more detail, and are divided into four main blocks.

The first block asks about the existing approaches to school evaluation and related policies within countries. The second block deals with the understanding of the tool from the perspective of the country in question. The third block requires a synthesis assessment of how the tool is viewed from the perspective of the existing evaluation system within a country. The final fourth block requests ideas on how the use of the European material could be promoted. These ideas should serve as possible starting points for practical work in the respective countries. The following list shows the guiding questions in detail:

1. **School evaluation in your country**
   1.1. Does your country perform school evaluations?
      - If so: what kind of evaluation is conducted? (Internal versus external; inspections and/or standardised assessment of achievement.) Please describe the typical procedure;
      - If not: is there an ongoing debate on the evaluation of schools?
   1.2. To what extent are methods of evaluation an issue in teacher training programmes?
   1.3. How are the results of evaluation treated in schools?
      - How are the results of assessments discussed in schools? What groups within the school participate in the discussion? What does the typical procedure look like?
      - To what extent are school administrators and external counsellors involved in the treatment of evaluation results?

2. **The "Tool for Quality Assurance of Education for Democratic Citizenship in Schools"**
   2.1. To what extent is the tool comprehensible and coherent? (If possible, refer to the individual chapters of the tool, and specify problems.)
   2.2. Does similar material exist in your country already? (If so, please describe it.)

3. **The tool as an instrument of school evaluation in your country**
   3.1. Conditions for using the tool in schools
      3.1.1. What circumstances might promote the use of the tool?
      3.1.2. What difficulties do you anticipate? Where do the obstacles lie?
      3.1.3. What parts of the tool appear to be particularly apt for use in schools in your country?
      3.1.4. Whom do you regard as the target group of your tool (pupils; teachers; school heads; school board; administration; ministries; other)? Please explain.
   3.2. Systemic conditions of use
      3.2.1. How does the tool (its design, procedure) match the objectives and ideas of quality assurance and evaluation in your country?
         - Does the tool contain aspects that might cause a problem in the context of your country? Which? Why?
      3.2.2. Considering the background of teacher training in your country, can you imagine teachers working independently with a translated version of the tool, or with the original English language version?
         - What kind and scope of training or counselling would be required?
         - What kinds of material might contribute to the use of the tool?

> 3.2.3. What other measures might facilitate its use?
> - Resources?
> - Incentives?
> - Adaptation of the tool to the national context?
> - Deletion of aspects for the national context?
> 3.2.4. How can the tool be applied to different school types?
> - For what school types does the tool seem to be particularly apt?
> - What problems occur for the other school types?
>
> **4. Ideas for an implementation process**
> 4.1. How should a process be designed for the schools so that they experience the use of the tool as relevant and helpful?
> - What could be the first steps in implementing the tool?
> - Who might be the local contact persons or agency?
>
> 4.2. How could the use of the tool be integrated into international school partnerships (exchange of teachers/students)?
>
> 4.3. What kinds of alternative scenarios can you imagine for using the tool?

3.3. Working processes

After obtaining the services of experts under contract in each country, drafts of country-specific reports have been written from August 2006 onwards. During a conference in Frankfurt (Germany), the first drafts were discussed in November 2006. At this event authors could compare their own work with the work of experts from other countries. Additionally a blind review process was introduced, which allowed each expert to receive feedback on his or her report. Scientists with experience in the respective country but not resident there were chosen as reviewers. On the basis of the discussions during the conference and these reviews, the country reports were revised by the experts. For most countries, a second review was made by the national EDC co-ordinator, who is responsible for linking the work of the Council of Europe with that of the national administrations. These second reviews centred on correctly describing the legal structure of the educational system within each country. Overall, this ensured an iterative process of finalising the country reports, mainly during 2007.

The final versions of the country reports were analysed as follows. First, the material from country reports was ordered in the way of juxtaposition. For this, the guiding questions and further theoretical considerations were used. After this, a comparison was made, which was first presented in parts at the 13th Congress of the World Council of Comparative Education Societies in Sarajevo (Bosnia and Herzegovina), in September 2007.

Country reports differ in the extent to which they represent the official position of a country's administration. Things may look different when viewed from the outside (for example, Wulf and Malerius, 2007). Nevertheless, although the working procedures within the project may allow for a certain number of evaluations that are specific to the political situation of countries, it is important to integrate these positions as part of the self-perceived situation in a country and to use this as a starting point in the implementation work.

4. Overview of the following chapters

The following chapters contain the country-specific reports as provided by the relevant experts. First, we present reports from Council of Europe member states, and then the reports about the two additional UNESCO member states selected for this study.

Thereafter follows a comparative part that comprises three chapters. One chapter examines the tool and current approaches to evaluation from the perspective of evaluation theory. A second chapter analyses the conditions for implementing the tool according to country reports, while a third chapter puts together ideas with the aim of enhancing implementation.

References

Abs, Hermann Josef and Klieme, Eckhard (2005). "Standards für schulbezogene Evaluation" (Standards for School Evaluation), *Zeitschrift für Erziehungswissenschaft*, 4/2005, 45-62.

Argyris, Chris and Schön, Donald (1978). *Organizational Learning: A Theory of Action Perspective*, Reading, MA: Addison Wesley.

Ausubel, David P. (1968). *The Psychology of Meaningful Verbal Learning*, New York: Grune and Stratton.

Bîrzea, César (ed.) (2004). *All-European Study on Education for Democratic Citizenship Policies*, Strasbourg: Council of Europe Publishing.

Bîrzea, César; Cecchini, Michela; Harrison, Cameron; Krek, Janez; Spajić-Vrkaš, Vedrana (2005). "Tool for Quality Assurance of Education for Democratic Citizenship in Schools". Paris: UNESCO, Council of Europe and CEPS.

Bray, Mark (2007). "Actors and Purposes in Comparative Education", in Bray, Mark; Adamson, Bob; Mason, Mark (eds.), *Comparative Education Research. Approaches and Methods*, Dordrecht: Springer, 15-38.

Chelimsky, Eleanor (1997). "Thoughts for a New Evaluation Society", *Evaluation*, 3. 97-118.

Dalin, Per and Kitson, Katherine (2005). *School Development. Theories and Strategies. An International Handbook*, New York: Continuum International.

Döbert, Hans (2007). "Germany", in Hörner, Wolfgang; Döbert, Hans; von Kopp, Botho; Mitter, Wolfgang (eds.), *The Education Systems of Europe*, Dordrecht: Springer, 299-325.

Döbert, Hans; Klieme, Eckhard; Sroka, Wendelin (eds.) (2004). *Conditions of School Performance in Seven Countries*, Münster: Waxmann.

Eurydice (2005). *Citizenship Education at Schools in Europe*, Brussels: European Commission.

Fend, Helmut (2008). *Schule gestalten: Systemsteuerung, Schulentwicklung und Unterrichtsqualität*, Wiesbaden: Verlag für Sozialwissenschaft.

Giedraitienė, Elvyra; Kiliuvienė, Dalia; Brauckmann, Stefan (2007). "Lithuania", in Hörner, Wolfgang; Döbert, Hans; von Kopp, Botho; Mitter, Wolfgang (eds.), *The Education Systems of Europe*, Dordrecht: Springer, 451-469.

Hellwig, Wolfgang and Lipenkowa, Janna (2007). "Ukraine", in Hörner, Wolfgang; Döbert, Hans; von Kopp, Botho; Mitter, Wolfgang (eds.), *The Education Systems of Europe*, Dordrecht: Springer, 808-825.

Hörner, Wolfgang; Döbert, Hans; von Kopp, Botho; Mitter, Wolfgang (eds.) (2007). *The Education Systems of Europe*, Dordrecht: Springer.

Hörner, Wolfgang and Nowosad, Inetta (2007). "Poland", in Hörner, Wolfgang; Döbert, Hans; von Kopp, Botho; Mitter, Wolfgang (eds.), *The Education Systems of Europe*, Dordrecht: Springer, 590-606.

Marinova, Dora and Phillimore, John (2003). "Models of Innovation", in Shavinina, Larisa V. (ed.), *The International Handbook on Innovation*, Kidlington, Oxford: Elsevier, 44-53.

Postlethwaite, Thomas Neville (ed.) (1995). The Encyclopaedia of Comparative Education and National Systems of Education (2nd edn), Oxford: Pergamon.

Průcha, Jan (2007). "Czech Republic", in Hörner, Wolfgang; Döbert, Hans; von Kopp, Botho; Mitter, Wolfgang (eds.), *The Education Systems of Europe*, Dordrecht: Springer, 166-183.

Rajangu, Väino (2007). "Estonia", in Hörner, Wolfgang; Döbert, Hans; von Kopp, Botho; Mitter, Wolfgang (eds.), *The Education Systems of Europe*, Dordrecht: Springer, 237-248.

Recommendation Rec(2002)12 of the Committee of Ministers of the Council of Europe to member states on education for democratic citizenship (adopted by the

Committee of Ministers on 16 October 2002 at the 812th meeting of the Ministers' Deputies).

Rogers, Everett M. (2003). *Diffusion of Innovations* (5th edn), New York: Free Press.

Sanders, James R. and Davidson, E. Jane (2003). "A Model for School Evaluation", in Kellaghan, T.; Stufflebeam, D.L. (eds.), *International Handbook of Educational Evaluation. Part Two: Practice*. Dordrecht: Kluwer, 806-826.

Schmidt, Gerlind (2007). "Russian Federation", in Hörner, Wolfgang; Döbert, Hans; von Kopp, Botho; Mitter, Wolfgang (eds.), *The Education Systems of Europe*, Dordrecht: Springer, 646-668.

Scriven, Michael (2003). "Evaluation Theory and Metatheory", in Kellaghan, T. and Stufflebeam, D.L. (eds.), *International Handbook of Educational Evaluation. Part One: Perspectives*, Dordrecht: Kluwer, 15-30.

Spillane, James P.; Reiser, Brian J.; Reimer, Todd (2002). "Policy Implementation and Cognition: Reframing and Refocusing Implementation Research", *Review of Educational Research*, 72, 387-431.

Sroka, Wendelin (2007). "Belarus", in Hörner, Wolfgang; Döbert, Hans; von Kopp, Botho; Mitter, Wolfgang (eds.), *The Education Systems of Europe*, Dordrecht: Springer, 85-103.

Sternberg, Robert J.; Pretz, Jean E.; Kaufman, James C. (2003). "Types of Innovations", in Shavinina, Larisa V. (ed.), *The International Handbook on Innovation*, Kidlington, Oxford: Elsevier, 158-169.

Stufflebeam, Daniel L. (2003). "Professional Standards and Principles of Evaluations", in Kellaghan, T. and Stufflebeam, D.L. (eds.), *International Handbook of Educational Evaluation. Part One: Perspectives*, Dordrecht: Kluwer, 279-302.

Weiss, Carol H. and Bucuvalas, Michael J. (1980). "Truth Tests and Utility Tests: Decision-makers' Frames of Reference for Social Science Research", *American Sociological Review*, 45, 302-313.

Wulf, Annegret and Malerius, Stefan (2007). *Demokratiebildung in Belarus, Russland und der Ukraine. Rahmenbedingungen und Beispiele* (Education for Democratic Citizenship in Belarus, Russia and Ukraine. Constraining Factors and Examples), Berlin: Stiftung "Erinnerung, Verantwortung und Zukunft".

Žogla, Irēna; Andersone, Rudīte; Černova, Emilija (2007). "Latvia", in Hörner, Wolfgang; Döbert, Hans; von Kopp, Botho; Mitter, Wolfgang (eds.), *The Education Systems of Europe*, Dordrecht: Springer, 418-437.

Chapter 2 – Country-specific reports
Member states of the Council of Europe

Czech Republic
Viola Horská

1. School evaluation in the Czech Republic

1.1. The education system in the Czech Republic

The Czech education system consists of a preschool level of education provided by nursery schools (*mateřská škola*, usually for children aged 3-6); a primary level of education comprising primary schools (*základní škola*, ages 6 to 15) and general lower secondary schools (*osmileté gymnázium*, ages 11 to 15); a secondary level of education comprising general upper secondary schools (*gymnázium*, ages 15 to 19), technical or vocational upper secondary schools (*střední odborná škola*, ages 15 to 18 or 19); and a tertiary level of education provided by technical post-secondary schools (*vyšší odborná škola*, usually for students aged 18 or 19 to 24), plus higher education institutions (*vysoká škola*, starting at 18 or 19; the studies are not limited by age). The education system also includes institutions providing basic art education (*základní umělecká škola*), special schools designed for children with special educational needs (*speciální škola*) and educational institutions serving various educational and special purposes.

1. Nursery schools or kindergartens (*mateřská škola*) ensure care for children usually aged 3 to 6. The percentage of 6-year-old children at this type of preschool institution is high, as more than 20% of parents choose to postpone the start of school of their children and attendance at a kindergarten is highly recommended before starting school.

School selection at pre-primary level is up to the parents, the only limitation being the capacity of the schools and their network. The municipality acts as the organising body for nursery schools/kindergartens and decides on a child's admission if the number of applicants exceeds the school's capacity.

The total participation rate in pre-primary education in the Czech Republic is around 75% of the whole age-group of 3-year-old children, 90% of the age-group of 4 year olds, and 95% of the age-group of 5 year olds. The number of children under 3 is considerably smaller at around 25%.

Due to their accessibility, preschool institutions have been historically the most numerous and consequently the smallest types of educational establishment. Owing to massive social changes, their number declined over the period 1990-95. The stipulation of a minimum number of pupils in these institutions and classes in 1995 represented an objective criterion for further reducing the preschool institution network, which was designed to correspond to the marked demographic decrease.

In 2002/03 the number of preschool institutions was sharply reduced. In general they were not abolished, but rather consolidated into larger institutions that could better comply with the demands of legal entities. In 2000/01 the demographic decrease slowed down, while at the same time the number of parents who were interested in having their child attend a preschool institution increased. However, in spite of the declining number of children, it has not proven possible to place them all in preschool institutions.

Preschool institutions enjoy a high degree of organisational flexibility. In pre-primary education, there are a variety of private and denominational (religious) pre-primary schools and other alternative types of preschool establishments (for example, Waldorf, Montessori, Dalton and other types of pre-primary schools) besides the state's preschool network. The number of private and denominational schools is low, and private schools exceed denominational ones. Their geographical distribution is uneven: the highest concentration is in northern Moravia (there is a balance between the large number of institutions and children) and in Prague (which has a high percentage of private institutions but a low percentage of children).

2. Primary schools (*základní škola*) combine primary and lower secondary levels of education in one organisational unit and provide compulsory education. They provide nine years of education and correspond to the length of compulsory schooling. Primary school is divided into a five-year first stage and a four-year second stage. Upon completion of the first stage, pupils who show interest and pass the admission procedure may transfer to a multi-year general secondary school (*gymnázium*). They may continue in an eight-year *gymnázium* after the fifth year or a six-year *gymnázium* after the seventh year and complete their compulsory schooling there.

Primary schools enjoy a high degree of organisational flexibility. Primary education consists of private and denominational primary schools as well as other alternative types of primary school establishments besides the state primary school network. The existing alternative structures comprise several primary schools of the Waldorf type, others with elements taken from the Montessori or Dalton system, etc.

The number of private and denominational (religious) schools is very small (approximately 3% of all types of primary schools); in this figure, private schools are twice as numerous as denominational ones (2% compared to 1%). Private and denominational primary schools are usually smaller than public primary schools. Their geographical distribution is uneven: the highest concentrations are in northern Moravia (where there is a balance between the large number of institutions and children) and in Prague (which has a high percentage of private institutions but a low percentage of children). Private schools often follow alternative educational programmes.

Due to their accessibility, primary schools are the most numerous type of educational establishment, exceeding the number of secondary schools by 120%. Owing to the massive demographic decrease and social changes in the period 1990-2000, the number of primary schools has declined sharply. In general they were not abolished but instead consolidated into larger institutions that could better comply with the demands of the public administration reform (which was launched in 2000). Since 2000/01 the demographic decrease has slowed down, although between 2001 and 2006 the number of primary school pupils declined by nearly 15%.

3. Secondary schools (*střední škola*) provide secondary education, which can be either general or vocational. Vocational education consists of two levels: vocational secondary education (*střední odborné vzdělání*), ending with a compulsory vocational final examination (*závěrečná zkouška*); and a comprehensive vocational secondary education (*úplné střední odborné vzdělání*), which ends with a compulsory final examination (*maturitní zkouška*). Vocational education is provided at both levels.

The compulsory final examination in all types of secondary schools entitles pupils to seek admission to post-secondary education. A person holding a vocational final certificate (*vysvědčení o závěrečné zkoušce*) can attend extension courses (*nástavbové stadium*). After completing these studies, they can sit the compulsory final examination that is necessary before entering higher education.

Secondary schools are divided into the following three types:
- general upper secondary schools (*gymnázium*), providing a comprehensive secondary education (*úplné střední vzdělání*) and ending with a compulsory final examination (*maturitní zkouška*) that primarily prepares pupils for higher education. The studies may last four years (only at the upper secondary level), or six or eight years (including lower and upper secondary education);
- technical upper secondary schools (*střední odborná škola*), providing four-year courses leading to comprehensive secondary education (*úplné střední vzdělání*) ending with a compulsory final examination (*maturitní zkouška*), after which pupils may apply for admission to higher education. Pupils who pass this examination are qualified to enter certain technical, economic and other occupations. A small number of two to three-year courses provide vocational secondary education (*střední odborné vzdělání*). Some schools also provide extension courses (*nástavbové studium*).

- One special type of technical secondary school is the *conservatoire* (*konzervatoř*). Pupils attending a *conservatoire* receive a technical post-secondary education with a specialised focus on art, which ends with an *absolutorium*.
- vocational upper secondary schools (*střední odborné učiliště*) provide qualifications for manual occupations and similar professions in two and three-year courses and in a small number of four-year courses leading to a final examination. These schools provide training for highly skilled workers and operators as well as open the way to higher education; some schools also provide extension courses (*nástavbové studium*).

Vocational schools (*učiliště*) are not formally recognised as secondary schools. They offer one-year or two-year courses to pupils who have completed their compulsory schooling before the ninth year or did not complete their ninth year successfully, and who did not use the opportunity offered by the 2000 School Act Amendment to apply to study at a secondary school.

Technical and vocational upper secondary schools predominate in the Czech secondary school system. Many of their educational programmes can be considered as an obstacle for comparative evaluation purposes. Considering this, new framework educational programmes for vocational secondary education are in the course of being elaborated and implemented in schools (see below in sub-section 1.2).

Practically all primary school-leavers (almost 95%) continue their studies at post-compulsory educational institutions. In view of the considerable predominance of vocational/technical schools over general education schools (80% compared to 20%), a considerable proportion of pupils at the upper secondary level gain a vocational qualification that is recognised by the labour market.

Secondary education contains private and denominational secondary schools in addition to state ones. The number of private and denominational schools is relatively higher in comparison to the primary school network (approximately 20% of all types of secondary schools); private schools predominate over denominational ones (18% compared to 2%) in this figure.

4. Special schools (*speciální škola*) are designated for children with various health (physical or mental) or social disabilities who cannot be integrated into the mainstream schools. These schools run in parallel to the mainstream primary and secondary schools (*speciální základní škola, speciální gymnázium, speciální střední odborná škola, speciální střední odborné učiliště*), and pupils reach a level of education equal to that achieved in the relative mainstream schools. Follow-up special education is provided by vocational schools (*odborné učiliště*) or by practical schools (*praktická škola*).

5. Technical post-secondary schools (*vyšší odborná škola*) prepare pupils for demanding, skilled professions. They offer post-secondary vocational educa-

tion (*vyšší odborné vzdělání*) ending with an *absolutorium* for secondary school graduates who have passed the compulsory final examination (*maturitní zkouška*). Technical post-secondary education is regarded as tertiary education.

Conservatoires (*konzervatoř*) are similar to technical post-secondary schools as they are of longer duration (usually six to eight years) and end in an *absolutorium*.

Primary schools, general, technical and vocational upper secondary schools, special schools and technical post-secondary schools have similar management and financing, and are collectively called regional schools.

6. Higher education institutions (*vysoká škola*) provide education at three levels: bachelor, master and doctoral (following a master). Bachelor programmes are aimed to prepare students for a profession or to continue to master programmes. The standard duration is three to four years. Master programmes aim at developing theoretical knowledge based on current scientific findings, research and development, at mastering their application and developing creative skills. Master programmes follow on from bachelor courses, and last between one and three years. If the nature of the study programme requires, accreditation can be granted to master courses that do not follow on from a preceding bachelor course; in this case, the course will last between four and six years (usually five years, or six years in the case of medicine and veterinary medicine).

Doctoral programmes focus on scientific research and independent creativity in research and development, and independent theoretical or creative activity in art. The standard duration of studies is three years. All three types of programmes may be studied on a full-time, part-time or distance basis or as a combination of these.

1.2. New features of the Czech education system

The conditions for implementing a new evaluation system were created by important reform activities that have taken place in the Czech Republic since 2000.

The public administration reform was launched in 2000 with the aim of decentralising the educational system by inducing school autonomy, enhancing new forms of participation in school management, promoting new approaches to partnership and leadership, etc. One of the most important objectives was to provide a legal basis for wider pupil/student involvement in decision making and participation in the life of the school and the local community.

The Medium-term National Programme for the Development of Education in the Czech Republic (White Paper) drawn up under the responsibility of the Ministry of Education, Youth and Sports was approved in 2001. This strategic document set up and outlined the overall framework, purpose and aims of educational reform. The 2002 Long-term Programme of Education and Education System Development in the Czech Republic (*Dlouhodobý záměr*, 2002) defined a coherent strategy and objectives to be accomplished by 2005, and included proposals for the concrete coherent steps necessary for the development of the Czech educational system (with some objectives proposed before 2010).

Recently, a new Long-term Programme of Education was elaborated in 2005 (*Dlouhodobý záměr*, 2005), which evaluated the degree to which goals defined in 2002 had been accomplished, and defined new objectives and concrete steps to be accomplished by 2008 (following a time perspective until 2010).

According to objectives formulated both in the White Paper and the long-term programme of education, a number of fundamental changes in the aims and content of education have been launched. In co-ordination with different activities shaping the educational reform, important discussions were linked with the proposed new act on educational staff, and mainly with a bill for the new Education Act. Both acts were approved in September 2004 and came into effect in January 2005.

The new Education Act replaces the three existing and frequently amended acts: the School Act, the Act on State Administration and Autonomy, and the Act on Educational Establishments. It defines the basic aims and principles of education, as these were not included in the previous School Act. In comparison with the previous approach, more attention is paid to the education process than to the educational institutions. The act increases transfers within the education system, strengthens the inclusion of pupils with special educational needs, and ensures equality in access to education. Free education at public schools is extended to the final year of preschool education. School organising bodies of all kinds have the same rights and responsibilities. The act specifies the process of the decentralised system of governing through the long-term policy of the Ministry of Education, Youth and Sports, while at the same time preserving a level of consistency throughout the system.

In response to decentralisation, a new information system on pupils has been established alongside the school network – the school register. It also defines the role of social partners, which has until now been insufficient. It specifies the rights and responsibilities of pupils, which have so far been set by regulations. A new legal form for a school is proposed – the school as a legal entity. This stresses its non-profit character, as private schools with the same legal form are viewed as enterprises. The financial flows are specified and made more transparent. Participatory management at all levels is strengthened.

The new Education Act underlines the principles of the White Paper, initiates curricular reform activities launched by different institutions and bodies, and introduces a new multilevel system of educational programmes. In addition to that, new features have been introduced into the curriculum, such as the concept of key competences as an instrument for transforming the academic conception of traditional Czech education. An internal transformation process at the school level was initiated so that schools can convert themselves into democratic learning environments and/or local democratic communities, making it possible to create the best possible conditions for pupils to learn about and through democracy in the school and within the local community.

The National Programme of Education (or State Educational Programme; the term "national curriculum" is also frequently used) represents the highest level of the system. It sets out the main principles of national curricular reform and the requirements of state curricular policy, which are generally binding.

Framework educational programmes for pre-primary, primary and secondary schools represent a lower level of curricular documents. They aim at modernising both the shape and the content of education with an emphasis on a competence-based and child-centred approach. These programmes set out generally binding requirements for individual levels and branches of education and define the compulsory core content, the attainment targets (or standards) for key stages of education for different school levels, and general guidelines for their implementation.

School educational programmes (or school curricula) are the lowest level of the system. Individual schools will have to elaborate their own school curricula in accordance with the framework educational programme for the corresponding school level. Framework educational programmes are designed in such a way that schools can shape their school curriculum according to the needs of pupils, parents, local communities or specific conditions. Schools are free to choose their own teaching/learning methods and to design educational content in compliance with their own educational philosophy. Pupil-centred teaching, competence-based learning, new methods of active and participative teaching/learning and various forms of cross-curricular integration are widely promoted.

There is an opportunity for schools to involve more partners in decision making and assessment processes (including pupils/students) and to run their own projects.

In the course of elaborating a school curriculum, schools are obliged to assist pupils/students in acquiring key competences. One area of these key competences is civic competences; other key competences are interrelated with civic competences (learning to learn competences; competences to solve problems; competences to communicate effectively; social and interpersonal competences; competences to work effectively and co-operate with others).

1.3. The school evaluation system in the Czech Republic

School evaluation in the Czech Republic focuses mainly on public administration and on educational tasks carried out by schools at various education levels.

Public administration in education is highly decentralised; different levels of the administration and the schools have a high degree of autonomy.

The state administration of education is carried out by the Ministry of Education, Youth and Sports or in stipulated cases by other central government bodies (for example, the Czech School Inspectorate), regional authorities, local authorities of municipalities with extended competences, school organising bodies and school heads. Self-government in terms of education is carried out by regions, municipalities and school councils.

Primary and secondary schools and educational establishments are evaluated on a systematic basis by the Czech School Inspectorate (*Česká školní inspekce*), regional school inspectorates and other administration authorities and bodies (the Ministry of Education, Youth and Sports, and school and educational establishment bodies). Other controls (budgetary issues, economic and personnel management, etc.) are carried out by the Department of Internal Audit and Control of the Ministry of Education, Youth and Sports.

The Czech School Inspectorate is an independent institution that is separate from the administration of education. In 1997 a decree was issued concerning the organisation, performance and tasks of the Czech School Inspectorate.

The Czech School Inspectorate carries out inspections of all types of schools and educational establishments, regardless of their organising body. These inspections concern namely educational and training results, especially in the context of the content of approved teaching documents; personnel, material and technical conditions for education; and economic management.

The Czech School Inspectorate also checks compliance with generally binding legal regulations and requirements; submits proposals to an authorised body to exclude schools from the network; takes part in discussing annual reports on school activities submitted by school heads to the school board if their first drafts have been rejected; and takes part in the preparation of a summary report on education.

Some employees of the Czech School Inspectorate act as controllers whose task is to control the finances allocated to schools from the state budget. Control is also exercised at the level of the Ministry of Education, Youth and Sports by the Department of Internal Audit and Control in particular cases (ministerial projects and European Social Fund projects run by primary and secondary schools). The ministry also carries out a financial audit of public higher education institutions. In relation to laws on budgetary rules (No. 218/2000 Coll.), on the property of the Czech Republic (No. 219/2000 Coll.) and on financial control in public administration, the education sector is controlled on the basis of the Directive of the Minister for Education, Youth and Sports No. 9/2003.

The inspection carries out four types of activities:
- comprehensive inspections (carried out by a team of inspectors), which monitor all the above components of schools' activities and are conducted at the instigation of the ministry, the Department of Education or the

inspectorate itself. A full inspection consists of a complete audit of both educational and administrative activities;
- focused inspections, which represent the most common type of inspection. They differ from comprehensive inspections in the breadth and depth of inquiry and aim at investigating specific events;
- topical (thematic) inspections, which deal with a certain theme determined either by the Ministry of Education, Youth and Sports or by the inspectorate itself. They are carried out on a designated sample of schools and educational facilities;
- inquiries into complaints and suggestions from parents, citizens, schools and municipalities.

The results of inspection findings and evaluations are recorded in an inspection report (*inspekční zpráva*). The conclusion of the inspection report contains an overall evaluation, a description of the relations and causal connections between the elements inspected where relevant, statements concerning any infringements and a statement with recommendations for correcting shortcomings. An evaluation of how effectively the school has used its allocated state funding comprises an independent part of the report. Developments since the last inspection can be mentioned.

The written report is sent to the school head as soon as possible, who has fourteen days in which to comment on it. These comments become part of the report. The final version of the inspection report is sent to the school head and to the organising body of the school (the local community/municipality in the case of pre-primary institutions and primary schools; the regional authority in the case of secondary schools and technical post-secondary schools; the Ministry of Education, Youth and Sports in the case of higher education institutions, etc.). Inspection reports are made available to the public on the Internet, in the school or educational facility, at the regional authority and at the relevant inspectorate body (depending on the area) for a period of ten years.

The results of the school inspection and inquiries are followed up by the school head, the regional authority and the organising body. A selective follow-up inspection is carried out when a reasonable period of time has elapsed, enabling the school head (or other addressees of the inspection report or record) to adopt measures to remedy any deficiencies. In case any deficiencies and/or shortcomings have not been corrected/set right, punishment measures of different levels of seriousness (according to the level of infraction or the gravity of the consequences) are applied. The most frequent punishment measure is a financial penalty imposed on the person in question (namely, the person liable for adopting measures to remedy any deficiencies).

The 1995 amendment to the Law on State Administration and Self-government in Education laid down the obligation for all schools and educational facilities to carry out internal evaluations. They have to compile annual reports on their activities and management of resources. This obligation also concerns all levels of the school administration, including the Ministry of Education, Youth and Sports, the Czech School Inspectorate and other institutions, for example, research institutions.

The quality of higher education is assessed by the Accreditation Commission, which carries out comprehensive evaluations of educational, academic, research, developmental, artistic and other creative activities of higher education institutions. In particular, it evaluates the activities of higher education institutions and the quality of all accredited activities and programmes, publishes the results and judges other matters concerning higher education submitted to the commission by the Minister for Education, Youth and Sports and publishes its views.

According to the 1995 amendment to the Law on State Administration and Self-government in Education, the whole of the education system is assessed and evaluated by the Ministry of Education, Youth and Sports, which issues an annual report on the state and development of the education system in each year.

The ministry and its specialised institutions (for example, the Institute for Information in Education) provide educational statistics and pedagogical research, in the fields within their scope of competences, for the purposes of evaluating the education system and making decisions concerning its development. Further research is carried out independently by higher education institutions. Since 1990 there have been various international activities in the field of evaluation.

Growing interest in evaluation and self-evaluation issues is evident from various international conferences and symposiums that have been held in Prague, for example, the Prague Forum in 2003 on Quality in Education and the Democratic Agenda, the International Conference on Self-evaluation and its Contribution to Continual School Development in 2006, etc.

1.4. Modes of school evaluation

School evaluation in the Czech Republic can take the form of external and/or internal evaluation of schools and educational establishments.

External evaluation is provided by the Czech School Inspectorate, officials of the Ministry of Education, Youth and Sports, and regional educational departments. Internal evaluation of a school falls within the responsibility of the school heads. At the school level, school boards (*rada školy*) and other self-governing bodies (for example, school parliaments, representatives of the school founding body, etc.) exercise a public control function.

Recently, with the introduction of new binding pedagogical documents, the so-called framework educational programmes, all schools are obliged to introduce evaluation and self-evaluation into their school educational programmes and into daily school life.

The long-term strategy for the development of education and the education system (*Dlouhodobý záměr*, 2005), which was prepared on the basis of a new Education Act, increases the importance of evaluation to balance the high level of autonomy of regions and educational institutions as far as the content and form of educational work are concerned.

In February 2004, the Minister for Education, Youth and Sports approved a Framework Project for Education Monitoring and Evaluation, which specifies three areas:
- pupil/student assessment: assessment of the key points of the educational career of pupils in the 5th and 9th years of primary school from 2005/06 (especially regarding their choice of educational pathway); ending studies at secondary school: a new school-leaving examination for general, technical and vocational upper secondary schools (*maturitní zkouška*) in school year 2007/08; testing a new model for the final examination of short-term vocational and specialised upper secondary schools, especially in the field of apprenticeships (*závěrečná zkouška*); monitoring the transition of school-leavers into working life, etc.;
- evaluation at the school level: external evaluation by the Czech School Inspectorate, the provision of objective tools, internal evaluation of the school (for example, assessment of existing methods of evaluation and preparation of the proposed indicators in 2005/06) and its interconnection with the external evaluation by the Czech School Inspectorate, evaluation by other institutions, etc.;
- evaluation and comparison of the whole education system and its parts: involvement of the Czech Republic in international research extended by evaluation and monitoring for national purposes; the evaluation of regions, various sectors, sorts and types of schools, etc.

The national priorities concerning the above-mentioned tasks are supported by projects co-financed by the European Social Fund.

In line with launching this framework project, a new educational institution was established in January 2006: the Centre for Assessment of Outcomes in Education (*Centrum pro zjišťování výsledků vzdělávání*). The centre carries out many activities and projects concerned with external evaluation, namely projects Kvalita I (Quality I) and Kvalita II (Quality II). At the same time, it is developing quality indicators for the new school-leaving examination for general, technical and vocational upper secondary schools starting in the school year 2007/08 and prepares so-called catalogues (or checklists) of school-leaving examination requirements for different subject areas, which represent educational standards in these subjects. It also stipulates the terms of successful standards of student attainment. Two catalogues are compiled, for civic basics and civic and social science basics (*Katalog požadavků k maturitní zkoušce: Občanský základ*, 2004; *Katalog požadavků k maturitní zkoušce: Občanský a společenskovědní základ*, 2005), both of which comprise many aspects of education for democratic citizenship (EDC).

The Kvalita I project aims at elaborating a new and comprehensive system of monitoring and evaluation of outcomes at the primary and secondary levels of education. There is still no integrated national system of education monitoring and assessment in the Czech Republic. The new system of external evaluation will introduce greater objectivity and will provide schools with evaluation instruments enabling them to compare themselves with other schools; pupils/students will be given an opportunity to compare their achievements against other pupils/students of the same age-group; while heads of schools and school administrations will be able to access information about other schools' levels of attainment. The main purpose of the Kvalita I project is to improve the quality of education.

The first source of information will be the outcomes of the new national assessment examination carried out at key points of the education of primary school pupils in the 5th and 9th years and of upper secondary school students finishing secondary general, technical and vocational schools by means of didactic tests. A second source of information will be so-called personal pupil/student portfolios, which are understood as containing complex information about educational pupil/student outcomes (for example, consisting of various activity records, background papers, reports, etc.). Pupil/student portfolios at the lower primary school stages are usually completed by the teacher; at senior primary school stages are produced by both the pupil and the teacher; while in secondary schools, individual student work on the portfolio is most common (sometimes students are provided with general guidelines for shaping their portfolio in advance).

The Kvalita II project aims at setting up a self-evaluation system including the implementation of national surveys and at providing a number of support activities. New self-evaluation instruments will be elaborated and introduced in schools. The project expects to interconnect external evaluations carried out by the Czech School Inspectorate and internal evaluations launched in schools by different stakeholders (teachers, heads of schools, school administrations, pupils, parents, etc.), to provide support for the reflection process and to help school administrations to determine the school development plan, and to define effective strategies to realise this plan.

The main objectives of self-evaluation activities could variously be self-reflection on the part of the school; or increased capacity on the part of teachers and school administrations to analyse the outcomes of their activities, to reveal its possible reasons and to stipulate performance conditions, to work with information obtained and to opt for new strategies leading to higher quality.

The 1995 amendment to the Law on State Administration and Self-government in Education set down the obligation for schools and educational establishments to compile and present annual reports on their activity, which were until recently the only instrument of self-evaluation.

The annual report on the school's activities should primarily include the following:
- an overview of timetables used that have been approved by the ministry;
- data on the school staff, their qualifications, professional experience and competences;
- a survey of the educational achievements of pupils (broken down by classes, fields of study, years);
- data on results of final examinations in secondary schools; and
- data on the results of inspections carried out by the Czech School Inspectorate.

The annual report has to be made public and must be available to every stakeholder.

If the school uses resources from the state budget (as is the case for practically all schools including private and denominational ones), it is obliged to present an annual report on its management of resources. This report is submitted and approved according to the same rules as for the annual report on the school's activities.

The annual reports on activities and management of resources are submitted to the school board, where the school head discusses the annual report on the school's activities at a meeting of the staff and other bodies represented (parents, school founding body or school organising body).

The decision on whether to approve the annual reports on the school's activities and management of resources is taken by the school board within one month of its presentation. If it is not approved, the school board must justify its decision and invite an inspector to attend a new discussion. If the report on the management of resources is not approved, an inspector and an employee of the regional authority are invited. The school head presents the report once again within a month. If the report is not approved even after the second discussion, the organising body (or the founding body) must state its opinion as to why the approval was not granted and decide on further steps.

In accordance with the Higher Education Act, higher education institutions are obliged to evaluate their activities and publish the results and at the same time prepare, present to the ministry and publish an annual report on their activities and an annual report on the management of their resources.

The new Education Act, which was approved by the Parliament of the Czech Republic in September 2004, modifies the evaluation of schools. Besides assessments provided by the Czech School Inspectorate, it includes a new internal evaluation of the school. A ministry regulation stipulates the structure, rules and deadlines of internal school evaluations. The obligation for primary and secondary schools to carry out evaluations and self-evaluations was set down in law as late as in 2005 (Public Notice No. 15/2005 Coll.).

Internal evaluation (or self-evaluation – there is still no distinction between these two words in the Czech professional/specialist literature dealing with evaluation issues – see Vašťatková, 2006) is a new and challenging phenomenon in the Czech education system. The concept of internal evaluation/self-evaluation carried out by educational institutions only appeared after 1990, initially in higher education and later, to a varying degree, at lower levels of the education system. Self-evaluation as a means of self-reflection is still not common in schools and is most frequently used in internal discussions among teaching staff.

There are also some non-state evaluation activities that take place at schools. These are voluntary, and the schools that decide to undertake such evaluations must cover the costs themselves. Schools are increasingly interested in the results of evaluations carried out at central or international levels and in tests organised on a commercial basis.

Primary and secondary schools can take part in an evaluation project called Kalibro, which offers them an opportunity to obtain a qualified measure of their teaching results. The tests cover the following study areas: Czech language, mathematics, social sciences, science, English language and German language. The school concerned obtains, besides the students' achievements, comprehensive results for classes and the school as a whole (these results are only given to the relevant school), as well as overall average results for the Czech Republic, individual regions, types of schools or categories of students. They serve the school as a measure for assessing their own results. On top of this, the overall results and the students' answers in particular are analysed, which assists teachers in their pedagogical work.

The SCIO project is ranked among the evaluations but focuses both on individuals and schools on a commercial basis. It offers so-called national comparative examinations of knowledge at the level of primary and secondary schools as well as comparative tests, practice exercises for entrance examinations to secondary schools and higher education institutions, etc. SCIO tests are used by hundreds of schools at all levels. Some secondary schools and higher education institutions take the results into account in their admission procedures. A large number of primary and secondary schools including multi-year *gymnázia* use the tests to assess educational achievement and to find out how to increase quality.

Between 1996 and 2000 technical post-secondary schools had the opportunity of entering the EVOS evaluation programme, which was run by the Association of Schools of Professional Higher Education (Sdružení škol Vyššího studia), and is designed to assist schools in enhancing the quality of their services. The starting point in this case is school self-evaluation. The programmes have not, however, continued since then.

Some schools take part in international projects and/or surveys aimed at evaluating the education systems of participating countries. Many schools in the Czech Republic were involved in the PISA Study run by the OECD, and some schools took part in the Civic Education Study (CivEd) run by the Association for the Evaluation of Educational Achievement (see Torney-Purta et al., 2001; Křížová, 2001; Torney-Purta, 2002). Project conclusions from the IEA CivEd project have been summarised by Ivana Křížová; however, her survey is deposited in the archive of the Institute for Information in Education (Prague) and concerns only an internal final report from the project.

The 1999 methodology of inspection tends to support self-evaluation, as the school head can express his or her opinion regarding the conception both before and after the inspection. The Czech School Inspectorate continuously undertakes so-called "thematic inspections" focused on new elements introduced in school life (for example, introduction of new forms of evaluation, starting up a self-evaluation process, implementing new content elements, etc.), enabling school administrations to check the state and development of their school.

The evaluation and quality assessment system is still a very new issue in the Czech education system. It is not possible to summarise any expert commentary on it since it has not been verified over the long term by schools and commented on by various stakeholders. The strong and weak points of the evaluation and quality assessment system will be tested by schools in the implementation phase of school evaluation and self-evaluation processes.

1.5. Evaluation as an issue in teacher training

In universities, students preparing themselves for a teaching career and in pre-service training become acquainted with a wide range of topics concerning school pedagogy, teaching methodologies, classroom/school management, etc. There is no common framework or common syllabus for teachers' undergraduate study. The teachers' undergraduate study content is set by the faculties themselves. It consists mostly of preschool or school pedagogy (depending on the branch of study), educational psychology and other pedagogical and psychological disciplines (for example, social psychology, didactics and teaching methodology in the relevant subject(s), etc.). Topics relevant to evaluation and assessment are usually part of these courses, or sometimes represent a separate part of undergraduate teachers' study syllabuses.

There are many different publications and study materials for these students, which cover a huge variety of topics. Some publications deal with issues of pupil/ student evaluation in this context, with practical instruction topics and/or models (for example, Štech, 1992; Beran, 1996; Rýdl, 1996; Pasch et al., 1998; Švarcová, 2005). A separate publication concerning EDC, its methodology, concepts and approaches used in preparatory, implementation and evaluation stages has been published in the first half of 2007 (Horská, Hrachovcová and Zouhar, 2007).

The Act on Educational Staff approved by the Parliament of the Czech Republic in September 2004 (effective from 1 January 2005) stipulates the ways in which individual categories of educational staff can acquire professional qualifications. It also regulates the obligation of educational staff to undergo in-service training and defines the conditions for this, including for the possibility of applying for study leave of twelve working days each school year. The act sets up accreditation rules and bodies for relevant educational institutions and programmes of in-service training. And, finally, it institutes a career system that sets out the rules of professional advancement and incorporates further education. Implementing regulations are being prepared.

This legislative document gives teachers the opportunity to enrich their professional experience, develop new teaching skills and learn about new concepts in education. As the concept of self-evaluation is very new in the Czech educational environment, teachers need support to be able to accomplish the task and fully understand the objectives of self-evaluation and its benefits for their daily work. In-service training centres in the Czech Republic are still not fully prepared for this. There are not many professionals active in the field of evaluation and self-evaluation. It is hoped that more professionals will become involved in the field of evaluation and self-evaluation and will produce and disseminate new ideas.

1.6. The use of evaluation results in schools and in the educational system

The use of evaluation results in schools still differs from one school to another. As there is no common evaluation framework (for example, widespread comprehensive reference material on evaluation, an integral national assessment scheme with an elaborated system of indicators, etc.), it is very difficult to estimate the number of schools using evaluation results for school development purposes.

In an effort to find out how schools perform evaluation and self-evaluation processes, several surveys have been carried out. Some of them represent thematic (or topic-focused) inspections accomplished by the Czech School Inspectorate, which concern self-evaluation in primary and secondary schools (*Tematická zpráva*, 2004) and individual primary and secondary school assessments (*Tematická zpráva*, 2005). These two inspections monitored the scope, focus, methods and impact of internal evaluation on school performance (and in 2005, also its application to school life).

The conclusions of these two thematic inspections match the previous assumptions of the Czech School Inspectorate. They contain information on the following survey findings:

- most schools have only just started to create assessment systems within the whole school; only a few schools have elaborated a system of quality indicators or have adopted the existing system of indicators;
- approximately only a third of school heads are aware of the significance and possibilities of school self-evaluation and estimate its outcomes as good feedback for the school and an excellent opportunity to detect the state of school development in achieving set educational objectives, to eliminate possible drawbacks and/or shortcomings, to draft out an improvement strategy, etc.;
- approximately two-thirds of school heads use evaluation and self-evaluation outcomes to establish the priorities of an improvement strategy, to take measures and necessary steps to overcome possible problems and weaknesses and to supervise corrections and possible error resolutions;
- many schools focus above all on the formal aspects of pupils' educational outcomes (for example, the rate of successfully accomplished upper secondary school entrance proceedings; further study continuation in the higher levels of the educational system and/or successful applications on the labour market);
- primary schools find it important to obtain information concerning pupils' behaviour and the quality of social relations in school; some schools do not see any use for general comparative testing of pupils' performance;
- in many schools, the effectiveness of educational strategies is not analysed with regard to set educational objectives; for many schools, fulfilling the curriculum requirements is of relatively little importance;
- the results of self-evaluation are presented and discussed in most schools with the teaching staff, but there are not always systematic measures leading to an improvement of the quality of the educational process;
- self-evaluation only has an effective feedback function in a smaller number of schools; few schools take measures and necessary steps on the basis of self-evaluation findings to improve their performance (for example, by setting up new objectives, educational strategy options, etc.);
- schools monitored in the survey did not prepare individual self-evaluation reports; their findings were embedded in school annual reports.

An individual and highly informative survey was carried out by Jana Vašťatková and Michaela Prášilová from Olomouc University (Vašťatková and Prášilová, 2005). According to its findings, a substantial number (approximately half) of respondents participating in the survey do not understand the nature (and thus the meaning) of school self-evaluation within the whole context of school-work quality assessment. School management and head administrators are interested above all in how best to meet the requirements placed on schools by legislative regulations (namely educational framework programmes and Public Notice No. 15/2005 Coll.) because of their binding character.

Based on the responses of head administrators monitored in the survey's teamwork and debates, the survey found that many schools focus above all on areas of school work defined by Public Notice No. 15/2005 Coll. and thus obtain data for a comprehensive overview of the whole school performance. When obtaining feedback data on particular educational areas or problems, these data are used by head administrators mainly as a source of information about the current state of school development. Sometimes they discuss these findings with other members of the school management and teaching staff. There is no rule, however, that particular corrective measures are always applied based on the information obtained during the evaluation and self-evaluation process. The school heads or school administrations purely acquaint teachers with the information obtained during the evaluation and self-evaluation process and expect them to take their own corrective measures if they feel that this is necessary or desirable. No feedback monitoring or supervision measures are consequently put in place by school heads or school administrations in order to check quality improvement in education (Vašťatková and Prášilová, 2005).

As the evaluation and quality assessment system in the Czech Republic is still a very new issue in the Czech education system, hopefully this situation will change in the near future with increased experience of good implementation on the part of different stakeholders and the schools themselves with daily practices and exercised procedures of school evaluation and self-evaluation like SWOT analysis, STEP analysis, marketing audit, TQM Excellence Model, EFQM Excellence Model, Q-analysis, and various questionnaires for parents, students and other stakeholders.

2. The "Tool for Quality Assurance of Education for Democratic Citizenship in Schools"

The "Tool for Quality Assurance of Education for Democratic Citizenship in Schools" can be considered a very useful and important reference tool for the purpose of launching school evaluation and self-evaluation, as it consists of various parts that are of primary importance when dealing with the topic. The tool represents an intermediate outcome of European debates in the field of quality assurance of EDC in schools arising from the Council of Europe Education for Democratic Citizenship project. It meets the findings of other contemporary European initiatives in the field of quality indicators as well (for example, the *European Report on the Quality of School Education*, 2005).

The team of authors is composed of well-known and notable professionals who are active in the field of EDC. Their professional experience is a guarantee of document quality and might be considered as an advantage in terms of the structure of the tool, its elaboration and suggestions offered.

2.1. Comprehensiveness and coherence

The tool is comprehensive and coherent, the language style used is adequate for the purposes of implementing the tool, and the scope of problems solved is very wide and instructive. The tool should be comprehensible not only to specialists working in the field of quality assurance, evaluation and self-evaluation, quality indicators elaboration, etc., but also to school administrations, school heads and to some extent also to ordinary teachers familiar with presented topics.

The most valuable parts of the text are the ones covering school development planning (Chapter 4), quality indicators for EDC (Chapter 5) and general guidelines for school self-evaluation (Chapter 6). Especially useful is the synoptic table showing the use of quality indicators and a clearly arranged description of defined EDC quality indicators (sub-sections 5.1 and 5.2), revealing step-by-step the school development planning process (sub-section 6.1), indicating the use of the quality indicators of EDC (sub-section 6.2), explaining general principles for evaluating EDC and illustrating these guiding principles by means of several synoptic tables (sub-section 6.3), calling attention to the analysis and interpretation of data obtained during the evaluation and/or self-evaluation process and identification of the school's strengths and weaknesses in terms of EDC in order to establish the priorities of an improvement strategy (sub-section 6.4) and, finally, presenting a step-by-step approach to EDC development planning (sub-section 6.5).

The tool and all of its aspects are very informative and useful. It represents a consistent summary of the main findings in the field of evaluation and self-evaluation and its application to EDC. The tool could thus be considered as a primary source of information about EDC evaluation strategies and school development planning from an EDC perspective. The presented tool fits into the collection of Council of Europe texts dealing with EDC issues and other important works in the field of EDC.

2.2. Corresponding material in the Czech Republic

In the Czech Republic, there is no material available like the assessed tool (mainly in terms of its wide applicability in the field of EDC). There are some comprehensive and coherent materials available, but these are mostly general and do not address ordinary teachers and their needs. Most publications covering issues of evaluation and/or self-evaluation are designed for specialists in this field, university professionals and for a school management audience.

A primary theoretical framework for the forthcoming efforts concerned with evaluation issues has been developed by Jan Průcha (Průcha, 1996). However, there is almost a complete lack of professional literature written in Czech that systematically and adequately deals with school evaluation and self-evaluation issues with the aim of meeting school practice needs. At present, certain sources of information are available (for example, Rýdl et al., 1998; Nezvalová, 2002; the Methodical Portal focusing on issues of framework educational programmes – the school self-evaluation section; and other Internet sources) from which schools may gain some information, but it is an open question as to whether these are adequate in terms of content, availability and quantity of usable materials. Well-funded support (for dissemination of materials, consultancy, etc.) is needed to bridge this gap.

There are several individual publications dedicated to the topic of school evaluation and/or self-evaluation (for example, Skalková, 1995; Průcha, 1996; Beran, 1996; Rýdl, 1996; Rýdl et al., 1998) and many partial and/or fragmentary reports dealing with some aspects of school evaluation and/or self-evaluation (Grecmanová, 2004; Kitzberger, 2004b; Kovařovic, 2004; Vašťatková and Prášilová, 2005; Vašťatková and Prášilová, 2006). None, however, is dedicated especially to EDC. There is a huge gap between general approaches to evaluation and their implementation in concrete evaluation tools for assessing pupil/student development in various fields of study (or school subjects), the effectiveness and appropriateness of the educational strategies used, the attainment level of key competences, and so on.

Many of the Czech publications concerned with issues of quality management, quality assurance, evaluation and/or self-evaluation pay attention to defining total quality management (TQM) in schools (Nezvalová, 1999; Obst, 2000; Albert, 2001; Nezvalová, 2002; Michek et al., 2006). In addition, some introduce individual concepts such as marketing audits in schools (Světlík, 1996; Eger et al., 2002), school development and change management (Pol and Lazarová, 1999; Nezvalová, Prášilová and Eger, 2004), different forms of self-evaluation and self-assessment tools for micro-analysing educational processes, SWOT analyses, etc. (Švec, 1998; Albert, 2001; Michek et al., 2006).

There are some theoretical background study materials that are available to students, teachers and other interested readers that concern the psychology of school accomplishment and success (Helus et al., 1979), topics of pupil/student school achievement and the tools for measuring this (Byčkovský, 1988), issues concerning different ways of assessing pupils/students (Schimunek, 1994; Číhalová and Mayer, 1997; Kolář, Navrátil and Šikulová, 1998; Slavík, 1999; Tondl, 1999), etc.

The most recent publications in this field deal with more complex issues such as quality management in schools, school quality indicators, application of ISO norms in education, the EFQM self-evaluation model, etc. (Roupec, 1997; Kunčarová and Nezvalová, 2006a; Kunčarová and Nezvalová, 2006b; Michek et al., 2006). Unfortunately, these publications are not widely disseminated and thus accessible to ordinary teachers. They serve mainly as a primary source of information for in-service training programmes for school managers and heads of schools.

There are some foreign publications that address issues of evaluation and/or self-evaluation that are available to teachers in the Czech Republic, for example, the pupil/school portfolio (MacBeath, 1991; Bernhardt, 1999; MacBeath and McGlynn, 2002; MacBeath et al., 2006). The Eurydice series concerning topics of evaluation in schools, key competences, citizenship education and other relevant issues is also accessible via the Internet or in printed versions (in English: *Key Competencies: A Developing Concept in General Compulsory Education*, 2002; *Evaluation of Schools Providing Compulsory Education*, 2004; *Citizenship Education at School in Europe*, 2005; in Czech – see www.uiv.cz/clanek/379/701).

Publications and documents concerned with evaluating EDC have only been produced by international projects run by the International Association for the Evaluation of Educational Achievement (IEA) or by national projects run by various private agencies. These comprise a final report from the IEA study conducted in the Czech Republic (Křížová, 2001) and in all 26 countries (Torney-Purta et al., 2001; Torney-Purta, 2002), and a final report on micro-expertise in the field of EDC and social studies (Mičienka et al., 2002).

3. The tool as an instrument of school evaluation in the Czech Republic

The tool could prove a very useful instrument for school evaluation in the Czech Republic since it meets the actual needs of teachers and addresses their motivation to learn more about both the evaluation and self-evaluation processes and about appropriate tools for assessing pupil/student performance.

Such a document dealing with both EDC and quality assurance is very challenging and new. The topics mentioned in the document (mainly school development planning of EDC, quality assurance elements from an EDC perspective, and a system of EDC quality indicators) are particularly topical and of primary importance. The usefulness of the document lies in its wider scope of presented topics and its comprehensive step-by-step approach revealing evaluation practice as performed by schools.

3.1. Conditions for using the tool in schools

Conditions for using the tool in schools have been created by important reform activities that have taken place in the Czech Republic since 2000.

In accordance with the new Education Act, binding principles of school evaluation and self-evaluation were set out by the law in 2005 (Public Notice No. 15/2005 Coll.). This legislative document defines six areas of school evaluation (1. material, technical, personal and other conditions of education; 2. the course of education; 3. pupil/student educational outcomes; 4. the quality of school and personal management, offered courses and in-service training for educational staff;

5. support of gifted pupils/students, assistance for pupils/students with special educational needs, co-operation with parents and other social partners; 6. the whole-school outcome level and added education value). The document also stipulates an obligation for schools to determine a time schedule for evaluation and self-evaluation activities.

3.1.1. Circumstances that might promote the use of the tool

The use of the tool might be promoted by the new rules, principles and requirements laid down by various legislative documents that have gradually elaborated various elements set out in the new Education Act, namely the framework educational programmes and Public Notice No. 15/2004 Coll. These legislative documents define the conditions and requirements for school evaluation, school self-evaluation and school development planning.

According to the Framework Educational Programme for Primary Education and the Framework Educational Programme for Gymnasia (that is, general upper secondary school), which is partly concerned with the structure of the school educational programme, schools have the duty to embed an evaluation system into their school educational programmes. This means that they have to explain which evaluation and self-evaluation instruments are used in daily school practice in six defined areas. Moreover, they have to determine a time schedule for evaluation and self-evaluation activities.

Appropriate support mechanisms to facilitate the local implementation of framework educational programmes are under way. A manual for the development of school curricula will help heads of schools and teachers to create their own programmes step by step. An interactive virtual forum (the so-called Electronic Methodical Portal for Teachers) will offer schools effective help and methodological support in the course of elaborating their school curricula. Participative ways of implementing the framework curricula into school curricula will be widely recommended. Teachers will be encouraged to use stimulating, participative and interactive teaching/learning approaches, challenging assessment and evaluation strategies, and working methods (for example, discussions, teamwork, project work, learning by playing, learning by doing, etc.). Samples of project work and/ or interdisciplinary approaches, examples of content integration and specific ways of elaborating content in different domains, and various evaluation tools suitable for different purposes will be presented.

In addition, the portal will serve as a forum for exchanging best practice examples from various schools. Teachers are invited to present their best practice examples of teaching and learning in different subjects, of various projects, evaluation and self-evaluation strategies used, etc.

3.1.2. Prospective difficulties and obstacles

Introducing any innovation at schools may face a number of problems. The implementation and incorporation of any new concept concerning teaching/learning strategies, evaluation and self-evaluation activities, etc. tend to be time-consuming. Teachers need sufficient time to familiarise themselves with these new concepts and to start to use them in their daily work. In addition, they need to be provided with background materials, in-service teacher-training courses and specialised counselling.

Unfortunately, there are no national indicators for the external and/or internal evaluation of educational outcomes elaborated so far that could help teachers to become acquainted with evaluation and self-evaluation strategies. Such indicators are currently being prepared (with the assistance of the Czech School Inspectorate and the Centre for Assessment of Outcomes in Education). Only a list of framework evaluation criteria was set out in Public Notice No. 15/2005 Coll. concerning the rules of evaluation and self-evaluation system in schools. These general criteria must be elaborated in the school curriculum in accordance with requirements defined in the framework educational programmes.

Due to the lack of common national evaluation standards, each school defines its own evaluation criteria, which thus vary from one institution to another. In compliance with the framework educational programmes, schools are free to create their own syllabuses according to their needs and to the personal qualifications of their staff. They must fulfil so-called expected outcomes (*očekávané výstupy*), which are understood as prescribed and binding attainment targets (or pupil/student performance benchmarks), as well as evaluation criteria of pupil/student attainment in different educational areas (or specialised subjects).

Expected outcomes are interconnected with so-called key competences (*klíčové competence*). The definition of these key competences is very broad, and they must be elaborated into concrete actions, behaviours, etc. of pupils/students. As teachers are not entirely familiar with the concept of key competences and their implementation into daily school life, it is very difficult for most to define comprehensive and coherent evaluation tools for pupil/student assessment and to evaluate the key competences acquired by learners. This could be the main obstacle facing any implementation of this tool in the Czech Republic, but it also represents a great challenge.

Another problem is that in the Czech Republic until recently, there was no evaluation tradition or culture. This is a new approach for dealing with educational processes and their outcomes, whereby schools can develop on their own.

3.1.3. Parts of the tool with particular applicability

Many parts of the tool seem to be particularly apt for use in schools in the Czech Republic, especially the parts dealing with school development planning (Chapter 4), the definition and use of quality indicators for EDC and a description of defined EDC quality indicators (Chapter 5), and general guidelines for school self-evaluation and the school development planning process in EDC (Chapter 6).

For teachers, the most instructive parts are synoptic tables illustrating the use of EDC indicators in school evaluation and/or the self-evaluation process and detailed descriptions of the self-evaluation process and school development planning. Other parts of the text are also useful and suitable for users in the Czech Republic; however, the more abstract and difficult the explanations in the text are (particularly Chapter 3), the more uninteresting the whole text could be to users. As the tool has obvious qualities, it might be useful to find some practical Czech examples to demonstrate the nature of quality assurance and quality control in schools in order to bring the topic closer to Czech users.

For Czech teachers, Chapter 2 appears very important, especially with regard to the wide ("umbrella") concept of EDC and capacity-building for EDC in schools. The same is valid in terms of highlighting the need to have a self-evaluation team (sub-section 6.2); to implement EDC evaluation and self-evaluation strategies successfully, team-building and capacity-building are crucial.

Among the most important suggestions are the necessity and importance of data analysis and interpretation, the identification of school strengths and weaknesses in the field of EDC, and the setting of priorities for an improvement strategy. The latter (that is, the existence of a corrective action plan and an improvement strategy) is still often omitted by school administrations and sometimes even by individual teachers in the Czech Republic, a startling fact that emerged from the thematic inspection carried out by the Czech School Inspectorate (*Tematická zpráva*, 2004).

3.1.4. Target groups of the tool

The target groups could be very diverse, as the tool addresses important and ever-present components of school life. The tool might be very useful for school heads, school managers, school administrations, school boards, head teachers and, at some point, EDC teachers (see sub-section 4.1). It could also be used for the purposes of pre-service and in-service teacher training, for academic study by professionals operating in the field of EDC (for example, researchers, university teachers, methodology providers, methodical support trainers, etc.) and as reference material for the Czech School Inspectorate, the Centre for Assessment of Outcomes in Education and the Czech Ministry of Education, Youth and Sports.

The tool seems to be particularly apt for primary and upper secondary technical and vocational schools, as there are some attempts to implement evaluation and self-evaluation for school development purposes on an everyday or a regular intermediate basis. According to thematic inspections carried out by the Czech School Inspectorate (*Tematická zpráva*, 2004; *Tematická zpráva*, 2005), which concern self-evaluation in the assessment of primary and secondary schools and individual primary and secondary schools, primary schools are best prepared for implementing various evaluation and/or self-evaluation instruments in daily school life as these schools are the most motivated to change their approaches to education (for example, in terms of content, methods, forms and/or educational strategies, using new evaluation tools, etc.). Upper secondary technical and vocational schools are very motivated to perform evaluations and self-evaluations due to their close links with the labour market, the outcome expectations and attainment criteria of which they have to fulfil. These schools are the most flexible in terms of change because they have to react instantly to market developments. They do not therefore need special incentives to introduce evaluation and self-evaluation processes: rather, they see them as something natural and challenging.

The situation in upper secondary general schools (gymnasia) is slightly different. These schools were formerly considered to have a distinct academic profile and thus enjoy higher social prestige than other types of schools. For this reason, they were not aware of the necessity to make any changes in their content, methods, educational strategies, etc. or to modify their approaches to student outcome evaluation and/or the whole school evaluation. Until recently, the majority of these schools did not use any self-evaluation tools, either adopted ones or their own (*Tematická zpráva*, 2004).

In terms of applicability, the tool could represent an initial and the most important source of information and methodical guidance for understanding and implementing evaluation and self-evaluation for school development purposes in upper secondary general schools. It could also become a very interesting experience enriching the working material of other types of schools.

3.2. Systemic conditions for using the tool

The systemic conditions for using the tool in the Czech Republic are quite good with regard to implementation of evaluation and self-evaluation strategies, leading to the possible elaboration of a school development plan in various types of schools.

With regard to EDC, the situation is rather complicated. EDC is still regarded as being a single teaching subject that is not applicable to the whole school climate, to democratic school management, to evaluation and self-evaluation processes carried out by various stakeholders, etc. However, some slight changes have been initiated by the approval of the Framework Educational Programme for Primary Education (*Rámcový vzdělávací program pro základní vzdělávání*, 2005). In this document, EDC is defined as a separate educational area or field (education for citizenship; *Výchova k občanství*), as one of several cross-curricular themes (education of democratic citizens; *Výchova demokratického občana*), and as one of several key competences (civic competence; *občanská kompetence*).

Regarding civic competence, more detailed competences have been elaborated in the scope of its broad definition. The most important sub-competences related to EDC are as follows: respect for others and for their opinions, way of life, values, cultural background, etc.; awareness of and respect for the rules and democratic principles that govern life in pluralistic societies, appreciation and acceptance of these rules and principles; legal awareness; awareness and protection of human rights; respect for and protection of cultural heritage; responsibility for oneself, one's decisions and behaviour; tolerance, openness and flexibility but at the same time a critical approach to the opinions of others, and so on. All these aspects of civic competence must be embedded in all subjects referred to in the School Educational Programme project.

Concerning the cross-curricular theme of EDC, it is recommended to integrate its objectives and content into various subjects. Ideally, it could be represented in all subjects taught in school. In accordance with the experience of pilot schools, many schools integrate this cross-curricular theme into education for citizenship. This indicates that there is no common understanding of the concept and objectives of EDC in the school environment.

The following additional cross-curricular themes contribute to EDC: personal and social education; the European dimension and global education; multicultural education; media education; and environmental education (in terms of taking responsibility for our world). Hopefully, the experience of pilot schools will show other schools the need to implement civic competences within the scope of all cross-curricular themes and all subjects taught in school.

Education for citizenship represents social, human, cultural, economic, political, legal, European and global dimensions. All modules defined in this subject area are compulsory components of the whole domain and are interrelated. However, teachers are free to choose their own order, scope, depth, methods used, etc. Teachers are advised to use participative methods of teaching/learning and to show pupils society from different perspectives. The key element in education for citizenship is to develop a democratic atmosphere in the classroom and the school; to create an open space for dialogue, discussion and mutual co-operation; to create opportunities for active pupil/student participation in school life and the life of the local community; to involve pupils/students in decision making; and to promote their personal engagement in the life of the community they belong to.

According to the new Education Act, pupils/students in the Czech Republic should be given the opportunity to exert their democratic rights in school. Pupils/students have the right to set up and run pupil/student self-governing bodies (for example, school parliaments, pupil councils); the right to vote in these self-governing bodies, and to be elected as representatives of these bodies at school, municipal, regional or national level; and the right to express their opinions, suggestions and/or complaints openly within the school. It is crucial to involve pupils/students in the evaluation and self-evaluation processes at school.

Some schools already enable pupils/students to have a say in school matters by means of pupil/student parliaments, school councils, etc., and thus to exert an influence on school life and overall school development. Pupils'/students' participatory evaluation can serve as an excellent instrument for self-evaluation purposes. It could enhance the education quality offered by school and change existing school cultures by encouraging more evaluation and self-evaluation.

However, despite these new open rules and a wider concept of EDC, most schools still only see EDC from a very narrow perspective. Many teachers (especially those teaching technical and science-oriented subjects) are unable to cope with democratic approaches in education, for example constructive and participative ways of teaching, learning and evaluation, open partnerships between teachers and pupils, etc.

The lack of support for the EDC concept still apparent in the Czech Republic could jeopardise the effective use of the tool.

3.2.1. The connection between the tool and the quality assurance and evaluation system

As already noted (see especially sub-sections 1.1 and 3.1), the Czech national system of quality assurance is still in its initial stages. Nevertheless, many schools are already implementing evaluation and self-evaluation strategies in their daily practice. This gives the tool a good chance of being understood by those who are familiar with the concept of evaluation and self-evaluation processes carried out in schools and who are open-minded in terms of considering school to be a "social laboratory" for pupils/students. These professionals will undoubtedly accept the tool as good reference material (especially in those aspects concerning quality indicators, school development planning and initiating a self-evaluation process).

The tool could become a good starting point for many schools in terms of deepening their understanding of and concern about the evaluation and self-evaluation processes carried out in daily practice. For those who do not see the concept of EDC as being an umbrella concept in education, the tool could help teachers change their perspective of looking at EDC and may encourage them to find possible ways of integrating EDC into other subjects, activities, governance practices, etc.

3.2.2. Preparing teachers to work with the tool

If teachers of EDC or other subjects are to use the tool efficiently, they should be offered special training. In the case of the Czech Republic, there is a language barrier and to some extent a shortage of teachers prepared to use evaluation and/ or self-evaluation tools in their daily work, which could make it difficult to work independently with the tool. Even if a translation of the tool is offered, special training will be needed in order to enable teachers to work with the tool.

In the Czech Republic, especially in-service training centres should offer teachers specialised courses concerned with evaluation, self-evaluation and benefits, the need and reality of school/teaching development planning, elaborating and using various quality indicators in the field of EDC, etc. At the same time, they should be given the opportunity to learn about the EDC concept and to change their view of EDC.

For the purpose of familiarising teachers with the tool, more practical materials could contribute to its wider use. Teachers should be trained in the practical use of educational objectives and expected outcomes related to key competences. A publication concerning EDC, its methodology, concepts and approaches used in preparatory, implementation and evaluation stages could help teachers in this respect (Horská, Hrachovcová and Zouhar, 2007).

3.2.3. Other possible facilitators

The first thing that might facilitate the use of the tool is translation into the Czech language, as many teachers do not have a good command of English. If the tool is not translated, a large number of possible users will be excluded.

Another possible factor that would facilitate the use of the tool could lie in offering schools a wide range of resources: specialised materials introducing the concept of evaluation and self-evaluation in school; a list of EDC quality indicators and levels of their performance; specialised guidance for teachers in the field of EDC evaluation and self-evaluation; team-building and capacity-building concerning EDC, etc.

It would be very useful to ask various primary and secondary schools to try the tool out and verify its applicability in daily practice. These schools might serve as facilitators for other schools and as a primary source of information about the tool and the benefits of its use for school development.

4. Ideas for the implementation process

If the tool is to be implemented successfully in different countries, it must be adapted to country-specific conditions in each of them. This means that the tool has to be translated into the respective national languages in order to be fully understood, and could be amended by some kind of a "personalised" preface (for example, why the tool is useful in that country's context; what its links are with existing national documents, standards, indicators, etc.; how it can be used in the national context, etc.).

4.1. How to make working with the tool valuable for schools

If the tool is to be successful and valuable for teachers, it has to be enriched by examples of practical quality indicators used in school as a whole and in the classroom as well. There is a need to provide teachers with a tool that is specifically designed for monitoring and evaluating pupil/student activities and their progress in various fields of education. Quality indicators have to address key competences as well.

The first steps in implementing the tool in national environments should be its translation into the mother tongue or official national languages (depending on the specific context) and the wide dissemination of the translated tool. The tool should be disseminated to school administrators first; then it could be discussed with subject teachers and other stakeholders. For this purpose, a school seminar or some kind of specialised training course would be useful.

The next steps could be more flexible according to education conditions in different countries. In any case, it would be suitable to invite schools (for example, by means of a special tender) to test the tool in practice and verify its applicability in daily school life. Teachers already using the tool could become mentors or serve as multipliers of specific evaluation and self-evaluation strategies for other schools.

This scenario could be used in the Czech Republic as well, with the proviso that the Czech Ministry of Education, Youth and Sports and other relevant institutions would promote the tool and its use. A good translation of the tool into Czech is needed, and a major information campaign should be launched, covering topics such as the EDC concept in school education with regard to school content and school governance. Such a campaign could serve as general evaluation and self-evaluation reference material; without it, it would be difficult to introduce the tool for EDC purposes.

4.2. How to integrate the tool into international partnerships

It would be both beneficial and effective to make it possible for schools to set up partnerships with other schools (maybe even have some specialised website or a blog that could serve as a discussion forum), providing them with an opportunity to exchange ideas about implementing evaluation and self-evaluation strategies in schools and to present best practice examples in this field.

With regard to school partnerships, it would be interesting to enable teachers to undertake study visits to other (foreign) schools and to invite them to present their experience in the field of evaluation and self-evaluation. This could be enriching for both schools and their staff. Possibly, school seminars or partnership conferences could be organised for the staff of both schools during the holiday period.

The only inconvenience and/or constraint might be the language competence of teachers. In the Czech Republic, relatively few professional teachers with foreign language expertise (especially English) are active in the field of EDC and/or social science. Moreover, many teachers are not computer-literate. Some schools, moreover, lack access to the Internet (however, there are relatively few of these schools).

4.3. Alternative scenarios for working with the tool

One alternative possibility for using the tool could be through follow-up measures. New, more precise quality indicators in the field of EDC could be elaborated by various national or international groups of experts (for example, the Council of

Europe, the European Commission, UNESCO or OECD expert groups, etc.). A brochure of good practice examples across Europe could be compiled. A special Council of Europe website aimed at collecting good practice examples, theoretical background materials, etc. could be set up as a useful reference point.

National administrations could create similar websites focused on evaluation and self-evaluation issues. The tool should be presented there in official national languages and accompanied with a national preface.

Another possibility for making good use of the tool and its qualities is to offer it to national experts dealing with quality assurance and/or quality indicators in the EDC field.

References

Act No. 561 of 24 September 2004 on Preschool, Basic, Secondary, Tertiary Professional and Other Education (the Education Act), Prague: Ministerstvo školství, mládeže a tělovýchovy ČR. Retrieved on 17 October 2006, from www.msmt.cz/_DOMEK/default.asp?ARI=103274&CAI=3255.

Albert, Alexander (2001). *TQM manažérstvo kvality v škole*, Dunajská streda: Lilium Aurum.

Bacík, František et al. (1995). *Úvod do teorie a praxe školského managementu*, Prague: Karolinum.

Belz, Horst and Siegrist, Marco (2001). *Klíčové kompetence a jejich rozvíjení. Východiska, metody, cvičení a hry*, Prague: Portál.

Beran, Vít (1996). *Jak si udělat školu na míru*, Prague: Agentura Strom.

Bernhardt, Victoria L. (1999). *The School Portfolio. A Comprehensive Framework for School Improvement* (2nd edn), Larchmont: Eye on Education.

Byčkovský, Petr (1988). *Základy měření výsledků výuky*, Prague: ČVUT.

Chlebek, Petr (1999). Vlastní hodnocení školy (Osobní zkušenosti ředitele školy), Plzeň: PC Plzeň.

Číhalová, Eva and Mayer, Ivo (1997). *Klasifikace a slovní hodnocení*. Prague: Agentura Strom.

Citizenship Education at School in Europe (2005). Brussels: Eurydice.

Dlouhodobý záměr vzdělávání a rozvoje výchovně vzdělávací soustavy České republiky (2002). Prague: Ministerstvo školství, mládeže a tělovýchovy ČR.

Dlouhodobý záměr vzdělávání a rozvoje vzdělávací soustavy České republiky (2005). Prague: Ministerstvo školství, mládeže a tělovýchovy ČR. Retrieved on 17 October 2006, from www.msmt.cz/_DOMEK/default.asp?ARI=103259&CAI=2802.

Education System in the Czech Republic 2005/2006 (2006). Brussels: Eurydice. Retrieved on 9 May 2007, from www.eurydice.org/ressources/Eurydice/pdf/eurybase/2006_DNCZ_EN.pdf.

Eger, Ludvík et al. (2002). *Strategie rozvoje školy*, Plzeň: CECHTUMA.

European Report on the Quality of School Education (2005). 16 Quality Indicators. Brussels: European Commission.

Evaluace škol poskytujících povinné vzdělání v Evropě (2005). Prague: Ústav pro informace ve vzdělávání. Retrieved on 18 October 2006, from www.eurydice.org/ressources/eurydice/pdf/0_integral/042CS.pdf.

Evaluation of Schools Providing Compulsory Education (2004). Brussels: Eurydice.

Georgi, Viola B. (2005). *Expert Workshop: Quality Assurance in Terms of Education for Democratic Citizenship*, Bonn: Bundeszentrale für Politische Bildung. Retrieved on 15 September 2006, from www.eduhi.at/dl/NECE_Workshop_Vienna_Bericht_Georgi_fuer_Website.pdf.

Grecmanová, Helena (2004). "Evaluace školního klimatu", *Řízení ve školství*, Vol. 12, No. 5, 4-29.

Helus, Zdeněk et al. (1979). *Psychologie školní úspěšnosti žáků*, Prague: SPN.

Horská, Viola; Hrachovcová, Marie; Zouhar, Jan (2007). *Manuál ke tvorbě učebních osnov v ŠVP. Příručka pro učitele občanské výchovy*, Prague: Práce.

International Conference on Self-evaluation and Its Contribution to Continual School Development (2006). Retrieved on 17 October 2006, from http://194.228.111.171/files/konf1/KONFERENCNI_SBORNIK.pdf.

Katalog požadavků k maturitní zkoušce: Občanský základ (2004). Prague: Ústav pro informace ve vzdělávání.

Katalog požadavků k maturitní zkoušce: Občanský a společenskovědní základ (2005). Prague: Ústav pro informace ve vzdělávání.

Key Competencies: A Developing Concept in General Compulsory Education (2002). Brussels: Eurydice.

Kitzberger, Jindřich (2004a). "Autoevaluace školy", in Slavíková, Lenka; Kučera, Radoslav; Linhart, Petr et al., *Vedení školy v praxi. D.2.6*, Prague: Raabe.

Kitzberger, Jindřich (2004b). "Jak si ředitelé vytvářejí obraz o kvalitě své školy? Výzkumná sonda – zdroje informací o kvalitě školy a indikátory kvality podle ředitelů škol", *Učitelské listy*, Vol. 11, No. 10, June, 1-4. Příloha pro ředitele Číslo 10.

Klíčové competence. Vznikající pojem ve všeobecném povinném vzdělávání (2003). Prague: Ústav pro informace ve vzdělávání. Retrieved on 18 October 2006, from www.eurydice.org/ressources/eurydice/pdf/0_integral/032CS.pdf.

Kolář, Zdeněk; Navrátil, Stanislav; Šikulová, Renata (1998). *Školní hodnocení a jeho současné problémy*, Ústí nad Labem: Univerzita J.E. Purkyně.

Koucký, Jan et al. (1999). *České vzdělání a Evropa. Strategie rozvoje lidských zdrojů při vstupu do Evropské unie* (Czech Education and Europe. Pre-accession Strategy for Human Resource Development), Prague: Sdružení pro vzdělávací politiku.

Kovařovic, Jan (2004). "Evaluace v práci školy", in Walterová, Eliška et al., *Úloha školy v rozvoji vzdělanosti. Part II*, Brno: Paido, 403-439.

Krek, Janez (2004). *Quality Assurance in Education and for Education for Democratic Citizenship: An Institutional Overview*, Ljubljana, Centre for Education Policies Studies. Retrieved on 15 September 2006, from www.coe.int/T/e/Cultural_Co-operation/Education/E.D.C/Documents_and_publications.

Křížová, Ivana et al. (2001). *Znalosti, dovednosti a postoje Čtrnáctiletých žáků v oblasti výchova k občanství. Zpráva o výsledcích mezinárodního výzkumu*, Prague: Ústav pro informace ve vzdělávání.

Kunčarová, Jitka and Nezvalová, Danuše (2006a). *Kvalita školy. Ověřování kvality školy*, Ostrava: Ostravská univerzita.

Kunčarová, Jitka and Nezvalová, Danuše (2006b). *Kvalita školy. Soubor ukazatelů kvality školy*, Ostrava: Ostravská univerzita.

Kvalita I. Systémový projekt (2005). Retrieved on 17 October 2006, from www.esf-kvalita1.cz.

Kvalita II. Systémový projekt (2005). Retrieved on 17 October 2006, from www.msmt.cz/_DOMEK/default.asp?ARI=103490&CAI=3219.

Kvalita a odpovědnost. Program rozvoje vzdělávací soustavy České republiky (1994). Prague: Ministerstvo školství, mládeže a tělovýchovy ČR.

Kyriacou, Chris (2004). *Klíčové dovednosti učitele. Cesty k lepšímu vyučování* (2nd edn), Prague: Portál.

MacBeath, John (1991). *Schools Must Speak for Themselves. The Case for School Self-evaluation*, London: Routledge Falmer.

MacBeath, John and McGlynn, Archie (2002). *Self-evaluation. What's in It for Schools?* London: Routledge Falmer.

MacBeath, John et al. (2006). *Serena aneb Autoevaluace škol v Evropě*, Žďár nad Sázavou: Fakta.

Michek, Stanislav et al. (2006). *Příručka pro sebehodnocení poskytovatelů odborného vzdělávání*, Prague: Národní ústav odborného vzdělávání.

Mičienka, Marek et al. (2002). *Mikrosonda občanský a společenskovědní základ. Závěrečná zpráva projektu.* Prague: Ústav pro informace ve vzdělávání.

Národní program rozvoje vzdělávání v České republice. Bílá kniha (2001). Prague: Ústav pro informace ve vzdělávání.

National Programme for the Development of Education in the Czech Republic. White Paper (2001). Prague: Ústav pro informace ve vzdělávání. Retrieved on 17 October 2006, from www.msmt.cz/files/pdf/whitepaper.pdf.

Nezvalová, Danuše (1999). *Řízení kvality*, Prague: Univerzita Karlova.

Nezvalová, Danuše (2000). *Reflexe v pregraduální přípravě učitele*, Olomouc: Univerzita Palackého.

Nezvalová, Danuše (2002). *Kvalita ve škole*, Olomouc: Univerzita Palackého.

Nezvalová, Danuše; Prášilová, Michaela; Eger, Ludvík (2004). *Kurikulum, řízení změn a tvorba vize školy*, Plzeň: Západočeská univerzita.

Obst, Otto (2000). *Základy školského managementu pro učitele*, Olomouc: Univerzita Palackého.

Pasch, Marvin et al. (1998). *Od vzdělávacího programu k vyučovací hodině. Jak pracovat s kurikulem*, Prague: Portál.

Pol, Milan (2001). *Plánování rozvoje školy s použitím specifického systému posuzování práce školy*, Brno: Filozofická fakulta Masarykovy univerzity.

Pol, Milan and Lazarová, Bohumíra (1999). *Spolupráce učitelů – podmínka rozvoje školy. Řízení spolupráce, konkrétní formy a nástroje*, Prague: Agentura Strom.

Prášilová, Michaela (2006). *Tvorba vzdělávacího programu*, Prague: Triton.

Prášilová, Michaela and Vašťatková, Jana (2005). "Pracovníci školy jako důležitý zdroj informací o stávající situaci školy", *Pedagogická orientace*, Vol. 2005, No. 2, 53-59.

Print, Murray; Ornstrom, Susanne; Nielsen, Henrik Skovgaard (2002). "Education for Democratic Processes in Schools and Classrooms", *European Journal of Education*, Vol. 37, No. 2, 193-210.

Průcha, Jan (1996). *Pedagogická evaluace. Hodnocení vzdělávacích programů, procesů a výsledků*, Brno: Masarykova univerzita.

Průcha, Jan (1997). *Moderní pedagogika*, Prague: Portál.

Rámcový vzdělávací program pro základní vzdělávání (2005). Ed. by Jeřábek, Jaroslav and Tupý, Jan, Prague: Výzkumný ústav pedagogický v Praze.

Rámcový vzdělávací program pro gymnázium (2006). Ed. by Jeřábek, Jaroslav; Krčková, Stanislava; Hučínová, Lucie, Prague: Výzkumný ústav pedagogický v Praze (pilot version).

Roupec, Petr (1997). *Vedení školy. Autoevaluace*. Prague: Raabe.

Rýdl, Karel (1996). *Cesta k autonomní škole*, Prague: Agentura Strom.

Schimunek, Franz-Peter (1994). *Slovní hodnocení žáků*, Prague: Portál.

Rýdl, Karel; Horská, Viola; Dvořáková, Markéta; Roupec, Petr (1998). *Sebehodnocení školy. Jak hodnotit kvalitu školy*, Prague: Agentura Strom.

Skalková, Jarmila (1995). *Za novou kvalitu vyučování. Inovace v soudobé pedagogické teorii a praxi*, Brno: Paido.

Skalková, Jarmila (2005). "Rámcové vzdělávací programy – dlouhodobý úkol", *Pedagogika*, Vol. 15, No. 1, 2005, 4-18.

Slavík, Jan (1999). *Hodnocení v současné škole. Východiska a nové metody pro praxi*, Prague: Portál.

Štech, Stanislav (1992). *Škola stále nová*, Prague: Karolinum.

Švarcová, Iva (2005). *Základy pedagogiky*, Prague: Vysoká škola chemicko-technologická v Praze.

Švec, Štefan (1998). *Metodológia vied o výchove*, Bratislava: IRIS.

Světlík, Jaroslav (1996). *Marketing školy*, Zlín: EKKA.

Tematická zpráva. Tematická inspekce zaměřená na autoevaluaci základních a středních škol (2004). Prague: Česká školní inspekce. Retrieved on 18 October 2006, from www.csicr.cz/upload/autoevaluace_ZS_SS.pdf.

Tematická zpráva. Vlastní hodnocení základních a středních škol (2005). Prague: Česká školní inspekce. Retrieved on 18 October 2006, from www.csicr.cz/upload/vlastni_hodnoceni_ZS_SS.pdf.

Tondl, Ladislav (1999). *Hodnocení a hodnoty. Metodologické rozměry hodnocení*, Prague: Filosofia.

Torney-Purta, Judith (2002). "Patterns in the Civic Knowledge, Engagement, and Attitudes of European Adolescents: The IEA Civic Education Study", *European Journal of Education*, Vol. 37, No. 2, 129-141.

Torney-Purta, Judith et al. (2001). *Citizenship and Education in Twenty-eight Countries: Civic Knowledge and Engagement at Age Fourteen*, Amsterdam: IEA.

Vašťatková, Jana (2004). "Autoevaluace jako prostředek k trvalému rozvoji školy", *Pedagogická orientace*, Vol. 2004, No. 3, 73-78.

Vašťatková, Jana (2005). "Podstata autoevaluace školy", *Učitelské listy*, Vol. 13, No. 1, September, supplement *Ředitelské listy*, 1-3.

Vašťatková, Jana (2006). *Úvod do autoevaluace školy*, Olomouc: Univerzita Palackého.

Vašťatková, Jana and Prášilová, Michaela (2005). "Jak jsou školy z pohledu ředitelů připraveny na zavádění autoevaluace/vlastního hodnocení?" in Vašťatková, Jana (ed.), *Pedagogický výzkum: reflexe společenských potřeb a očekávání? Sborník z XIII. konference ČAPV*, Olomouc: Univerzita Palackého, 335-339.

Vašťatková, Jana and Prášilová, Michaela (2006). "Vlastní hodnocení školy a realita", in *SCHOLA 2006. Kvalita výchovy a vzdelávania*, Bratislava: Slovenská technická univerzita, 443-450.

Výchova k občanství ve školách v Evropě (2006). Prague: Ústav pro informace ve vzdělávání. Retrieved on 18 October 2006, from www.eurydice.org/ressources/eurydice/pdf/0_integral/055CS.pdf.

Vyhláška Č. 15/2005 Sb., kterou se stanoví náležitosti dlouhodobých záměrů, výročních zpráv a vlastního hodnocení školy (2005). Prague: Ministerstvo školství, mládeže a tělovýchovy ČR. Retrieved on 17 October 2006, from www.msmt.cz/_DOMEK/Default.asp?ARI=103113&CAI=3257&EXPS="VYHLÁŠKA*"%20AND%20"15/2005*".

Zákon Č. 561/2004 Sb., o předškolním, základním, středním, vyšším odborném a jiném vzdělávání (školský zákon). Prague: Ministerstvo školství, mládeže a tělovýchovy ČR. Retrieved on 17 October 2006, from www.msmt.cz/_DOMEK/default.asp?ARI=103001&CAI=3255.

Web references:

- www.esf-kvalita1.cz/evaluace.php (basic information about Kvalita I project – school evaluation and self-evaluation).
- www.scio.cz/tvorba_testu/teorie_testu (test elaboration in Scio).

- www.scio.cz/tvorba_testu/hodnoceni_kvality (quality assessment of admission exams in secondary schools led by Scio).
- www.webparking.cz/kalibro.cz/index.php?lang=en&sec=about_us (basic information about the Kalibro project).
- www.rvp.cz/sekce/511 (portal, school self-evaluation section).
- www.scv.upol.cz/Studium/FS_2/rizeni_kvality/Riz_kval.doc (quality management – an in-service study programme for head teachers and school managers).
- http://web.pedf.cuni.cz/uprps/vzdel-kbs.php (quality management – an in-service study programme for head teachers and school managers).
- www.cermat.cz (Centre for Assessment of Education Outcomes).

Estonia
Anu Toots

1. School evaluation in Estonia

The school system in Estonia

Estonia has a comprehensive school system with a compulsory national curriculum and a single-track structure. Pre-primary education is not compulsory in Estonia, although 80% of 4-year-old children go to kindergarten (COM, 2006: 28). Compulsory education lasts until the end of lower secondary education or until the age of 17. After completing basic schooling, students can continue in general upper secondary education (gymnasium) or in vocational education. Admission to higher education is based on a secondary education certificate and the candidate's assessment score.

Most students attend public sector schools, which are funded by the national government and maintained by the local governments. In the academic year 2005/06, 89% of pupils attended municipal schools, 5% state schools and 7.5% private schools (Eurydice, 2006). State schools include educational establishments for children with special needs (often mentally or physically disabled), where the learning process is based on the adjusted curriculum. Private schools usually follow the national curriculum and receive some financial support from the government. Nevertheless, parents have to pay fees. Religious schools are almost non-existent in Estonia. Municipal schools have their own school districts and guarantee a place for each pupil close to his/her home. Parents can also choose another school if there is a vacant place available. Some of the most popular schools use various admission exams or tests; at upper secondary level this is quite a common practice.

Municipalities have quite a large degree of autonomy in running schools in their own territory. They make decisions on whether to open or close a school, on administrative matters and on the language of tuition. Since Estonia has a large Russian-speaking minority residing mainly in the capital, Tallinn, and in the northeast, many Russian-speaking schools can be found there. For example in Tallinn 27 out of 69 municipal schools (39%) are Russian-speaking. In 2006 16% of all general educational institutions in Estonia had Russian as their language of tuition (Eurydice, 2006). In all those schools Estonian is a compulsory subject; students must also pass a public exam in Estonian language at the end of lower and upper secondary education. Aiming at more efficient integration of non-Estonian minorities into Estonian society, a special national programme on ensuring the transition of Russian-speaking upper secondary schools to Estonian as the language of instruction has been developed. The Ministry of Education and Research (MER) has determined five subjects (Estonian literature, citizenship education, geography, Estonian history and music) in which tuition must be carried out in Estonian. The new system will be implemented step by step starting on 1 September 2007 and ending in 2014. Although the public authorities have undertaken many efforts to prepare the reform, public opinion on the issue is still divided. Some parents, students and teachers support the reform because it creates better career opportunities for non-native students; others fear the decline in quality of teaching and in students' performance indicators.

In addition to the planned movement towards Estonian-speaking schools, there is also a clear bottom-up initiative in this area. An increasing number of non-Estonian parents are now deciding to send their children to an Estonian-speaking kindergarten and further to an Estonian school. Thus the number of Russian-speaking educational establishments is decreasing. This trend is amplified by the overall sharp decrease in the school-age population in Estonia. The number of pupils is expected to decrease by 44 000 by 2010. This means that many schools will be closed down, and others merged or rearranged as combined preschool and primary school establishments.

1.1. Modes of school evaluation

Estonia uses several different modes of school evaluation – external inspections, standardised assessment tests and public exams, and internal evaluation. All these procedures are stipulated in national primary and secondary legislation, and thus the system can be regarded as transparent and comprehensive. The main legal acts that regulate all kinds of school evaluations are the Act on Basic and Secondary Schools; the Act on Vocational Educational Institutions; the Act on Pre-primary Educational Institutions and the Act on Private Schools.

External evaluation has a long tradition in the Estonian educational system dating back to the Soviet era. There are two main modes of external evaluation – state inspections and national assessment of students' achievement. In the last decade more attention has been put on assessment, with school inspections becoming less important. The aim of state inspection is to control how schools follow governmental legal acts, which regulate education and training activities. A detailed procedure of implementation of the state evaluation is enacted in a decree of the Minister for Education and Research. Formerly, each school had to pass a total inspection once every six years, but since 2006 the system has been amended. Now the evaluation has a thematic approach, which means that each year certain priorities are selected for inspection. In 2006, for example, the focus was on the work of the school educational board (*õppenõukogu*). The regularity of meetings, their content and decisions, and the engagement of different parties in the work of the board are all subject to evaluation.

Since Estonia has a unified administrative system, the representative of the national government in regions, the county governor, bears responsibility for executing governmental control in schools. The county governor nominates, out of the county administration staff, people to inspect schools; educational experts must be also involved. A team of inspectors visits sampled schools for five days and conducts interviews, observations, tests and studies school documents. Ten days after the visit the school receives a written evaluation report and can comment on it. Annually in spring, county governors compose a summary report on site visits they have performed according to the indicators stated in the decree, and forward it to the MER. The results of the supervision of educational institutions at the state level are analysed and published. An electronic version of the document is published on the MER's website. The MER uses the results of the analysis to amend legal acts and to prepare strategic documents for educational policy.

The external inspection of schools organised by the county governments deals mainly with their financial, legal and administrative accountability. Another important aspect of external evaluation – control upon learning achievements – is the responsibility of the National Board of Examinations and Qualifications (NBEQ). The board, which is a semi-independent body subordinated to the MER, organises external assessments in three different modes: level tests, final centrally set exams at the end of lower secondary school (grade 9, end of compulsory schooling) and national exams at the end of upper secondary school (grade 12). The system of external assessment was implemented in 1997 and at that time prompted much argument for and against. Today, the general opinion is supportive, although some criticisms have been voiced that educational assessment relies overmuch upon quantitative measurement and grading.

The definition of exams and their aims are enacted by a decree of the Minister for Education and Research (https://www.riigiteataja.ee/ert/act.jsp?id=968652). The objectives of final and public exams are:
- to assess the extent to which curriculum objectives have been achieved;
- to obtain feedback on the efficiency of tuition;
- to guide the teaching and learning process;
- to receive reliable data to enable comparison of students' achievements.

The higher the level of assessment, the stricter and more advanced the procedures are. So, level tests are carried out in sampled schools, test items are composed by the staff of the NBEQ, but grading is carried out by the teachers of the tested schools. For final exams in lower and upper secondary schools, special commissions are responsible for developing items and creating the assessment guide. Different parties are members of the commissions, such as teachers, staff of the NBEQ and university teachers. At public exams in upper secondary schools, an external observer must be present.

The content of exams follows the national curriculum; basically all content areas of the subjects are covered since the aim of any exam is to evaluate how efficiently the curriculum is being implemented. In addition to knowledge of the subject matter, the exam also assesses general educational competences such as students' ability to evaluate relations and situations and to take actions and the ability of self-reflection. To assess all these various aspects the exam includes different types of questions. Some questions are based on work with statistical or documentary sources, some presuppose analytical skills or the ability to see the relationship between facts and developments. Argumentation skills, as well as the capacity to formulate a personal viewpoint and to defend it, are also assessed.

There is strong evidence that the introduction of final exams in civic education at the end of lower and upper secondary school has changed attitudes towards the subject. Schools and teachers now allocate more time and effort to teaching, while students take learning more seriously. As a result of these changes, the number of students who choose to take the exam in civic education is increasing year by year. When this exam was first introduced in 2002, 995 students chose it. By 2007 the number had increased to 5 460, comprising about 30% of high school graduates in Estonia.

Nevertheless, not everything works perfectly. The format of final exams is continuously improved as a result of feedback analysis, but curriculum and textbook development rarely takes messages from exams directly into account. This is partly a consequence of poor co-ordination between the different departments of the NBEQ. The exams are the responsibility of the Department of Curricula and Exams, but development and improvement of the national curriculum is the function of another unit – the Department of Curriculum Development. Another shortcoming of the national assessment system is its very rapid development and assessment rules that change too frequently. This complicates comparison across years and subjects and challenges the reliability of findings. According to the research literature, the latter seems to be a common problem in educational systems that rely heavily upon external testing (Apple, 2004).

Speaking about internal evaluation of schools in general terms, the increasing attention of educational authorities should be noted. Referring to the European experience (Eurydice, 2004), the Estonian MER started active work on implementation of internal evaluation in schools. A voluntary internal audit was first introduced in 2001. Five years later, relevant educational acts were amended and internal evaluation became obligatory for all types of educational establishments (including pre-primary, vocational and private schools).

According to national law, internal evaluation is a permanent process that aims to create a good environment for students' development and to secure continuity in a school's educational work. As a result of self-evaluation, the strengths of the school as well as opportunities for improvements should be determined. The findings of self-evaluation must be included in the school's development plan and into its three-year action plan (see the Act on Basic and Secondary Schools). Although the school's head teacher is the person who decides the precise procedure of self-evaluation, he or she must also consider the opinions of the school board (*hoole-*

kogu) and the school holder (the municipality or private owners). They both must approve the self-evaluation report before the head teacher can sign it.

Efforts of the MER to prepare carefully the implementation of this new initiative must be pointed out. The ministry has organised various projects, seminars and meetings to introduce the idea of internal evaluation, such as the Omanäoline Kool (Unique School) project in the 1990s, the joint project of the Estonian MER and Canada on the learning community, and the projects of the MER and the British Council on internal appraisal of educational institutions. The MER also takes care of providing training and methodical support to the schools in performing self-evaluation. According to the Development Plan of General Education 2007-13, 80% of schools should pass relevant training by 2010. Special advisers will be employed by the NBEQ to consult schools on evaluation issues. The MER will also support projects to involve parents and students in school activities, as engagement is regarded as a powerful tool that can make the self-evaluation process work (MER, 2007). In 2006 the MER issued guidelines for performing internal evaluations in schools, which provide a detailed tool and indicators applicable for different educational levels (kindergarten, general educational establishments and vocational schools). The methodological departing point combines the whole-school approach, the conception of the learning organisation and EFQM.

Internal evaluation is performed in two parts. Firstly, an online database on educational information (EHIS) (www.ehis.ee) was launched in 2005. It collects annually basic performance indicators of schools such as class size, the student–teacher ratio, the number of teachers, their qualifications and demographic characteristics, etc. The aim of this online database is to make all information necessary for evaluation transparent and easily accessible. Secondly, every three years each school composes a self-evaluation report according to the indicators and targets set by the guidelines. Since internal evaluation has only been introduced very recently (in July 2006), the first self-evaluation reports do not have to be accomplished until September 2010. Thus, there is sufficient time for preparation and learning. The crucial moment today is awareness-raising among teaching staff and increasing their motivation for self-evaluation. Teachers often complain about their steadily rising administrative workload, and thus may regard the self-evaluation process as an additional administrative burden.

Recent trends in school evaluation are clearly affected by developments in the EU educational policy. This means greater emphasis on internal self-evaluation instead of classical external inspection. The main aim is to build up a synergetic system of school evaluation. In addition, the financial support of the European Social Fund (ESF) allows various activities to be expanded, such as training advisers, developing guidelines and tools, carrying out studies, etc. In 2006 an ESF project Koolikatsuja 2006+ (School Tester 2006+) was launched in co-operation with the MER and universities aiming to provide a complex solution to school evaluation. In the course of that project, a handbook for internal evaluation will be elaborated and teams from 36 schools will be trained during 240 hours of schooling to carry out self-evaluation in schools. The handbook includes sample questionnaires for appraising the satisfaction of students, staff and parents and the software required for analysing the results.

Although there are many legal norms already in force, the issue of school evaluation is still highly topical and the subject of lively debate in educational circles.

1.2. Evaluation as an issue in teacher training

Initial teacher training in Estonia is carried out by two large public universities – Tartu University and Tallinn University. Universities enjoy remarkable autonomy in Estonia, especially regarding curriculum policy and teaching practices. Thus the subject content and titles of the curricula in the same field may vary significantly. Nevertheless, the policy on teacher education is somewhat stricter. All teacher education curricula must be composed according to the Government Decree Framework Requirements for Teacher Education (2000). The decree states that the aim of the initial teacher training is to prepare teachers who are competent to realise a school's developmental and curriculum objectives. Subjects included in the teacher education curricula should provide future teachers with competences in leadership and management, including the skills to cope with a multicultural environment. All curricula in Estonian higher education are subject to international accreditation, and thus as a starting premise, it is likely that the objectives of the framework requirements will be pursued.

Nevertheless, a detailed analysis of curricula in the field reveals that effective training is not so advanced and follows a rather traditional subject-centred approach. This means that future mathematics and science teachers mainly study different subjects on maths, also including didactics. Lecture courses that provide knowledge and skills in quality management are not part of every curriculum in teacher training and education. As a rule, these topics are primarily addressed at the MA level, and especially in curricula oriented towards managers and policy makers. For example, in Tallinn University there is a curriculum called "Educational Management", which includes subjects on the development of the school curriculum and on school performance management. In the University of Tartu one can find an MA curriculum on "School Management", which includes several subjects on management and quality assurance. Ordinary student teachers can freely choose to take these subjects, which only comprise a very insignificant portion of their study plan. It is interesting to note that "School Management" as a curriculum belongs to the area of business and administration, whereas curricula in the area of education do not contain anything on management or evaluation procedures. Thus, the existing initial teacher-training system does not equip graduates with sufficient competences to carry out quality assurance in schools. Among the older generation of teachers, relevant knowledge is even scarcer.

Teacher education in general terms has been focused on by decision makers for many years now. However, no complex reform has been carried out since the collapse of the Soviet regime. The current system of teacher training is highly fragmented and lacks a reliable monitoring system. This is especially true for in-service teacher training. Therefore a working group representing various educational stakeholders and interests was set up in order to develop a National Development Plan for Teacher Education. A draft version of this document was presented in 2003, but unfortunately has still not been enacted. Despite this, teacher-training institutions are already taking the stipulations of the draft version into account. Another positive factor is the system of professional standards for teachers, which was enacted in 2004. To obtain high qualification standards, applicant teachers must demonstrate to the special Professional Council of Education that they possess all the required knowledge and skills, including those of conducting self-evaluation. Although this system of professional qualification is voluntary, it is a good motivator for teachers to pay more attention to personal professional development.

The Development Plan for Teacher Education also highlights some weaknesses of the current situation in teacher education. The rather general character of the framework requirements is criticised for causing considerable variance within different teacher education curricula (see also the current report above). According to the authors of the development plan, some important aspects such as citizenship education, teamwork in the school and curriculum development are not sufficiently represented in current teacher education curricula (MER, 2003).

When comparing the two legal documents that deal with school evaluation (the Framework Requirements for Teacher Education (2000) and the Developmental Plan of Teacher Education (2003)), one can note a somewhat more explicit focus on quality and evaluation issues in the latter. For example, knowledge of the basics of management and leadership, as well as the ability to master methods of assessment, feedback and analysis, are mentioned there as required pedagogical competences of the teacher. Unfortunately, the whole school approach is not visible in that document either; instead, the focus remains on individual teachers within single classes.

1.3. The use of evaluation results in schools and the educational system

It is hard to estimate the real use of evaluation practices, since the relevant information is very fragmented and poor. The picture is somewhat better at the system level concerning external evaluation of achievements. Every year the NBEQ analyses the data of final national exams within subjects, regions and school types. The results of this analysis are published annually in a separate collection of articles and made public on the website of the NBEQ. Additionally, each school receives an analysis of their students' results. The findings also serve as a basis for improving the format and context of exams and for adapting in-service training courses to the teachers' needs. Commissions that prepare national exams usually start work on the next exam after a profound analysis of the last year's results.

Since there is considerable media attention on exam results, schools are very sensitive about this issue. Estonia has eagerly followed neo-liberal educational reforms in the UK, and therefore many problems that concern British citizens are also familiar to Estonia. So-called league tables, which rank schools according to their performance, are often published in Estonian newspapers and cause similar popular interest and sharp criticism to that in the UK. The majority of teachers and parents regard ranking schools purely on the basis of national exam results as unfair and unreliable. Nevertheless, league tables continue to appear in the press and many parents make their choice of school based on them.

The MER has recognised the problem of an excessive focus on exam results among the general public, but the proposed measures can only be regarded as attempting to remedy the situation, while not changing it radically. The main concern of the MER is the reliability of exam results across school years and subjects. To enhance reliability, more extensive participation in international student assessments, such as the Programme for International Student Assessment (PISA) and the International Association for the Evaluation of Educational Achievement (IEA) studies, is planned (MER, 2007). Estonia is also engaged in elaborating quality indicators in education at the EU level (including indicators on active citizenship).

Putting more value on internal evaluation as an inclusive and multidimensional process can lead to more fundamental changes. In this aspect the philosophy of education for democratic citizenship (EDC) and quality assurance in EDC (EDC-QA) can be helpful, since these stress not so much the final outcome in terms of learning achievement, but rather various factors of democratic educational governance (Bîrzea et al., 2005: 100).

Internal evaluation in the Estonian educational system is still in its initial stages today, and therefore it is hard to assess whether complex results of internal evaluation can outweigh the dominance of exam league tables. To make this happen, carefully designed PR activities are needed.

2. The "Tool for Quality Assurance of Education for Democratic Citizenship in Schools"

2.1. Comprehensiveness and coherence

The authors of the tool have taken all materials produced within the EDC project into account so far. This allows them to keep in line with the mainstream principles of EDC ideology and show the strengths and weaknesses of the EDC process itself. In my opinion, one of these weaknesses is the broad definition of EDC. As stated in the tool, "EDC is learning throughout life in all circumstances, and in every form of human activities" (Bîrzea et al., 2005: 26). This approach brings EDC very close to the concept of lifelong learning. What seems to be the main problem here is the difficulty of linking such a vague concept to quality assurance. The latter presupposes operationalisation of the concept and definition of measurable indicators. Since the key concept (EDC) is not operationalised, the evaluative framework also remains quite general. So Table 1, which shows EDC quality indicators, does not provide any measures of these indicators. Instead, "sub-themes" to indicators are provided, which are even more abstract than the quality indicators themselves. For example, how are "EDC learning outcomes" (p. 60) measured? What are actually these "learning outcomes"? Illustrating the methodology with some concrete examples will help readers to grasp the logic of the evaluation framework.

I do agree with the authors that keeping the wide variety of situations in Europe in mind, one cannot go very far with concrete indicators. Nevertheless, remaining too abstract means reducing the practical value of the tool. One must agree that educational systems in Europe are very different, but despite that, the European Commission still succeeded in defining common benchmarks in education and training. Indicators for active citizenship are in the process of being developed.[1] Thus, my suggestion is to elaborate a system of indicators and their measures somewhat further.

The second problem of a general character concerns the relation of EDC to QA. According to the tool, the QA approach means that all parties are engaged in the process, which is by its very nature collaborative and supportive (Bîrzea et al., 2005: 35). The same characteristics are stressed as key aspects of EDC (Bîrzea et al., 2005: 24-25, 100). Thus, EDC and QA as methodological approaches to the quality of education seem to blend or amalgamate. Although some headlines promise to explain what the peculiarity of EDC is in terms of QA, I was unable to discover it. Table 9, dedicated to this issue, does not provide any convincing answers in this regard (Bîrzea et al., 2005: 106).

My third suggestion for improving the tool is to target it better at different user groups. The total stakeholder approach must be highly appreciated and promoted, but its realisation will be more feasible if each stakeholder can find perspectives in it that are precisely relevant to him or her.

There are different groups involved in EDC-QA – students, teachers, parents, school administrations and municipality governments. Additionally these groups are hierarchically structured – some students, parents and teachers are socially active, and often members of representative bodies; whereas others, so-called rank-and-file members, are not so eager to participate or to speak up. Heads of

---

1. A network comprising key interdisciplinary experts from across Europe was established in 2006 jointly by the Council of Europe and the Centre for Research on Lifelong Learning (CRELL) based on indicators and benchmarks of the European Commission. The aim of this research project, Active Citizenship for Democracy, was to contribute to the analysis of data needs, the development of the survey modules and the selection of indicators. On the basis of this work, an Active Citizenship Composite Indicator was developed, which was included in the 2008 "Report on Progress Towards Lisbon Objectives in Education and Training". Further information is available at: http://active-citizenship.jrc.ec.europa.eu.

schools and head teachers represent authority even in a very democratic school and probably bear the main responsibility for evaluation and QA. Thus, it will help to achieve broad and effective engagement if the roles and possibilities for the intervention of different stakeholders are explicitly stated in the tool. It also seems to be of primary importance that the patterns of interaction between different parties are described in the document.

As a matter of secondary importance, some contradictions and repetitions can be found in the text. For example, on one page (p. 101), accountability measures related to market competition approaches are criticised, but shortly afterwards, the results of national assessment tests are praised as providing valuable information (p. 103). I also found the constant reference to various chapters, stating where to go or what to look at, somewhat confusing. This raises the question of whether the organisation of the material can be improved.

2.2. Corresponding material in Estonia

Important similarities can be found between the tool and the national guidelines for internal evaluation (see p. 2.1). These concern the engagement of different parties and the total quality management (TQM) approach. Unlike the tool, the guidelines provide separate recommendations for different educational institutions. Also, the guidelines are more formalised and concrete in terms of evaluation criteria, indicators, measures and quantitative targets. Indicators are classified according to the main parties in the educational system – ones linked to the students, to the school staff, to external interest groups and to the school as an organisation.

As discussed above, it is hard to make international documents very concrete, but the guidelines are nevertheless easier to use than the tool in this regard.

The main difference between the national and European documents is in approaching democratic governance and citizenship issues. For the latter this is at the very core, whereas in the former these aspects are almost completely neglected. Since this difference is highly substantial, I will discuss it more deeply in the following chapters.

3. *The tool as an instrument of school evaluation in Estonia*

3.1. Conditions for using the tool in schools

3.1.1. Circumstances that might promote the use of the tool

Policy incentives tend to be successful if they fit well into existing practices and ways of thinking. In Estonia, increasing attention is being paid to quality assurance and internal evaluation in schools, and this creates a good premise for the implementation of the tool. The focus on internal evaluation has not remained hollow rhetoric; some tools and systems already exist that support the implementation of

QA in schools. The issue of school evaluation and quality of education is explicitly dealt with in the following recent strategic policy documents and legal acts:

- Developmental Plan of General Education 2007-13 (draft);
- Revised National Curriculum 2007 (draft);
- Act on Basic and Secondary Schools (amended in 2006).

In addition to the endogenous factors, there are also some exogenous factors that may promote introduction of EDC-QA in schools. Firstly, QA is becoming increasingly important in the business sector. Understanding and know-how about performance evaluation gained there can be disseminated via parents and alumni to the school system. Secondly, educational systems have witnessed the growing concern of parents and employers in quality of education. As Mintrom demonstrates, recent school reforms focused on quality improvement have opened up new avenues for exercising democratic practices and engagement in schools (Mintrom, 2001). This commensurability between reform efforts motivated by quality and accountability concerns and education for democracy create good premises for efficient use of EDC-QA.

3.1.2. Prospective difficulties and obstacles

Until now, understanding of the importance of QA has very clearly come from top officials at the central level of government. No comprehensive bottom-up movement has yet emerged. When such a compliance gap exists between decision makers and practitioners, the very core idea of self-evaluation could be under attack, since schools may regard QA as simply one additional mode of bureaucratic control. Thus awareness-raising within schools, at the grass-roots level (including students and parents) is extremely important. One must send a very clear message as to how students, parents and teachers will profit from the self-evaluation process.

In addition to the limited awareness at the grass-roots level, some other difficulties must be mentioned.

The burden of administrative tasks placed on teachers and school staff is already heavy. It is quite obvious that the implementation of a QA system will increase it even more. At the same time, schools do not have any possibilities or resources to hire a temporary workforce to carry out internal evaluations. Nor can they temporarily reduce the workload of teachers and students actively engaged in the self-evaluation process.

The competence level of school staff in QA procedures is not high, and in many cases is even inadequate. The problem is explicitly linked to the in-service training system. The vast majority of training courses involve tuition fees and take place in two main cities – Tallinn or Tartu. This means that rural schools with fewer resources (money, replacement teachers, etc.) often cannot participate in schooling. Consequently, variation in the level of competence might increase.

EDC has promoted the "whole school" approach for several years now, but this concept has not yet become a tradition in Estonian schools. Issues of democracy and citizenship are still regarded as the responsibility of civic education teachers and to some extent of classroom teachers. As a result of this approach, the trust of students towards schools is declining and they tend to become less interested in participating in discussions about school life. According to the nationwide survey, only 46% of 8th graders and 50% of 9th graders would like to discuss how their school works (Toots, Idnurm and Ševeljova, 2006: 73). The same survey also revealed a large gap between pupils' willingness to participate in decision making in the school and effective possibilities of doing so. In this situation, it will be quite challenging to apply EDC-QA, which presupposes the engagement of the entire school community.

Last but not least, the link between EDC-QA and national curriculum development must be pointed out. As stated in the tool, "clarity of definition of what is meant by educational quality" is necessary for an effective QA system (Bîrzea et al., 2005: 46). Unfortunately, this is not the case in contemporary Estonian educational policy. The reform of the national curriculum is in a state of stalemate largely because no consensus has been reached about the general aims and principles of the educational process.

3.1.3. Parts of the tool with particular applicability

The chapters of the tool each have a different content focus, which is useful for different tasks and activities. Their applicability also depends on the user's characteristics: in what position is he or she in his or her school? What are his or her previous knowledge and skills in terms of EDC and QA? Does he or she have some concrete tasks with regard to performing self-evaluation in school?

Since material about EDC and QA already exists, I found Chapters 2 and 3 less essential. However, although literature about development planning is quite accessible as well, I appreciated the clear and coherent presentation of the topic (especially sub-section 4.3).

Taking the modest level of teachers' skills into account in carrying out sociological research, chapters devoted to research methods seem to be especially needed. When encouraging schools to carry out surveys or tests, one should also explain what kind of risks and limitations are related to these research tools. Indeed, EDC "is primarily concerned with changes of values, attitudes and behaviour" (Bîrzea et al., 2005: 80). However, measuring such latent constructs as attitudes is an advanced research task that requires professional skills. Badly constructed research instruments or unreliable samples can lead to wrong conclusions and, all in all, harm the whole self-evaluation process. Thus, the application of relevant research methods and making use of various data sets should be described in even greater depth.

For example, triangulation as a good method for checking reliability of data and comparing internal and external data can be useful for school evaluation teams.

3.1.4. Target groups of the tool

As suggested above in sub-section 3.1, the tool will be more user-friendly if the material is structured according to the different target groups. Currently, it is designed for everyone, which makes it difficult to see the specific role of various stakeholders. I do not entirely share the authors' view that all parties are equally engaged in EDC-QA. In my opinion, parents or local interest groups (municipality, non-governmental organisations (NGOs)) have quite specific interests in the process, and also specific intervention possibilities. Within the current structure it is hard to imagine that the tool could attract or encourage even well-educated parents to take action. Therefore, I suggest considering whether the typical design of public websites, oriented towards different user groups, is applicable here.

The main target groups of the current version of the tool will most likely be civil servants dealing with the topic, heads of schools and head teachers. Experienced teachers who carry out research together with their students can use Chapter 6.

3.2. Systemic conditions for using the tool

3.2.1. Correspondence of the tool and the system of quality assurance and evaluation

The tool corresponds to the national guidelines in basic principles, but differs in terms of the level of instrumentality (see sub-section 3.2). National guidelines are more concrete, but they are not developed from the EDC perspective. Thus the question is how to integrate EDC into existing national guidelines. Three important issues can be given here as examples of possible problems:
- firstly, the national guidelines do not see students as active participants in the process; rather, they are the objects of evaluation. This standpoint differs significantly from the ideology of EDC-QA;
- secondly, the national guidelines evaluate decision making in school mainly from the perspective of efficiency and satisfaction. Democratic values of decision making, such as transparency, accountability, representativeness and respect towards different opinions, are not mentioned as indicators of school performance;
- thirdly, Estonian educational policy typically regards the school as purely an institution for transmitting knowledge, and not as a place for living. Accordingly, "living and learning democracy" is not considered to happen inside the school. The national guidelines suggest measuring the school environment by just one mathematical indicator – square metres per pupil (MER, 2006).

These problems make the implementation of EDC-QA in Estonia more difficult, but at the same time open up new perspectives for improving the existing national evaluation system. The added value of EDC-QA can be found in its focus on the school as a holistic democratic community, not on individual actors within the education process. The latter constitutes the traditional Estonian pedagogic approach, and only a few schools have succeeded in developing a working school ethos.

The table below provides an example of how the current technocratic approach to school evaluation could be supplemented by the evaluative framework of the tool:

Result area	Indicators	Measures
Educational institution (the school)	Student–teacher ratio *Student–teacher collaboration*	*Modes of collaboration Share of engaged students and teachers Frequency of activities*
	Students' participation in learning	Number of missed lessons *Possibility to choose topics and learning methods*
	Learning environment	Square metres per student *Opportunities for participation and self-expression*

Sources: National Guidelines for Internal Evaluation of Schools; "Tool for Quality Assurance of Education for Democratic Citizenship in Schools"; and author's contribution.

Note: the provisions of the tool and the author are in italics.

In addition to the issue of fitness in "spirit", the question of compulsion should be brought up when speaking about implementation of the tool. The national system of evaluation is enacted with mandatory regularity (once every three years), but EDC-QA is a voluntary undertaking. In these circumstances one must be careful not to build duplicate policies in QA.

If the added value of EDC-QA is not explicitly clear for the schools, they will not practise it widely (see also critical notes in sub-section 3.1). The best feasible solution here seems to be better co-ordination with national QA policies.

3.2.2. Preparing teachers to work with the tool

Analysis of the initial teacher-training curricula reveals that graduates are not sufficiently equipped with the skills and knowledge to perform self-evaluation. Therefore it is necessary to train them in two aspects: (1) to raise awareness about QA; and (2) to train them in applied research and in the evaluation of research results.

One specific aspect must also be mentioned. Since the tool only gives general guidance and not measurable indicators, it is necessary to show how to operationalise and adapt EDC quality indicators. Put differently, how can one measure the value of European indicators in concrete terms in a school? In my opinion, this is crucial for ultimate success. At the same time, this task is too difficult to be left to teachers and schools alone. In this respect it is unlikely that teachers can work with the tool independently without special training or good guidance materials.

For the school staff and parents, it is necessary to translate the tool into native languages. In the case of Estonia, translation into Russian is also needed, since 16% of schools are Russian-speaking. The Russian-speaking community (both inside and outside the school) will probably need more intensive work in raising awareness and building capacity, since it is not very actively involved in new initiatives in quality education at the national level.

3.2.3. Other possible facilitators

In addition to the promoting and demotivating factors analysed above, it is also worth thinking about two additional aspects.

Firstly, how is it possible to make more efficient use of resources (time, know-how)? Is it feasible to import relevant know-how into schools?

On the one hand, every school is unique, but on the other, there are also many commonalities. It seems reasonable to ask professionals to develop a standard survey instrument for all schools (or school types) and to contract field operations to polling companies. In this case, schools would receive data ready for analysis and save time otherwise spent in developing instruments and carrying out fieldwork. Obviously, extra funding must be available for contract work. However, reducing the risk of unreliable data is far more important than extra money.

Secondly, publicity is an extremely powerful facilitator of policy reform. In the information society, publicity means first of all websites. According to Estonian law, every school has to have its own website. Schools' websites are extremely popular and often visited by pupils and parents. Thus, if one wants to make EDC-QA common practice, a special link to the self-evaluation materials should be created on a school's website or at the national online educational database (in Estonia, EHIS). This allows schools to compare themselves to others and to learn lessons; parents and students will get an easy tool to monitor school performance.

It is obvious that implementation of EDC-QA will be easy or difficult depending on the school ethos. School size, language of tuition or students' achievement level do not seem to be significant variables here. Primary schools, however, comprise a special case, given that their students are very young. However, even primary school pupils should be engaged in self-evaluation as active partners, although in a suitably age-relevant way. In this regard, there is remarkable room for improvement both in the tool and in the national guidelines for self-evaluation.

4. Ideas for the implementation process

4.1. How to make working with the tool valuable for schools

Considerable work must be done before QA is common practice in schools. The first step in this process is to raise awareness among all parties, demonstrating clearly what differences – if any – the implementation of regular self-evaluation can make to them.

It is also important to plan all activities well in advance. For example, the school should know a year ahead that self-evaluation will be on the agenda. This allows schools to make sufficient preparations (to compose the team, to organise training, to allocate time and resources) and to integrate QA activities smoothly into other undertakings of the school community. It would be good if schools had some flexibility in choosing the time frame over which to carry out the self-evaluation. Once again, it should be stressed that EDC-QA must be carried out in conjunction with the general self-evaluation process in the school; there cannot be two separate processes or any duplication.

The nomination of the people responsible for self-evaluation is one of the key steps in preparatory work. Formally, the headmaster of the school bears responsibility for self-evaluation. At the same time, self-evaluation should be a collective process. Two problems concerning leadership arise here. On the one hand, the leader must be an "insider" familiar with the school. At the same time, researchers point to the risk of "going native". This means that a person with very close links to the organisation is not always able to provide a truly non-partisan picture of the situation. It is human nature that staff try to show the situation as being somewhat more optimistic than it is. Heiki Lyytinen, a Finnish expert, suggests combining internal review with the work of external experts, who ensure an independent evaluation (Lyytinen, 2006). MER has taken this suggestion into account and the staff member responsible for the self-evaluation will be assisted by a councillor from outside the school. As far as EDC in self-evaluation is concerned, it would be wise for the teacher of civic education to act as subject-matter adviser. Members of NGOs active in the field of citizenship education can also be involved in this role.

Another, probably even more crucial, problem in the management of the self-evaluation process is that of teamwork. How to ensure the collective and co-operative character for self-evaluation? Unfortunately, all Estonian documents dealing with school evaluation are extremely brief on this question. Here again, the community spirit of EDC can play a supportive role because the tool is a good power-sharing device.

4.2. How to integrate the tool into international partnerships

Participation in various EU youth exchange programmes (Comenius; Twinning Schools) is very popular in Estonia. Activities within these projects are excellent examples of good teamwork between students and teachers in one school; this experience can be applied to carry out EDC-QA as well. Additionally, European school exchanges can be used as an instrument to learn best practices of self-evaluation from partner schools abroad.

To make self-evaluation more attractive, some kind of bonuses or awards could be granted for those schools that have performed self-evaluation effectively. This would mean adding a new component to the Comenius exchange, where currently schools are awarded a trip to the partner school on the basis of an impressive project or learning product. As a first step in Europeanisation, a European website for the end-users (namely, the schools) of the tool could be launched.

4.3. Alternative scenarios for working with the tool

The best way to implement EDC-QA into schools is to merge it into the existing national internal evaluation structures. Nevertheless, given the significant barriers in doing so, it is wise to think about alternative scenarios. Three such alternatives are described and assessed below.

Thematic approach. This idea comes from the current system of schools' external evaluation in Estonia. As mentioned in sub-section 2.1, certain priorities are set for each school year. The same pattern can be applied in EDC-QA, especially in the first years of the policy. This will give schools the possibility to introduce the new system step by step, and also decreases the workload related to self-evaluation.

Entirely pupils' business. According to this scenario, EDC-QA will be totally delegated to the students' organisations, which should then receive the relevant mandate (and of course training and advice). It can be expected that students are more interested in critical evaluation of their school than teachers or the headmaster. They are not afraid of losing their job or of "wage punishment". A short overview of policy documents and public letters of the Estonian School Students Councils' Union (ESCU) confirmed that they are highly interested in participating in quality assurance. "The role of students and parents in school life must be increased. These interest groups must be treated as a potential resource in improving the quality of education" (ESCU, 2006).

Europeanisation of EDC-QA. In the last few years, the European Commission and Eurydice have paid increasing attention to citizenship education in schools (Eurydice, 2005; COM, 2006). In their eyes, "school plays an important part in educating young people for citizenship. It may contribute to their grounding as active citizens through the content of teaching, but also in encouraging pupils to assume responsibilities in the mini-societies that schools represent". As stated in Pointers to Active Citizenship, "new forms of evaluation" for pupils and teachers with regard to EDC "are essential given the cross-curricular status of EDC and importance attached to the developing practical skills" (Eurydice, 2006b: 4).

Engaging students in self-evaluation according to the tool may become one of these new forms of evaluating the achievement in citizenship education.

References

Apple, M. (2004). "Creating Difference: Neo-Liberalism, Neo-Conservatism and the Politics of Educational Reform", *Educational Policy*, Vol. 18, No. 1, 12-44.

Bîrzea, C.; Cecchini, M.; Harrison, C.; Krek, J.; Spajić-Vrkaš, V. (2005). "Tool for Quality Assurance of Education for Democratic Citizenship in Schools", Paris: UNESCO, Council of Europe, CEPS.

COM (2006). "Progress Towards the Lisbon Objectives in Education and Training", Brussels: European Commission.

ESCU (2006). Website of the Estonian School Student Council's Union (Eesti Õpilasomavalitsuste Liit): www.escu.ee.

Eurydice (2004). *Evaluation of Schools Providing Compulsory Education in Europe*. Retrieved on 5 January 2007, from www.eurydice.org/portal/page/portal/ Eurydice/showPresentation?pubid=042EN.

Eurydice (2005). *Citizenship Education at School in Europe*.

Eurydice (2006). *National Summary Sheets on Education Systems in Europe and Ongoing Reforms. Estonia*. Retrieved on 21 December 2006, from www.eurydice. org/portal/page/portal/Eurydice/showPresentation?pubid=047EN.

Lyytinen, H. (2006). *New Directions in Educational Evaluation in Finland*. Retrieved on 22 October 2006, from www.hm.ee/index.php?popup=download&id=4430.

MER (2003). *Õpetajakoolituse riiklik arengukava. Tööversioon. 2003* (National Development Plan of Teacher Education. Draft. 2003). Retrieved on 29 October 2006, from www.hm.ee/index.php?popup=download&id=5202.

MER (2006). *Õppeasutuse sisehindamine. Soovitusi sisehindamise läbiviimiseks õppeasutustes* (Guidelines for Internal Evaluation of Schools). Retrieved on 26 October 2006, from www.hm.ee/index.php?popup=download&id=4125.

MER (2007). *Üldharidussüsteemi arengukava aastateks 2007-2013. Tööversioon.* (Developmental Plan of General Education). Retrieved on 2 January 2007 from www.hm.ee/index.php?03236.

Mintrom, M. (2001). "Educational Governance and Democratic Practice", *Educational Policy*, Vol. 15, No. 5, 615-643.

NBEQ (2006). *Riikliku õppekava materjale* (Draft of Revised National Curriculum). Retrieved on 18 December 2006, from www.ekk.edu.ee/oppekavad/ arendus/oppekavad_2006-6.pdf.

Õpetajakoolituse raamnõuded. VVm. 2000 (Framework Requirements for Teacher Education 2000, Government Decree).

Õpitulemuste välishindamise põhimõtted, riigieksamitööde, põhikooli lõpueksamitööde ja üleriigiliste tasemetööde koostamise, hindamise ja tulemuste analüüsi alused. Haridusministri määrus nr. 18, 23.01.2002 (Ministry Decree on National Assessment and Exams).

Õppeasutuse riikliku järelvalve prioriteedid, temaatilise riikliku järelvalve läbiviimise, selle tulemuslikkuse vormistamise ja tulemustest teavitamise kord 2006/2007 õppeaastal. Haridus- ja Teadusminiteeriumi määrus nr. 22, 04. aug. 2006 (Ministry Decree on Carrying out External Evaluation).

Põhikooli ja gümnaasiumi seadus (2006) (Act on Basic and Secondary School).

Toots, A.; Idnurm, T.; Ševeljova, M. (2006). *Noorte kodanikukultuur muutuvas ühiskonnas*, Tallinn: Tallinn University.

Germany
Tobias Diemer

1. School evaluation in Germany

The education system in Germany

The educational system in Germany is characterised above all by two distinguishing features that must be taken into consideration by any project aiming at a successful implementation of instruments like the "Tool for Quality Assurance of Education for Democratic Citizenship in Schools". The first of these features is the strongly federal nature of the educational system in Germany at the political and governmental levels, which concerns legislative and administrative powers in the field of education. The second distinguishing feature is the tracking system in the area of secondary education that determines implementation by clearly defining and practically adapting the tool to several types of schooling environment.

Let us look at federalism first. According to the National Constitution (Grundgesetz) of the Federal Republic of Germany and the constitutions of the *Länder* (states in the Federal Republic of Germany), the legislation of the educational system is basically the responsibility of the 16 *Länder*. The *Länder* have the superior right to legislate education as far as the constitution does not award legislative powers to the federation. Effectively, according to the law in force, the legislative powers of the *Länder* apply to the school sector, the higher education sector, adult education and continuing education.

Furthermore, every *Land* has its own particular administrative apparatus that carries out legal and academic supervision (*Rechts- und Fachaufsicht*) as well as supervision over staff (*Dienstaufsicht*). In most cases, the administrations are structured in a two-tier system with the State's Ministry of Education on the top tier and lower-level supervisory authorities (*Schulamt*) on the lower tier. In addition, in each Land (state) there is at least one institution, for the most part named the State Institute (Landesinstitut), which fulfils several support and executive duties ranging from in-service and further teacher training to designing and developing concepts and tools for teaching, to quality assurance and school development.

Against this background, it should be noted that there is no single school system in Germany, but rather 16 separate ones. These systems, however, share a certain number of basic common features such as school types, graduations or terms of school attendance. On the basis of an agreement among the *Länder*, these systems co-ordinate activities and regulations with each other through the Standing Conference of the Ministers of Education and Cultural Affairs of the *Länder* in the Federal Republic of Germany (Kultusministerkonferenz, KMK). This organisation brings together the policy makers of the *Länder* responsible for education, research and cultural affairs to deal with and to decide on policy matters that are of common nationwide relevance. One central purpose of the conference is to guarantee a certain measure of shared and comparable structures that either are required by rights, especially those of the constitution, or are necessary with regard to the wider supra-regional public good. Finally, at the national level of the Federal Republic of Germany, there is a further institution, the Federal Ministry of Education and Research (Bundesministerium für Bildung und Forschung). Because of the authority held by the *Länder* in the case of educational and cultural affairs, the responsibilities of this ministry are indeed limited to developing foundational law in the area of vocational training outside school, state fellowships for students from a low socioeconomic background, the provision of scholarships for outstanding students and researchers, research funding, and the promotion of international exchanges.

In Germany co-operation in the field of educational policy between the federation and the *Länder* is restricted to the possibility of co-operation in the assessment of efficiency of the educational system in international comparison and in the production of reports and recommendations relating thereto (Grundgesetz, Article 91b (2)).

The political, legislative and administrative structures outlined above may indicate some diversity amongst the various school systems themselves, which indeed both differ from and resemble each other in various respects. Nonetheless, they all share one key aspect, namely the tracking system of secondary education, which comprises the longest part of school education. In the majority of the *Länder* this tracking system consists of three tracks and students are assigned to a certain track according to their performance after primary school, namely, upon the completion of grade 4 in the majority of the *Länder*. This assignment can be revised, if uncommon decreases or increases of performance occur. The three tracks are offered in different schools, like basic schools (*Hauptschule*, up to grade 9), middle schools (*Realschule*, up to grade 10), academic secondary schools (*Gymnasium*, up to grade 12 or 13 and leading to the university-entrance diploma), or in comprehensive schools (*Gesamtschule*, integrating the various tracks in one organisation). Moreover there are special schools for students with special educational needs (*Schule mit sonderpädagogischen Förderschwerpunkten*). (For a short overview of these types of schools and the basic structures of the German school system from preschool to primary, secondary and tertiary, and on to continuing education, see KMK, 2006a; KMK, 2006b).

Particularly with regard to EDC, the education systems of the *Länder* provide several well-established institutions. Two aspects in particular stand out: (1) all school legislations and school constitutions of the *Länder* provide several participation rights and structures for students as well as parents and teachers. The participation structure that is allocated by law to students is called the *Schülervertretung (SV)*.

This comprises the election of class and school representatives amongst students who deputise with a certain parity in the school conference (in some *Länder*, one third next to teachers and parents) when it comes to taking decisions on important organisational affairs; and (2) in secondary school, and in part in primary school as well, there are some subjects specially designed for the purpose of teaching EDC such as *Gemeinschaftskunde, Sozialkunde, Politik*, or as combinations of social science subjects. Since the early post-war period, when these subjects were first established, they have undergone several conceptual changes in parallel with the development of different trends in civic education in Germany.[1] One such trend was based on political theory and emphasised the necessity of analysing society using political concepts (Litt, 1955). This stood in parallel with an alternative trend based on a tradition of pragmatism, which emphasised the aspect of living together in communities (Oetinger, 1951). While the first of these had its roots in the domain of political science, the second was rather grounded in educational science (Detjen, 2007).

Political science itself was re-established as a German university discipline after the war and in those early years saw its main objective as civic education. Thus, political science provided the basis for the various school subjects on civic education within the German *Länder*, with political scientists dominating the commissions for curricula development (Detjen, 2007). In the context of the so-called didactical turn of the late 1950s, the new sub-discipline "didactic of politics" (*Politikdidaktik*) emerged from the domains of education-oriented political science and political pedagogy, taking over the scientific reflection of civic education (Gagel, 1994). This subject-specific didactic, as constituted by the founding generation of, among others, Wolfgang Hilligen, Kurt Gerhard Fischer and Hermann Giesecke, was subsequently institutionalised in the form of university chairs. To this day, this discipline continues to orient its objectives and content mainly towards political science, although some groups of scientists have also tried to integrate discourses from educational science (as well as, since about 1989, empirical research on teaching and learning).

With the arrival of the millennium the old controversy between scientists promoting the imparting of rather general social competences and those in support of an analytical, political concept-based approach to civic education had erupted anew. The central question was how much emphasis should be given to a critical understanding of the political system and political actions, and how much to the individual's adaptation to the system and subsequent development into an active member of society. Unlike some educationalists, researchers with a political science background are much less confident that school and family can be used as a model of society. They point out the distinctive features of the political field and fear that the students' ability to analyse public life as a system with particular structures

---

1. The author thanks Professor Dr Georg Weisseno for his assistance with the subsequent historical and conceptual outline.

and functions will be lost out of sight if civic education is reduced to promoting a certain way of life (Massing, 2004). This position is supported by empirical findings that show that social participation is no predictor of political knowledge or even interest in politics (Biedermann, 2006).

Nevertheless, supporters of this reasoning do not disapprove of direct (or simulated) experience with democracy as a part of civic education, but are convinced that categories such as participation, sense of belonging, respect, social awareness and responsibility do not cover the political field sufficiently. Therefore, in their view, designers of learning environments should also focus on granting opportunities for more analytical approaches.

1.1. The school evaluation system in Germany

Evaluation has increasingly become a key issue in connection with the ongoing major transition from once dominantly input-oriented approaches of system control and regulation towards increasingly output-oriented ones. For this purpose, initiatives have been taken by the KMK, which oblige all *Länder* to develop, implement and institutionalise several forms and modes of evaluation.

The fundamental and to a certain extent already established elements of the currently developing evaluation system are in essence the following:
- the accomplishment of system monitoring through participation in national and international studies of student achievement;
- the formulation of educational standards by the KMK and the design and development of appropriate standardised tests in the *Länder*;
- the development of quality assurance frameworks (*Qualitätsrahmen*) and the establishment of inspectorates that accomplish external summary evaluations;
- the promotion of quality assurance and organisational development processes in schools through working out school profiles or programmes and implementing formative self-evaluations.

The Standing Conference of the Ministers of Education and Cultural Affairs of the *Länder* (KMK) declared in a resolution of October 1997 that quality assurance and improvement processes were matters of special interest. This resolution also comprised participation in PISA 2000. However, these matters only began to receive wider attention after the publication of the first PISA results in 2001. PISA is certainly the most discussed and most influential system monitoring study that Germany is participating in at the moment. Besides PISA, the German *Länder* have participated at international level in the Third International Mathematics and Science Study (TIMSS, see Baumert, Bos and Lehmann, 2000) and in the Progress in International Reading Literacy Study (PIRLS, see Bos et al., 2007). In addition, several studies of students' achievement have been carried out Germany-wide that focus on several further competences. Due to its volume the most notable of these is DESI (Deutsch Englisch Schülerleistungen International, see Klieme and Beck, 2007), a large-scale study of competences in German and English of grade 9 students, which was commissioned in 2001 by the KMK and carried out from then until 2006 by DIPF (the German Institute for International Educational Research).

In addition and in parallel with conducting system monitoring, the KMK took the initiative after the above-mentioned resolution and the first PISA results to formulate binding educational standards (*Bildungsstandards*). Taking into consideration an expert report (Klieme et al., 2003), these standards were adopted by the conference in 2004 for several subjects in the primary sector for grade 4 and in the secondary sector for the basic certificate after grade 9 (*Hauptschulabschluss*), as well as for the middle certificate after grade 10 (*Mittlerer Bildungsabschluss*). These standards determine the subject-specific competences that students should have achieved at the respective stage of their school career. In order to further develop these standards for better testability, in 2004 the KMK established the Institut zur Qualitätsentwicklung im Bildungswesen (Institute for Quality Development in Education, IQB), which is a research institute located at Humboldt University Berlin. On top of this, in many *Länder*, comparative test instruments are being developed that are designed to help administrations, schools and teachers to diagnose to what extent the standards have been met, and at the same time to equip them with information that can be used for quality assurance and development processes in classrooms and schools. For this reason these tests, unlike PISA and similar monitoring studies, are not designed to be representative, but rather as full sample studies that can provide statistical information at the levels of classrooms and students. The generic and untranslatable term used for such tests is *Lernstandserhebungen* ("standard achievement tests"), whereas due to the autonomous status of the *Länder* different terms are used that designate similar designs and concepts (for further information see Deutscher Bildungsserver, 2007a).

In 2006 the KMK passed a comprehensive strategy about the monitoring of the educational system (*Gesamtstrategie der Kultusministerkonferenz zum Bildungsmonitoring*, see KMK, 2006c) that integrates the preceding developments. The strategy consists of four cornerstones (*Säulen*) of a future monitoring system:

- international studies of student achievement;
- centralised tests of the achievement of national educational standards comprising inter-state comparison;
- decentralised standard tests in the *Länder* comprising intra-state comparison;
- joint reporting about the educational system in parallel by the federal government and the *Länder*.

Regarding the third and fourth elements of this emerging evaluation system, various endeavours are ongoing in all *Länder* that are designed to establish measurements for external and internal quality assurance and improvement processes. In many

Länder such endeavours include the establishment of quality frameworks that define criteria as well as indicators concerning several aspects of good school quality. These frameworks are designed to serve a twofold purpose: providing orientation to schools for their own formative work, and offering the basis for external school evaluations that deliver qualitative and quantitative information to administrations as well as to schools themselves, which they can work with in the course of various formative processes. This latter purpose is served by special quality agencies or inspectorates that bear different names and are institutionalised in different ways in the different *Länder* (for further information, see Deutscher Bildungsserver, 2007b).

For the second part of the observable quality assurance and improvement endeavours, formative self-evaluation activities are being initiated in all *Länder* as a basis for strengthening planning and development activities within individual schools. In some *Länder*, therefore, schools have recently been obliged to undertake self-evaluations in conjunction with establishing systematic quality management systems or in the context of the obligatory task of developing individual school profiles or programmes. The latter essentially include guiding principles, an analysis of the situation, the formulation of objectives and projects as well as corresponding plans and schedules for the realisation of these objectives and projects.

1.2. Evaluation as an issue of teacher training

Regarding the special relation between evaluation and teacher training, it should be noted that the actual value of evaluation in this field is still less pronounced than in the other fields outlined above. Thus teacher training is still more discussed as an issue of evaluation than evaluation is as an issue in teacher training. After the Mixed Commission Teacher Training (Gemischte Kommission Lehrerbildung) and the Science Council (Wissenschaftsrat) had pointed out critically that teacher training had for too long been neglected with regard to evaluation and quality assurance, in 2004 the standing conference also adopted Standards for Teacher Training: Educational Science (*Standards für die Lehrerbildung: Bildungswissenschaften*) (KMK, 2004). These standards define several essential requirements for teacher activities in and outside the classroom, and form the basis for regular evaluations of teacher-training courses in the *Länder*, including an up to two-year-long preparatory period of training (*Vorbereitungsdienst*) that candidate teachers have to attend after completing their graduate studies, and in-service teacher-training courses.

Beyond this, numerous field reports have been published since the turn of the millennium that document various approaches to self-evaluation and quality assurance instruments applied by institutes that are responsible for the in-service phase of teacher education. These reports show that in some teacher education institutes, considerable efforts at self-evaluation have already been undertaken. The range of adopted instruments is wide, covering questionnaires, several feedback approaches, and evaluation workshops lasting several hours. Another remarkable finding is that such evaluation processes are often confronted with serious difficulties such as teachers' existential or personal fears, or problems regarding restricted financial, temporal and professional resources (Speck, 2006: especially 325-328).

Concerning the topic of evaluation as an issue of teacher training, evaluation has not yet been introduced as a systematic part of teacher education, either in the first phase at university or educational academies or in the second preparatory phase at state institutes for teacher education (Speck, 2006: 332). However, as increasing attention is being paid to the more general issues of school development and quality assurance, the more specific issue of evaluation is presumably already to some extent part of teacher education in the first as well as in the second phase.

1.3. The use of evaluation results in schools

The exploration of the procedures and possibilities as well as the difficulties of using evaluation results in schools has begun simultaneously with the accomplishment of the first system monitoring studies as well as in the course of the introduction of standard achievement tests (*Lernstandserhebungen*). With respect to the particular case of system monitoring, some studies already exist about the reception of their results (Klieme, Baumert, and Schwippert, 2000; Kohler, 2005; Schwippert, 2004). In general, these investigations demonstrate only moderate interest on the part of teachers, whereas interest among supervisory officials is significantly higher. Kohler (2005) shows high values among teachers regarding patterns of external attribution in cases of poor results. The fact that these values correlate negatively with values of the appreciation of the monitoring results indicates complex patterns of reservation against external evaluation among teachers. In contrast to these findings, some more recent studies concerning the use of standard achievement test results show that there might be a positive development with respect to the acceptance of results from external evaluations (Kühle and Peek, 2007; Nachtigall and Jantowski, 2007; Maier, 2008).

If one asks not only for acceptance, but for use, especially as far as teaching methods or school development are concerned, things remain more difficult (Kühle and Peek, 2007; Nachtigall and Jantowski, 2007). As Stamm (2003) aptly put it, we still need to work on the development and implementation of "ways of more efficient utilisation", as well as "more efficient ways of utilisation" of evaluation results in schools.

2. The "Tool for Quality Assurance of Education for European Democratic Citizenship in Schools"

2.1. Comprehensiveness and coherence

With its focus expressly directed towards quality assurance rather than quality control, the "Tool for Quality Assurance of Education for European Democratic Citizenship in Schools" primarily seems to be addressing itself to one half of the circumstances and developments that have been outlined in the preceding chapter, namely the parts concerning: (a) the development of quality assurance frameworks and the establishment of inspectorates for external evaluation, on the one hand; and (b) the promotion of quality assurance and organisational development processes in schools through working out individually customised school profiles or programmes and implementing formative internal self-evaluation, on the other.

The first of these two issues is dealt with by the tool through the formulation of a "Framework to evaluate EDC" in Chapter 5. With the specification of areas, quality indicators and sub-themes this chapter provides a framework that can be utilised as an instrument for feeding EDC into the proceeding formulation of quality assurance frameworks in the different German *Länder*. In conjunction with the conceptual framework on EDC provided in Chapter 2 and the conceptualisation of quality assurance from the point of view of EDC in Chapter 3, the tool furthermore provides conceptual resources for determining purposes and procedures of external evaluation executed by the respective inspectorates.

Admittedly, the main emphasis of the tool is placed on the second thematic area, namely that of quality assurance and development processing as well as formative self-evaluation. By addressing these issues through conceptualising school development planning and self-evaluation in Chapter 4 and by supporting implementation through the provision of a toolbox containing several instruments for dealing with these matters in Chapter 6, the tool covers both necessary conceptual issues as well as required practical resources for implementing EDC-specific self-evaluation procedures in schools.

Overall, although the chapters about quality assurance and self-evaluation certainly build the core component of the tool in terms of being directly addressed to schools and school development operators and advisers, they are apparently closely intertwined with the other sections of the tool concerning external evaluation processes and structures. The connecting piece can be found in the "Framework to evaluate EDC" in Chapter 5, with the formulation of quality indicators that could (or should) be seen as a hinge between the inner-school section of self-evaluation and development planning, on the one hand, and the designing of quality assurance frameworks and the way of executing external evaluations through state inspectorates or quality agencies, on the other.

2.2. Corresponding material in Germany

Since the issues of school quality, school development and internal as well as external evaluation have become increasingly more important over the last ten or twenty years, many conceptual as well as practical materials have been created. However, although aspects of EDC are regularly broached in part or implicitly, the issues of school quality, school development and evaluation are not conceptualised with special regard to EDC. A current example of conceptual and practical work dealing with school quality, school development and evaluation from a perspective directed specially towards EDC has been published within the project "Democracy Learning and Living". On the basis of experience and expertise gained through that programme, a quality framework for EDC (de Haan, Edelstein and Eikel, 2007) has been developed that covers similar objectives and topics to the tool.

This quality framework deals with the two major issues that must be addressed by any approach to EDC, namely the issues of fostering democratic competences in students, and the task of building democratic school quality. Thus, the quality framework provides a comprehensive approach to democratic quality assurance in schools that simultaneously contains conceptual basics as well as practical tools and thus is intended for heads of schools and for teachers as well as for administrative officials, inspectorates for external evaluation and professional school development advisers.

After outlining the basic principles, concepts and topics of EDC (Booklet 1), the framework for one major part provides an extensive definition of democratic competences through a systematic formulation of concrete competences that should be acquired by the end of grade 10 (Booklet 2). It additionally contains 30 exemplary descriptions of ways and opportunities to acquire these competences based on selected practices that have been proven to work within the programme (CD-Rom). As a second major part, the framework then presents a procedure to develop and ensure democratic school quality (Booklet 3). The first of two tracks concerns the issue of school programme development (Booklets 4 and 5). The second track contains a so-called democracy audit (*DemokratieAudit*), which describes a programme for self-evaluation of schools on the basis of a catalogue of criteria and indicators that define democratic qualities of schools (Booklets 6 and 7). With respect to their applicability in schools, the descriptions of the two procedures are divided into two sections, one in each case describing the procedures themselves, and the other containing practical methods and instruments that may help realise these procedures.

Furthermore, the framework presents a list of criteria for defining the democratic quality of schools which, together with the extensive definition of competences for acting democratically, forms one of the two cores of the whole framework. This list has been developed against the background of several international as well as national concepts and procedures of quality assurance inside and outside the school sector, including the "Tool for Quality Assurance of Education for Democratic Citizenship in Schools".

In addition to this example, a wide range of conceptual as well as practical materials has been developed concerning several particular features of the tool. With respect to EDC, considerable efforts have been made in recent years to define and explain the concept of EDC. In 2002 an expert group developed as an expert contribution for the KMK a core curriculum for two subjects, politics and social science for A-level education in secondary schools. This was published in 2004 along with core curricula in mathematics, German, English, biology, chemistry, physics and history (Behrmann et al., 2004). According to this curriculum concept, EDC essentially aims at developing five democratic competences: role-taking capacities (*Perspektivenübernahme*), conflict-solving capacities (*Konfliktfähigkeit*), the ability to judge in the domain of politics (*politische Urteilsfähigkeit*) and to analyse social phenomena (*sozialwissenschaftliches Analysieren*), and the ability to participate and act democratically (*Partizipationsfähigkeit/demokratische Handlungskompetenz*) (Behrmann et al., 2004: 337 ff.). Additional concepts have also been published. Particularly remarkable in this regard are two (partly complementary, partly competing) approaches advanced by the German Association for Political Didactics and Political Youth and Adult Education (Gesellschaft für Politikdidaktik und politische Jugend- und Erwachsenenbildung (GPJE), see GPJE, 2004), and by Himmelmann (2003). They differ in that whereas the GPJE approach distinguishes between the ability to judge politically (*politische Urteilsfähigkeit*), the ability to act politically (*politische Handlungsfähigkeit*) and methodological competences, Himmelmann shifts the main focus of EDC from policy learning to democracy learning (Himmelmann, 2006: 139) and launches a subject-related core concept in terms of a core curriculum (*fachliches Kernkonzept i.S. eines Kerncurriculums*), democracy-related cognitive abilities in terms of knowledge and understanding (*allgemeine kognitive Fähigkeiten*), affective and moral commitments and attitudes (*affektiv-moralische Einstellungen*) as well as practical and instrumental skills and strategies (*praktisch-instrumentelle Fertigkeiten*).

On top of this conceptual material, a lot of practical material has been published describing instructional and pedagogical approaches concerning several aspects of EDC. The "Online resources" section provided by the German Education Server already contains 247 links under "Demokratie", mostly to practical online material or portals with further online resources (date of query on www.bildungsserver.de: December 2007). For this reason, this study purely refers to one publication edited by the State Institute for School Development of Baden-Württemberg (LiS, 2006), which provides a practical repertory for EDC in schools. It is not exhaustive, but rather presents some of the key approaches for EDC in schools with some best practice examples, for instance participation within the framework of representative student councils (*Schülervertretung*), so-called dilemma discussions, regular class conferences (*Klassenrat*) and school-wide community conferences (*demokratische Gemeinschaftssitzungen*), training courses in civil courage and conflict mediation, service learning, the participative development of school programmes, and networking with external partners.

Regarding the topics of school development, school quality and education, the situation resembles that of EDC. A wide range of conceptual as well as practical contributions to these topics can also be found in books and support materials issued by state institutes; in addition, considerable professional expertise has been built up, for example through experimental school development programmes. The German Education Server also provides a good overview as well as access to such materials under titles like "School evaluation and school inspection in the *Länder*", "School evaluation and quality research" and "School development:

institutions and material of the *Länder*" (see Deutscher Bildungsserver, 2007b; Deutscher Bildungsserver, 2007c; Deutscher Bildungsserver, 2007d).

A key publication is that of Brackhahn and Brockmeyer (2004), which documents in six volumes the extensive expertise in this field gained in the course of the pilot programme QuiSS – Qualitätsverbesserung in Schulen und Schulsystem (Quality Improvement in Schools and School Systems). Their study covers several important dimensions, such as fundamental conceptual and organisational issues (Vol. 1), the issue of developing learning processes and assessing students' performance (Vol. 4), external supervision and school management (Vol. 5), and standards, competences and evaluation (Vol. 6).

Finally, there is a multitude of conceptual and practical material that has been elaborated by approaches aimed at internal school reform (*innere Schulreform*) (see among others Rolff, 2007; Rolff, 2000; Kempfert and Rolff, 2005; Fend, 2001; Schratz, Iby and Radnitzky, 2000; Eikenbusch, 1998; Burkard and Eikenbusch, 2000; Klippert, 2000; Ruep, 1999). Although this material does not focus explicitly on EDC, it does tacitly cover many EDC-related aspects of school development and evaluation (see Schröter, Diemer and Kohle, 2003-06; Ulrich and Wenzel, 2003).

3. The tool as an instrument of school evaluation in Germany

Although many essential and important facts have been established in recent years, it is still true that quality assurance and evaluation in the educational system and especially in German schools are mostly still in a start-up stage. Efforts concerning the implementation of quality assurance measures for EDC in schools can be conceptualised as innovations involving several typical challenges as well as some special ones for schools and for the persons concerned, who are predominantly heads of schools, teachers, students and, to some extent, also parents.

Such challenges can be described as felicitous or necessary conditions for succeeding in school development processes. Concerning the special case of democratic school development processes, conditions of these kinds have recently been investigated through a qualitative interview-based study (Giesel, de Haan and Diemer, 2007), in the course of which about 120 teachers, heads of schools and students in 30 schools were interviewed about their views, expertise and knowledge of EDC and school development. The findings of this study permit some empirically enriched appraisals of school-related as well as systemic conditions for using the tool of quality assurance for EDC in schools.

3.1. Conditions in schools for using the tool

3.1.1. Circumstances that might promote the use of the tool

Several types of circumstance that could promote the use of the tool can be identified. The first is whether it is compatible with existing values, objectives, customs, etc. in schools. This means that some basic and shared beliefs about the importance of EDC must exist as a goal of education in general and of schooling in particular. This seems to be a necessary prerequisite in the sense that without it, the tool will not be recognised by schools as representing an interesting and relevant instrument that may help improve school quality. In this regard, it is important to stress the fact that the school laws of all *Länder* mention democracy as a high-ranking educational goal of schools in general. Consequently, it can be argued that schools are committed as an overall goal to taking EDC into consideration.

Based on this there are actually two further potentially beneficial circumstances of a regular institutional kind. One is the legally guaranteed and defined system of active representative participation of students and parents concerning various organisational domains. This system of students' and parents' participation, which is usually called *Schülervertretung*, could eventually work as an important organisational element in the event that the tool is implemented in individual schools. The other is the existence of specific subjects in primary and secondary schools that were especially established for the purpose of teaching EDC, for example *Gemeinschaftskunde*, *Sozialkunde* or *Politik*. Such subjects may, *inter alia*, play an important role with respect to implementing the tool in terms of form and content.

A further circumstance that might prove crucial with regard to the prospective use of the tool consists of the practical value it can offer. The debate as to whether an innovation brings about or even is merely suspected of bringing about relief or synergies with regard to existing duties and tasks is often a very sensitive issue for schools. This topic is considered simply in terms of time, which is seen as a scarce and hence limiting resource. On the other hand, it is also commonly understood that innovations are evaluated in view of their usefulness for subject-related instruction. Therefore, in the special case of democracy, heads of schools and teachers tend to grant innovations importance inasmuch as they foster tolerance, self-reliance or self-confidence in students, simply because such characteristics make their work in and outside the classroom easier.

Finally, a circumstance that is increasingly important, at least from an organisational point of view, is that the concept of EDC in general as well as the tool in particular can be of special interest for schools insofar as they contribute to the formation of the pedagogical and public profile of a school. Many *Länder* increasingly require schools to develop and continually work on individual school programmes that simultaneously function as planning or co-ordinating tools as well as tools for self-portrayal, which present guiding principles for learning and living both for the school and for the public. In this context the tool could be promoted if it proves helpful with regard to accomplishing the task of establishing and continually working on the evaluation and further advancement of school programmes.

3.1.2. Prospective difficulties and obstacles

Parallel to the potentially beneficial circumstances outlined above, there are also some circumstances that could have adverse effects on the prospective use of the tool or might raise difficulties of varying severity. One such circumstance that is regularly reported by teachers and heads of schools as being exceedingly difficult is the existence of a vast number of different reform directives and expectations that have been targeted at schools in recent years. What appears problematic to many is that these reforms may overtax teachers as individuals as well as schools as organisations, either because of the perceived complexities of the reforms (which may moreover be perceived as incoherent or even inconsistent), or because the perceived high number of demands made on schools is often seen as being too vast a task to work on at the same time. In some cases, this can easily lead to negative reactions to innovations like the tool.

Another potentially challenging circumstance concerns the intra-systemic conditions of schools. The case studies mentioned above show that successful democracy-related school development processes were essential for the emergence of multiple formal as well as informal ways of communication and co-operation among teachers and between heads of schools and teachers, teachers and students, and teachers and parents. This is a condition that has certainly not been met everywhere. Even if it is an aim of democracy-related school development, it is also an issue that has to be taken care of separately in the context of the implementation of the tool. The studies show that schools that have in place working methods in school management, planning of instruction and in the organisation of school life perform better in terms of democracy-related school development than schools that lack such prerequisites.

3.1.3. Parts of the tool that are particularly applicable

Concerning the applicability of parts of the tool, it is logical to distinguish between those parts that are applicable to concrete work in school, and those that are not. The latter appears to be true with regard to the "what is" chapters (1 to 4), which primarily serve the purpose of defining and explaining concepts and developing concepts. The former applies to Chapters 5 to 7, which present short manuals with appendices of relevant methods.

By comparison with the quality framework for EDC (de Haan, Edelstein and Eikel, 2007), it should be noticed that these manuals for evaluating EDC via quality indicators for EDC (Chapter 5), for self-evaluation and development planning of EDC (Chapter 6) and for establishing a quality assurance system of EDC (Chapter 7) still seem to require more concrete formulations in order to be genuinely operational for schools and their staff. In their current state, these parts still seem to require considerable developmental work, which presumably many schools are not capable of accomplishing on their own.

With respect to such concrete work in schools, it seems not only desirable but also necessary to extend the tool in at least two directions. One urgent requirement consists in further operationalising the "indicators" of the evaluative framework. Although each indicator is explained through several sub-items, these sub-items again seem to be in need of further operationalisation in terms of clear and concrete concepts and descriptions. A second important requirement consists in providing a practitioners' toolbox containing various types of material such as practical method descriptions, step-by-step tutorials, best practice examples, worksheets as master copies, etc. Appendices 2 to 4 of the tool merely represent a rudimentary step in such a direction, but do not yet appear to be sufficiently developed for this purpose.

3.1.4. Target groups of the tool

In view of these limitations of the current version of the tool, not treating heads of schools and teachers as the main or primary target groups of the tool should be considered. Offering the tool to them in its current form could entail the risk of refusal. The tool appears to represent a conceptual basis for operations that may appeal to groups outside schools working on conceptual matters concerning several parts of the school system. The spectrum of groups to be taken into consideration then turns out to be quite wide, comprising various groups with differing powers and competences that accordingly have to be addressed in appropriate ways. The plurality of groups that need to be taken into consideration comprises the following:

- policy makers and decision makers in state ministries as well as those responsible in state institutes;
- quality agencies and inspectorates recently established under the authority of the respective *Länder*;
- curriculum development and school development departments in the state institutes of the *Länder*;
- university departments and state institutions engaged in preparatory teacher education, as well as further providers of vocational training that work in the field of in-service teacher training;
- professionals and institutions offering consulting and co-ordinating services in the context of organisational school development processes;
- the Federal Agency for Civic Education (Bundeszentrale für politische Bildung) and the agencies for civic education of the *Länder*;
- governmental and non-governmental organisations involved in relevant educational subject matters, such as human rights education, peace education, education for sustainable development, etc.

Basically, there seem to be two functions for which these groups could be addressed. One consists in influencing official and administrative regulation activities, and the other in implementing the tool or parts of it into the practice of schools by developing it further, making it more concrete, promoting it in the course of multiplying activities and applying it in schools. Due to the fact that the tool aims at internal evaluation and school development rather than at external inspection and quality control, such external efforts should predominantly be aligned towards providing consulting and assisting services that help teachers as well as heads of schools to work with the tool or an accordingly advanced version of it. Issues that might prove critical in this context are examined below in sub-sections 3.2.2 and 4.1 respectively.

3.2. Systemic conditions for using the tool

3.2.1. Correspondence of the tool and the system of quality assurance and evaluation

In general, the tool features essential links to some common key elements and recent developments in the German system of quality assurance and evaluation. As already outlined (see sub-section 2.1), some promising linking areas are: (a) the development of quality assurance frameworks and the establishment of inspectorates for external evaluation, and (b) the promotion of quality assurance and organisational development processes in schools through the working out of individually customised school profiles or programmes and implementing formative internal self-evaluations.

Regarding the issue of quality frameworks and external evaluation, the relevant conditions with respect to the use of the tool essentially pertain to its formal and substantive connection to those frameworks. This concerns the question whether (and if so how) the areas of the evaluative framework match the areas of evaluation defined by the respective state-specific quality frameworks. Against the backdrop of the strong federalism that regulates the educational system in Germany, the existing variability in conceptual and structural composition among the existing state-specific quality frameworks must be taken into account. Thus, with regard to the concrete use of the tool, it will be necessary to ensure its formal and substantive connection individually for each framework. However, irrespective of whether or not this is desirable, a number of differences seem to exist at the level of terminology and formal structures, if not in the conceptual substance of the frameworks. At least this is suggested by a simple juxtaposition of the quality areas (*Qualitätsbereiche*) demarcated by the quality frameworks of several *Länder*. Comparing these areas with the areas of the tool, as Table 1 does, reveals considerable overlaps. The table shows that the tool appears to stand a good chance of being well received by the quality assurance and evaluation system.

Table 1: Comparison between quality areas demarcated by quality frameworks of several *Länder*, the Quality Framework for Education for Democratic Citizenship and the "Tool for Quality Assurance of Education for Democratic Citizenship in Schools". Bracketed numbers denote chapters

Quality Framework for Education for Democratic Citizenship	European Foundation for Quality Management	Quality frameworks in Berlin, Brandenburg Niedersachsen	Quality framework in Hamburg	Quality framework in Hessen	"Tool for Quality Assurance of Education for Democratic Citizenship in Schools"
Competences	Key Performance Results, Society Results, People Results, Customer Results	Results and Successes (1)	Effects and Results (3)	Results and Effects (7)	**I. Curriculum, teaching and learning** *Students and teachers acquire understanding of EDC and apply EDC principles to their everyday practice in school and classrooms (2)*
Learning Group and School Class	Processes	Learning Culture (2)	Literacy and Education (2)	Teaching and Learning (6)	*Design and practice of assessment within the school is consonant with EDC (3)*
Learning Culture					
School Culture		School Culture (3)		School Culture (5)	**II. School ethos and climate** *School ethos reflects EDC principles (4)*
School and Local Community	Partnerships and Resources	Sub-chapter of (3): School Culture: School, Local Community and Public Partners (3, 4)	*No proper area, but covered within other areas*	Sub-chapter of School Culture: 5.4. Co-operation and Public Communication	
Personal Development	People	Teacher Professionalisation and Personal Development (5)	*No proper area, but covered within other areas*	Professional Competence (4)	
School Management	Leadership	School Management (4)	Leadership and Management (1)	Leadership and Management (3)	**III. Management and Development** *Effective school leadership is based on EDC principles (5)*
School Programme and Development	Policy and Strategy	Goals and Strategies (6)	Part of Leadership and Management (1) as well as Literacy and Education (2)	Developmental Goals and Strategies (2)	**I. Curriculum, teaching and learning** *Adequate place for EDC in the school goals, policies and curriculum plans (1)*
				Prerequisites and Conditions (1)	**III. Management and Development** *Development plan reflects EDC principles (6)*

3.2.3. Preparation of teachers to work with the tool

Against the background of the judgment that the tool in its current form does not yet appear to be sufficiently suitable for being addressed directly to teachers (see sub-section 3.1.4), preparing teachers to work with the tool will prove crucial in the context of any of the indirect implementation methods outlined above in terms of suggested target groups. Any strategy project aiming at disseminating the tool should always be sensitive to the question of if and how its outcomes are helpful to teachers and schools as organisations.

According to evidence produced by Giesel, de Haan and Diemer (2007), two major paths need to be identified whereby innovations concerning EDC and democratic school development processes can enter schools, both of which are directly focused on the preparation of teachers. The first path is in-service training for teachers and, notably, of heads of schools. Most teachers felt that this had proven to be the most important and effective way by which innovations reached them. The second path consists in providing continuous external process assistance via skilled school development advisers. Against this background it is thus essential to promote the creation and institutionalisation of corresponding assistance and programmes at the level of the *Länder*. This is important with regard to starting basic school development projects, as well as with regard to more advanced and ambitious democratic school development processes.

3.2.4. Applying the tool to different schools and school types

As a framework defining key quality indicators and formulating structural guidelines, the tool is apparently applicable to every school type. Due to its comparatively high level of abstraction, it might seem ideal for a wide degree of application, yet the need for further operationalisation and concretisation (see sub-section 3.1.3) suggests that contingencies certainly exist that should be taken into account.

One such contingency, though definitely not the only one, is the difference among school types (tracks). In fact, on the strength of the tracking principle of the German school system, this is a rather complex issue. One must be aware of the existence of firm distinctions between the various school types concerning educational self-conception and practice. These types exhibit different didactic, pedagogical and organisational cultures that must be carefully reflected in the course of developing appropriate material. In addition, there are other parameters as well that have to be taken into consideration, such as different local and regional environmental conditions that generate specific needs, and key aspects of activity in schools. For this reason it appears advisable to undertake efforts to explore such diversity in connection with actions aiming at further operationalising the tool. At the same time, it should be discussed in advance whether the tool should be further developed as a general tool that applies to all school types, or whether school type-specific versions of it should be created.

4. Ideas for the implementation process

4.1. Making schools aware of the range of purposes

With regard to how working with the tool could prove valuable for schools, two approaches that differ analytically, but are not entirely independent of each other, can be considered. One is oriented towards and motivated primarily by content-related issues, that is issues concerning the various aspects of EDC as described by the tool. The corresponding type of motivation that forms the basis of working with the tool can be characterised as intrinsic motivation. The other form of perceiving the tool as valuable for schools relates to rather extrinsically motivating issues such as the duty of continually working out and revising school programmes, and of continually carrying out obligatory quality management and self-evaluation activities.

In respect of possible intrinsic motives, a huge variety of constellations of school-specific purposes certainly have to be taken into account that to some extent are conditioned by aspects like those outlined in the preceding chapter, for example, school types with their characteristic self-conceptions, as well as several specific environmental conditions. In general, intrinsic motivations are either based on negatively formulated living problems such as bullying, high rates of violence, a bad school climate, regular conflicts between teachers and students, or on positively formulated pedagogical intentions such as civic education, improving teaching and learning processes, realising higher standards of fairness and transparency concerning the rating of students' performance at school, providing opportunities to learn social and democratic accountability through practising democracy inside and outside the classroom, changing and improving co-operation among teachers, teachers and students as well as between the school and the students' parents, entering into co-operative activities with partners in the local community, and so on. Such motives will probably have to be identified in advance in each case when working with the tool in individual schools so that it can be perceived as a chance to work effectively on such issues. Furthermore, the identification of an intrinsic motivation to work with the tool is a demanding task that certainly requires further exploration. Probably, it would be advisable to undertake some qualitative and quantitative empirical investigations to accompany a pilot phase of implementing the tool in order to obtain more detailed impressions of the intrinsic motivation schools really experience when working with it.

Concerning the extrinsic motivation and motives of schools, it should first of all be noted that at present schools usually tend to evaluate the innovations to be adopted strictly in terms of the involved expenditure. Innovations tend not to stand a good chance of being adopted if they are not perceived as being helpful in view of the obligatory amount of work schools have to deal with. Conversely, the question becomes increasingly crucial if an innovation such as the tool can prove advantageous in comparison with previous practice. Further extrinsic motives that could make working with the tool valuable may consist in the provision of assistance through external mentors, critical friends, etc. It could possibly prove useful to refer to this to provide such assistance services in conjunction with mutual agreements or contracts.

4.2. How to integrate the tool into international partnerships

Further work on the tool and how to improve it, both in a national and a European context, is recommended as this symbolises a common European effort. However, at the level of partnerships between schools, this could prove a rather ambitious goal. As the case studies mentioned above suggest, co-operative networking of schools is usually well appreciated but rarely realised to a great extent (see Giesel, de Haan and Diemer, 2007: 123 ff.). This applies both in regional and in local settings, where conditions in principle allow co-operation. But other conditions, especially limited resources in terms of staff, time and money, mean that co-operation among schools in most cases remains selective even where there is interest in sharing ideas and working together. Against this background, integrating the tool into international partnerships at the level of schools requires special efforts if such partnerships are to be established and animated. This task can either be accomplished by using ways that already exist at the European level, such as the European Commission's Comenius School Partnerships Programme (Comenius, 2007), or eTwinning, a programme for forming school partnerships through the Internet, which is part of the European Commission's Lifelong Learning Programme (eTwinning, 2007). A special programme for partnerships between schools that wish to work with the tool could also be established.

With respect to how the tool could be integrated into international partnerships at the level of the various target groups mentioned above (see sub-section 3.1.4), it seems highly advisable to co-operate with stakeholders that share similar goals and purposes. Partners could for example comprise national and international organisations engaged in human rights education and in promoting educational engagements based on the Convention on the Rights of the Child (for example, UNICEF, UNESCO, etc.). Another possible partnership could be found within the OECD, with special regard to its Defining and Selecting Key Competencies project (DeSeCo, see Rychen and Salganik, 2001; OECD, 2002). And last but surely not least, consideration should be given to developing strategies with the aim of integrating the tool systematically.

4.3. Alternative scenarios for working with the tool

Finally, it may prove fruitful to think about two further scenarios that could surround strategies aiming at supporting as well as promoting the use of the tool. The first scenario could be a low-threshold award campaign, which would publicly give recognition to schools that perform well according to the quality indicators of the tool. In Germany such a campaign could be modelled on several existing awards such as the German School Award (Deutscher Schulpreis) or the Acting Democratically programme (Demokratisch Handeln); similar awards exist in other European countries.

A second scenario relates to the issue of sharing information, knowledge and experience. This could involve offering relevant information services such as an Internet platform with appropriate functionality, or could comprise opportunities for sharing and discussing ideas such as at network meetings, conferences and symposia. In this regard a promising development would be to establish connections and co-operative partnerships among various stakeholders in adjoining and partly overlapping areas, ranging from initiatives and organisations that work on education for sustainability to activities and discourses concerning aspects of quality assurance.

References

Baumert, J.; Bos, W.; Lehmann, R. (eds.) (2000). *TIMSS/III: Dritte Internationale Mathematik- und Naturwissenschaftsstudie - Mathematische und naturwissenschaftliche Bildung am Ende der Schullaufbahn*, Opladen: Leske + Budrich.

Baumert, J.; Cortina, K.S.; Leschinsky, A. (2003). "Grundlegende Entwicklungen und Strukturprobleme im allgemein bildenden Schulwesen", in Baumert, J.; Cortina, K.S.; Leschinsky, A.; Mayer, K.U.; Trommer, L. (eds.), *Das Bildungswesen in der Bundesrepublik Deutschland: Strukturen und Entwicklungen im Überblick*, Reinbek bei Hamburg: Rowohlt, 52-147.

Behrmann, G.C.; Grammes, T.; Reinhardt, S.; Hampe, P. (2004). "Politik. Kerncurriculum Sozialwissenschaften in der gymnasialen Oberstufe", in Tenart, H.-E. (ed.), *Kerncurriculum Oberstufe II. Expertisen im Auftrag der KMK*, Weinheim: Beltz, 322-406.

Biedermann, H. (2006). *Junge Menschen an der Schwelle politischer Mündigkeit. Partizipation: Patentrezept politischer Identitätsfindung?* Münster: Waxmann.

Bîreza, C.; Cecchini, M.; Harrison, C.; Krek, J.; Spajić-Vrkaš, V. (2005). "Tool for Quality Assurance of Education for Democratic Citizenship in Schools", Paris: UNESCO, Council of Europe, CEPS.

Bos, W.; Hornberg, S.; Arnold, K.-H.; Faust, G.; Fried, L.; Lankes, E.-M.; Schwippert, K.; Valtin, R. (eds.). (2007). *IGLU 2006. Lesekompetenzen von Grundschulkindern in Deutschland im internationalen Vergleich*. Münster: Waxmann.

Brackhahn, B. and Brockmeyer, R. (eds.) (2004). *QUISS - Qualitätsverbesserung in Schulen und Schulsystemen. Konzept – Organisation – Ergebnisse*, Vols. 1-5, Neuwied: Luchterhand.

Burkard, C. and Eikenbusch, G. (2000). *Praxishandbuch Evaluation*, Weinheim: Beltz.

Comenius (2007). *Lifelong Learning – Sectoral programmes: Comenius*, Brussels, Luxembourg: European Commission, Directorate-General for Education and Culture. Retrieved on 30 April 2007, from http://ec.europa.eu/education/programmes/llp/structure/comenius_en.html.

de Haan, G.; Edelstein, W.; Eikel, A. (eds.) (2007). *Qualitätsrahmen Demokratiepädagogik. Demokratische Handlungskompetenz fördern, demokratische Schulqualität entwickeln. Schuber mit 7 Heften und CD-ROM*, Weinheim: Beltz.

Detjen, J. (2007). *Politische Bildung. Geschichte und Gegenwart in Deutschland*, Munich/Vienna: Oldenbourg.

Deutscher Bildungsserver (2007a). *Standard Tests in the Länder*, Frankfurt-on-Main: DIPF. Retrieved on 30 April 2007, from www.bildungsserver.de/zeigen_e.html?seite=4452.

Deutscher Bildungsserver (2007b). *School Evaluation and School Inspection in the Länder*, Frankfurt-on-Main: DIPF. Retrieved on 30 April 2007, from www.bildungsserver.de/zeigen_e.html?seite=2652.

Deutscher Bildungsserver (2007c). *School Evaluation and Quality Research*, Frankfurt-on-Main: DIPF. Retrieved on 30 April 2007, from www.bildungsserver.de/zeigen_e.html?seite=1264.

Deutscher Bildungsserver (2007d). *School Development: Institutions and Material of the Länder*, Frankfurt-on-Main: DIPF. Retrieved on 30 April 2007, from www.bildungsserver.de/zeigen_e.html?seite=5079.

Eikenbusch, G. (1998). *Praxishandbuch Schulentwicklung*, Berlin: Cornelsen.

eTwinning (2007). *What is eTwinning?* Bonn: Schulen ans Netz. Retrieved on 30 April 2007, from www.etwinning.de/en/index.php.

Fend, H. (2001). *Qualität im Bildungswesen. Schulforschung zu Systembedingungen, Schulprofilen und Lehrerleistung*, Weinheim: Juventa.

Gagel, W. (1994). *Geschichte der politischen Bildung in der Bundesrepublik Deutschland 1945 – 1989*, Opladen: Leske + Budrich.

Giesel, K.; de Haan, G.; Diemer, T. (2007). *Demokratie in der Schule. Fallstudien zur demokratiebezogenen Schulentwicklung als Innovationsprozess*, Frankfurt-on-Main: Peter Lang.

GPJE – Gesellschaft für Politikdidaktik und politische Jugend und Erwachsenenbildung (2004). *Nationale Bildungsstandards für den Fachunterricht der politischen Bildung an Schulen*, Schwalbach am Taunus: Wochenschau Verlag.

Gries, J.; Lindenau, M.; Maaz, K.; Waleschkowski, U. (2005). *Bildungssysteme in Europa. Kurzdarstellungen*, Berlin: ISIS Berlin e.V. (Arbeitsmaterialien/ISIS Berlin e. V).

Himmelmann, G. (2003). "Fragile Fachidentität der politischen Bildung und Standards des Demokratie-Lernens", in Himmelmann, G. (2005), *Demokratie-Lernen als Lebens-, Gesellschafts- und Herrschaftsform*. 2nd edn. Schwalbach am Taunus, 312-343; and published as "Expertise zum Thema 'Was ist Demokratiekompetenz?' Ein Vergleich von Kompetenzmodellen unter Berücksichtigung internationaler Ansätze" by the Council of Europe. Retrieved on 30 April 2007, from www.coe.int/t/dg4/education/edc/Source/Pdf/Documents/By_Country/Germany/Expertise%20zum%20Thema%20Was%20ist%20Demokratiekompetenz.PDF.

Himmelmann, G. (2006). *Leitbild Demokratieerziehung. Vorläufer, Begleitstudien und internationale Ansätze zum Demokratie-Lernen*, Schwalbach am Taunus: Wochenschau Verlag.

Kempfert, G. and Rolff, H.-G. (2005). *Qualität und Evaluation. Ein Leitfaden für Pädagogisches Qualitätsmanagement*, Weinheim: Beltz.

Klieme, E.; Avenarius, H.; Blum, W.; Döbrich, P.; Gruber, H.; Prenzel, M. et al. (2003). *Zur Entwicklung nationaler Bildungsstandards. Eine Expertise*, Berlin: Bundesministerium für Bildung und Forschung. Retrieved on 30 April 2007, from www.bmbf.de/pub/zur_entwicklung_nationaler_bildungsstandards.pdf.

Klieme, E.; Baumert, J.; Schwippert, K. (2000). "Schulbezogene Evaluation und Schulleistungsvergleiche", in Rolff, H.-G. (ed.), *Jahrbuch der Schulentwicklung*, Band 11, Weinheim: Juventa, 387-438.

Klieme, E. and Beck, B. (ed.) (2007). *Sprachliche Kompetenzen - Konzepte und Messung*, DESI-Studie (Deutsch Englisch Schülerleistungen International), Weinheim: Beltz.

Klippert, H. (2000). *Pädagogische Schulentwicklung. Planungs- und Arbeitshilfen zur Förderung einer neuen Lernkultur*, Weinheim: Beltz.

KMK – Secretariat of the Standing Conference of Ministers of Education and Cultural Affairs of the *Länder* in the Federal Republic of Germany (2004). *Vereinbarung zu den Standards für die Lehrerbildung: Bildungswissenschaften (Beschluss der Kultusminister-konferenz vom 16.12.2004)*, Bonn: Sekretariat der Ständigen Konferenz der Kultusminister der Länder in der Bundesrepublik Deutschland. Retrieved on 30 April 2007, from www.kmk.org/doc/beschl/standards_lehrerbildung.pdf.

KMK – Secretariat of the Standing Conference of Ministers of Education and Cultural Affairs of the *Länder* in the Federal Republic of Germany (2006a). *The Education System in the Federal Republic of Germany 2005. A Description of the Responsibilities, Structures and Developments in Education Policy for the Exchange of Information in Europe*, Bonn: KMK. Retrieved on 30 April 2007, from www.kmk.org/dossier/dossier_en_ebook.pdf.

KMK – Secretariat of the Standing Conference of Ministers of Education and Cultural Affairs of the *Länder* in the Federal Republic of Germany (2006b). *Basic Structure of the Education System in the Federal Republic of Germany – Diagram*, Bonn: KMK. Retrieved on 30 April 2007, from www.kmk.org/doku/en-2006.pdf.

KMK – Secretariat of the Standing Conference of Ministers of Education and Cultural Affairs of the *Länder* in the Federal Republic of Germany (2006c). *Gesamtstrategie der Kultusministerkonferenz zum Bildungsmonitoring*, Bonn: Sekretariat der Ständigen Konferenz der Kultusminister der Länder in der Bundesrepublik Deutschland. Retrieved on 30 April 2007, from www.kmk.org/schul/Bildungsmonitoring_Brosch%FCre_Endf.pdf.

Kohler, B. (2005). *Rezeption internationaler Schulleistungsstudien. Wie gehen Lehrkräfte, Eltern und die Schulaufsicht mit Ergebnissen schulischer Evaluation um?* Münster: Waxmann.

Kühle, B. and Peek, R. (2007). "Lernstandserhebungen in Nordrhein-Westfalen. Evaluationsbefunde zur Rezeption und zum Umgang mit Ergebnisrückmeldungen in Schulen", *Empirische Pädagogik*, 21, 4, 428-447.

LiS – Landesinstitut für Schulentwicklung Stuttgart (2006) (ed.). *Demokratie durch Handeln lernen. Beiträge und erprobte Materialien zur Demokratieerziehung an Schulen*, Stuttgart: Landesinstitut für Schulentwicklung.

Litt. T. (1955). *Die politische Selbsterziehung des deutschen Volkes*, Bonn: Schriftenreihe der Bundeszentrale für Heimatdienst.

Maier, U. (2008). "Rezeption und Nutzung von Vergleichsarbeiten aus der Perspektive von Lehrkräften", *Zeitschrift für Pädagogik*, 54, 1, 95-117.

Massing, P. (2004). "Der Kern der politischen Bildung?" in Breit, G. and Schiele, S. (eds.), *Demokratie braucht politische Bildung*, Schwalbach: Wochenschau, 81-98.

Nachtigall, C. and Jantowski, A. (2007). "Die Thüringer Kompetenztests unter besonderer Berücksichtigung der Evaluationsergebnisse zum Rezeptionsverhalten", *Empirische Pädagogik*, 21, 4, 401-410.

OECD (2002). "Definition and Selection of Competences (DeSeCo): Theoretical and Conceptual Foundations. Strategy Paper", Paris: OECD. Retrieved on 30 April 2007, from www.portal-stat.admin.ch/deseco/deseco_strategy_paper_final.pdf.

Oetinger, F. (1951). *Wendepunkt der politischen Erziehung. Partnerschaft als pädagogische Aufgabe*, Stuttgart: Metzler.

OHCHR – Office of the United Nations High Commissioner for Human Rights (eds.) (2007), "Report of the Special Rapporteur on the Right to Education, Mr Vernor Muñoz Villalobos – Mission to Germany (A/HRC/4/29/Add.3)", Geneva: OHCHR. Retrieved on 30 April 2007, from http://daccessdds.un.org/doc/UNDOC/GEN/G07/117/59/PDF/G0711759.pdf?OpenElement.

Peek, R. (2004). "Qualitätsuntersuchung an Schulen zum Unterricht in Mathematik (QuaSUM) – klassenbezogene Ergebnisrückmeldungen und ihre Rezeption in Brandenburger Schulen", *Empirische Pädagogik*, 18, 1, 82-114.

Rolff, H.-G. (2000). *Manual Schulentwicklung. Handlungskonzept zur pädagogischen Schulentwicklungsberatung (SchuB)*, Weinheim: Beltz.

Rolff, H.-G. (2007). *Studien zu einer Theorie der Schulentwicklung*, Weinheim: Beltz.

Ruep, M. (1999). *Innere Schulentwicklung. Schule als lernende Organisation - ein lebendiger Organismus. Theoretische Grundlagen und praktische Beispiele*, Donauwörth: Auer.

Rychen D.S. and Salganik L.H. (eds.) (2001). *Defining and Selecting Key Competences*, Göttingen: Hogrefe & Huber.

Schratz, M.; Iby, M.; Radnitzky, E. (2000). *Qualitätsentwicklung. Verfahren, Methoden, Instrumente*, Weinheim: Beltz.

Schröter, K.; Diemer, T.; Kohle, V. (2003-06). *Demokratiebausteine "Selbstevaluation"*, Berlin: BLK-Programm Demokratie lernen & leben. Retrieved on 30 April 2007, from www.blk-demokratie.de/materialien/demokratiebausteine/selbstevaluation.html.

Schwippert, K. (2004). "Leistungsrückmeldungen an Grundschulen im Rahmen der Internationalen Grundschul-Lese-Untersuchung (IGLU)", *Empirische Pädagogik*, 18, 1, 62-81.

Speck, K. (2006). "Stand und Perspektive der Evaluations- und Qualitätsdebatte in der zweiten Phase der Lehrerbildung (Referendariat)", in Schubarth, W. and Pohlenz, P. (eds.), *Qualitätsentwicklung und Evaluation in der Lehrerbildung. Die zweite Phase: Das Referendariat*, Potsdam: Universitätsverlag Potsdam, 321-337. Retrieved on 30 April 2007, from http://opus.kobv.de/ubp/volltexte/2006/696/pdf/pbl02.pdf.

Stamm, M. (2003). *Evaluation und ihre Folgen für die Bildung. Eine unterschätzte pädagogische Herausforderung*, Münster: Waxmann.

Ulrich, S. and Wenzel, F.M. (2003). *Partizipative Evaluation. Ein Konzept für die politische Bildung*, Gütersloh: Verlag Bertelsmann Stiftung.

Latvia
Irēna Žogla and Rudīte Andersone

1. School evaluation in Latvia

Background information and general evaluation of the tool

The Law on Education (1998, revised 2001) and the Law on Comprehensive Education (1999, revised 2002) outline the main educational reform process towards democratisation (Law on General Education 1999), which is further detailed in the documents of the Ministry of Education and Science and which specify:
- decentralisation of education by providing schools with the right to choose the way they want to reach their desired goals;
- the autonomy of schools in choosing or creating programmes and textbooks to meet the needs of learners and ensure the quality of their academic achievements and skills;
- quality assurance and management of the improved system, from control to internal evaluation and self-evaluation, to external evaluation and accreditation;
- development planning based on investigation, self-evaluation, external evaluation, and discussions with stakeholder participation;
- collaboration and partnership within and among schools to ensure quality of education and learners' success.

Schools are now working towards creating learning communities and becoming cultural centres of communities in order to make better use of local possibilities for the benefit of learners (Ministry of Education and Science, 2006).

The state education standards specify key aspects in the development of the education system according to the Law on Education (the strategic goals and main tasks of educational programmes, compulsory curricula, basic principles for QA and the procedure for assessing the level of education reached by learners). These standards meet the regulations of the Cabinet of Ministers (Regulations on the State Basic Education Standard 2000, No. 462) and provide the main objectives of different types of education. They also redirect programmes/curricula from the knowledge domain to an outcome based on learners' knowledge, skills and abilities. They denote the core subjects, namely the sciences, mathematics and civic education; special attention is also paid to modern languages. Schools with Russian and other minority languages of instruction are obliged to learn Latvian. Specialists from the Ministry of Education and Science in co-operation with the

Advisory Board on Ethnic Minority Education Issues have developed a support plan to help educational institutions prepare for transition to studying in Latvian (Ministry of Education and Science, 2005). Textbooks are released in at least two languages of instruction – Latvian and Russian.

The overarching goal of educational development is to carry out the necessary changes in the education system that would enhance the building of a knowledge-based, democratic and socially integrated society, make the Latvian population and economy more competitive, and simultaneously preserve and develop typically Latvian cultural values (Ministry of Education and Science, 2005; OECD, 2000).

The timeline of qualitative stages in the development of the Latvian education system is as follows:
- 1991-95: redirection of the system towards that of an independent country;
- 1995-2000: development of a coherent system of legislation;
- 2001 onwards: the system of education has reached another stage of development – to ensure educational quality and democratisation in co-operation with policy makers, stakeholders and non-governmental organisations.

The reform is implemented by the following state administration institutions:
- the Ministry of Education and Science;
- the Curriculum Development and Examination Centre (development of the curriculum, evaluation of textbooks, preparation of centralised tests, monitoring of teaching/learning outcomes in accordance with the standards, co-ordination of teachers' in-service education);
- the State Education Inspectorate (state control and monitoring of education);
- the State Youth Initiative Centre (implementation of youth policy, provision of methodological assistance in the area of hobby education, organisation of teachers' in-service training for out-of-school activities);
- town and regional educational boards (operation of educational institutions in the regions, methodological support for teachers and community).

The ministry co-ordinates the operation of the central public administration institutions, as well as municipal education boards and establishments. At the end of each year, the ministry submits a progress report to the Cabinet of Ministers (government), which is prepared together with the local school boards. Democratic management is ensured by school councils in co-operation with the municipalities, the community, parents and school (teachers') councils (which deal with teaching/learning issues).

The notion and phenomenon of democracy have always been understood as the power of the people. However, people's understanding of this topic often differs according to which part of the population they represent. Those who identify with it usually experience real or anticipated activity and participation, though the very content of the notions of citizenship, democracy and education might have different culturally based understandings, a peculiarity that is characteristic of Latvia.

Latvia became democratic after many years under a totalitarian regime, where the ruling ideology also called itself democratic, and certain groups of people used to be recognised by officials as not only being loyal to the political system, but also as having brought freedom and democracy to the country. After the political changes in 1991, these people experienced the feeling of lost positions and values. The majority of the government has come to power with the experience of life and loyalties under the previous system, and as a result, some political parties do not always accept positive initiatives promoted by their opponents.

From time to time the government appears to perceive the positive energy of the population as a threat, not as a positive confirmation of their activities, and therefore a number of people still experience isolation or even alienation. Different loyalties exist in the country, and achieving mutual understanding is not easy. In a truly democratic society, developments at national level cannot take place if individuals do not legitimise their activities and do not act consistently with those developments (Pabriks, 2002: 43-45). Democracy is related to certain key basic freedoms: freedom of religion, speech, association, identity, using one's own language and developing one's own culture – freedoms that are declared to be basic democratic issues in Latvia, but are still understood and accepted differently by different groups of people, while parents or political parties have different values with regard to school.

One of the most discussed issues related to EDC is the language policy. In 1992 the Latvian language was proclaimed the official state language (www.gov.lv/likumi), and a ten-year period of preparation to switch to Latvian as the language of instruction at schools started. Ethnic minority learners in grades 10-12 who attend state and local schools have a guaranteed opportunity to acquire up to 40% of the total curriculum of general secondary education programmes in an ethnic minority language. The knowledge and skills of a native language, along with the acquisition of a minority culture and ethnicity, are provided through education programmes and special interest-related education activities at schools and in communities (Ministry of Education and Science, 2004). Ethnic and linguistic diversity has specific features in education and society: Latvian in education; the two main languages (Latvian and Russian) in communication; English as the main foreign language in schools; and a multi-ethnic society (with about 100 ethnic groups being represented in Latvia). The languages of instruction in school reveal the multicultural reality that Latvia faces:

- schools with Latvian as the language of instruction (72.9%, and 64.1% of learners) – previously almost mono-ethnic, now multi-ethnic – are attended by Latvian children and children from other ethnic groups with the aim

of better integrating them into society or seeking possibilities to continue tertiary education;
- schools with Russian as the language of instruction (the second largest group of schools, 14.9%, and 23% of learners) have always been multi-ethnic with a Russian cultural domain. They are attended by pupils who choose Russian as their mother tongue, and follow the traditions, cultural identity or political orientations of their families;
- 11.4% of schools have classes in both Latvian (8% of learners) and Russian (4.3% of learners);
- schools for other ethnic minorities – Belorussian, Ukrainian, Polish, Hebrew, Roma, Lithuanian and Estonian – are small, comprising only 0.4% of the total number of learners. These schools are free to choose their language of instruction to reach the level of academic achievements and skills required by the state standards, with pupils learning Latvian as well (Central Board of Statistics of Latvia, 2006; more information in Žogla, Andersone and Černova, 2007).

Attitudes to language policy differ according to the different identities of social groups, and the choice of language of instruction reflects different loyalties and cultural domains (Baltic Institute of Social Research, 2000). The historical background impacts education in many ways with regard to legislation, the activities of the political parties, parents' political and cultural orientation, parents' value domain, the predominant attitudes and loyalties of community stakeholders, attitudes towards the EU, the processes of an open society, etc. Many factors have little to do with schools – while implementing the tool, this peculiarity might cause less difficulty at schools, but could complicate co-operation with the community and with stakeholders. These circumstances point towards the need to modify the tool accordingly.

Considerable disagreement exists regarding the nature and practical implementations of democracy in society and in schools. There are opposite and even conflicting views on the basic issues: some consider that a democratic society and a free market are two components of one perspective, and that education should cultivate human capital so that society is economically competitive; however, others, especially people involved in education and the cultural sphere, argue that education in a democratic society should seek to cultivate human values and potential, and foster personal development to ensure active inclusion in all social processes – which corresponds to the basic aim of education as defined in the Law on Education. Therefore, education in Latvia is on its way towards combining both these approaches with the main aim of developing human values, empowering individuals for life in a democratic society by creating inclusive schools, and fostering learners' competitiveness.

Accountability, benchmarking and evaluation practices at schools are the major issues for discussion in the context of educational quality – that is, what learners and teachers ought to be held accountable for, what are the most productive ways of accountability in the situation when stakeholders participate in development planning and evaluation leading to school accreditation, how to assess and evaluate the social dimensions of education as cultural and equality issues, or how to assess the attitudinal development of learners.

The above-mentioned social peculiarities seem on the one hand to be the most complicated obstacle for the implementation of the tool in Latvian schools, yet on the other hand it is precisely why a tool like this is needed in order to tackle the existing problems.

The diverse nature of Latvian society and recent political changes are reflected in the types of schools:
- state schools, attended by the majority of the learners and financed by the state budget: this group also comprises schools for children with disabilities;
- schools run and financed by local authorities;
- private comprehensive schools, which offer an alternative to the state schools in terms of their curriculum (private schools receive financial support from the state or municipal budget that only covers staff salaries).

Adherence to the state standards ensures that these schools follow common goals, though the way chosen by the schools and their stakeholders do result in differences that are sometimes considerable. The implementation of the tool might differ considerably among state/municipality schools, private schools, and schools for children with limited abilities and a need for special pedagogical assistance. Modification of the tool will need the values of democratic citizenship to be integrated into the culture of each school, as well as into subjects (content, strategies and organisational settings), out-of-class activities and teacher education, to ensure the targeted use of the tool.

The relationship between the conception of the tool and its general usefulness for Latvian schools emerges from comments on the main ideas it contains:
- the tool is a powerful means of capacity-building: it can be identified and modified to integrate EDC into the existing QA experience in order to foster further development of the education system. It aims at ensuring QA in development planning so as to improve the effectiveness of education, as well as to guarantee the comparability of the system within the country and among other countries. Capacity-building by EDC should be contextualised with other national values;
- quality assurance and development planning: the tool has already been introduced in Latvian schools and included into school evaluation criteria. The practice presented by the tool can be used for the explicit integration of EDC, and the tool can serve as a model for planning and methodological issues in all spheres of education;

– self-evaluation and progress report: in the system of school evaluation, the tool has already been implemented in practice, and evaluation criteria for internal and external evaluation are available at schools. The characteristics as well as the quality indicators of EDC will make evaluation of educational outcomes more explicit. Suggested step-by-step implementation of EDC in the existing QA system and development planning will make integration of EDC easier.

1.1. Modes of school evaluation in Latvia

The Latvian education system is being developed in accordance with the general educational development trends that have been defined by the European Parliament and the Council of Europe: co-operation to develop QA and assessment, creating open QA and evaluation systems, facilitating development of self-evaluation and internal evaluation, ensuring stakeholder participation, exchanging experience among schools. These initiatives are developed in the special instructions on evaluation, and thus ensure self-evaluation as the main process of evaluation and comparability. They also keep the discussion in Latvia going towards further democratisation of schools (Regulations on the State Basic Education Standard, 2000; Ministry of Education and Science, 2004a; Ministry of Education and Science, 2002). This background provides a facilitating environment for the implementation of the tool.

To obtain credible and reliable data for the analysis and development of the education policy, a unified education quality assessment system was introduced in 2005 (Ministry of Education and Science, 2004b). The quality of education is assessed according to 22 criteria (Ministry of Education and Science, 2004a) and lead to: identifying the advanced components of the pedagogical process of the particular school; identifying earlier valuable results that further developments can be based on; distinguishing the most necessary improvements as well as possible ones; and providing research-based planning for school development. These criteria are already being used in all Latvian schools, and the implementation of the tool will require considerable attempts to introduce a new set of criteria related to EDC, as well as to integrate them into existing practice. Teachers' views are nevertheless very supportive towards the system of criteria that they have recently mastered.

To ensure quality of education and effective school evaluations, in 2002 the ministry published a Handbook for *School Evaluation and Development Planning* (Ministry of Education and Science, 2002) with an explicit description of areas and parameters according to which schools are evaluated. Internal and external evaluations use the same criteria. To assure correct use of the criteria, the handbook clarifies the aims and procedure of evaluation, the main items to pay attention to in SWOT analyses, evaluation criteria and parameters, methods and organisation of evaluation, data collection and processing, and the possible structure of a progress report. The criteria represent seven areas of educational process and school activities with desired achievements: content of education, process of teaching/learning, learners' achievements, learners' supporting systems, school environment, resources and school management (Ministry of Education and Science, 2004c). The handbook provides detailed instructions on the modes of evaluation and development planning – the possible structure, demands and explicit instructional materials. Some 12 appendices give recommendations and details for QA, development planning and the progress report. They also include evaluation sheets for seven areas: analysis sheets and an evaluation of the final state examinations, recommendations for self-evaluation of the progress report, a database collection of learners' achievements, patterns observed from experiences in the country, questionnaires for stakeholders and observation sheets.

EDC qualities described in the tool are represented in each of the above-mentioned areas, though they are not as explicitly addressed as in the tool. The criteria are open to implementation of EDC in the school subjects most related to it, as well as the possibility to integrate it as a cross-curricular issue. Several criteria for school activities can be considered as the most favourable background issue for implementing the tool: participation of learners in decision making, development of learners' social skills, maintenance of equal rights for all learners, facilitation of co-operation among learners, inclusion, etc.

The basic education standards (Ministry of Education and Science, 1998) include four blocks of school subjects, one of which is called "society and myself". They aim at developing learners' social competence – their understanding of social systems and processes, co-operation skills, participation in social processes, features of democratic citizenship, etc. The desired academic achievements and skills of the learners are described in detail for all grades from 1 to 9 of basic school. Qualities related to democratic citizenship, for example, social life skills, are also described in the programmes for secondary schools and included in the evaluation criteria with instructions in the handbook (Ministry of Education and Science, 2002).

Centralised single examinations and tests take place by the end of grades 9 and 12; in grades 3 and 6 diagnostic tests of the teaching/learning process take place. The current scores for evaluations used at the centralised examinations range from 1 (lowest) to 10 (highest), and the system of level evaluation ranges from A (highest) to F (lowest). The scores and levels are described in detail. The results of the final centralised examinations (grade 12) are recognised by the tertiary educational institutions upon admission.

The challenging quality of the tool lies in its detailed description of democratic citizenship, as well as its stages of development and the relationship to school development planning. The introduction of the tool would mean duplication with the handbook (which is not cheap), it would also require new guidelines to be prepared containing material on EDC. This would be very valuable, but at the same time time-consuming, resource-intensive and financially costly.

A common technology of school evaluation has been launched, and the suggested unified system of evaluation is related to QA and ensures comparability of results. Internal evaluation is the main procedure in the evaluation system, and includes self-evaluation, evaluation by stakeholders (state and municipalities, parents, learners, other non-governmental organisations) and experts, and is carried out on a systematic basis. Analysis and evaluation is a precondition for school development planning. A typical procedure of internal evaluation at school is a two-phase process – a general overview and detailed evaluation, followed by a discussion and improvement of development planning:

- the preparatory stage for explicit self-evaluation (usually a week is allocated) by the principals and his or her assistants, groups of the most experienced teachers and other staff members to formulate a general background view of the pedagogical process and out-of-school activities – main data revealing achievements in general and conclusions based on teachers' experience and observations. The main aim of this procedure is to assume the development of the school in general, as a whole system, as well as to single out the most advanced spheres and to choose items for detailed analysis;

- a detailed investigation of the achievements (this usually lasts for several months) in selected spheres of school functioning – data collection according to the schemes (included in the handbook – statistics, learners' and parents' views, teachers' views, detailed observation and analysis of the process, analysis of the outcomes, and evaluation of the teaching technologies and equipment; namely, data collection that will reveal the main trends). This is a long-lasting process that involves all staff and resources. The process itself is conducted by a special group that plans the internal assessment procedure, and brings together stakeholders (learners and parents) and experts (usually the most experienced teachers, and those who lead methodological teams of subject teachers). The team prepares draft conclusions for discussion in the subject teacher groups, parents' council, staff meetings, etc. The main aim of this investigation is to spotlight the strongest areas and those that need special attention to ensure quality. Schools practice this kind of evaluation once a year unless there is a special need for more frequent evaluation. Internal evaluation takes place prior to every school accreditation, resulting in a progress report that covers all areas of school activities.

The internal evaluation procedure in general does not contradict the idea of the tool. Nevertheless, evaluation of EDC appears be problematic for several reasons. The tool deals with democratic citizenship and human rights – only one of the thematic areas of education and values to be acquired – while schools in Latvia according to the national standard are evaluated in seven areas. All modes of evaluation use data collected by international evaluation programmes. Since 1992 Latvia has participated in 10 international comparative studies, such as IES, TIMSS, etc., and data collected provide a good basis for comparing achievements. Since 2000 Latvia has participated in OECD research, and the ministry has prepared 182 tables with data on the system of education that should prove sufficient for the State Agency of Evaluation of Quality of General Education (hereafter "the agency") to judge the main trends of development and quality assurance (Šmite, 2006). Currently, the OECD's Programme for International Student Assessment 2006 is used to determine pupils' achievements in the European context. Consequently, an overall assessment of the interaction among the economic, social and education fields can be carried out. This aspect of evaluation goes beyond the competence of the country: the integration of the tool in this context can hardly depend on a school or country, and therefore needs special consideration.

The issues for evaluation follow the idea that self-evaluation cannot be substituted by chains of figures. The two kinds of investigation – qualitative and quantitative – are seen as supplementing each other, and descriptions of the real state of affairs, viewpoints and attitudes are revealed in narratives and contextualised descriptions of situations. Therefore an essential part of internal evaluation is learners' self-evaluation and their direct or indirect participation in school evaluation and decision-making – their reflections, portfolios and descriptions are to this end used (Šmite, 2006). Learners' achievements are assessed individually with detailed analysis of school quality. Their self-evaluation, peer and teachers' evaluation and assessment form part of every lesson. Assessment of EDC can be integrated into the procedure of self-evaluation, and internal and external evaluation as far as it is a competence of a given school or the country.

External evaluation is carried out in three ways: accreditation, activities of the inspectorate, and centralised tests. The agency was established to ensure unified school quality evaluation: to organise school quality evaluation; to gather and analyse data related to the quality of general education; and to propose ways of improving the evaluation methodology and of the education policy. Institutionalising the evaluation ensures the accessibility of information, the transparency of the evaluation process and the impartiality of results in the field of education. The agency uses the same evaluation criteria as the schools do. If the tool is recommended by the ministry and accepted by schools, the agency should be asked to include EDC evaluation into the system of school evaluation and accreditation. If so, instructions for evaluation and accreditation will accordingly need to be modified.

The maximum period of school accreditation is six years. If a school is accredited for a shorter period (between one and five years) because a considerable improvement might be needed, internal evaluation will take place before every accreditation. The procedure is similar to the second phase of internal evaluation, and is described in detail by Regulation No. 612 of the Cabinet of Ministers, 16 August 2005 (Ministry of Education and Science, 2004a).

To carry out external evaluation and accreditation in Latvia, 368 experts had been trained by the agency by the end of 2005/06 (Šmite, 2006). These and the newly selected experts will need additionally financed courses to familiarise themselves with the tool, as well as the practice of EDC assessment in the school QA system, evaluation and accreditation.

The State Education Inspectorate is a state supervisory body that administers education quality. It examines on a regular basis whether educational institutions are operating in compliance with the regulations, and ensures the observance of public rights in the field of education. Therefore the staff of the ministry, the inspectorate, and central and local administration institutions should be acquainted with the tool, and its implementation should become a component of the administration's procedures.

1.2. Evaluation as an issue in teacher training

Pre-service teacher education is provided by two types of tertiary educational institutions: universities with teacher educational programmes, and pedagogical higher educational establishments. These are state or private institutions. Students completing a pedagogical programme are awarded a Bachelor of Education with a teacher's qualification in the chosen track: preschool, subject teacher, etc. The number of these institutions is sufficient, though there is a real shortage of teachers in Latvia, as a considerable number of graduates do not start work in school (mainly because of the low salaries and because the quality of the programmes they have graduated from enable them to find more lucrative jobs in the private sector) – students pay educational fees, and graduates feel free in their career choices. Therefore the academic staff of schools is constantly ageing, and faces a heavy workload. Issues like the tool are welcomed by teachers – if modified, it could save time.

Pre-service education includes a wide range of subjects concerning psychology and school pedagogy, teaching/learning theories and technologies, subject didactics, classroom and school management, the organisational basis of out-of-class and out-of-school activities, the theoretical background and practices of assessment and evaluation, etc. There is no common framework for Bachelor of Education studies in Latvia: although educational institutions that run teacher educational programmes usually compare curricula with one another, the scope of the main subject clusters is similar, and school hours are similar for all pre-service tertiary teacher education programmes, reaching 22-26 credit points (33-29 European). The assignments for school practice include the full procedure of evaluation and accreditation, as well as a survey of the enabling documents. Thus theory plus practice of assessment and evaluation are included in training programmes in three ways: special subjects to acquire skills of evaluation and self-evaluation; part of several subjects that are related to the methodology of teaching-learning; and part of students' school practice.

Teaching is considered an important profession in Latvia, and teachers' professional development is planned – teachers are supposed to hold higher pedagogical education or study towards a diploma (a Bachelor, professional and/or Master's degree). In-service training is planned on a regular basis and widens teachers' options. Teachers without a higher pedagogical education are strongly recommended to take courses in educational sciences at least once every three years. The atmosphere in schools is highly demanding with regard to teachers' professional qualifications, and pre-service students during their practical training are involved in school internal and external evaluation alongside permanent staff.

The tertiary programmes aim at developing students' skills to assess and evaluate the success of learners (instructions for all modes of evaluation are provided): to reflect and self-evaluate during the studies and school practice, as well as to evaluate textbooks in compliance with the standards and learners' needs.

The Master's programmes include courses on theory and practices of quality assurance, and trends of school development and planning, leadership, assessment and evaluation. These programmes are designed to develop students' skills to ensure their participation in internal evaluation and to develop their career further towards achieving an expert competence. Specialised management programmes are designed that lead to a Master's diploma for a manager of an educational establishment.

In the last decade several papers have been published by the ministry on school management, development planning, assessment and evaluation that contain definitions, theories and practices of self-evaluation, internal and external evaluation, practices of accreditation, learners' and parents' participation in school evaluation, management of changes and leadership. The published materials comprise monographs, methodological papers, and evaluations of experience. For instance, the *Management of an Educational Establishment* (Šmite, 2006) has been released in four parts (the last one in 2006). These publications are used on a regular basis by teachers and students.

It would be possible to prepare an optional course on EDC for pre-service and in-service education, as well as to integrate the ideas of the tool into existing programmes and subjects. A seminar for educators is needed.

1.3. The way evaluation results are used in schools and in the educational system

The main areas for evaluation and self-evaluation, criteria as well as levels of the learners' academic achievements and skills, plus their detailed description, all serve as a background for a unified system of evaluation – common criteria, methods of collecting comparable data to make comparable conclusions, etc. – and give discussions at schools a common vocabulary with regard to the main issues and ensure up-to-date professional language. The system of evaluation and accreditation described above was introduced several years ago, and schools still combine it with the earlier experiences with discussions regarding evaluation results. Experiences may well therefore be individual and specific to a particular school.

A typical procedure is as follows: the most experienced teachers and vice-principals (depending on the competence that is most needed to analyse the evaluation results) are asked by the school principal or the council to reflect on the items that have been highlighted as the strongest or the weakest ones, to collect the necessary data and then to formulate the main items for discussion at the school or in the teachers' or parents' council. Usually, external counsellors or inspectors participate in these discussions. The main direction is towards further improvement, the ways this should be done and the people to be involved. The most effective way of using the evaluation results is to improve the pedagogical process during the evaluation wherever possible: improvements during the internal assessment are evaluated as a special item. Discussions distinguish between those spheres that are advanced and those that need improvement, denoting priorities for further QA (where we are, where we want to be, what we know about our possibilities and what we can achieve). After this stage, objectives are corrected and planning improved for the forthcoming period for the whole school and for each teacher.

Local bodies and the ministry analyse the results of the external evaluation and accreditation and use the conclusions as a background for further activities. School accreditation material and progress reports are accessible for teachers, parents and community representatives, and can be obtained from schools. General conclusions on the education system and country progress reports can be downloaded from the ministry's site (www.izm.gov.lv) or obtained in printed form.

Despite being comparatively recently introduced, this system is already accepted by the majority of teachers and stakeholders, who have developed their own practices. However, the considerable workload that teachers face and uncertainty about innovations in general (which are very frequent in Latvia) could result in the usual reaction to the implementation of the tool if it is poorly modified to local needs – mixed emotions resulting in resistance.

2. The "Tool for Quality Assurance of Education for Democratic Citizenship in Schools"

2.1. Coherence and comprehensiveness of the tool for schools in Latvia

The EU's Ministers for Education have agreed on three major goals to be achieved by 2010 for the benefit of the population and the EU as a whole:
– to improve the quality and effectiveness of EU education and training systems;
– to ensure its accessibility to all;
– to open up education and training to the wider world.

These goals are accepted in Latvia and are reflected in various documents on education.

To reach some conclusions with regard to the coherence and validity of the tool for schools in Latvia in the EU context, teachers' and school principals' views on the tool were addressed. Teacher-students on the Med programme at the University of Latvia comprises the largest number of respondents (162). They assessed the system of evaluation, QA and development planning in Latvian schools. Seven school principals and vice-principals, and 13 teachers from 20 schools (randomly chosen) were acquainted with the tool and their views assessed. The majority (73.6%) of teacher-students were either positive or very positive about the evaluation system (internal, self-evaluation, external evaluation), as opposed to those partly satisfied, 21.3%; unsatisfied, 0.23%; or who made no judgement, 4.87%. The majority of additional comments revealed that the system of QA, development planning and evaluation is too new to yield any detailed conclusions.

Their level of satisfaction with the printed matter on school evaluation is even higher – 88.7% were positive or very positive; 10.9% considered themselves not competent enough to evaluate the issues; and 0.4% did not answer. All respondents admitted that their possibilities for participating in school evaluation and development planning are unlimited, and that they depend on personal initiative and motivation. The collected data support the judgments of the authors of this expertise, and illustrate viewpoints and statements that are grouped according to the most important items in this chapter and the next. Two main conclusions can be reached at this stage:

- the tool is very well targeted and provides a learners' learning-centred pedagogy that describes the main components of a pedagogical process in detail with relevant quality indicators and clearly stated desired outcomes;
- the tool provides an easy-to-use description of the essence of education for democratic citizenship, as well as the way it can be included into the educational process of a school. Especially relevant in this context is the chapter on school development planning as a means of implementing the tool.

Evaluation in Latvia assesses learners' civic knowledge and skills by regular tests and content evaluation (internal and external). School evaluation includes such criteria as meeting learners' social needs, developing their social skills, ensuring inclusion, etc. (Ministry of Education and Science 2004a). The tool can be considered as a way of providing a detailed and explicit description of democratic citizenship – a system-making quality in the social development of a person. To use the tool productively, schools will need specific content and methods for each grade from 1 to 12.

In 2008/09 it is planned to update the content of secondary education and the final centralised test in mathematics for grade 12 (school-leavers). This activity can be combined with the introduction of EDC if an official decision is taken on the tool.

2.2. Corresponding material in Latvia

No materials of this kind on EDC are available in Latvia. However, there is a set of materials on building an inclusive school, quality evaluation criteria with a detailed description of levels, criteria of teachers' professional qualification, etc., which provide background and can help in implementing the tool. Implementation will cause these issues to be revised in due course.

Principals and vice-principals who are acquainted with the tool admit that in Latvia no special issues are needed for evaluation, QA and development planning as the possibilities of the existing ones have not yet been exhausted, and there are still many teachers whose knowledge of these issues is poor. They report a need for instruction, seminars, translation of the tool, and hands-on sessions to explain the idea behind the tool and how to implement it. This would, however, have to be agreed to by the ministry which, because of its system-making power, affects the whole process of school education. To make these changes to the tool and introduce it into the current system would need the support of a large number of specialists, plus considerable financial support for this and for preparing administrators, teachers and stakeholders. The principals also pointed out that implementation of the tool still requires many modifications for each grade and subject in order to integrate the new content into the existing system.

The respondents expressed their awareness of a possible imbalance in value education: teachers have to deal with other important values held or needed by their learners and parents, while only EDC has such an explicit description. They also reported on the need to collect comparable and reliable data.

3. *The tool as an instrument of school evaluation in Latvia*

3.1. Conditions for using the tool in schools

During the years of transition the content of teaching/learning, school evaluation and self-evaluation in Latvia followed the idea of creating a democratic learning-centred, humanistic, inclusive school with the aim of moving towards an integrated society (Baltic Institute of Social Research, 2000; Secretariat of the Special Assignments Minister for Social Integration Affairs, 2005). Based on the principle of a democratic school and the humanistic pedagogical process, the tool thus provides a theoretically based issue with detailed instructions for practical implementation.

We examined the results from this reflection on the tool in several groups to understand better its essential characteristics, as well as possibilities to implement it in Latvian schools. These reflections are organised according to the main items that characterise a modern school, and indicate the main directions in which it could develop in Latvia.

Democratisation and modernisation of schools for the learners' self-directed development, creating a powerful tool for developing cultured citizens, empowering learners to meet the challenges of globalisation and mobility, and increasing their compatibility by using QA in schools (Ministry of Education and Science, 2004b; Ministry of Education and Science, 2006). Latvia's education system has emerged through crucial changes and still is in a process of fostering teachers' and learners' decision making, self-assessment, and inclusive participation in development planning. The tool addresses one of the most topical items and relevant targets of the state standards – in Latvia democratisation in education has started in a decentralised fashion, and teachers had to learn about democracy by doing and taking responsibility for their choices.

> *As a teacher notes: "This sort of issue (the tool) would have been extremely important when we started the redirection process. Sometimes there is only some evidence of inclusion – a democratic game which ends as soon as the time of a current activity is over. EDC, if it were included in the school development plan (as per the tool), would function as a constant means of school QA and would achieve the target. It would also prevent schools from functioning in a fragmented way, and would provide a constant means of including or of experiencing self-directed involvement. The tool can be used as a pattern for EDC as well as for other qualities included in the targets of school education."*

Schools in Latvia are working towards increasing learners' efficiency and equality in a mobile world in which cultures exert enormous mutual influence. The inclusion of learners, as well as the prevention of gender, social or other discrimination, is one of the targets. The validity of the tool is achieved by a clear assumption of democratic citizenship nowadays and the possibility of modifying the multicultural and specific settings of a particular country. Recognition of diversity and provision of multiple choices are two of the tool's assets.

> *To quote another teacher: "The tool ... is a good means of evaluating the quality of a school if it preaches diversity and if it is able to facilitate diversity."*

> *This assessment is supported by another teacher: "At our school we have a programme for multicultural education, and the tool brings a good portion of certainty – attempts by colleagues in other countries are following the same understanding of education in a multicultural setting."*

Constant development offers certain key incentives such as appropriate democratic models of governance, leadership and partnership in education, and synergies arising in schools. The tool improves educational governance, initiates the development of leadership and partnership within a school and among schools. Distinguishing between development planning and planning of everyday work towards the main target is relevant for a school's capacity building.

> *The importance of this is reflected in teachers' comments: "The tool is relevant for the principals to learn how to perform democratic governance. They sometimes find it difficult to distinguish between good understanding of*

> *democratic governance and its everyday appearance and evidence. Quality indicators can be used to learn this lesson."*
>
> Another teacher points out that: *"Issues of this kind are needed by teachers and managers – we have not got the time to work out instructions and perform effective participation in the processes directed towards school development, especially if the school is experiencing constant change."*

Areas of constant improvement include the shift from learning input to learning outcomes in formal educational settings, and distinguishing and following up the key competences and learners' abilities by targeted curricular development on the basis of shared experiences and partnership among teachers, schools and countries. The tool is a well-structured manual that introduces the idea, defines the essence of this innovation, and suggests clearly presented possible ways of implementation in a learning-centred setting.

> *Teacher comments: "Well-defined components of a quality assurance system and indicators provide the relevant background for co-operation with colleagues within a school, among schools and even countries – it will help to develop and share a common professional language. Nevertheless, the national context should be addressed."*
>
> *"The tool is a good basis for discussion among colleagues. Quality assurance, planning of school development, EDC in the whole-school setting, and guidelines for self-evaluation constitute a 'reasonable textbook' for teachers and principals to learn democracy and initiate the participation of learners and teachers in decision making."*

A topical issue is the development of schools as centres for co-ordinating and initiating learners' formal and informal learning as a system, creating learning communities. The value of the tool lies in the approach of the authors – it successfully follows a "whole school" approach, and its implementation might develop into a targeted discussion based on its ability to improve the performance of schools as learning communities.

> *A vice-principal's view: "The tool can help in targeting the development of schools as attractive institutions to initiate learning 'to know', 'to do', 'to be' and 'to live together', if modified in the context of existing issues in this country."*

Incentives are needed to ensure lifelong learning and professional development for teachers in order to meet the challenges of the epoch and implement appropriate innovations given the rapidly changing Latvian social context. Understanding the essence of the tool, using it as a system and building capacity can strengthen teachers' openness to innovation as well as their resistance to immediate and unprepared or incompetent and destructive changes. As with any innovation, its implementation needs guidance.

A school principal comments that this is a "good pattern to follow. Teachers often get innovative ideas through different forms of professional development, such as seminars, courses, hands-on sessions, etc. Alongside measures introduced by the ministry and the universities, the tool can be used as a holistic means of introducing innovations at school due to its structure, definitions and clear main notions and central idea".

3.1.1. Circumstances that promote the use of the tool

Educational targets in Latvia follow the idea of differentiation and diversity. The main aims and principles are defined in the Law on Education (1998) and Law on General Education (1999), the concept of education in Latvia and the state standard of basic and secondary education. Educational development has been concentrated on implementing an educational concept that aims at building knowledge and providing a skills-based, competent development of the younger generation with the aim of creating a democratic, socially integrated society that provides opportunities for everyone to develop his or her physical and spiritual abilities, leading to free and responsible, creative and cultured individuals capable of lifelong learning and responsible participation, and possessing the basic skills for their future professional education and compatibility, and empowered by democratic values (Ministry of Education and Science, 2004b; Ministry of Education and Science, 2005).

In 1918 the Republic of Latvia was proclaimed, and among the first laws passed by the new government were ones that declared the importance of a democratic, humanistic education, aiming at equal rights in education and learners' individual development, as well as developing the culture and identity of the Latvian nation and all minorities. Since the end of the 19th century, the standards and prestige of education had been traditionally high and schools were in place for ethnic minorities. Education was one of the most important criteria for national progress. The country's lack of natural resources and multicultural character emphasised the importance of education as a background for national development, competitiveness in the labour market, and social integration. In the post-Soviet period, however, this process became contradictory and complicated for many reasons, making it extremely important to have pedagogically sound laws to improve schooling and strengthen democratic processes, as well as encourage social integration and inclusion in a multi-ethnic country (Secretariat of the Special Assignments Minister for Social Integration Affairs, 2005).

The Ministry of Education and Science monitors schools, assures their autonomy, and prepares and conducts the process of decentralisation through such strategic programmes as Education 1998-2003 and the Main Directions of Educational Development in 2007-2013 (Ministry of Education and Science, 2006). The latter is a plan for constant strategic development in all spheres of education (structure, content of education, financing, etc.). Publications like the tool that are designed to develop school autonomy and responsibility for quality education are needed and are widely accepted by teachers.

Public control, supervision and school's self-government are carried out by school councils, which consist of representatives of local authorities and parents. Every school has its pedagogical (teachers') council, as well as a learners' parliament or council. The tool could be useful for these bodies for several reasons:

- it can provide better understanding of the main educational trends in a multicultural and increasingly mobile society;
- it specifies parental and community activities to support schools, and creates a system of formal and informal education;
- it facilitates children's upbringing and fosters values for life in a democratic society;
- it can further improve the school system and out-of-school activities for the benefit of learners, and can help develop a "cultured" community.

To accomplish the main ideas of reform, schools need updated recommendations and tools like this one – to complete the transition from a knowledge-centred curriculum to one that is centred on pupils' skills and abilities, one which applies knowledge and practical skills, strengthens learners' performance and encourages participation, active citizenship and responsibility. This problem is directly connected with schools' constant need for up-to-date textbooks and technological material. These are the main topical items being discussed in schools around the country.

Since 2002, in-service courses for teachers and school principals, as well as discussions on teachers' professional further development and implementation of the standards, have been organised in Latvia with the main emphasis on productive strategies of teaching/learning, evaluation of learners' success and quality management in schools. Since 2004 discussions on the practices of the implementation of the standards have continued in the context of making teaching/learning more productive, and strengthening learners' academic achievements and skills towards creating a well-functioning QA system. The tool could in the context of these discussions be offered for teachers' consideration.

The state policy on education of minorities is being implemented in accordance with a special state programme designed to strengthen citizenship (Secretariat of the Special Assignments Minister for Social Integration Affairs, 2005). Since then the concept of integration has been expanded to embrace qualities of inclusion, which comprises, inter alia, recognition of learners' cultural needs as well as the need to acquire the Latvian language. In 2002/03, 11% of minority schools reported their readiness to teach all subjects in Latvian, and 77% aimed to be ready by September 2004 in this regard. By 2004, 85% of parents and pupils in grade 8 confirmed their readiness to have Latvian as the language of instruction. In spite of the results achieved, however, this period was, and still is to a certain extent, marked by tension at such schools. The topic remains an emotionally and politically charged one, especially among parents. In this regard the introduction of the tool could represent an opportunity to improve the situation with regard to the language policy, as well as learners' attitudes too in some cases. It should be noted that many people from ethnic minority groups have not yet applied for Latvian citizenship. Strengthening EDC at schools would therefore be a relevant activity.

To support the state programme in this respect, as reported by the State Agency of Evaluation of Quality of General Education, 27.4% of original programmes for minority schools are licensed for basic education, and 36% for secondary education (State Agency of Evaluation of Quality of General Education, 2006). These activities reveal the socio-political situation in education as well as the ways in which actual problems are solved. We assume that the tool might be accepted by minority schools as an issue that could help teachers, learners and their parents to meet expectations better. Such schools function on the basis of the learners' or parents' choice, and they might wish to have the tool adjusted to their specific needs and possibilities. Translation into these languages is not necessary as both teachers and learners speak fluent Latvian.

The state standards for basic and secondary education (1998, modified in 2002) were fully introduced by 2005, and fundamental redirection is considered to be finished by now. The autonomy of teachers in designing the curriculum is assured, and the only obstacle that could appear is teachers' will and ability. Nevertheless, some details could still be improved further, and the tool could function as a supporting activity designed to strengthen the curricula.

The structure of the national standards is as follows: strategic aims and objectives of the programmes; compulsory content; main principles; and the evaluation procedure of learners' success. They comprise the main areas of school subjects, learners' achievements and the criteria for these. The way the desired and planned achievements are attained is up to each school and each subject teacher. These standards therefore imply an obligation to tailor teaching/learning to learners' needs and expectations. Teachers themselves, as highly competent professionals, expect assistance to improve teaching/learning. They tend to be open to new ideas, and welcome well-prepared materials that can save time and energy. To ensure that the tool with due modifications is accepted by teachers as a valuable means of assistance, advice by teachers, administrators and stakeholders on how to use it would be welcomed.

The standards of the school subjects have been worked out by the ministry with the participation of school principals, teachers, teachers' professional organisations and teacher educators. Parents and pupils were also involved in this process. The programmes are registered at the ministry in accordance with the Law on Education, and only accredited programmes are allowed to be implemented. The programmes of subjects are worked out by the Curriculum Development and Evaluation Centre, with the assistance of teachers' professional associations, subject teachers' associations, scientists, textbook authors, and other competent specialists. Teachers are welcome to elaborate their own subject programmes as long as these correspond to the state standards, or choose existing ones and to adapt them to the learners' abilities and needs. Each subject programme covers the requirements of the standard, though its content can be wider than it is defined by the standard in order to provide the learners with options and facilitate their individual development. The programmes and textbooks prepared by teachers are then approved by the school principals. Thus the improvement of the programmes and textbooks is an ongoing process. The structure of programmes (curriculum) comprises the aims and objectives of the programme (whole school or a particular subject); the requirements to join the programme; the content of education comprised by the integrated content of the subjects; the programme's plan of implementation; and the criteria for evaluating the pupils' success. Considerable changes also require adequate staff education, technologies, appropriate teaching materials, as well as additional financial support.

To meet the above-mentioned targets, schools constantly expand opportunities for their pupils:

- more than 80 school subject programmes (curriculum) have now been elaborated and are functioning, many of which offer alternative content design and methods of teaching/learning. The literature programme for grade 5, for instance, has three options. Textbooks are also designed with options – for example, teachers can choose among two or three textbooks (State Agency of Evaluation of Quality of General Education, 2006);
- every year the ministry releases a list of recommended literature and textbooks. It includes all the textbooks and other texts that are available and have been recommended by teachers' professional or subject teachers' associations;
- secondary schools choose their profile and expand the scope of the compulsory or additional school subjects to provide opportunities for pupils to start specialising or taking the subjects they like best.

In addition to the subject programmes (curriculum), out-of-class activities are extremely popular among pupils – 46% out of the total number of learners are currently involved in these activities (Central Board of Statistics of Latvia, 2006). The tool should be modified for senior learners to empower them and ensure lifelong social participation by suggesting the desired knowledge, skills and values of democratic citizenship. The tool should be modified for self-evaluation as well.

Learners have the right to choose between programmes (in city schools this option is wider); methods of teaching and organisational forms (a variety are offered); individualised teaching/learning; additional subjects or activities after regular classes, etc. By introducing the tool to learners, this will enable them to target their options, expand their social experience, and widen their abilities.

Cultural values have always been held in high estimation by the population of Latvia. Aesthetic education is integrated into all possible school subjects and is provided by a number of creative out-of-class activities – especially choir singing, folk dances, handicrafts and other activities. Every four years the national festival of choir singing and dancing takes place (with 10 000 participants selected for the final festival). School pupils constitute the majority of the participants, and the wide-ranging involvement of the population in these activities helps transmit and develop national cultural values. Pupils of the ethnic minorities take part in these activities with their specific ethnic cultural values.

The background of involvement is therefore well prepared for EDC. Moreover, EDC's specific orientation towards social inclusion and active participation could represent a good complementary initiative.

Quality assurance and the evaluation of learners' success are based on the following principles:
- open criteria and demands towards the learners' achievements;
- acquired education reflected in scores that measure knowledge, understanding, application of knowledge and creative skills;
- compliance of the test with all levels of achievement as represented in the score system;
- a variety of test tasks – written and oral, individual and group achievements, different forms that reveal varying dynamics of success, etc.;
- regular controls and assessment to promote progress;
- compulsory assessment (except in cases when pupils have the legal right not to take examinations or tests according to the Law on Education).

The tool will support this practice with a well-structured and clear means of implementation if supplemented with due instruction.

3.1.2. Prospective difficulties and obstacles

Difficulties might be related to teachers' understanding of the tool and its validity. It could also prove extremely time-consuming to restructure the content of teaching/learning and select the appropriate technology. This obstacle could be overcome by a targeted programme of implementing the tool, but the following constraints would have to be addressed:
- although initial teacher feedback on the tool collected in Latvia is very positive, concrete and ongoing implementation might cause misunderstandings or lead to practical problems, as the tool requires teachers to make considerable changes to their usual practices (there are always many teachers who hesitate to change their approach or ones who need more time to get used to the idea);

- preparing teachers to use the tool in an appropriate way so that the idea is implemented properly (via seminars, hands-on sessions, instruction, appropriate technology, etc.) is time-consuming;
- constant assistance will be needed to help teachers and educators in the form of hands-on sessions, handouts, etc. so that the tool can be integrated into the teaching/learning process;
- the tool is designed for all levels of educational management, and therefore all levels of management should be involved in mastering the idea of the tool and ways of integrating it into the existing education system. The means to ensure managerial readiness to conduct implementation as a long-lasting affair should also be in place.

3.1.3. Parts of the tool that are particularly applicable in Latvian schools

Quality assurance can be used to enrich experiences and to compare them with the ones presented in the tool, as well as to create new experiences, especially based on QA systems in school education, the QA process, accountability, etc.

Guidelines for school self-evaluation and quality indicators of EDC can be used as a means of involving teachers in the process of self-evaluation, as well as for revising existing practices in schools.

EDC in combination with QA and school development planning is a very topical theme, and definitions and a detailed description of implementation of the idea of this tool could also prove useful in this context.

3.1.4. The possible target groups
- staff at the Ministry of Education and Science, the Curriculum Development and Examination Centre, the State Agency of Evaluation of Quality of General Education, the State Youth Initiative Centre, the State Educational Inspectorate, regional educational boards, as well as the Ministry of Culture, the Ministry of Children and Family Affairs, the Ministry of Social Integration Affairs – a letter from the co-ordinating institution (preferably) with the recommendation to implement the tool into the educational system of Latvia, as well as seminars, workshops, etc. for staff on the co-ordinated implementation of the tool;
- the Institute of Pedagogical Science, University of Latvia – for a project aimed at the adaptation of the tool to the needs of schools, preparation of educators, principals and school teachers – by using the existing programme for further pedagogical development of educators and by working out new programmes for administrators and teachers. The institute is able to co-ordinate institutional efforts in this country by using existing experience. However, the context with international programmes such as TIMSS, IES, OECD, etc. should be clarified;

- universities and tertiary education institutions that have programmes for teacher education and in-service training – conferences, seminars, hands-on sessions to show how existing programmes could be improved, introducing special courses for EDC in schools, as well as including the ideas of the tool into the programme of students' school practice;
- principals and vice-principals of schools – a recommendation on how to implement the ideas of the tool, and workshops to change the educational system of the schools and the way in which the community and parents co-operate;
- parents' councils will need information and instruction in order to develop an understanding of the ideas of the tool and how activities could be best conducted among parents;
- subject and class teachers will need seminars, hands-on sessions, etc. to acquire the essence of the tool and to see how it could be used as a system in the context of other equally important values at national level and in minority schools;
- specialists who work in the regional initiative centres – initiatives are needed to help them prepare for the implementation of the tool in their specific context;
- learners at each grade in basic and secondary general schools, special and professional schools – their activities should be facilitated towards encouraging the development of democratic citizenship as a personal quality.

3.2. Systemic conditions of use

3.2.1. *Correspondence of the tool with the objectives of QA and evaluation in Latvia*

The tool matches the objectives of QA and evaluation in Latvia in the following ways:
- the idea of the tool corresponds to the democratisation of education and educational aims, and their orientation towards the development of the individual potential of learners;
- the development of the idea of the inclusive school, the policy of multicultural education and the development of minorities' schools to preserve ethnic diversity;
- the curricula include citizenship education at different levels of schooling as special subjects in the cluster of humanities, as well as a component in other subjects;
- implementation can be adjusted to the system of quality assurance, school evaluation and accreditation.

A more detailed description is provided in parts 1 and 2.

3.2.2. Possibilities of teachers' independent work with the tool

Possibilities of independent work are limited, as the modification and implementation might be too time-consuming and varied in different schools, and runs the risk of going against the idea of the tool. The following kinds and scope of training/counselling are required:

- introductory activities to prepare the regional school boards and/or school principals with the aim of creating supportive bodies in regions and schools. Discussions, seminars and hands-on sessions might take up to ten or twelve hours;
- a series of about twelve to sixteen hours (unless there is another means of implementing the tool) comprising hands-on sessions, seminars for groups of teachers (subjects, class teachers) conducted by a specialist in citizenship education, as well as by those who know how to use and implement the ideas of the tool according to local peculiarities in terms of education, social inclusion, participation and perspectives of ethnic or cultural minorities. Local specialists can be of use in this regard.

Materials that might contribute to the use of the tool should mainly be of a methodological character:

- translation of the tool into Latvian;
- ways of integrating the tool into the process of teaching/learning of a particular kind of school, subject, sphere of activities in the community – a guided elaboration of these issues by groups of specialists and teachers in the particular sphere. This co-operation will help teachers adapt the tool better;
- instructional materials for planning, counselling and evaluating – these could also be elaborated by groups of specialists and managers, in order to help understand the idea of the tool and its system-making function better;
- ways of involving learners in the implementation of the tool, recommendations for learners' organisations, etc. – these could be elaborated by groups of specialists and learners, thereby involving them in the decision-making process;
- the experience of those who have implemented the tool, which could be presented at seminars, hands-on sessions or as printed materials.

3.2.3. Other possible measures to facilitate the use of the tool

Resources should be raised by international projects, the first one preferably as a continuation of the DIPF project to prepare for the investigation of the implemented tool and to collect comparable data. International project bids can be prepared by the Institute of Pedagogical Science (University of Latvia), together with other co-operation partners, to investigate specific aspects of the tool in different types of school. Local projects can support the implementation process.

Incentives for Latvian schools are that the tool can be adapted without crucial changes to the curricula in specific national educational settings. Additional incentives include the fact that teachers will receive printed materials designed to acquaint them better with the tool; the tool will be modified for local needs according to the cultural context of Latvia, and for Latvian and minority schools in particular; and teachers and school managers will be well prepared for the tool.

However, if the tool is accepted, the following will be needed:
- translation into Latvian as well as resources to cover expenses – at present there are no spare resources available;
- financial support for printed materials, seminars, hands-on sessions, etc., all of which are a significant precondition for implementation.

The necessity of deleting or modifying some aspects according to the national context has also not been highlighted before modification and implementation.

3.2.4. The way the tool can be applied to different school types

Two types of school are most prepared to implement the tool: general (comprehensive) two-stage schools (primary and lower secondary), and secondary schools, based on their standards, curricula, management and experience of evaluation. Nevertheless, to strengthen incentives for the use of this tool, some modifications will be needed, especially as the tool does not distinguish between these two school types.

The tool will also need to be modified for the following school types:
- private schools: these might be especially supportive and could accept the tool as an innovative initiative. Nevertheless, these will also need the same preparatory activities;
- schools for ethnic minorities with their language and specific cultural domains (Russian, Belarusian, Ukrainian, Polish, Jewish, Roma, Lithuanian, Estonian): these will need some specific assistance;
- vocational schools: in Latvia these are run by different ministries (education and science, agriculture, welfare, culture), which must each be addressed, and modifications made in accordance with their specific programmes. Teachers' and managers' in-service training should also be targeted accordingly;
- special schools for children with disabilities and who need special pedagogical assistance: these already have specific programmes and curricula. Modifications will be needed for all of these schools, as their learners' needs are very specific. Social and special pedagogy is also being developed by the Institute of Pedagogical Science (medical programmes, doctor-student investigations, research projects, and co-operation with other national and external institutions).

4. Ideas for the implementation process

4.1. The way a process should be designed for Latvian schools to experience using the tool as being relevant and helpful

As with any innovation, guidance will be needed – introduction, instruction, modification to local needs, preparation of staff at different levels of education, and school management. The first steps to be taken in implementing the tool comprise the following:

- publications addressed to teachers and school managers to make them aware of the essential characteristics of the tool and how it functions, as well as possibilities of implementation (in 2008/09);
- translation into Latvian, and the printed matter distributed to schools to acquaint teachers and principals with the ideas behind the concept, and to prepare them for seminars, hands-on sessions, and courses (2008/09, if funding is found);
- in-service courses (these could be conducted by the Institute of Pedagogical Science), which would be offered to teachers, school managers and others involved in organising education (in 2008/09);
- conferences and a research project launched by the Institute (prepared and submitted for funding in 2009).

Possible local contact persons or agencies

The Institute of Pedagogical Science (PZI) at the University of Latvia is ready to start this project in Latvia: use can be made of existing co-operation (as annual seminars for teacher educators at universities and pedagogical higher educational institutions of Latvia; exchange of educators to deliver some courses; traditional conferences, etc.). The institute is prepared to initiate further co-operation with its partners to include the tool in joint research projects.

Other possible bodies include the Ministry of Education and Science, the Curriculum Development and Examination Centre, the Ministry of Social Integration Affairs, and the State Agency of Evaluation of Quality of General Education. Other institutions might need to be addressed during the step-by-step implementation of the tool.

4.2. Possible integration of the tool into international partnerships

Some experience has already been gathered following a discussion on national and international perspectives of citizenship education in Latvia:

- an international conference (CiCe, Children Identity and Citizenship in Europe) took place in Riga in May 2006. The PZI is an institutional member of this organisation;

- an international conference on citizenship education has already taken place at a regional higher educational institution (Rēzeknes augstskola) in February 2007. The authors of this report have made a presentation and introduced the tool as part of the results of an international research co-operation project, and discussed problems for further investigation;
- the PZI is ready to implement the tool in Latvia and to initiate further international co-operation with its existing bilateral partners. To discuss the tool and further co-operation, the institute intends to prepare a concurrent session for the traditional ATEE (Association for Teacher Education in Europe) international conference in Riga in May 2008, which is held once every two years. The conference usually has 10 to 12 concurrent thematic sessions. The title of this conference is "Teacher of the 21st Century: Quality Education for Quality Teaching".

To continue investigating the tool, it should:
- first be integrated into the existing experience of the countries (via a pilot project in several schools);
- be added to existing international research co-operation as one of the items to be investigated;
- be investigated further: to implement the tool, explicit methods and investigation approaches must be worked out in order to obtain comparable data;
- be the subject of an international research project initiated by DIPF to investigate its implementation in pilot schools in different countries.

4.3. Alternative scenarios for working with the tool

The tool is the result of the hard work of its authors, and therefore is first of all worth modifying to meet the specific needs of the country, and to test its validity for the cultural context of Latvia. A pilot phase might suggest further improvements to the tool or the need for alternative scenarios.

References

Baltic Institute of Social Research (2000). *Towards the Civic Society*, Riga.

Central Board of Statistics of Latvia (2006). *Educational Institutions in Latvia at the Beginning of School Year 2005/06*, Riga.

Law on Education (1998). LR Saeima. Retrieved on 10 November 2006, from www.izm.gov.lv.

Law on General Education (1999). LR Saeima. Retrieved on 10 November 2006, from www.izm.gov.lv.

Ministry of Education and Science, Curriculum and Examination Centre (1998). *Valsts pamatizglītības standarts* (The State Standard for Basic Education), Riga. Retrieved on 10 November 2006, from www.izm.gov.lv.

Ministry of Education and Science, ISAP (2002). *Skolu vērtēšanas un attīstības plānošanas rokasgrāmata* (Handbook for School Evaluation and Development Planning).

Ministry of Education and Science (2004a). *Kārtība, kādā akreditē vispārējās izglītības programmas un izglītības iestādes, kā arī atestē valsts un pašvaldību dibināto vispārējās pamatizglītības un vispārējās vidējās izglītības iestāžu vadītājus. LR MK 2005. gada 16 augusta noteikumi Nr. 612* (Instruction for programmes', schools' and principals' accreditation to implement the government's decision (Cabinet of Ministers, No. 612, 16 August 2005). Retrieved on 9 November 2006, from www.izm.gov.lv.

Ministry of Education and Science (2004b). *Development of Education: National Report, 2004*. Retrieved on 10 November 2006, from www.izm.gov.lv.

Ministry of Education and Science (2004c). *Skolu darbības kvalitātes vērtējuma līmeņi un to apraksti* (Quality Levels of Schools and Their Description), Riga.

Ministry of Education and Science (2005). *National Report on the Progress of Implementation of the European Commission's Programme Education and Training 2010 in Latvia*. Retrieved on 19 November 2006, from www.izm.gov.lv.

Ministry of Education and Science (2006). *The Main Directions of Educational Development 2007-2013*. Retrieved on 11 November 2006, from www.izm.gov.lv.

OECD (2000). *Examens des politiques nationals d'education: Lettonie*, Paris: OECD.

Pabriks A. (2002). "Political Culture: Identity and Participation", in *Towards Civic Culture in Central and East European Countries. Materials of the International Conference*, Latvian National Commission for UNESCO, Ministry of Education and Science, Soros Foundation, 43-45.

Regulations on the State Basic Education Standard (2000, No. 462), Regulations on the State General Secondary Education Standard (2000, No. 463), Regulations on the State Professional and Vocational Education Standard (2000, No. 211). Retrieved on 3 November 2006, from www.izm.gov.lv, "General education 1 and 2".

Secretariat of the Special Assignments Minister for Social Integration Affairs (2005). *Pilsoniskās sabiedrības striprināšana 2005-2009.gads. Sabiedrības integrācijas programma* (Strengthening of Citizens' Society in 2005-2009. Programme for Social Integration in 2005-09). Retrieved on 10 November 2006, from www.integracija.gov.lv.

Šmite A. (2006). *Izglītības iestādes vadība. Vadītājs izglītības sistēmā, IV daļa* (Management of an Educational Establishment. Manager in a System of Education. Part IV), Riga: Raka.

State Agency of Evaluation of Quality of General Education (2006). *Izglītības kvalitāte Latvijā: Vispārējās izglītības kvalitātes novērtēšanas valsts aģentūras apkopojuma ziņojums par 2005/2006 mācību gadu* (Quality of Education in Latvia in 2005/06), www.izm.gov.lv.

Žogla, I.; Andersone, R.; Černova, E. (2007). "Latvia", in Hoerner, W.; Doebert, H.; Kopp, B.V.; Mitter, W. (eds.), *The Education Systems of Europe*, Dordrecht: Springer, 418-437.

Lithuania
Elvyra Acienė

1. School evaluation in Lithuania

Basics of education policy in the context of school reform in Lithuania

In 1990 Lithuania declared its independence. School reform, however, started earlier, because of the democratic processes that began in 1985 in the former Soviet Union and led to the emergence of progressive ideas. The *Concept of the National School* was first published in 1988 and became the basis for the future Lithuanian school reform process.

The Law on Education, published in Vilnius in June 1991 (amended in 1998 and 2003) defines the "common foundations of the structure, operation, and management of the education system".

The main principles of the Lithuanian education system were confirmed by the Constitution of the Republic of Lithuania in 1992. In November 1992 the Minister for Culture and Education announced the Educational Reform Programme and the General Concept of Education in Lithuania (the "general concept"). It was presented to the government and parliament for approval. The general concept was published in 1994. It determined the major goals and tasks that would guide and form Lithuanian education in the years to come and reflected the ideas already announced by the Law on Education, which stated that the education system should "develop a sense of civic duty and understanding of personal rights and obligations to the family, nation, society and the State of Lithuania ... and create conditions for the development of individuality" (*General Concept of Education in Lithuania*, 1994: 8).

The main goal of the general concept was to provide "a unique opportunity for Lithuania to join the community of democratic European nations, fully liberate the creative energies, which were repressed during the years of occupation, and form a modern, open, pluralistic and harmonious society of free citizens .... Education is a fundamental factor in the development of the society, the basis for all social reforms" (*General Concept of Education in Lithuania*, 1994: 8).

To prepare for eventual membership of the European Union and therefore to base the educational reform on the "educational experience of democratic Lithuania and Europe", the "Principles of Lithuanian education" were outlined in the general concept, complementing the four goals announced earlier by the Law on Education: humanism, democracy, nationality and renewal (*General Concept of Education in Lithuania*, 1994: 10-11).

The Government of the Republic of Lithuania presented a new proposed Education Law to the Parliament of the Republic of Lithuania in June 2002; afterwards a strategy of long-term education development for the years 2003-12 was presented to Lithuanian society.

1.1. Modes of school evaluation

In January 2001 the European Parliament approved the recommendations of the European Council regarding collaboration on evaluating the quality of education. The members and candidate members of the EU were recommended: "to introduce a transparent system of evaluation of education quality; to introduce and induce internal audit of the schools; to introduce and improve the system of schools' external audit; to induce involvement and participation of the school's communities and partners in the activities of the school; to support and induce exchange of the schools' experience in their own country and in the context of the EU" (www.europarl.eu.int/home/default.en.htm; cited in *Internal Audit Methodology for Comprehensive Schools. Part I*, 2002: 17). The main means of school evaluation in the Lithuanian educational system as well as in other post-Soviet countries was that of external inspection organised by inspectors of the education departments of the municipalities and the Ministry of Education and Science. The reform of schools has proposed new evaluation tasks that reflect the requirements of contemporary democratic society. The 2003 Resolution of the Parliament of the Republic of Lithuania on the National Strategy of Education for the Years 2003-12 entrenched attitudes regarding the creation of a management system for education quality.

In creating such a system, the following four main goals are pursued:
- to create an information system of education management that embraces the organisation of timely data gathering and the creation of databases, and guarantees its accessibility;
- to create a permanent system of educational monitoring and to strengthen the structures of various levels responsible for the formation of educational policy at various levels.
- to create a national system to evaluate children's achievements, reflecting the content of pupil learning and training, and to improve these;
- to create and introduce a well-balanced system of internal and external school audits, and to teach teachers and auditors of the state (municipalities) how to apply it.

At present there are two types of evaluation (audits) applied in Lithuanian schools: internal and external. Both types of audit have to supplement each other. However, it is too early to speak about their balance, as internal audit has only been applied in Lithuanian schools since 2002. External audits, on the other hand, have a long-standing tradition as these were systematically carried out both during the Soviet era and since the declaration of independence up until today. An external audit was understood as constituting an inspection of a school's activities. However, evaluation criteria varied according to the character of the school reform. These inspections were often seen as a means used by the state to highlight any shortcomings. The performance of a school (external audit) was evaluated by the local (city or regional) authorities, that is the departments of education took over the function of inspection. Evaluation reports were sent to the Ministry of Education and Science (MES). For a long while, the main criteria for school evaluation were the academic achievements of pupils and the number of pupils who managed to enter university and higher education institutions.

Nevertheless, attitudes to audits have changed. Whereas before they were seen as an element of quality management, with the primary goal of facilitating the school's activities and inducing improvements, now inspections are also increasingly seen as a means of effecting positive educational changes.

Both types of audit are inseparable from the strategic plans of the state's education policy. Today, four types of state plans can be identified, which have to be evaluated from the perspective of both internal and external audits:

- long-term strategies (visions). The current vision is defined in the Resolution of the Parliament of the Republic of Lithuania on the National Strategy of Education for the Years 2003-12;
- mid-term strategic plans of activities (future allocations). These form the basis for the annual state budget and set out the needs of education, including allowances requested for reforms;
- annual working plan. This can be understood as a delegation of responsibility to all educational structures. It is announced on the website of the MES (www.mtp.smm.lt);
- realisation of programmes and projects (this part is related to the mid-term strategic plans).

Therefore, during the education reform, the question of the school's internal evaluation did not dominate, but rather such factors and processes as: the renewal of teaching and education content as well as evaluation of the exams, reform of pedagogical preparation and improvement of qualifications, computerisation of schools and modernisation of libraries, reorganisation of the types of school nets, the introduction of profile learning, and the provision of social services. These were the main aspects according to which the city and county departments of education evaluated school performance.

The MES of the Republic of Lithuania, the School Development Centre (which was established in 1997), together with certain schools that showed the initiative to be involved in this process, have created an internal audit methodology for schools since 1999.

In 2001 the internal audit methodology project for schools took place. This received recognition from academia. Some 28 schools in Lithuania took part in the experiment, which became the basis for confirming the audit methodology for the schools. This methodology was published in four editions (see the appendix).

The internal audit methodology was approved on 28 February 2002, by Order No. 302 of the Minister for Education and Science. Now all schools (both secondary and vocational) can use it in their self-evaluation processes.

This methodology is based on the Scottish model, as presented in detail in the publication *How Good is Our School? – Self-evaluation Using Performance Indicators* (1996). This model was chosen after analysing the different experiences of self-evaluation models in various countries. It was adopted taking into account the situation and demands of Lithuanian education, common evaluation, self-evaluation, and the national reporting culture. The Scottish self-evaluation model is attractive because it is based on the application of school activity indicators, namely a system of features is created according to which each school might self-evaluate its quality of work in different fields. Internal audit facilitates the function delegated to the city or municipality departments of education by the MES – to supervise the education system. The MES and the departments of education administer external audits which, since the implementation of internal audits, have lost their primary function of control and are increasingly similar to the function of consulting. In 2005 a new Methodology of External Auditing for School Improvement (www.mtp.smm.lt) was prepared, which is used as an instrument for external accreditation of schools. Now, internal and external audits are based on the same principles and have the same seven areas of evaluation: content of education; achievement of learning; learning and education; help to pupils; ethos; resources; management of school and quality assurance (see the appendix).

An audit might be "wide" (evaluating all seven areas) or "partial" (evaluating only certain areas). Schools usually fulfil a wide audit every couple of years, whereas the departments of education often apply partial audits in order to inspect priority or problematic areas.

Internal school audits are a permanent and thorough process of reflection, which involves all school employees and departments. Their goal is to analyse aspects of school work, to emphasise advantages and disadvantages, and to prepare a plan of action on how to improve the school's performance.

The internal audit process comprises the following elements:
- preparation: acquaintance with the main principles of an internal audit, and the organisation of a working group;
- wide audit: an evaluation of the entire performance of the school, analysing the audit methodology, performance indicators, subsidiary indicators, the seven performance areas, data gathering and a summary;

- partial audit: analysis of a chosen area (one of seven);
- preparation and presentation of the report;
- planning: preparation and presentation of the future strategic plan of the school, analysing the results of wide or partial audits.

The appendix to this chapter contains the scheme of a school's internal audit, indicators of school performance, principles of self-evaluation and some specific examples.

External audit experts use the results of the internal audit and evaluate them in the context of comparative attitudes to the situation of education in Lithuania in general.

Conclusion: a quality assurance (QA) system exists in Lithuania.

1.2. Evaluation as an issue in teacher training

First of all, it has to be emphasised that the methodology of evaluation (internal and external audits) is not a main topic in teacher-training programmes. Presently, three universities and eight colleges provide teacher training in Lithuania. Analysing the BA and professional qualification programmes of teacher training at Lithuanian universities and colleges, it is apparent that aspects of methodology of internal and external evaluation in the study programmes can only be traced in the "Management of education" courses. However, they usually account for no more than four national credits (6 ECTS points – 1 credit in Lithuania = 1.5 European credits), and their content is based on general knowledge of school management, although the teachers' competence includes the development of management skills.

The author of this article would like to emphasise that the methodology of internal and external (particularly international) audits has only recently been implemented as a form of self-assessment at the level of schools, universities and colleges in Lithuania. The self-evaluation of universities and colleges study programmes is authorised by the Centre of Studies' Quality, which is under the control of the MES. An evaluation methodology was prepared by the employees of the Centre of Studies' Quality that corresponds to international requirements for accreditation of teacher-training programmes. The first international accreditations of teacher-training programmes in Lithuanian universities showed that these programmes lack credits for educational management. This means that requirements for teacher-training programmes in the context of educational management will have to be dramatically improved in the near future and the content of educational management could be added, according to the demand for teacher competences.

Nevertheless, teachers at schools that are implementing internal evaluation are receiving external support in various forms, for example, consultations and methodological material, where methods of data gathering and organisation of qualitative and quantitative research are presented. Seminars are organised for the co-ordinators of internal evaluation, where they can become acquainted with how to prepare the report for a school's internal and external audits. It is believed that the methodology of carrying out these audits will become one of the main topics in the education management programme of teachers who include education quality methodologies in their study programmes. Two institutes of continuing studies have been established in Lithuania. They belong to two universities (Šiauliai and Klaipėda) and are responsible for developing an integral and profitable system of lifelong learning. One of the areas of their strategy is to improve teachers' level of qualifications in compliance with European educational standards.

On 25 May 2006, Resolution No. 468 of the Lithuanian Government was approved regarding the reorganisation of teacher training and improvements in the levels of qualifications. This programme was prepared while implementing the National Strategy of Lisbon, which was approved by Resolution No. 1270 of the Lithuanian Government on 22 November 2005 (Valstybės Žinios, 2005: No. 139-5019). The above-mentioned programme will be carried out during the period 2006-08 in collaboration with the counties (there are 10 such counties in Lithuania) and municipal administrations, and the universities and institutions that offer programmes in improvement of teaching qualifications. It is emphasised in the document that while analysing the present situation of teacher training, "there is a gap between university teachers who train students and teachers, and practitioners at schools; the system of teacher training is not practically accommodated to the needs of lifelong learning; and the content of studies is not orientated towards nurturing new skills and competences – critical thinking, problem-solving, information literacy" (Resolution No. 468, 2006: 1-4). According to Order No. ISAK-1155, which was signed by the Minister for Education and Science on 14 August 2003 (Valstybės Žinios, 2003, No. 81-3709), the Teachers' Competency Centre was established, which has successfully integrated itself into the implementation process of the above-mentioned programme.

There is sufficient room in the programme to incorporate the methods of internal and external evaluation into teacher-training programmes, thus leading to improvements in qualifications. Professor Ramutė Dobranskienė claims that pedagogical and management functions are interlaced in teachers' work (Dobranskienė, 2002: 34). The professional performance of a teacher influences all aspects of school life, pupils' maturity, harmony and public spirit. As long ago as 1998, students at the Education Faculty of Klaipėda University had already affirmed that future teachers need to learn about management as this helps them to understand the basis of a school's organisation, a teacher's place in the life of the school community and the life of society in general (Dobranskienė, 2002: 143).

The situation on MA programmes is, however, quite different. In 1994 Klaipėda University implemented an Education Management MA programme in the field of educology. Since then, four other universities have created MA programmes in the field of educology. The Management of Education Quality project receives financial support from EU structural funds. The title of the programme – "Management of education quality" – looks like a very narrow aspect of educational management. However, the programme includes a wide range of content concerning the methodology of internal and external evaluations.

Conclusion: the methodology of internal and external evaluation is one of several very important teacher-training issues in the framework of education management.

1.3. The use of evaluation results in schools and the educational system

School audit reports (internal and external) are one of the most important parts of the audit process, as these reports enable users to acquaint themselves with the school's academic and social life in detail. The school community as well as the parents' council may acquaint themselves with all the documents: reports, research, interviews and recorded material of the meetings. Parents are informed during class meetings or general school community meetings.

After all the information has been presented, the results are discussed with all interested groups. Before that, schools can publish information in the press, as well as preparing or updating their website. The public discussion of reports helps to plan ways of improving school performance as well as receiving support.

After the interview with parents, the school director discusses the generalised data once again with his deputies, the school council, the methodological council, representatives of the pupils' self-government institutions, a working internal audit group, social pedagogues, a special pedagogue, and the heads of classes.

Generalised information is presented to the community of the city and region. A given method in managing the school education process can be designated.

Reports are also presented to the local departments of education (city municipalities and county administrations) and to the MES. These reports help the authorities understand how education works in the city, county and throughout the country. The reports also enable "good experience" to be disseminated and help to plan state education policy.

The results of internal evaluation are used to develop the school's strategic plan. They influence a school's performance strategy and the way the annual programme is formulated, and improve the activities of the teachers' council. Interviews with specialists among the school's founders (in the respective municipal department of education) help to understand the results in the context of other schools' results. At the same time, the founders of the school (the municipality of the city or county) support the programme on the basis of the self-evaluation results.

An in-depth audit analysis facilitates the design of a school's future programme. The fact that the external audit results virtually coincide with the results of the internal audit proves the objectivity of the evaluation. This is vitally important when the external audit turns from a control mechanism into part of the school improvement process.

Conclusion: the results of the audit allow evaluation methods to be improved, help to prepare education policy documents, and contribute to teachers' professional qualifications in the context of lifelong learning.

2. The "Tool for Quality Assurance of Education for Democratic Citizenship in Schools"

2.1. Comprehensiveness and coherence

The tool is fairly comprehensive and coherent. Parts 1 and 2 are very informative. The authors introduce aspects of the tool concerning EDC, QA and QA of EDC (EDC-QA). Other parts of the tool I tried to understand from the point of view of the existing Lithuanian evaluation methodology. In this way, I think that the tool could be better understood and greater insight into its possible implementation in Lithuania could be obtained. Every country has its own experiences and, as the authors of the tool stress, it needs to be adapted to each country's context (Bîrzea et al., 2005: 9). Chapters 3 and 4 can be linked to the principles of internal audit methodology as used in Lithuanian schools. Chapter 3, "What is quality assurance and why is it important?" (Bîrzea et al., 2005: 33-42), corresponds to the content of one of the parts ("The context of the schools' audit") of the audit methodology (Part I, 2002) used in Lithuania. In both the Lithuanian audit methodology, as well as in the methodology of the tool (Bîrzea et al., 2005: 33), certain questions are raised, such as why have audits become so popular nowadays, what management tasks do they solve in the context of general management, what quality can be attained through audits, and how far are audits adapted to the changing requirements of today's schools. Educational management specialists in Lithuania claim that audits are inseparable from the management of education quality, and explain what makes QA different from inspection and control. The same point is emphasised in Chapter 3, Part 1 of the tool (Bîrzea et al., 2005: 33-34). Two main goals can be identified:
 – to determine the school's strengths and weaknesses;
 – to identify priorities for the school's improvement plan.

It is possible to expect effective results from educational reform, while carrying out audits of the educational system. At the same time, audits reflect the needs of all participants in the educational process (the school community, principals, teachers, students, parents and ministry leaders and local authority officials).

I found Part 2 of Chapter 3 (Bîrzea et al., 2005: 35), "Quality control and quality assurance", very impressive because the authors pay attention to a simple but very important dictum in the context of evaluation methodology: "quality control" and "quality assurance" cannot be used synonymously.

Part 3 of Chapter 3 (Bîrzea et al., 2005: 35-37) describes the characteristics of QA systems in school education. For example, the goals and values of the school, of the state education policy and of the regional education policy; plus scholars' evaluations of the development tendencies in Lithuanian schools in the context of educational reform, other viewpoints and insights into the future of society. These characteristics are similar to the ones presented in the Lithuanian audit methodology (Internal Audit Methodology for Comprehensive Schools. Part I, 2002: 7).

The table presented in Part 6 of Chapter 3 (Bîrzea et al., 2005: 41) reflects the presentation of the audit methodology in Lithuania in the first chapter of this report and its appendix. The audit process is divided into five phases: preparation, wide audit, analysis of a chosen area, reports and information planning. Every phase includes corresponding components of the QA system (Bîrzea et al., 2005: 41).

Lithuanian schools have a school development planning strategy. Its main principles are its universality, thorough evaluation of the school and openness. Another important principle is compatibility, which has to be understood in the context of education reform both at state level and in terms of school performance.

According to recommendations made by the Lithuanian methodology (Internal Audit Methodology for Comprehensive Schools, Part I, 2002: 65), a strategic plan can be made out of conclusions drawn from the school's problematic areas as designated by the internal audit, priorities for improvement, the school's goals, tasks to achieve these goals, and predicted results. This plan relates to the questions presented in Chapter 4 of the tool (Bîrzea et al., 2005: 48-51), because the methodology also raises questions in the context of the audit, such as: How are we succeeding? How do we know this? What do we plan to do in the future? How will we do it?

The strategic plan of the school is not a finished and explicit document, but rather a general collection of ideas resulting from an evaluation of the internal audit, which suggests how the school has to change. A mid-term strategic plan is prepared for a three-year term. The strategic plan has to link internal and external priorities into a solid sequence.

The creators of the Lithuanian audit methodology refer to Stoll and Fink (Internal Audit Methodology for Comprehensive Schools, Part 1, 2002: 48), who stress that each school is unique. Therefore planning may reveal the political dynamics of the school and the degree of motivation to improve the life of the school's community.

To illustrate Tables 3 and 4 (Bîrzea et al., 2005: 53), we have to introduce the specific experience of Lithuanian (or other countries') schools first. As internal and external audit methodologies have recently been introduced into Lithuanian schools, we can expect this process to become universal and thus planning strategies of the schools will progressively improve.

The first part of the tool (Chapters 1-4) is I think interesting, but gives information about general educational management more in the context of QA and less in that of EDC. But in spite of such a positive comparison in the context of QA, I must emphasise that all concurrences are only structural and not related to content of EDC. Audit methods in Lithuania (internal and external) are not highlighted in EDC.

An analysis of the tool's methods allows us to state that the authors are responsible for the data analysis of their projects, which means therefore that experts encounter certain difficulties trying to convey the content of this instrument to teachers and education policy specialists in their own country. I must apply the methodological structure used in Lithuania in order to find possibilities for applying EDC content. During meetings with teachers, principals, university professors and officials from local authorities, I introduced the tool. The teachers raised many questions. The first question was about the EDC concept itself. I agree that in the Baltic countries, the concept of EDC has not been formed in a general context "which encompasses knowledge, skills, attitudes and action ... it is based more around knowledge 'about' citizenship" (Mikkelsen, 2004: 85). This implies the possibility of a different understanding of quality indicators, while concrete examples could eliminate ambiguity. All six indicators are described on pages 59-70 of the tool, but it is rather difficult to talk about the tool's applicability without EDC evaluation examples from several schools in different countries (for example, methods of internal evaluation in Lithuania were represented as an experiment by 28 schools with detailed inventories). Without this, we face the problem of relating EDC and QA. A detailed explanation on how to assess the results is missing, especially when the concept of EDC itself is interpreted in different ways.

I should like to emphasise one more factor (life out of school) – it is rather difficult to involve parents in school activities. Even internal evaluation results are only submitted to active parents. Children, especially from risk group families, also tend to be very passive. I think that the tool should highlight the responsibility levels of EDC and QA players, such as the heads of schools, teachers, parents, pupils, local authorities and the MES. Furthermore, possible problems in the context of relations among these groups should be provided for as well. At present, the tool methodology only belongs to the school community inside school.

The last part of the tool – recommendations by policy makers – seems very normative and fairly distant from reality.

Conclusion: the tool is fairly comprehensive and coherent assuming that a country has some experience in EDC and QA.

2.2. Corresponding material in Lithuania

The main materials that correspond to the tool in Lithuanian schools are their QA systems (external and internal audits), well-developed educational law and strategic planning.

No specific EDC evaluation methodologies are presented in Chapters 5, 6 and 7 of the tool. At present only the main documents that have influenced the development of EDC can be introduced. However, citizenship education has been important at all stages of education reform. The aim of a civil society goes back to the preamble of the Lithuanian Constitution, which was approved in 1992. The general principles of the state policy on civic education are determined by the Law on Education.

The third chapter ("Goals of education") of the Adjustment Law of Education Law (17 June 2003, No. IX, 1630) says that it is necessary to "create conditions for a person to acquire traditions of democracy, which embody the basis of civic and political culture, and to develop skills and experience that are essential for a person, competent as a citizen of Lithuania and a member of the European and World community, multicultural society".

In 2004, the General Programme on Citizenship Education in Schools was approved in Decree No. ISAK-1086 of the MES. This programme was designed according to the European dimensions of EDC and still plays a very important role in the formation of civic self-awareness among the younger generation in Lithuania.

Resolution No. 1105 regarding the Implementation of Civic Education in Educational Institutions was approved by the Government of the Republic of Lithuania in 1998, and the orders of the MES on such programmes as Patriotic Education of the Pupils and Performance of Holocaust Education were declared in 2000 and 2003 respectively.

The Implementation of Civic Education in Educational Institutions programme includes:

- alternation in terms of the content of education, including citizenship education;
- democratisation of educational institutes, and education regarding the democratic way of life at school;
- knowledge of European integration.

Since the European Council proclaimed 2006 to be the Year of Public (Civic) Spirit, Lithuania has been involved in several general civic performance programmes in Europe. A working group led by the Secretary of the MES, A. Puodžiukas, prepared a Long-term Programme of Civic and National Education for 2006-11. This programme was prepared after evaluating educational projects and programmes that were or still are being implemented in Lithuania (From Civic Initiative Towards Civic Society, Constitutional Values for Youth, Civitas, etc.). At the same time, research results were analysed (during the period 1996-2000, the International Association for the Evaluation of Educational Achievement (IEA) carried out a study to evaluate the civic maturity of young people in 28 European countries; in 2004 another research project, Participation of Young People in the Activities of Public Organisations and Municipalities, was realised).

The content of citizenship education is laid out in detail in the general programmes of Lithuanian Comprehensive Education (1997). Some Lithuanian schools also follow the guidelines determined by the Council of Europe in the project Education for Democratic Citizenship.

To summarise, EDC is an important issue in the life of the school and in educational management. Research results are reflected in the content of programmes (for example, a special course, the "Basics of Civic Society", was introduced in 1995 for pupils in grades 7, 8 and 10); however, not enough attention is paid to this discipline in methodology. This shows that using the tool really could become reality at educational institutions in Lithuania.

However, for the moment, EDC in Lithuanian schools is only based on implementation programmes or on taking part in projects, and not on a methodical process of evaluation and how it influences pupils; although, as mentioned above, many good documents, programmes and projects exist that could solve this problem. A very small number of schools have experience with pupils' self-government, which is directly related to skill consolidation in the field of EDC. It is one thing to adopt documents and programmes, and quite another to implement them in real life with positive results. Schools are not able to do this alone, taking into consideration the fact that the present social/demographical and economical processes in Lithuania are not favourable for consolidating citizenship in Lithuanian schools, because society's problems reflect school life like a mirror. The family has a great impact on a child's civic maturity, but is not active in the context of citizenship education. It shows that families also need special training in the field of EDC.

Conclusion: material related to EDC in general exists in Lithuania, but schools lack the methodology needed to evaluate it.

3. The tool as an instrument of school evaluation in Lithuania

3.1. Conditions in schools for applying the tool

3.1.1. Circumstances that might promote application of the tool

There are certain potential factors that could promote application of the tool in Lithuanian schools: first, there are internal and external evaluation methodologies in school education, and, second, considerable attention has started to be paid to citizenship education. This is related to the high migration levels of Lithuanian people. It can be said that the appearance of such a tool affects training on citizenship and democracy in Lithuania, especially when one bears in mind that one of the main priorities of education reform is to firmly establish civic education. It is even more important in the context of the Long-term Civic and National Education

Programme for the Years 2006-11, and developing the Programme of Patriotic Education further (www.smm.lt/veiklos_planai_ir_programos/docs/prg6.htm).

Democratisation of society, EU entry and other factors mean that the Lithuanian education system needs to be open and compatible with EU standards. This is even more important regarding the compatibility of evaluation (audit) criteria. One of the four components of the Programme of School Improvement, prepared by the MES, is the Formation of the Quality Management System of Education. Its implementation has already produced good results, such as: constant improvement of monitoring of the education system, which enables the content of education policy to be defined; and the introduction of internal and external audit systems to train school communities to fulfil audits, and the auditors of the municipalities to apply it. One other very important condition is to improve constantly the legal database of education policy, reflecting the needs of society.

Conclusion: it can generally be affirmed that the Lithuanian education policy is favourable to EDC implementation, but that this process can only be successful in the event that the tool's methods are introduced into existing evaluation methodologies (the author of this article bases this statement on the reflections of teachers who took part in the preparation of internal school audits). The policy should also be able to create criteria that could fix knowledge, skills, attitudes and action results, which should practically reflect the social behaviour of pupils in the context of EDC.

3.1.2. Prospective difficulties and obstacles

As mentioned above, we have a sufficient basis for data that can determine the content of citizenship.

The climate of the entire school is extremely important in this context as it may ensure the realisation of the content of civic concepts. Citizenship in the school is understood as: civic participation, value (civic) judgments, knowledge required for citizens that may familiarise pupils with the realities of national or global political and cultural life so as to understand social and political conflicts, and the possible problems residing in the democratic constitutional system, as well as civic/national identity. This description is, however, very abstract.

There are also some hidden obstacles, such as civic indifference, disappointment with democracy and public life, decreasing activity during elections, and emigration processes. These can be monitored based on the research data (for example, research co-ordinated by the European Commission, Eurobarometer 2005, showed that only 33% of Lithuania's residents are content with the way democracy operates in the country). In the first fifteen years of independence, nearly 400 000 inhabitants out of a total population of 3.5 million left Lithuania. At present the country badly needs a workforce, with unemployment at only 3.2%. The level of social activity is also very low, especially among young people.

Few people take part in the activities of non-governmental organisations (NGOs), which reveals the shortage of political and juridical education. Such a social environment represents a huge barrier when seeking to implement evaluation methodologies.

Lately, the importance of citizenship has been much discussed. Lithuania faces the following problems regarding the implementation of the tool's methodologies:
- there is a shortage of co-ordination at all levels of citizenship education;
- the implementation of new methodologies is related to the problem of financing;
- human resources – teachers – are of great importance as well. They have just mastered internal audit methodologies; any new methodologies will not be accepted so readily. Though we talk about the importance of EDC, teachers of citizenship education and supervisors are the only ones bearing the responsibility for citizenship education;
- EDC is not treated as a constituent part of QA;
- it will take quite a long time to improve teachers' preparation programmes in the context of education, as accreditation of programmes of studies is positive but still highly bureaucratic;
- the weakest point in EDC methodologies is the problem of measuring results. How can these results be measured? Not only knowledge needs to be monitored, but actions as well. This necessitates concrete examples;
- the whole process will take a lot of time, especially for those chains that still have not mastered the methods of internal and external evaluation;
- we need to translate the tool into Lithuanian (and even at this level I have encountered problems discussing the problem of implementing the tool with teachers);
- the EDC evaluation process needs to be co-ordinated at all levels (local, national and European);
- more instruments need to be prepared to support the tool with examples of good experience.

3.1.3. Parts of the tool with particular applicability

Lithuanian schools can now master the tool thanks to the recently implemented internal and external audit methodologies. It is possible to anticipate in this context the parts that are particularly applicable. Otherwise, this would be a process lasting several years. The adaptation of some new parts into existing audit methodologies will itself be relatively time-consuming.

Chapter 5 is a particularly applicable part of the tool (Bîrzea et al., 2005: 55-68). Specific areas (Bîrzea et al., 2005: 58, Table 1) interrelate with the areas (presented in the first chapter of this report) of the wide audit, as applied in Lithuanian schools. Areas 1-4 ("Content of education", "Achievements of learning", etc., see appendix) surround such areas of the tool as "Curriculum" and "Teaching and learning"; or Areas 5, "Ethos", and 6, "Resources – School ethos and climate"; and Area 7, "Management of the school and assurance of its quality – Management and development". The main and subsidiary indicators of area performance could be addressed by quality indicators.

The above-mentioned idea can be explained further: it is possible to apply the tool, while adapting its content to the existing audit methodology in Lithuania. Certainly, instead of mechanically "mounting" artificial indicators, this could be done by evaluating the development of EDC. Only then is it possible to find space for implementing the idea of EDC. This could broaden the content of existing training programmes in the context of today's EDC.

3.1.4. Target groups of the tool

In her book, Professor Dobranskienė (Dobranskienė, 2002) underlines the structure of school communities, stretching from the pedagogues as leaders of the school community (from principals of schools to teachers of citizenship education), to pupils as members of the school community, and on to parents as an inseparable part of the school community. All three groups are important in the framework of EDC evaluation; however, while introducing components of EDC in general in the audit methodology of Lithuania, it is important to involve representatives of the MES, Teachers' Competency Centre, officials of local authorities, universities and colleges that are preparing teachers and researchers. Also, NGOs play an important role by taking an active part in projects concerning citizenship education.

3.2. Systemic conditions for applying the tool

3.2.1. Correspondence of the tool and the system of quality assurance and evaluation

The author of this report has discussed the question of quality assurance and evaluation with employees of the Department of Education of Klaipėda City Municipality, who are responsible for implementing quality controls and introducing a new audit methodology in schools. It was also discussed with the principals and teachers of schools and representatives of various NGO projects. These discussions had more of a pilot or informative character, resembling an exchange of opinions rather than a deep analysis. The tool itself, however, is appreciated as a valuable instrument, which could be adapted to the general audit methodology by expanding the audit's areas and quality indicators that now exist in Lithuania.

Whereas the first round regarding the methodology of internal and external audits in Lithuania is just finishing, and various procedures to improve it are taking place at the moment, there is no major problem foreseen in expanding the content of audits, even if the authors of the audit methodology are still reflecting on the first results of the audit. It will, however, be more difficult to encourage teachers to start a new evaluation process in the context of EDC. This will require incorporating the tool into the remit of the co-ordinating group of the project – the Formation of a School's Inner Audit Methodology and the MES.

3.2.2. Preparation of teachers to work with the tool

As already mentioned in sub-section 1.2, management of education is not an important issue in Lithuanian teacher-training programmes. To prepare teachers to work with the EDC tool, special training is needed (in EDC-QA).

As there are a number of teachers who do not know any foreign languages, this instrument has to be translated into Lithuanian. As the structure of the tool is clear and its methodology is logical, there should not be any problems with using it as long as Chapters 5, 6 and 7 of the tool are adapted to the existing QA methodology in Lithuania (this observation applies to all chapters of this report). Referring to training courses on using the tool and its ease of use, seminars and consultations might be necessary. Nevertheless, it would be very useful to be able to refer to documents (with examples) from a country that has already implemented the tool. Principals and teachers need more precise examples of the eight steps from QA to EDC (Bîrzea et al., 2005: 71). The short examples introduced in the tool cannot illustrate the wide content of EDC indicators. A similar document is now being used in Lithuanian schools following the internal audit experiment. Other materials encompassing the content of EDC in the context of Lithuania and Europe (the documents from Lisbon and Bologna, the European Council, Lithuanian Education Policy and the National Strategy of Education for the Years 2003-12), are accessible for all Lithuanian teachers as they are published on the website of the MES, and have been explained at various methodological seminars and conferences, and in scientific articles and periodicals.

We only have experience with teacher training in the framework of EDC content, but this nevertheless represents useful experience. In 1998, the Implementation of Civic Education in Educational Institutions programme was created. The priority of this programme is to train teachers involved in a new discipline, "Basics of civic society". This entails running seminars for teachers of citizenship education and seminars on European integration issues. The MES has recommended various seminars (Content and Methodology of Teaching Citizenship Education in Grades 7 to 10, Methodology of Educating a Democratic School Community, etc.) for teachers who intend to teach the new discipline. In 2004, the General Programme on Citizenship Education was approved. It pointed out the aims and objectives of citizenship education, how to implement this, and defined the cognitive and practical skills that schools have to build up.

In conclusion: Lithuania has a methodology of external and internal QA and an understanding of EDC content (from the point of view of the Lithuanian definition), as programmes on citizenship education are part of school life. The QA methodology that exists in Lithuania, however, has to be adapted to the EDC-QA and introduced to teachers, as was the case with implementation of the internal audit methodology. It also could be an experiment in some schools. Institutes of continuing education, universities and local administrations (for example, education departments) have to work together to prepare teachers to work with the tool (via seminars, e-learning courses, published materials, websites, etc.).

3.2.3. Other possible facilitators

The author of the report will answer this question by presenting Order No. 302 of the MES, as approved on 23 February 2002, regarding the Methodology of Internal Audit Applied to Comprehensive Schools. This document establishes an internal audit methodology in all national and municipal comprehensive schools from the school year 2004/05 onwards, as well as in primary schools (encompassing grades 1 to 4), with the aim of ensuring continuity.

The creators of the audit methodology claim that it is very flexible and may be adopted by all educational institutions after evaluating the context of their performance and goals.

Special attention should be paid to the particular situation of special teenagers' schools containing young pupils that lack either the motivation to learn or the requisite social skills.

In order to implement the EDC tool, I think that NGOs with experience of training volunteers would be a good platform to initiate citizenship activities in society.

4. Ideas for the implementation process

4.1. How to make working with the tool valuable for schools

While discussing implementation of the tool with school directors, local authorities, education institutions, teachers and university lecturers, one realises that the idea of EDC evaluation is extremely important and has to be discussed and evaluated at all levels of education.

As a first step, the departments of education of the city municipalities and county administrations have to discuss this idea with the school directors. Afterwards, the directors have to discuss their findings with teachers and pupil representatives (from self-governing student institutions). Then, after receiving feedback, the departments of education have to summarise the discussion on how to implement this idea and present it to the MES, which is responsible for the Long-term Civic and National Education Programme for the Years 2006-11. The authors of the above-mentioned programme have to initiate the expansion of the present internal audit methodology so that it clearly presents the activity and the subsidiary indicators enabling the assessment of the EDC situation in Lithuanian schools.

University and college lecturers who train teachers, together with scientists, may actively participate in this process, as can politicians, especially members of the parliament's Education Committee.

Regarding local authorities, those people that are closely involved in managing the quality of education could be appointed as contact people. The specialists in the Division of Primary and Secondary Education of the Department of Comprehensive Education at the MES should be mentioned in this regard.

The co-ordinators of already realised projects, such as CIVIC and others, should also be involved in the process as their competence may help prepare the quantitative indicators and sub-themes of all the above-mentioned spheres in the evaluative framework. This means we have to co-ordinate the existing audit methodology with the "Tool for Quality Assurance of Education for Democratic Citizenship in Schools".

4.2. How to integrate the tool into international partnerships

Lithuanian schools have reasonable experience in the sphere of international collaboration. In 2002, the Socrates programme celebrated its 20th anniversary, and has already been operating in Lithuania for ten years. In Lithuania it also co-ordinates the Comenius programme for schools (from 2006 on with the new title of the Lifelong Learning programme). Therefore, this programme may also get involved in the process of implementing the tool by supporting exchange programmes between teachers and pupils, seeking to assimilate good experiences, organising training courses for Lithuanian teachers and lecturers, and inviting foreign specialists who have experience in the development and implementation of the tool.

Conclusion: international projects represent a genuine way of implementing the tool at international level.

4.3. Alternative scenarios for working with the tool

It is always very difficult to propose alternatives, because any given alternative is an idea that seems good to its author, but is possibly completely unacceptable for other parties. Civic education is an integral part of some excellent projects and initiatives. I think we do not always fully exploit the existing opportunities. I have in mind the UNECE Strategy for Education for Sustainable Development and the Vilnius Framework for the Implementation of the UNECE Strategy for Education for Sustainable Development, both of which were approved during the meeting of the MES and the Ministry of the Environment on 17 and 18 March 2005.

The vision of this strategy states "that education is not only one of the human rights, but a required condition for a cohesive development and substantial means for good management, acceptance of well-founded solutions, and promotion of democracy" (UNECE strategy, 2005: 3). This strategy was also approved by the Government of Lithuania. In the context of this strategy, Lithuania is implementing several projects, such as Agenda 21, ELOS, etc.

I think that it is possible to find certain ways to implement the tool in the strategy of cohesive development, which interrelates with the development and strengthening of EDC content. Evaluation methodologies will only be effective if the content of training in schools is strengthened with EDC programmes regarding both formal and non-formal education.

To summarise, we may conclude that the tool is sufficiently clear and flexible and may have an impact not only in terms of evaluating the level of democracy and public spirit in one country or another, but also fixing attention on the development of the content of the problem and the possibilities of strengthening citizenship culture in general.

I would like to thank all the principals, teachers, school professors and universities in Lithuania who helped me to understand many interesting things in the field of EDC, enabling me to carry out this study.

References

Andriekienė, R.M. (2004). "Problems of Professional Competence of Teachers in the Context of Permanent Learning", in *Theory and Practice in Teacher Education II*, Riga, 5-16.

Bendroji pilietinio ugdymo programa. LR Švietimo ir mokslo ministerija, 2004 m. liepos 5 d (General Programme of Citizenship Education. Ministry of Education and Sciences, 5 July 2004). Retrieved from www.pedagogika.lt/puslapis/Pilietinis.pdf.

Bendrojo lavinimo mokyklos vidaus audito metodika, 2002. I dalis (Internal Audit Methodology for Comprehensive Schools. Part I, 2002). Vilnius: Švietimo ir mokslo ministerija.

Bendrojo lavinimo mokyklos vidaus audito metodika, 2002. III dalis (Internal Audit Methodology for Comprehensive Schools. Part III, 2002). Vilnius: Švietimo ir mokslo ministerija.

Bendrosios programos ir švietimo standartai, 2003 (General Programmes and Education Standards, 2003). Vilnius: Švietimo ir mokslo ministerija, 423-428.

Bîrzea, C.; Cecchini, M.; Harrison, C.; Krek, J.; Spajic-Vrkas, V. (2005). "Tool for Quality Assurance of Education for Democratic Citizenship in Schools", Paris: Council of Europe, UNESCO, Centre for Educational Policy Studies.

Dobranskienė, R. (2002). *Mokyklos bendruomenės vadyba* (Management of the School Community), Šilutė.

General Concept of Education in Lithuania (1994). Vilnius: Lietuvos Respublikos kultūros ir švietimo ministerijos leidybos centras.

Ilgalaikė pilietinio ir tautinio ugdymo programa 2006-2011 (2005) (Long-term Civic and National Education Programme for the Years 2006-11). Vilnius.

Jungtinių tautų Europos ekonomikos komisijos darnaus vystymosi švietimo strategija ir Jungtinių tautų Europos ekonomikos komisijos darnaus vystymosi švietimo strategijos įgyvendinimo Vilniaus gairės (2005) (UNECE Strategy for Education for Sustainable Development and the Vilnius Framework for the Implementation of the UNECE Strategy for Education for Sustainable Development). Vilnius: Švietimo ir mokslo ministerija.

Laurinčiukienė, L. (ed.) (2003). *Darbotvarkė 21 mokykloje* (Agenda 21 at School), Vilnius: VšĮ Regioninio aplinkos centro Centrinei ir Rytų Europai biuras Lietuvoje.

Lietuvos Respublikos Seimo Nutarimas Dėl Valstybinės Švietimo Strategijos 2003-2012 metų nuostatų, 2003 m. liepos 4 d. Nr. IX-1700 (2003) (Resolution of Parliament of the Republic of Lithuania on the National Strategy of Education for the Years 2003-12). Vilnius: Valstybės žinios.

Lietuvos Respublikos Švietimo ir mokslo ministro įsakymas dėl Neformaliojo vaikų švietimo koncepcijos patvirtinimo, 2005 m. gruodžio 30 d. Nr. ISAK-2695 (2005) (Resolution of the Minister for Education and Science on Approval of the Concept of Informal Children's Education). Vilnius: Valstybės žinios.

Lietuvos Respublikos Švietimo Įstatymo Pakeitimo Įstatymas, 2003 m. birželio 17 d., Nr. IX-1630 (2003) (Adjustment Law of Education Law). Vilnius: Valstybės žinios.

Lietuvos Respublikos Vyriausybės Nutarimas dėl Valstybinės Pedagogų rengimo ir kvalifikacijos tobulinimo pertvarkos programos patvirtinimo, 2006 m. gegužės 25 d., No. 468 (2006) (Resolution of the Lithuanian Government for Adjustments in the State Programme for Training Pedagogues and Improvement of their Qualifications). Vilnius: Valstybės žinios.

McLaughlin, T.H. (1997). *Šiuolaikinė ugdymo filosofija: demokratiškumas, vertybės, įvairovė* (Contemporary Philosophy of Education: Democracy, Values, and Variety), Kaunas.

Mikkelsen, R. (2004). "Northern Europe regional synthesis." in Bîrzea, C. (ed.). *All-European Study on Education for Democratic Citizenship Policies*. Strasbourg: Council of Europe, 83-90.

Mokyklos demokratizacija: problemos ir sprendimų paieškos (1998) (Democratisation of the School: In Search of Problems and Solutions). Vilnius.

Patriotinio ugdymo įgyvendinimo programa (Implementation of the Programme on Patriotic Education). Retrieved from www.smm.lt/veiklos_planai_ir_programos/docs/prg6.htm.

Peck, B.T. and Mays, A. (2000). *Challenge and Change in Education: The Experience of the Baltic States in the 1990s*, Huntington, NY: Nova Science Publishers, Inc.

School in Lithuania: the Past, the Present, the Future. Collection of Selected Papers Presented at the Conference (1997). Klaipėda: KU leidykla.

Subjektų, vykdančių vaikų ir jaunimo socializaciją, socialinės, edukacinės ir teisinės kompetencijos aprašas. LR švietimo ir mokslo ministro 2005 m. gruodžio 23 d. įsakymu Nr. ISAK-2636 (Description of Social, Educational and Juridical Competency in Subjects that Promote Socialization of Children and Youth). Vilnius: Valstybės žinios.

The Review of the Strategic Action Plan of the Municipality of Klaipėda City 2004-06 (2006). Klaipėda.

Towards Inclusion of Citizenship Culture in Teacher Education Programmes (2006). Prague: Faculty of Education, Charles University.

Ugdymo programų akreditacijos kriterijai ir jos vykdymo tvarka (2004) (Criteria and Procedure of Accreditation of Education Programmes). Vilnius: Švietimo ir mokslo ministerija.

Valstybės Žinios (2005). m. lapkričio 22 d. LR Vyriausybės nutarimas "Dėl Nacionalinės Lisabonos strategijos įgyvendinimo programos" (Resolution No.1270 of Lithuanian Government on 22 November 2005, "On Implementation of National Program of Lisbon Strategy") Valstybės Žinios, 2005, Nr. 139-5019. www.ceeol.com/aspx/getdocument.aspx?logid=5&id=c6A163B6-5220-4CAO-871B-D648E773F26D.

Valstybės Žinios (2003). m. rugpjūčio 14 d. LR Švietimo ir mokslo ministro įsakymas Nr. ISAK- 1155 "Dėl mokytojų kompetencijos centro steigimo" (Order No. ISAK-1155 of Lithuanian Minister of Education and Science on 14 August 2003, "On Establishment of Teachers Competences Center") Valstybės Žinios, 2003, Nr. 81-3709. www.smm.lt/prtm/docs/mkt/mokytoju_%20reng_ir_kvalf_tob_programa.doc.

Zaleckienė, I. *Pilietinio ugdymo socialinė dimencija* (Social Dimension of Citizenship Education). Vilnius.

Želvys, R. (2001). *Švietimo vadybos pagrindai* (Basics of Education Management), Vilnius: VU leidykla.

Appendix: Project on Internal Audit Methodology for Comprehensive Schools

Internal Audit Methodology for Comprehensive Schools. Part I presents a detailed internal audit model, the phases of fulfilling the audit, indicators of school activities and methods of their evaluation, the methodology of preparing the report, principles of school development planning, and the price of fulfilling the audit. This edition was enriched with various sources and documents (laws, resolutions, and orders of the Minister for Education and Science, standards, other legislation, the regulating system of education) that might be useful while evaluating the activities of the school.

The next part, Part II, presents the wide experience of the schools that participated in the project via various means of inquiry (questionnaires, interviews, etc.).

The final part, Part III, was dedicated to presenting the experience of 10 schools from the Moletai region. They created and adapted internal audit tools that could be used by all Lithuanian school communities.

The methodology was approved on 28 February 2002 by Order No. 302 of the Minister for Education and Science. Now all schools (both secondary and vocational) can use it in their work.

Principles of self-evaluation:
- evaluation is not a single act, but a process;
- the main subject of evaluation is the institution, not people;
- the evaluation process is accepted by the majority of teachers in educational institutions;
- evaluation is based on the internal rules and education goals of the educational institution that correspond to its mission;
- evaluation must be the principle of everyday perfection.

Possible sources of evaluation:
- the strategic plan of the school and its annual action plan;
- the regulations of the school;
- the educational plans of the school;
- material to ascertain the needs of pupils;
- educational programmes and plans of various periods prepared by teachers;
- timetables;
- class diaries;
- project documentation;

- activity documentation of methodological groups;
- pupils' homework;
- documentation of the school's self-government institutions;
- plans to improve qualifications;
- protocols of the teachers' council meetings;
- protocols of the meetings.

Possible evaluation methods:
- analysis of the documents;
- interviews;
- inquiries;
- discussions with members of the community;
- social research.

There are also some techniques (both quantitative and qualitative) of evaluation methodologies presented in the methodology of internal audits, namely how to prepare a questionnaire or interview, how to concentrate the attention of focus groups, how to carry out monitoring and how to record data.

Data from a school's self-evaluation are used:
- to create a strategy to improve the educational institution;
- to prepare reports for societies, sponsors of the educational institution and local politicians;
- to enlarge the databases of municipal or regional monitoring according to the determined order of laws (for more details, see *Internal Audit Methodology for Comprehensive Schools. Part I*).

The tables below show how internal audit methodology is applied in Lithuanian schools.

Table 1: Internal audit methodology (according to the *Internal Audit Methodology for Comprehensive Schools. Part I*, 2002: 20)

Areas of evaluation 1. Content of education; 2. Achievements of learning; 3. Learning and education; 4. Help for pupils; 5. Ethos (understood as the environment of the school, the relationship between teachers and pupils, school guidelines on the behaviour of pupils and teachers, etc.); 6. Resources; 7. Management of the school and quality assurance.	These seven areas of evaluation reveal the main aspects of a school's performance.
Indicators of performance	Each performance indicator is divided into one or more subsidiary indicators.
Levels 4 – very good – achievements predominate 3 – good – there are more achievements than shortcomings 2 – satisfactory – there are significant shortcomings 1 – insufficient – shortcomings predominate	A school's performance according to the subsidiary indicators is evaluated using four levels.
Illustrations are presented as examples in the methodological editions.	Illustrations of the 2nd and 4th levels are presented for each subsidiary indicator. On the basis of illustration, a school may think of questions to ask or may emulate the situation described.
Performance features	The methodology contains features of every subsidiary indicator. Relying on them, the school gathers its features or arguments, reflecting specific performance in the chosen area of evaluation.

Table 2: Specific example: area content of education (according to the *Internal Audit Methodology for Comprehensive Schools. Part I*, 2002: 22)

Performance indicators	Subsidiary indicators	Levels			
		4	3	2	1
1.1. Educational plans	1.1.1. Educational subjects and their relation to the plan of education				
	1.1.2. Interdisciplinary relations and integration				
	1.1.3. Meeting pupils' needs and workloads				
1.2. Educational programmes	1.2.1. The variety of programmes and their interconnection				
	1.2.2. Structure of educational programmes, their correspondence to the demands of subject content, general programmes and standards				
	1.2.3. Methodological assistance for teachers preparing programmes				
1.3. Planning of teachers' activities	1.3.1. Planning of programmes and everyday activities				
	1.3.2. Quality of planning procedures				

Table 3: Illustration of levels according to the first indicator in the area content of education (according to the *Internal Audit Methodology for Comprehensive Schools. Part I, 2002: 25*)

Performance indicators	Subsidiary indicators	Illustrations (examples)		Features
		4	2	
1.1. Educational plans	1.1.1. Educational subjects, their relation to the educational plan	The educational plan completely satisfies the goals of the school, the peculiarities of the region and place, and the recommendations of the state. The relationship between educational subjects completely corresponds to the recommendations of the state's education plans. It is well co-ordinated and comprehensive at the level of class and the stage.	The educational plan does not completely satisfy the goals of the school and the recommendations of the state and region. The relationship between educational subjects does not correspond completely to the recommendations of the state's education plans. It is neither well co-ordinated or comprehensive.	Compatibility, continuity, offer, demand, and expediency at the level of the class and the stage of the educational subjects. Subsidiary education hours are available and are compatible with the educational subjects.

Poland
Alicja Pacewicz

Remarks on the historical context of the report

Research for this report has been conducted in a specific historical and political context in 2006 and early 2007. At the time, the leader of the nationalist-populist party – the League of Polish Families – was head of the Ministry of Education. During this time, citizenship education was treated as redundant if not pointless. Democracy at school was dismissed as "paidocracy" – a dangerous Utopia. Quality assurance was gradually replaced by external control. Fortunately, most of the schools, principals and pupils were able to function in survival mode.

In the second half of 2007, the governing coalition collapsed, the new parliament was elected and a new government was formed. The present Ministry of Education considers both quality assurance and education for democratic citizenship as important backbones of the educational system, at least in its declarations. At the same time, however, there is no guarantee that the "Tool for Quality Assurance of Education for Democratic Citizenship in Schools" can now be easily adopted on a large scale. Educational authorities and schools are focused on a complicated and costly structural and curricular reform, including the introduction of formal education at the age of 6 (until 2008, mandatory school age was 7). At the same time, principals, teachers, students, parents and public opinion in general pay more attention to external exam results than to the process of school democratisation and quality assurance in this field. In summary we can say that while in June 2008 the general climate for introducing the tool is certainly more favourable than two years ago, developments in the Polish educational system are extremely difficult to predict. Hence, the report is not only of historical interest but will also serve as an example of challenges that transforming societies might face. The report shows possible strategies in such a context.

Introduction

Any expertise concerning the possibility of introducing quality assurance (QA) of education for democratic citizenship (EDC) into Polish schools must consider both the long-term changes that have taken place in Polish education since 1989, and the current political context.

In the last dozen or so years there have been two significant reforms of the educational system:
- the decentralisation of schools. The Ministry of Education handed over the administration of educational institutions to the local government authorities – municipalities (*gminas*) and districts (*powiats*);

– curricular and structural reform. The introduction of new guidelines for curricula and external examinations, and the change in the structure of education from a two to a three-tier system (for more information on the Polish system of education, see O'Brien and Paczynski, 2006; Horner et al., 2007).

All of the changes introduced in post-communist Poland have led from centrally administered schools with a uniform curriculum and identical textbooks, to schools with a greater degree of autonomy, managed by a director rather than a minister, in which the teachers are responsible for developing curricula and educational activities, after taking into consideration the voices of students and parents. Attempts were also made to increase the roles of the school council – a collective body comprising representatives of teachers, parents and students, parental committees – and of the student council. Much has been said about the need to set up proper procedures in order to protect the rights of students, and for several years schools and *Kuratoria Oświaty* (regional administration and evaluation bodies) even had students' ombudsmen.

The example of more than a thousand "non-public" schools created after 1989 (owned by parents' associations or private entities) also increased the influence of parents and students in school life, as did mounting pressure from national and local parental organisations, which wanted to have a greater say in how their children were being educated. Numerous attempts were made to encourage various forms of pupil participation in school life and to develop more egalitarian relationships between teachers and students based on mutual respect. Interactive teaching and learning methods were introduced by many teachers, allowing for authentic student activity and co-operation, and open communication and debate.

As a recent study entitled "The Education Systems of Europe" suggests, despite the major economic difficulties accompanying social change, educational reforms have been introduced persistently in parallel with the ongoing processes of the decentralisation and democratisation of educational structures. Decision-making prerogatives have been placed in the hands of head teachers and the competences of the local consulting structures have been broadened, especially those of parents (Horner et al., 2007).

In general it may be said that schools were becoming more democratic and more modern, though it was evident that there was still a long way to go. A document prepared in 2005 by the Ministry of Education entitled "Education and Competences" presented policies for 2007-13, and stated that transformation (in the field of politics, economy, society and civilisation) was taking place both outside the educational system and within it. It included both learners and teachers. Systemic solutions adequate to the new reality have not been formed, however. Schools have not kept pace with this transformation even though education has become increasingly important (Ministerstwo Edukacji Narodowej, 2005).

In the last couple of months, with the new Minister for Education, Roman Giertych (the leader of the Nationalist-Catholic Party, the Liga Polskich Rodzin (LPR)), the sector has found itself in completely new circumstances. The ministry has declared its wish to move away from the concept of an autonomous, open and tolerant school, and has announced its plans for the Programme of 4Ps – standing for prestige (of the teaching profession), orderliness, patriotism and truth (*prestiż, patriotyzm, porządek and prawda*). The minister has declared his preference for a tightening of control by a centralised authority. More recently, new legislation has been passed – self-evaluation by schools (in-house quality assurance) is to be limited and external control – conducted by the *Kuratoria Oświaty* (regional administrative bodies) directly under the ministry's jurisdiction – is to be reinforced.

In June 2006, the director of CODN (the National In-service Teacher Training Centre) was dismissed by the minister with immediate effect, under the accusation of "promoting homosexuality". The action was prompted by CODN's publication of the Polish version of the Council of Europe's handbook *Compass*. The minister took a dislike to the scenario of lessons on tolerance towards persons of different sexual orientations, especially to the possibility of inviting representatives of GLTB (gay, lesbian, transgender and bisexual) associations. The Council of Europe's Secretary General protested over this issue, sending two memoranda to the Polish Government, but to date has received no satisfactory reply.

The minister is keen to promote patriotism, which is understood as emphasising Polish traditions and building national pride. One of the ideas he had concerning the curriculum was to abolish a subject known as "knowledge about society" (which is the Polish equivalent of citizenship education) and introduce "patriotic education" instead. A proposal was also made to separate teaching the history of Poland from general history – with lessons about democracy placed in the latter. Fortunately none of these declarations was ever implemented. It is worth noting here that never before had any ministry been so active in announcing (although not necessarily introducing) changes and new regulations.

In reaction to several recent broadly publicised cases of school violence, Minister Giertych announced a "Zero tolerance of violence" programme, stressing the need to tighten school discipline and placing school staff under a legal obligation to report any example of abuse or violence to the police. The procedure of direct inspections by special commissions composed of three people (a *Kuratorium* inspector, local government employee and policeman or prosecutor), investigating the problems of safety and violence in every middle and high school, was also introduced by the Prime Minister, Jarosław Kaczyński. Public opinion partly supports these measures, frightened by a series of shocking school incidents.

As a result of all these activities, an aura of uncertainty or even fear has started to pervade the educational sector. Naturally it is difficult to believe that democratic processes in schools can be permanently reversed, but the current political situation has been a cause of anxiety and certainly does not favour the introduction of mechanisms supportive of EDC.

1. School evaluation in Poland

The changes that have taken place over the past eighteen years have not bypassed the school evaluation system. The country has slowly passed from a system of "hard control" to one of "soft supervision", and its control functions have been strongly limited to make way for consultancy and support. This found its expression in educational law: in 2004 a directive (Ministerstwo Edukacji Narodowej, 2004) was passed that no longer referred to inspection, but rather to measuring the quality of school performance. It was then decreed that in order to develop the educational system and especially to assist the qualitative development of schools and educational institutions, to support student development and the professional development of teachers, the bodies responsible for educational supervision should:

- conduct systematic, planned evaluations of the quality of performance of schools and other educational institutions;
- undertake activities to support schools and educational institutions in improving their performance;
- ensure that schools and educational institutions comply with the law with respect to organisation and performance;
- support teachers and directors of schools and educational institutions in meeting quality performance standards;
- support schools and educational institutions in determining the direction of their qualitative development;
- give schools and educational institutions access to information concerning changes in the law related to the functioning of schools and educational institutions.

From 2004 up to December 2006 two kinds of quality evaluation processes were conducted in Polish schools: external inspection through the ministerial monitoring system, and in-house evaluation or self-assessment, carried out by the school itself and co-ordinated by the head teacher. This situation changed in December 2006, when the minister issued the new law on pedagogical supervision, practically eliminating the latter process.

It should be added here that since the introduction of external exams in 2002, all school evaluations have had to include an analysis of the students' achievements. For inspectors, local governments and school principals, the results of the exams have become a very significant part of the external and internal evaluation. These results are often treated as a basis for comparisons and checking school progress. Thus the achievements of particular schools can easily be compared. This comparison is not only a means to assess their performance; it also, and more importantly, diagnoses their problems and provides a valuable overview, hopefully leading to substantial developments in the quality of education (Horner et al., 2007). Many experts warn, however, that analysis of students' results may oversimplify the complicated matter of school performance.

The problems of quality control in education were emphasised in the document "Operational Programme: Human Capital", which was accepted by the Polish Government as part of the national strategy of development for the years 2007-13. It will probably be one of the areas of education in which new tools and procedures will have to be introduced if school management and financing are to become more effective (Ministerstwo Rozwoju Regionalnego, 2006).

Polish schools take part in various international evaluation studies, such as PISA conducted by the Organisation for Economic Co-operation and Development (OECD) and research organised by the International Association for the Evaluation of Educational Achievement (IEA). Their results help evaluate different aspects of students' performance and school education, but not of individual schools.

1.1. Modes of school evaluation

External evaluation

External evaluations are conducted by the educational supervisory system, namely the 16 *Kuratoria Oświaty* (regional administrative bodies). It is often school principals who apply to the *Kuratoria* to put into motion the evaluation procedure. The inspection takes several days to complete, and consists of an analysis of documentation, interviews with the director and teachers, and visits to lessons. Almost all external evaluations conducted in such a manner end positively; negative opinions are very infrequent. Such controls should be conducted by inspectors at least once every five years, but due to insufficient personnel this condition cannot always be met.

More frequently, schools are subjected to a partial evaluation of certain aspects decided on by the *Kuratorium* – for example, in the area of extra-curricular activities, attendance or systems of student assessment. One of the participants in the Directors' Forum in the Learning Schools programme (a voluntary self-evaluation project described below) gave the following answer to a question concerning the frequency and course of external inspections:

> *"I have not had a large-scale inspection (quality control) or one on a smaller scale (evaluation of a chosen problem) for four years. I should probably be pleased about this as every inspection disorganises work! There are occasional brief topic appraisals – last year we were given three questionnaires to complete on the following subjects: 'implementing four hours of PE', 'the list of textbooks used by the school' and 'student attendance'. And then, no feedback whatsoever. This year, however, an inspection is almost certain, as I have applied for a performance evaluation" (CEO, 2006a).*

Inspections carried out as a consequence of circumstances other than an application made by the school, such as dissatisfaction on the part of the local administrative body responsible for the school, serious disciplinary problems or complaints made by parents, are of a different character. Such inspections consist of a discussion of the legitimacy of the complaints or allegations, and do not have to be announced prior to their occurrence.

The *Kuratorium* inspectors' work should support the school director and teachers in improving their performance, but this aspect does not always work as it should. Due to a lack of employees, visits to the schools are unsystematic. In addition, some of the inspectors are insufficiently prepared for this responsible and delicate mission, which breeds an air of uncertainty among both directors and teachers. The director of one school says: "There are inspectors and 'inspectors'. Some will come beforehand, talk, listen, give some advice, take into account the school's perspective. Others should be trained in how to support instead of obstructing someone else's work" (CEO, 2006b).

Evaluation in 2004-06

Under the directive of 2004 the main task of inspectors was defined as measuring the performance quality of schools and other educational institutions – assessing the state, conditions and effects of the school's tuition, educational and nurturing practice, as well as other of its statutory activities, and the evaluation of progress in these areas. The responsibilities of *Kuratoria* mainly included:

- conducting external quality measurement;
- verifying whether there was an in-house QA system in place in the school, that is whether the director was organising quality self-evaluations;
- evaluating the usefulness and efficacy of school practice in relation to goals set.

The external evaluation was above all concerned with the extent to which the school was meeting standards set in the directive, in certain cases modified by the appropriate regional *Kuratorium* (Kuratorium Gdańskie, 2005). Regional quality standards differed slightly, but all encompassed 16 standards relating to the four areas of a school's responsibility, namely:

- a scheme of work developed by the school or educational institution;
- management and organisation;
- instruction/tuition;
- education and nurturing.

The standards set in the directive were illustrated by examples of indicators that precisely defined what the inspectors should pay attention to in the process of controlling a school. These sample indices turned out to be more than mere examples – however, the *Kuratoria* and school directors began to treat them as mandatory. This in turn detracted from the independent search for quality criteria or indicators that would be more appropriate for the given school.

Most of the supervisors did not manage to implement the expectations expressed in the regulation: the *Kuratoria*'s approach to monitoring school quality and performance is sometimes criticised as being too centred on "box ticking", verifying the formal respect of criteria on teacher qualifications, equipment and so on, and neglecting a more careful evaluation of teaching performance and educational outcomes (O'Brien and Paczynski, 2006).

Directive of December 2006

The new directive put in motion in December 2006 does not mention school quality assurance, and in place of "external quality measurement" by *Kuratoria*, we find "diagnostic and evaluative activities". These activities include controlling legal aspects of school operation; examining, diagnosing and evaluating school operation in the areas of instruction, education and nurturing; and checking how teachers have fulfilled their tasks in these areas. There are no quality standards, which means that everything will rest in the hands of the individual inspectors who may have their own points of view, priorities and criteria. Obviously it is now impossible to foresee the consequences of the new regulation – many educators agree that it means less bureaucracy, but some add that it might also mean more control and less school autonomy.

It is also worth adding that in the last few years, some *Kuratoria* had established their own regional certificates and awarded them to schools that met regional standards of school performance (for example, Pomeranian Certificates of Quality given by the Gdańsk *Kuratorium* and European School Certificates awarded by the Kielce *Kuratorium*). Under the new circumstances, these regional standards and quality management procedures had to be suspended.

Self-evaluation

2004-06

Under the directive of 2004, quality assurance in schools constituted a key element of the whole quality management system. Responsibility for internal evaluations rested on the director, who – in co-operation with all teachers – developed and put into practice an in-house quality assurance system. He or she conducted the self-evaluation, including an assessment of students' results; chose diagnostic tools and techniques; and wrote a report on the in-house evaluation during the school year and presented it to the *Kuratorium*, school council, board of parents and the local body administering the school. He or she was responsible for creating programmes to develop the school, analysing the results of external examinations and launching remedial measures.

It was also stated that the principal's role was to support teachers in professional development and achieving high performance quality (Ministerstwo Edukacji Narodowej, 2004).

Unfortunately, the directive introducing the concept of an in-house quality assurance system, which had initially delighted specialists, fairly quickly turned out to be dysfunctional. Its goal had been to persuade schools to develop their own QA systems, but it instead forced them to produce vast amounts of documentation proving that the system had been put into operation. It is worth adding that the existence of documents proving that a quality measurement system was working formally constituted justification for the *Kuratorium* inspector to forego external control. So it was not surprising that directors and teachers alike threw themselves wholeheartedly into developing the relevant work plans, reports and analyses, rather than into developing QA systems (for example, *Organizacja Nadzoru Pedagogicznego w SP w Rososze*, 2005).

Since the appendix to the directive contained an exceptionally detailed catalogue of standards and illustrative indicators, it was absolutely impossible for schools to diagnose simultaneously their achievements and problems in all the areas thus defined and to undertake authentic corrective activities.

In a way, the system started to increasingly resemble a fictitious entity – directors created bureaucratic documentation that sometimes bore no direct relation to real-life operations. The *Kuratorium* – basing its actions on the 2004 directive defining methods of verifying in-house QA systems – then acknowledged their receipt. The problem also lay in the fact that the *Kuratorium* was in no state to analyse the reports. As one of the experts wrote: "If the *Kuratorium* supervises the work of a significant number of schools, for example well over one and a half thousand in the Mazowsze Voivodship, and each report is on average three pages long, the employees of this agency would have to read about 4 500 pages in a given year. Is that at all possible?" (Nowacki, 2006).

Directive of 2006

As already mentioned, the directive of December 2006 no longer refers to QA or self-evaluation. School directors are no longer responsible for managing QA systems; their function is confined to developing a yearly plan of school inspection (supervision), which has to take into account a plan of inspection prepared by the *Kuratorium* and the results of school inspections conducted in previous years. The plan is to include:
- the scope, topics and organisational aspect of measurements and analyses to be conducted in the school; an agenda of lessons that will be supervised;
- topics of training courses for the teachers' council;
- other significant information (Ministerstwo Edukacji Narodowej, 2006).

This plan should be presented to the teachers' council and school council (including parents) before the start of the new school year. Before the end of the school year the head teacher is to inform the same bodies about its implementation and conclusions concerning – among other things – an analysis of students' performance and decisions resulting from these conclusions.

Announcing the directive, the minister said that it would eliminate unnecessary bureaucratic work, which was greeted with real relief by many head teachers and teachers. How is the new law going to reshape school practices? Some principals will continue to conduct QA even without a formal obligation because many of them have learnt how effective it can be for school development. But probably most will limit their school activities to what is required by the directive. The coming months will eventually show how *Kuratoria* and inspectors are going to "define" what requirements the schools will really be obliged to fulfil.

Other evaluation systems

There are also at least several organisations outside the state supervisory system that conduct evaluations that schools and other educational institutions can participate in on a voluntary basis. These evaluations – usually in-house, but frequently supported by an external assessment conducted by bodies especially ordained for this purpose – are often part of a broader quality assurance system. They are frequently also a precondition for receiving quality certification and accreditation.

There are several other independent QA systems and/or endeavours operating in the country. The best known are the following:
- Learning Schools – a programme run under the patronage of the Centre for Citizenship Education (CCE) and the Polish-American Freedom Foundation (for more information, see below);
- Schools of Quality – certificates awarded for meeting standards in three areas: education, teaching and learning, management, awarded by the privately owned training centre EKO-TUR;
- ISO 9001:2000 – certificates of the International Organization for Standardization;
- Health Promoting School – a network of "healthy" schools ("healthy" as defined by the World Health Organization), co-ordinated by the Methodological Centre for Psychological and Educational Support;
- Polish Good School Now – an accreditation system for non-public schools that are members of the Civic Educational Association;
- Interkl@sa – a quality guarantee given to schools that can prove that they are ICT literate;
- Green Certificate – awarded to environmentally friendly kindergartens and schools by the Centre for Ecological Education EKO-OKO;

– European Label – a European certificate for schools introducing innovative language education with a European dimension.

It should be noted that under the 2004 directive, the *Kuratorium* supervisors could abstain from evaluating a school's performance, basing their decision on certificates and other documents that prove that the school has put into effect an in-house QA system. It is unclear whether participation in such voluntary QA networks can be beneficial for a school under the new directive.

The Learning Schools self-evaluation programme and network

Learning Schools is a programme, run under the patronage of the Centre for Citizenship Education (Centrum Edukacji Obywatelskiej) and the Polish-American Freedom Foundation, which already encompasses 500 schools. Its goal is to help schools improve performance quality and effectiveness, design and then implement the necessary changes. Schools define their own goals, the methods of achieving them and monitoring techniques in four major areas of school operation such as the effects of tuition and education, teaching and learning, the school as an institution, and the school and its environment (the standards are based on the European Project Evaluating Quality in School Education). Fundamental to the Learning Schools programme are: co-operation within teacher teams; defining tuition and educational goals in a manner that enables control of the degree in which they have been reached; a reliable system for monitoring performance effects; and building a local community incorporating teachers, students and parents (for more information, see CEO, 2006b).

Schools also network around the more significant educational challenges, such as motivating students to study and behave appropriately, strengthening responsibility, individualising work with students, preventing aggression and bullying, encouraging co-operation between the school and home, and working with children with behavioural problems (CEO, 2006a).

A school is awarded the title of a "Learning School" (which it is entitled to for a period of three years) only after it has organised a "collegial panel". The panel invites representatives of other schools in the LS programme, the local authorities and the local community, and functions as a forum for open debate on the school's priorities and working methods. It is also a space for working out new methods of dealing with previously identified problems.

It should also be added here that 15 schools from the Learning Schools programme also participated in the European Bridges across Boundaries project, cross-disseminating quality development practices for schools in southern and eastern Europe. Activities such as sharing self-evaluation models, action research and critical friends groups were carried out based on the earlier European pilot project and on the book entitled *Self-evaluation in European Schools: A Story of Change* (MacBeath et al., 2000).

The weak points of the debate concerning school evaluations

The debate on the subject of evaluation has been going on in Poland for many years, but its scope has been limited. Its participants included numerous experts from state and private agencies in educational issues, plus the appropriate ministerial departments and *Kuratorium* officials. Happily, some professional periodicals for directors and teachers have also been pulled in. There have been several publications, including a translation of John MacBeath's *How Good Is Our School?* and John Jay Bonstingl's *Quality Schools. Introducing TQM*, as well as several Polish ones (for a list, see Trojan, 2006).

It is worth adding that the British Council has become involved in disseminating the concept of quality in the Polish education system. Twice yearly a Quality Forum is organised in co-operation with the National In-service Teacher Training Centre and the Centre for Citizenship Education. It is addressed to managers at different levels of the educational sector and is devoted to promoting interesting initiatives that advance quality in education (British Council, 2004).

This discussion over the various approaches to school evaluation and their benefits has two singular weaknesses. The opinion is often raised that self-evaluation is the weaker form, as it is not objective. Opponents emphasise that listening to the voices of students and parents yields little as the students – "understandably" – are not sufficiently orientated to the school's goals and the principles on which it functions, and hence cannot be treated as a reliable source of information. For their part, parents – it is often argued – only act in their own best interests and are able to express only the most general of expectations ("to prepare the kids adequately for examinations"). In addition, everyone wants something different from the school (some are more interested in personal culture and tidiness, while others in the skills of independence and self-reliance). For this reason, the idea of abandoning QA and focusing on objective indicators (examination results) and external evaluations recurs periodically.

Unfortunately, the schools themselves are not firmly convinced of the usefulness of self-evaluations. Only a small percentage of schools know how to use self-evaluations as a performance improvement tool. The reason lies in the lack of simple tools for diagnosing quality, and dependable ways of solving typical (and atypical) problems. Many teachers still consider that it is not worth wasting time on meetings on such topics as "How to teach better?" or "Why students don't want student councils", or building project teams. The belief that "We are here to teach, and not to evaluate" is a common one. Add to this a perpetual sense of not having enough time and being overloaded by didactic work and the reporting they have to do – for teachers these are sufficient impediments to involvement in self-evaluation procedures. And for the same reasons, many of them have welcomed the directive of 2006.

So it is not strange that the second weakness of the debate is the fairly minimal participation in it of the schools themselves – directors and teachers. Many of them still treat school performance evaluations as a necessary evil, and not as a useful mechanism enabling more effective and satisfactory work.

At the same time, increasing significance is allocated to evaluating school performance quality on one single dimension – the results of the external examinations that the students sit. This indicator is objective, measurable and easily accessible and is beginning to be used as a measure of school performance and teacher competences. One forgets that it relates not so much to school performance quality, as to the "quality" of the students who attend the given school. Only a comparison of results year by year and an analysis of trends can yield any information concerning changes in the school's performance, and that only in the narrow aspect of preparing students for examinations.

To sum up, quality self-evaluation in Polish schools is still in its incubatory phase and there are many conditions that make its development difficult. This in turn may negatively influence the quality of school work.

1.2. Evaluation as an issue in teacher training

Evaluating school performance is still absent from teacher training curricula in colleges. Polish universities educate fine historians or biologists, but inadequately prepare teachers for the role of a teacher.

There are no courses on the subject of class management, modern teaching methods or educational skills. On-site teacher training is only marginally treated. At universities and teacher-training colleges the dominant view is still that the only valid evaluation is an external one, preferably severe as only such an evaluation can sufficiently motivate teachers to work harder. The teacher is to evaluate students; the director, in turn, teachers and, finally, state inspectors, the director. There is not much space here for self-evaluation or critical support from friends. Evaluating school performance is primarily the director's and inspector's problem, and not the teachers' responsibility – so why should one teach it in college?

Professional development courses deal with the issue of QA more frequently, but programmes dealing with quality management are usually attended by principals or administrators, and rarely chosen by "normal" teachers. After the directive of 2004 was published, postgraduate courses and management training courses of this kind were offered by many teacher-training colleges and universities. The risk is that now, since the Ministry of Education has undermined the importance of in-house QA systems, such courses will gradually cease to exist.

1.3. The use of evaluation results in school and the educational system

How are evaluation results used? Basing our opinion on fragmentary data we may state that in the case of external evaluations:

- the results are important for the school's director and often (especially if they are negative) have some effect on his or her career;
- teachers are informed about the results but do not always have any occasion to discuss them;
- students usually know nothing about evaluations carried out by the *Kuratorium* – they only see that "there are people walking about the school and sitting in on classes"; sometimes they are forewarned that there will be an inspection and that they should behave properly;
- parents are sometimes informed, albeit very briefly, unless the inspection is a reaction to a parental complaint or an accident occurring in the school, etc.;
- the results of the external evaluation become the basis for a report written by each *Kuratorium*, sent to the minister, regional authorities and local government bodies running the school.

In the case of self-evaluations for the purposes of QA projects, teachers, students and parents participate to a greater extent both during the diagnostic phase, as well as at the stage when conclusions are broadcast. In most schools a significant source of information about the school's problems and successes are opinion polls conducted among all the stakeholders – questionnaires, interviews and discussions on the topic of various areas of the school's work. The authenticity and significance of this process for the school's subsequent performance depends on the extent and manner in which teachers, students and parents are included in the process of working on the school development plan.

The voices of parents and students have a completely different standing when the school participates on a voluntary basis in the Learning Schools programme, or when it is applying for ISO certification or the EKO-TUR Quality School certification. In undertakings of this kind, the opinions of "clients" are considered the most important and are the point of departure for evaluating school performance, and building the development programme.

Representatives of the local authorities also often take part in discussion of the evaluation results. They are frequently interested in how "their" schools are working and which direction they should be taking. As an example, local government representatives – the mayor or president of the town, as well as district or regional representatives of the department of education – always participate in the evaluation panels organised within the Learning Schools programme. It is worth remembering that education often accounts for over half of local government expenditure; hence it is easy to understand the local authorities' interest.

The role of external experts and consultants is varied, but most often marginal. The school usually tries to deal with the task on its own, very often simply for financial or organisational reasons. Schools sometimes invite experts to help diagnose school problems or work out the evaluation tools. Some of them take part in training sessions or courses organised by universities, teacher training institutes, non-governmental organisations (NGOs) or private companies. Special computer programs are now available on the market which assist in the gathering of data on students and school performance.

However, it seems that due to a "genetic" flaw in the system of supervision, the help of specialists is more often treated as a means of fulfilling difficult requirements, and not as an opportunity to reflect on the school's problems and the methods of raising performance quality.

The situation is completely different when schools enter programmes on a voluntary basis, and when they have a longer period for evaluating quality and formulating a development plan. The schools see external experts as allies, not controllers, and are ready to divulge their real problems. All of the voluntary QA programmes mentioned above assume help for the school in diagnosing problem areas and developing corrective measures. In certain cases the schools (directors, school boards, task teams) share their experiences and examples of good practice with each other. Schools network to share thinking on how to solve the more typical school problems – this is happening for instance in the Learning Schools programme, which has developed various forms of co-operation between schools and also offers advice from consultants from Poland, Great Britain and the United States.

2. *The "Tool for Quality Assurance of Education for Democratic Citizenship in Schools"*

The tool is a very promising concept, both for evaluating a school with regard to its "democratic added value", and for planning activities that can increase this value. The tool not only indicates the areas of school life where EDC may explicitly or implicitly be present, but also gives examples of good practices in all of them. The idea of EDC being something more than a curriculum subject is worth promoting. Most Poles would agree that lessons in civics or political education are not sufficient preparation for young citizens – a large part of this job should still rest with parents, the media and politicians. And yet awareness that schools also transmit citizenship values and skills mainly through the everyday experience of students, teachers and parents, and not only during specific classes, is by no means common. Such principles as sharing responsibility, assuring transparency and accountability, or empowerment of all school stakeholders, are rarely connected with EDC.

The tool can also be treated as a gentle way of introducing QA to those schools that have no experience with such procedures, or for other reasons are reluctant to assess the processes and effects of their work.

2.1. Comprehensiveness and coherence

The tool is well constructed. Its structure is very clear and comprises all the necessary elements, including:

- the rationale for developing such an instrument – the gap between EDC policies and practice;
- explanation (and promotion) of QA principles and of self-evaluation, combined with development planning processes;
- a broad conceptual framework of EDC;
- an overview of QA as a system and a collaborative process, as opposed to an act of external control;
- the characteristics of school development planning and its stages;
- a strategy for using QA in evaluating and developing EDC in schools;
- a toolbox that can be of assistance to individual schools in self-evaluation and planning processes;
- the implications for the educational system, including policy measures at the level of the whole educational system.

The tool is conceived in such a way that it gives not only a theoretical background and conceptual framework, but also specific instruments and advice. It fits the general goal stated on page 15 of the publication: its objective is to provide those responsible for planning and carrying out EDC in formal education with principles, instruments, methodologies and options to agree on goals, evaluate their attainment, and improve EDC performance in schools and within the educational system as a whole (Bîrzea et al., 2005).

Part 2 of the tool entitled "What is EDC and what does it mean in schools" has – in my opinion – its own value as a concise and clearly stated definition of EDC as the overall quality of school life. Showing how the experiences of students can enhance or destroy citizenship virtues and skills is worth reiterating. In the Polish context, this section could even exist on its own – an attempt to summarise the tasks standing before both the school as a whole and its individual teachers, in a bid to eliminate or at least narrow the gap between democratic declarations and the real-life experience that school life provides.

I particularly value the catalogue on page 27 of learning situations in which EDC happens (even if their participants are not aware of it). Also instructive are the examples of knowledge, skills and values that the principal, teachers and governing bodies should strive to attain if the concepts of rights and responsibilities, participation and diversity are to be made real in a school and in the educational system as a whole. One can only ask why just these three general ideas have been chosen as the basic ones, and why – for example – empowerment, social justice or the common good are treated as less crucial. Maybe the list should be enlarged or it should be stated that these are only examples.

The chapter on the importance of QA is also enlightening, even for those who think they have already introduced this mechanism into their school. The list of characteristics of QA systems in school education should be printed and many copies distributed among Polish inspectors and school administrators as well as – even more importantly – among school directors and teachers. In Poland (and probably elsewhere), the notion of empowering schools to plan their own development, of creating simple, easy-to-use evaluative tools, of revising national and local in-service training arrangements still needs to be promoted. The graph illustrating the components of a QA system helps every reader to realise the complexity of the mechanism. It also provides an insight into the prospective difficulties it will meet with in Poland, namely the weaknesses of almost all of the elements of this structure of forces, and the lack of support we are now witnessing at the national policy level.

In my opinion the section of the tool devoted to development planning is the least revealing, especially in its opening paragraphs. However, the catalogue of core good practices may be useful for schools struggling with questions like: "We have gone through self-assessment. What can we do now? And do we really have to do anything more?". The stages of a planning cycle illustrate clearly why QA is an ongoing, never-ending story. This observation may be depressing to some, but it needs to be frequently reiterated. I also consider important the advice to focus – during the beginning stages – on priorities, rather than trying to improve everything at once.

Unrealistic goals will never be reached, and teachers, students and parents only become convinced that "school development planning" makes no sense whatsoever. I would risk a hypothesis – based on our experience with Polish schools participating in QA programmes – that two or three main goals might be enough for one school year. Even if a school decides to focus on one important aspect of school life, for example, assessment, all other areas of school life will start changing as a result. Students and parents will become involved, teachers will ponder whether assessment is transparent and just, and head teachers will have to change procedures concerning informing students (and parents) about the criteria of assessment and the possibilities of improving marks. Changing one aspect directly influences many other areas of school life.

Too many standards to be met at once is of course the type of mistake that the Polish Ministry of Education made when it published – albeit in good faith – the principles of internal quality management for schools (the directive of 2004). Four immense topics, 16 standards, several indicators and the a priori assumption that the school already has achievements in each of them, and knows how to proceed. Schools had no time to ponder what the directive was all about, to develop a QA system, organise topic teams, make an in-depth study of their problems, determine priorities, draw up a strategic plan, monitor achievements and reassess performance. The consequences of a law as unrealistic as this were logically ludicrous.

The chapter framework to evaluate EDC addresses the tool's central problem – "How to use the QA system to evaluate EDC in schools?". Considering that this strategic question only appears on page 55 of the book, which has 105 pages plus appendices, one might postulate shortening the first, introductory half of the publication and expanding the second. In my opinion, this might make the whole of the tool more useful. Chapters 5 and 6 are by far the most crucial to the goal set at the beginning of this endeavour: to provide educators with principles, instruments, methodologies and options to agree on goals, evaluate their attainment, and improve EDC performance in schools.

One of the most effective and promising aspects of the tool is the EDC indicators proposed by the authors. Here we come to real-life issues – we are offered six key indicators to help in evaluating EDC in three main areas of a school's operations: the curriculum, teaching and learning; the school ethos and climate; and management plus development. These indicators are unequal from the point of view of their generality – for example, the one concerning assessment is much more specific than the one dealing with school ethos, but maybe this is unavoidable.

It is clearly stated that these indicators reflect the judgment of the authors on the importance of specific school tasks and priorities. This choice is subjective and may on some points be questioned. For example, there is no clear mention of the content of citizenship education – is the kind of knowledge students will gain about democracy, its principles, procedures, problems and dilemmas really so self-evident or so unimportant? Of course, each country has its own national curriculum – some are very detailed, others extremely modest – but maybe it would be advisable to construct some "European core curriculum guidelines", obviously as a source of inspiration rather than obligation. Some attempts have already been made in this direction (the Council of Europe, Eurydice and other European Commission programmes, plus independent institutes), and it is rather a matter of consolidating approaches and documents and presenting them in a consistent way than starting work from the very beginning.

One could also point to the fact that the external world, that is the world beyond the walls of the classroom, is almost absent from this set – school is portrayed as an isolated entity, functioning apart from the real world with all its challenges. I would recommend making this connection stronger both in the indicators and sub-themes: the question is to what extent schools encourage students to get involved in social work, charity projects and key public issues at local, national and even global levels. I believe that if young citizens – pupils and students – do not become interested in and have access to public life and real-life problems, they can easily become discouraged from participating in civil society and political life when they become adults. If they are not given a chance to think how to make the world a better place now, they could become either cynical or helpless later.

This obviously does not mean that teenagers should be given full decision-making power. However, they should always be involved in public debate and be able to make their voice heard. Including this dimension in the tool would also inspire teachers to present pupils and students with more controversial public issues and encourage principals to allow for such activities as organising voting for students in parallel to national elections, conducting anti-corruption campaigns or consulting young people (and even conducting referenda in schools) on chosen public issues.

Finally, the indicators should be more precise – somewhat closer to the "sub-themes", which means that additional criteria of success or "sub-indicators" have to be formulated, if we want the tool to be operational and not just an awareness-raising device. Maybe descriptors and questions accompanying sub-themes can play this role, but in that case we should think of preparing a more complete set, not just some examples illustrating three chosen indicators (as in Table 5).

Nevertheless, in my opinion the evaluative framework for EDC is a very valuable instrument for anyone – policy makers, administrators, inspectors, local government officials, principals, teachers, students, parents and other members of society – who wants schools to become more democratic. From this perspective, the table on page 58 may be treated as a multi-purpose tool useful for diagnosis and planning in the area of EDC.

The section on school development planning for EDC seems to be that part of the book without which the whole project of QA of EDC is unlikely to be put into effect. It contains basic guidelines on how to make the tool work. The description of eight steps is consistent with the previous chapters – from the first step of building a culture of self-evaluation, through setting up an evaluation team, transforming indicators into evaluation issues, choosing evaluation methods, collecting and analysing the data, drawing conclusions, preparing and disseminating the report, to the final step of preparing a development strategy. The process, however, appears to be so long and complex that it can be discouraging – as it was for the teachers to whom we showed this material. They were afraid to start talking about it in their schools, as they were sure that other teachers would be reluctant to engage in such an ambitious project.

Of course, the authors offer some good advice in this respect – to begin with small goals, to set reachable targets – but it is hard to escape the fact that QA of EDC requires a lot of hard work and even sacrifice on the part of all school stakeholders. Perhaps it would be reasonable to prepare a two-step approach, based on the idea of pilot evaluations of classroom or school projects in EDC, as put forward on page 73. The EDC evaluation team could start as a smaller group and the goal would be more modest, making the whole endeavour less risky. This would also help to engage students and parents – who are usually more ready to get involved if the time frames are shorter. Having successfully negotiated a short-term pilot project, the school could engage in the complete QA of EDC procedure, with everyone in a better position to make it really work.

Tables 3, 4, 5 and 6 are the most operational component of the tool – only after reading them do we finally understand how it all can be done, what questions may be asked and what methods of evaluation might be used to find out answers. Unfortunately, these are all only introductory examples of questions and a list of descriptors that have to be translated into more practical ready-to-use instruments. For example, will a typical director or evaluation team know what clues to look for to check if the school policy on EDC is good or bad? I strongly doubt it. In the final version of the tool, some more hints would be helpful to make the work of the evaluation team easier and more predictable. I can already hear the voices of the critics saying that this would limit schools' creativity in inventing questions and methods of evaluation. Our experience proves, however, that teachers and students always show a great deal of inventiveness in adapting model questions or tools, ignoring some of them and searching for new ones – especially if they are encouraged to do so. The other option – purely leaving schools with examples – often turns out to be counterproductive, as elaborating them consumes the time and energy necessary for developing and implementing the plan itself.

The same suggestion concerns descriptions of a school's performance levels in the six areas corresponding to the indicators. It is always easier to start with a sample category that may or may not mirror the particular school's reality, but does give a clear idea of what criteria of success the school could use. Such a category does not have to be developed by experts – it is highly recommended that schools be asked to provide the materials, and then edit them to create a final version.

Figures 5 and 6 illustrate how evaluation results may be presented in a simple and comprehensible manner, and hung in a school corridor as a reminder of the steps that have to be taken to improve school performance in EDC. The first graph, however, has been turned "upside down" – one would prefer high levels to be higher than the low ones.

To sum up: the chapter on development needs to be refined and enlarged. Some additional examples and information could be drawn from other Council of Europe publications dealing with similar topics, such as *Democratic Governance of Schools* by Elisabeth Bäckman and Bernard Trafford, or other publications from the EDC/HRE Pack. Taken together and supporting each other, these books could become a tool kit, though some editorial work would be needed.

The last part of the tool contains recommendations for policy makers – which all sound convincing, but are extremely normative. It is hard to say what could be done if the educational authorities are not devoted to QA, EDC or both. Can then schools do anything at all?

2.2. Corresponding material in Poland

Polish schools have no direct procedure for diagnosing and improving education for democratic citizenship. The areas of school life encompassed by the tool are sometimes present in the QA instruments that particular schools use. For example, the principles and practice of assessing students are very often chosen as worth diagnosing, analysing and modifying, because of the lack of transparency or fairness in this area. This is an issue in many schools (probably not only in Poland), as students, parents and even the teachers themselves are usually dissatisfied with how assessment works. Sometimes debates of this kind lead to significant changes – such as the introduction of formative assessment. However, the practice of assessment is seldom considered an issue related to EDC – it is treated as pure assessment during maths or chemistry lessons.

Of course, in many schools students are encouraged to participate in some decision-making processes (although these are usually limited to marginal topics, such as when to organise a "school day"), and students' opinions about their role in school governance are collected. But again, this is rarely a planned and integrated effort to provide them with experience in the role of young citizens, or then to check whether they are satisfied, and to identify any other ideas for involvement they may have. Undertakings of this kind are usually an intuitive effort on the part of a director or teacher to find out what can be done in one or two isolated fields of school life, rather than part of a systemic approach to EDC. So – paradoxically – even if students are completing questionnaires about the school board or students' rights, this is usually done within a non-EDC framework.

It is worth noting that regulations concerning some aspects of EDC were included in the set of standards proposed by the Ministry of Education in the directive of 2004 (Ministerstwo Edukacji Narodowej, 2004). These for example included the institution's nurturing and preventive functions. The school/educational institution carries out educational and preventive programmes that, among other things, take into consideration students' developmental needs, universal values, patriotic and civic education, promoting respectful attitudes towards others and oneself, student self-governance, and the forms of psychological-pedagogical support offered. Students are encouraged to make an effort and work on their self-development, and their achievements are appreciated. Parents and all teachers are involved in the educational process, and the educational activities are homogeneous and congruous. Integrated educational and preventive measures are conducive to students respecting universal values.

And to take two examples of indicators suggested by the ministry:
- the school/educational institution's tuition, educational programmes and other activities promote respect for every human being, his or her intrinsic dignity, tolerance for diversity, justice and other universal values;
- relationships between teachers, students and parents are positive, and characterised by openness and mutual respect.

There are some schools in Poland that – in order to meet the criteria defined by this legislation – made an effort to find out how such standards were or could be put into effect. Unfortunately, there was not enough time to put any declarations into practice, and now, with the directive invalid, principals are holding their breath and waiting for new developments.

3. The tool as an instrument of school evaluation in Poland

Putting QA of EDC into practice could strengthen the changes taking place in the educational sector in Poland, among others:
- showing the value of authentic QA and self-evaluation;
- raising the quality of the education of young citizens;
- supporting the autonomy of schools and directors;
- overcoming the professional isolation of teachers through the teamwork it propounds;
- empowering all school stakeholders.

As I wrote earlier, however, the current political situation may delay, hinder or completely block the introduction of QA of EDC into schools. Nevertheless, we should not lose hope and need to search for schools or institutions that could attempt to implement the project at least on a small-scale basis, as a pilot study or "QA of EDC laboratory", then verify and develop it, to be able to teach the procedure to others in the future.

3.1. Conditions for using the tool in schools

We are now witnesses to the dynamics of an encounter between contradictory forces – on the one hand, the modernisation of schools and education, and on the other, reactionary trends expressing themselves in the desire (or nostalgia) for central government, limiting the autonomy of the school and the diversity of its projects and teaching styles, an authoritarian style of work with students, and a distrust of teacher and student responsibility or self-evaluation. There are factors that favour, as well as those that hinder, the introduction of the tool into schools, both of which will be mentioned below.

3.1.1. Circumstances that might promote the use of the tool

In general it can be stated that the following circumstances might promote use of the tool:
- emerging future political changes in the field of education leading to further democratisation of the school;
- maintaining decentralised governance in the educational sector, protecting the autonomy of schools and the director's position;
- changing the attitude of the *Kuratoria* and inspectors, abandoning external control for greater support of the school's development and increasing the status of self-evaluation;
- increasing the significance of civic education, broadly understood, at different levels of education; legitimising it in curricula through appropriate legislation;

- preparing directors and teachers sufficiently to use the QA procedure in general, and specifically QA of EDC;
- empowering students and their parents in everyday school life, giving them effective encouragement so that they can become involved in school matters;
- developing existing formal and informal structures that can enhance student and parent participation, for example, via school boards, parental boards, student councils, projects in civic education such as school elections, community projects, etc.;
- curing or alleviating some of the inherent problems of Polish education: schools that are too large, authoritarian traditions, insufficient training of teachers in establishing good relations with students, solving conflicts, supporting students with specific educational deficits, etc.

The introduction of QA of EDC will be supported by concrete undertakings that schools, NGOs and institutions supporting schools can engage in:
- offering training courses in the use of the tool, including online training (e-learning);
- running support groups for teachers and schools, and maybe even students, who decide to introduce the tool in their establishments;
- publishing a Polish language version of the tool, adapted to conditions in Poland, and additional material useful for its implementation;
- giving NGOs operating in the educational sector access to the tool, so that – independently of ministerial policy concerning QA and EDC – schools may use it on a purely voluntary basis;
- including debate about the procedure into the Quality Forum movement co-ordinated by the British Council;
- liaising with other undertakings to encourage the introduction of QA of EDC, such as creating national – or better yet, European – networks or associations of schools that use the tool.

In the next parts of this paper, I will develop the ideas and proposals suggested above.

3.1.2. Prospective difficulties and obstacles

Two types of prospective difficulties may be identified – the current educational policy, and long-term changes of an institutional and even cultural nature. We cannot count on the current ministerial authorities abandoning their approach. Rather, we may fear the introduction of successive legislation that will not serve QA of EDC, and an intensification of the aura of aversion surrounding the autonomy of teachers, directors and schools. The permanence of these negative factors is at the same time related to developments in the political scene in Poland, which is in turn rather unstable.

A second set of factors is related to processes with a longer time frame – institutional changes, above all changes in the attitudes of teachers and students, or even in the attitudes of society as a whole. Such changes will be helped along by the almost universal awareness of the importance of education for the future of young people and the whole country, and also by an opening up to European values. These will follow on the heels of progressive integration, the diffusion of European standards, both in the area of education, such as work culture and the principles of accountability applied to non-business settings. We can also assume that the slow but steady evolution in the identity of teachers over the past decade – from "imparters" of knowledge into "coaches" – will not be stopped. It is worth reminding ourselves that thousands of Polish teachers are now participating in European projects, thousands of students are studying at European universities, and hundreds of thousands of young people are working in Great Britain, Ireland, Sweden, the Netherlands, Spain and Portugal.

One more obstacle needs to be confronted. The most controversial aspect of the tool in our national context is now – paradoxically – EDC as its main focus. The language the Minister for Education and his deputy use reflects values that are conflicting, if not downright irreconcilable, with democratic values. The ministry emphasises obedience, order and tighter control, isolating students whose behaviour does not fit into the canon of correctness as defined by the categories of a traditional and authoritarian school. He has openly stated that there is no place for democracy in school: "Democracy is good for a society where adult citizens take responsible decisions. In a school it would mean paidocratia" (Portal Olsztyn, 2006).

A misinterpretation of Catholicism resulting in a questioning of Darwin's Theory of Evolution threatens to ridicule the entire Polish educational system. Despite objections on the part of public opinion and in scientific circles, examples of conforming behaviour have begun to emerge in certain schools – for example, in a Łódź high school, the director banned the hanging on the school walls of a poster illustrating the evolution of mankind from anthropoid ape to homo sapiens. The Deputy Minister, when asked whether there is some place for tolerance of different outlooks, stated: "The world has long survived without tolerance and will manage to go on without it" (Orzechowski, 2006).

In such an atmosphere, directors and teachers may be afraid to participate in activities that would make their school more democratic. There are rumours that in some schools, student councils that seemed too independent were dismissed and that "order and control" rhetoric is becoming more popular among many teachers and parents. However, it is difficult to assess the possible scope of such fears and the resultant conformism, as well as the extent to which the ministry will be able to build an effective system of controlling schools. Fortunately, in Poland the law gives directors significant autonomy, thanks to which they can continue to base their decisions on democratic and liberal values, especially as the position of the latter in the country is still strong.

3.1.3. Parts of the tool with particular applicability

It is difficult to say which parts of the tool are particularly applicable – to some extent it has been conceived as a coherent instrument. Of course, it can be deconstructed into smaller parts, which can also be useful. As already mentioned, the section concerning what EDC means in schools can be treated separately as awareness-raising material. The framework for evaluating EDC, combined with quality indicators, constitutes the real core of the instrument for checking how well a given school is doing in chosen areas. The section on planning school development in the area of EDC is a concise guide for those principals and schools who are ready to act and do not have to be persuaded of the value of QA and EDC.

3.1.4. Target groups of the tool

At present neither the ministry nor the educational supervisory system can be regarded as being interested in such an endeavour for reasons already explained. In the Polish context, school principals and teachers are the most promising targets, as they have the authority to introduce the tool without requiring official approval. In particular, schools where other QA systems are already in place might be ready to use it.

Teachers of citizenship education and teachers who are (or were in the past) responsible for supporting student councils and student civic projects can be regarded as potential leaders of the movement. There is one more target group – teacher counsellors working in regional and local in-service teacher-training centres, who have already been involved as trainers or participants in QA and/or EDC training programmes.

And last, but not least – the pupils themselves. In many cases they are the ones who really want to change their school into a more democratic and empowering place, and they have an acute understanding of its many weak points. There are numerous student councils which – if they are allowed to, are properly trained (maybe partially over the Internet) and supported – might become a powerful force for QA of EDC. Pupils cannot, however, be encouraged to use the tool without at least some approval and commitment from the principal and teachers – otherwise their initiative might be regarded as an anti-school action.

It is also worth taking note of NGOs active in the fields of citizenship education and quality in education as potential targets of this initiative – the Centre for Citizenship Education and the Polish Association of Directors and Managers in Education can, for example, be regarded as its natural allies. They both have long-standing relations with thousands of schools and principals and experience in educational projects.

3.2. Systemic conditions for using the tool

The preparation and execution of a "national plan of QA of EDC" does not seem at the present moment to be feasible. There is no chance of any policy frameworks or legislation favourable to QA and QA of EDC being passed. No official structures can be set up at present, and the existing ones may even be reformed in the opposite direction. Training policies and programmes have to be developed behind the walls of official governmental institutions, at least for the time being. The same refers to the networking of practitioners or the dissemination of the tool in schools.

There are, however, also some positive factors – the relative autonomy of Polish schools, the high degree of autonomy of their principals, the common sense of many teachers, pupils and their parents, the existence of independent educational organisations, and seventeen years of experience in introducing schools to different aspects of democracy. It has to be pointed out that exchanges and co-operation at the European level are ongoing and may support EDC in schools.

3.2.1. Correspondence of the tool and the system of quality assurance and evaluation

To some extent the tool is consistent with the goals of the QA system that has been operating in Polish schools since 2004. However, as previously said, this self-evaluation procedure was only in force for a short while, and was abolished by the new law. Considering the lack of clarity surrounding the future shape of the supervisory practice, it is difficult to judge right now the extent to which the tool will be reconcilable with the new guidelines for evaluating schools. Several variants are possible.

In the first, optimistic scenario, as the rigid principles of reporting are "loosened", schools will be able to define their priorities and the areas they would like to subject to closer scrutiny, and will have more time to improve their work. This would let directors and teachers choose EDC as a topic worth investigating and possibly shaping up, which might open the door to using the tool, especially in those school communities that believe in the desirability of democratic values, principles and procedures.

The second variant is less optimistic. With the self-evaluation requirement slackened, the school loses its motivation to implement the procedure in any area, and will return to its previous proven and trustworthy practices, with no need for teams reflecting upon processes or on the school's performance. Everyone will forget that there were ever any standards or ideas for assuring quality, and inspectors will audit schools on the basis of very general guidelines and exam scores.

Naturally there is also a third alternative – the new directive will only remain in force for a short while (a year or two), until the next change of power at the ministry. All in all, it would be better for this chapter if it were written by a soothsayer than an expert.

3.2.2. Preparation of teachers to work with the tool

As has already been mentioned, QA does not constitute part of a typical teacher-training curriculum, neither at pedagogical institutes nor during in-service teacher training. A serious training and counselling programme would be required to prepare teachers to use the tool. In our experience as an institution that has been training teachers for similar QA systems, teachers need a relatively long training period and sustained support to be able to introduce QA practice in the workplace, especially as this is not a task to embark on single-handed. A critical mass of teachers in a school have to devote themselves to the project and to be educated in the procedure, if its implementation is not to be a matter of pure fiction. It is also indispensable to start with the school principal – without his or her personal commitment and professional skills, nothing can be attained. As I have already stated, it is the directors who had the greatest chance of being trained or at least informed of QA procedures in connection with the 2004 law. All training should be synchronised with real-life school practices, so that participants soon have a chance to try out what they have just learnt at the course – to avoid engaging in a useless "training for training's sake" activity.

In the case of Poland, it is necessary to publish a translated version of the materials – as a rule only teachers of English are familiar with this language (and maybe also German language specialists). The good news is that the National In-service Teacher Training Centre has already translated the tool and the Polish version needs only some editorial work. A year ago, prior to the radical changes in political climate, the centre and the CCE jointly decided that the CoE initiative and publication might constitute valuable material for Poland's education system. We even organised two meetings of co-ordinators and teachers, active participants in the European Year of Citizenship through Education, to share this idea with them, and together think of ways of introducing the tool into the schools. They were all convinced of the utility of the instrument, but somewhat sceptical about the possibility of implementing it on a large scale, due to all the pressures that directors and teachers were victims of at the time – namely, external exams and the introduction of the 2004 QA system.

In order to implement the instrument, directors and teachers need more precise examples of school regulations, procedures and practices that can foster EDC. All publications from the EDC Pack elaborated by the Council of Europe can be useful in this respect – the "Tool on Teacher Training for EDC and HRE" and the "Tool on Key Issues for EDC policies" were presented to Polish educators and received positive comments. In addition, *Democratic Governance of Schools* (Council of Europe, 2007), a book addressed to principals, looks as if it could complement the tool well, as it gives a good representation of the different ways in which a director may act, and how this factor contributes to or hampers the citizenship experience not only of the students, but also of their parents and teachers.

Perhaps some sort of alignment is necessary, as the key areas are defined in a different way; however, connecting both approaches seems relatively easy. *Democratic Governance of Schools* presents detailed rubrics for school self-assessment, as well as a section with tips for principals on how to handle particular real-life problems. This advice corresponds to the different levels of democratic governance in the school, and therefore follows a three-step model. Such a strategy, showing the variety of possible attitudes and behaviours, gives us a chance to understand how many alternative versions of school reality exist and what their consequences for EDC could be.

The chapter of the book entitled "Democratic governance: patterns and common features" covers those aspects of school life that everyone using the tool should also be concerned with. These include both structural settings such as decentralisation of authority in education, goals not instructions as governing methods, teacher empowerment through formal committees or interest groups, student empowerment; and patterns of informal school life such as trust as a dominant attitude, active participation encouraged and revised, school newspapers, students involved in mediation and counselling, etc.

A very inspiring case study of a school from Helsinki exemplifies the kind of additional materials that might facilitate the use of different QA and EDC tools. Polish teachers like to be offered not only enlightened ideas of how school life should look like, but also practical tips and alternative solutions from among which they can choose. I understand that finding numerous examples of schools is not a simple matter, but even 10 case studies, possibly also illustrating the changes introduced as an effect of QA of EDC, would make a difference. Such examples could also be developed in the course of this initiative – if the CoE decides to endorse it, one of the possible results could be a catalogue of school cases.

There are of course other materials that might be helpful, such as:
- checklists for diagnosing how the school is doing in different areas of EDC, preferably adapted to the three levels of education and to different types of schools;
- materials available online – practices, tips, tools and examples from other schools;
- a website devoted to QA of EDC with links to schools and other institutions participating in this movement;
- a DVD or video material showing the possible forms that EDC can take in different countries and different types of school.

One of the ways of supporting schools is by providing them with an e-learning course for the principal and teacher team on how to implement the tool – the consecutive modules should be presented some time ahead of the actual activity taking place in the school (for example, a week or a month before), so that the course is closely aligned with the eight steps of QA of EDC.

3.2.3. Other possible facilitators

As far as incentives are concerned, there are various possibilities. However, it is not clear if these can effectively motivate schools and teachers trying to introduce

QA of EDC in a setting hostile to this idea. Here are some potential incentives, albeit with no guarantee of effectiveness:

- diplomas, both national and European, for teachers and principals participating in the programme (pilot programme?);
- "EDC Quality Badge". The QA of EDC badge could be awarded to schools implementing the tool, maybe in a two-step approach – a silver badge for those school units that have installed the procedures, and a golden one for those that have undergone some sort of verification (such as by an inter-school commission?);
- joint European projects. A European network of schools with QA of EDC, including seminars for school directors and QA teams, study visits and student leader meetings.

The tool will need some adaptation to the Polish context, but the changes do not seem to be fundamental or urgent – maybe they can be planned as one of the results of the pilot programme. For example, the passage describing the "responsiveness" of the school leadership has to be redefined in order to help schools to be "irresponsive" to policies that undermine EDC in school life. "Management of resources" as a collective and negotiated process is probably the sub-theme that should be reduced if we do not want the school leadership to get into trouble. Many decisions about the use of resources are made behind closed doors, and it would be a revolutionary idea to open them without prior preparation.

It is obvious that the chances of introducing the QA of EDC procedure depend to a large extent on the kind of school we are dealing with. Some factors will influence its probability: the size of the school, the level of education, the type of setting (urban, small town, rural), school culture (traditional versus modern) and kind of body running the school (public versus non-public).

It is evident that the tool will be easier to introduce in smaller units than in large ones, where there are hundreds of students and the possibility of building personal relations is non-existent. As far as the level of education is concerned, primary and middle schools look more promising. High schools are usually much more focused on preparing students for their final examinations than for democratic citizenship; however, there are probably many places where regardless of this enormous exam pressure, one could find school communities eager to work on EDC improvement. Technical and vocational schools seem to be the least inclined to engage in such projects.

It goes without saying that there is less place for joint decision making or collaborative efforts in schools where traditional culture is cherished. Although non-public schools offer more chances for QA of EDC, public ones ought not to be excluded, as they constitute the mainstream of Polish education. And finally, the schools where the principal is open to both the QA concept and the need for better EDC are the best partners in this initiative. Their commitment is unquestionably the most important factor here.

And one more remark – funding might be an important factor facilitating introduction of the tool. Financial means will be necessary to train trainers, prepare evaluation teams, counsel individual schools and to co-ordinate the whole project.

4. Ideas for the implementation process

At present, the implementation of the tool in Polish schools could be severely hampered by the hostile political climate and administrative environment. Nevertheless, some steps can be taken in order to prepare for more supportive conditions. Here are our preliminary ideas:
- identifying the institution that will co-ordinate the project in Poland (for example, the CCE or another NGO active in education);
- informing about the initiative in teacher and student-targeted media, and – if possible – in other places willing to co-operate;
- printing a leaflet promoting the project and distributing it in regional and local in-service teacher-training centres and NGOs;
- e-mailing schools already involved in QA and/or EDC initiatives (such as Learning Schools, Schools with Class, schools participating in the ELOS project, Bridges across Boundaries and other European networks);
- recruiting and preparing teacher trainers – facilitators of the implementation process (regional co-ordinators of EYCE and Learning Schools trainers should be approached);
- identifying 15-25 schools willing to participate in a pilot project: Laboratory of QA of EDC in co-operation with other European schools;
- starting a website with materials on QA of EDC, possibly preparing an e-learning pilot course and its moderators (two to four people);
- conducting preliminary training courses for principals and team leaders of QA of EDC;
- identifying the needs of the schools, constructing specific materials and workshops for problematic areas;
- supporting the schools through e-learning courses and seminars/ workshops;
- refining the Polish version of the tool and supplementing it with auxiliary materials;
- fund-raising for a larger-scale programme, in which the directors and teachers from the "laboratory schools" could serve as multipliers and experts;
- introducing the philosophy and practices of QA of EDC in all schools willing to join the project – hopefully already in a less hostile political environment.

4.1. How to make working with the tool valuable for schools

This question refers to the greatest obstacle in the implementation process in the case of Poland. Schools will have to "swim against the stream", as neither QA nor EDC are regarded as valuable by the ministerial and administrative authorities. On the contrary – both ideas may be even associated with the "Do what you like" approach to school governance that is openly criticised by the minister.

It can only be hoped that bodies running the school (both local governments and other "owners" of the schools), independent of the ministry, will in some places (if not everywhere) support this initiative. Incentives mentioned before, such as diplomas or quality badges, might also help teachers and schools take part in a "pilot" or "large-scale" programme of introducing QA of EDC. The European dimension of the project – seminars, networking, study visits – will certainly be seen as an extra source of motivation for joining the movement.

4.2. How to integrate the tool into international partnerships

This initiative has a very high potential for international co-operation, as it allows directors and teachers from different countries to overcome specific national contexts, and to look for the common core principles of education for democratic citizenship and of a democratic school. Such an approach is fully justified when it refers to member states of the Council of Europe, all of which have declared their commitment to the basic tenets of constitutional democracy and human rights, on which EDC is also founded.

The tool can be integrated into some of the existing programmes that Polish schools and institutions are involved in. One of them is ELOS: Europe as a Learning Environment in Schools funded by the European Commission, where at least some parts of the procedure and underlying philosophy could be incorporated. The QA of EDC dimension could also be introduced in Socrates/Comenius-type partnerships and exchanges.

The tool can act as a potential platform of discussion and co-operation between international governmental organisations and/or NGOs from Europe and other parts of the world – for example, Civitas International, with 100 members from all continents, may be interested in a joint project.

4.3. Alternative scenarios for working with the tool

The implementation plan presented above may prove to be unrealistic in the current systemic circumstances for two main reasons. First, because of political and administrative obstacles and, second, because many schools, directors and teachers are disappointed with recently introduced QA procedures, and – what is even more important – feel under strong pressure owing to the system of national examinations.

There are, however, other possibilities of working with the tool, waiting for a more convenient moment for all schools to develop a full-fledged plan for QA of EDC. Some parts can be incorporated into other initiatives. The following examples may be mentioned:

- starting on an awareness-raising campaign in the mass media, on educational websites and in the professional press;
- presenting the QA of EDC approach during conferences for school principals, and encouraging them to apply chosen aspects of the tool in their schools;
- inviting young school leaders and student councils to use parts of the tool to diagnose the situation in their school and to work out a plan for improvement;
- including the tool in pre-service and in-service education programmes for civics teachers;
- training local educational officials in basic aspects of EDC;
- conducting scientific research on EDC, then publishing the results and starting a debate on the strengths and weaknesses of Polish schools in this respect.

These alternative scenarios have one more advantage: they can be used simultaneously with the one envisaged previously. Different bodies may become part of the national but unofficial movement for QA of EDC. The survival strategy for QA and EDC requires all the possibilities to be tried out.

References

Bîrzea, C.; Cecchini, M.; Harrison, C.; Krek, J.; Spajic-Vrkas, V. (2005). "Tool for Quality Assurance of Education for Democratic Citizenship in Schools", Paris: UNESCO, Council of Europe, Centre for Educational Policy Studies.

British Council (2004). Quality Forum, www.britishcouncil.org.

Centrum Edukacji Obywatelskiej (CEO) (2006a). *Pomysły dobrej praktyki*. Retrieved on 3 October 2006, from www.ceo.org.pl/portal/pomysly_sus.

Centrum Edukacji Obywatelskiej (CEO) (2006b). *Szkoła ucząca się*. Retrieved on 3 October 2006, from www.ceo.org.pl/portal/sus.

Council of Europe (2007). *Democratic Governance of Schools,* Strasbourg: Council of Europe Publishing.

Hörner, W.; Döbert, H.; von Kopp, B.; Mitter, W. (2007). *The Education Systems of Europe*, Dordrecht: Springer.

Kuratorium Gdańskie (2005). *Pomorskie Certyfikaty Jakości*, Gdańsk. Retrieved on 3 October 2006, from www.kuratorium.gda.pl/index.php?c=72&d=128.

MacBeath, J. et al. (2000). *Self-evaluation in European Schools. A history of Change*, Routledge Taylor and Francis Group.

Ministerstwo Edukacji Narodowej (2004). Rozporządzenie Ministra Edukacji Narodowej i Sportu z dnia 23 kwietnia 2004 r. w sprawie szczegółowych zasad sprawowania nadzoru pedagogicznego. Retrieved on 3 October 2006, from www.men.gov.pl/prawo/wszystkie/rozp_288.php.

Ministerstwo Edukacji Narodowej (2005). *Plan Operacyjny "Wykształcenie i kompetencje". Strategia rozwoju edukacji na lata 2007-2013*, Warsaw. Retrieved on 3 October 2006, from www.men.gov.pl/oswiata/biezace/strategia_2007_2013.pdf.

Ministerstwo Edukacji Narodowej (2006). Rozporządzenie Ministra Edukacji Narodowej z dnia 15 grudnia 2006 r. w sprawie szczegółowych zasad sprawowania nadzoru pedagogicznego. Retrieved on 27 December 2006, from http://isip.sejm.gov.pl/servlet/Search?todo=file&id=WDU20062351703&type=2&name=D20061703.pdf.

Ministerstwo Rozwoju Regionalnego (2006). Program Operacyjny "Kapitał Ludzki". Narodowe Strategiczne Ramy Odniesienia, Warsaw.

Nowacki, J. (2006). "Mierzenie przeciętności", *Kierowanie Szkołą*, No. 9 (97).

O'Brien, P. and Paczynski, W. (2006). *Poland's Education and Training: Boosting and Adapting Human Capital*, OECD. Retrieved on 3 October 2006, from www.olis.oecd.org/olis/2006doc.nsf/43bb6130e5e86e5fc12569fa005d004c/7aba6dd8019b46e7c12571a3003c9834/$FILE/JT03211668.DOC.

Ogólnopolskie Stowarzyszenie Kadry Kierowniczej Oświaty (2005). Retrieved on 27 December 2006, from http://oskko.edu.pl/oskko/inicjatywyoskko.html.

Organizacja Nadzoru Pedagogicznego w SP w Rososze (2005). Retrieved on 3 October 2006, from www.klub.oficynamm.pl/publikacje/procedury.doc.

Orzechowski, M. (2006). Interview with the Deputy Minister by Aleksandra Pezda. Retrieved on 3 October 2006, from http://serwisy.gazeta.pl/wyborcza/1,34513,3684136.html.

Portal Olsztyn (2006). "Giertych spotkał się z nauczycielami". Retreived on 10 December 2006, from http://agencjaitp.pl/olsztyn_5554.html.

Trojan, E. (2006). "Jak badać i podnosić jakość placówki oświatowej", *Kierowanie Szkołą*, No. 7 (95). Retrieved on 3 October 2006, from http://scholaris.pl/Portal?secId=2M7N531B6A78JOT05I408780&refId.

Russian Federation

Galina Kovalyova and Elena Rutkovskaia

Introduction: the school system in the Russian Federation

Under the current Law on Education passed in 1992, the Russian educational system has become more decentralised in its decision making and funding. According to the Law on Education, the state guarantees citizens of the Russian Federation free general education and, on a competitive basis, free vocational education at state and municipal educational institutions.

The Law on Education gives considerable autonomy and responsibility to schools. According to the law, the main documents regulating school instruction include the education standards (the minimum content of education to be taught in class and the requirements for student achievement) and the programme of study.

The sources of financing for educational institutions are determined by their organisational legal forms: state (municipal and departmental) and non-state (private and religious). Approximately 99% of all primary, basic and secondary schools in Russia are state-municipal (60 771 out of 61 497 in the 2005/06 school year), meaning that the municipal budget is the main source of financing, with many decisions made at the regional level.

Current responsibilities of the federal education authorities include:
– making federal policy in the field of education and implementing it throughout the country;
– developing the legislative basis for the functioning of the educational system;
– establishing the federal component of the state educational standards;
– elaborating model curricula as well as model programmes of study for different school subjects on the basis of state educational standards (federal components);
– organising the publication of textbooks and supplementary literature for schools.

The educational programme at an educational institution is determined independently by the curriculum, the annual calendar study plan, and the timetable of classes developed and approved by the institution. The state, management bodies and local government bodies do not have the right to change the curriculum or study schedule of an educational institution once they have been approved, except for cases stipulated by the Russian legislature.

The tendency towards increasing variability of education can be illustrated by the growing number of textbooks for school subjects by different authors.

Since 2000 the Russian Government has begun to develop a new educational reform programme with the main directions as follows: modernising the structure and content of general education, raising the quality of education, providing equal access to education, developing effective mechanisms for transmitting social requests to the educational system, and broadening public participation in managing education.

The state system of education includes preschool education, general secondary education, secondary vocational training, higher education, postgraduate education and improvement of professional skills, and in-service training and retraining.

General secondary education, the core of the Russian education system, includes three stages: primary education (grades 1 to 4), basic or lower secondary (grades 5 to 9), and secondary (completed) or upper-secondary (grades 10 and 11). Basic general education is compulsory according to the constitution. The structure of the general education system is provided in Diagram 1.

Primary education may be provided by primary schools, by basic schools that include the primary stage, and by secondary education institutions that include all three stages.

In the 2005/06 school year total enrolment in the 60 558 general education institutions, which can comprise one, two or all three of the stages, stood at 15.07 million students and about 1.5 million teachers. These general education institutions included general schools, schools specialising in teaching specific subjects, gymnasiums and lyceums.

Urban schools make up only 33.4% of all general schools, but over 70% of all students study at them. Generally, rural schools are small with classes of less than five pupils. There are about 65 000 classes of this kind.

The system of schools with native language tuition (so-called "national schools") provides citizens with an education in their native language. In the 2005/06 school year, 3 091 general education institutions conducted lessons in 28 languages for a total of 201 732 students. In addition, there are 2 906 schools where at least one native language of 79 different ethnic groups is studied as a separate discipline.

A parallel non-state educational system is being created with the support of the Ministry of Education and Science. In 2005 non-state general education institutions comprised 1.2% of schools and catered to a mere 0.5% of students.

The general secondary education curriculum has three components: federal, ethno-regional and institutional. The federal component ensures the unity of general education in the country and contains the part of educational content that includes global and national values in school programmes of study. These core subjects are Russian language (as a state language), mathematics, IT, physics, astronomy and chemistry.

Diagram 1: Structure of the Russian education system

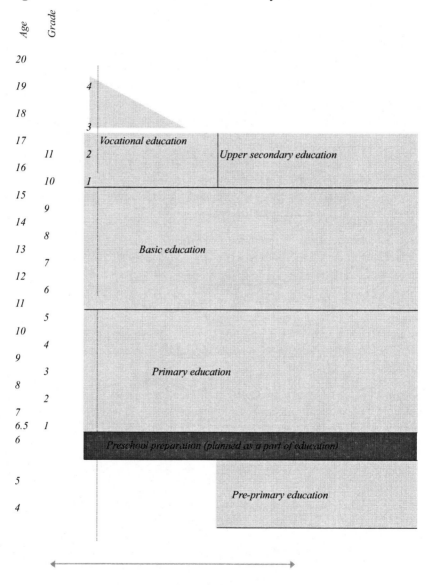

100% of age cohort

The ethno-regional component ensures that the specific interests and needs of people from different parts of the country are met. It contains educational content with ethnic and regional distinguishing features, such as the respective native language and literature, history and regional geography. Some fields of subject matter or subjects are presented both in federal and ethno-regional components, such as history, social studies, the arts, biology, physical education and technology.

The institutional or school-based component, which covers both compulsory and optional studies, emphasises the specific features of the educational institution and promotes the development of school activities.

The general education curriculum includes the following educational areas:
- philology (Russian language as the state language, Russian language as the mother tongue, literature and foreign languages);
- mathematics;
- social studies (social studies, history and geography);
- science (biology, physics, astronomy and chemistry);
- arts (fine arts, music);
- technology;
- physical education.

1. School evaluation in Russia

1.1. Modes of school evaluation

School evaluation in Russia is conducted in accordance with the Law on Education, the regulations on the state (summative) Attestation of Graduates of Grades 9 and 11 (12) of General Education Institutions of the Russian Federation (2003), and the document about the procedure of attestation and accreditation of educational institutions (1998).

Attestation is the main form of state and public control of the quality of education in schools. The goal of school attestation according to the Law on Education as external evaluation is to establish that the content, level and quality of students' achievement at a school correspond to the state's educational standards. The main principles of attestation are openness, competency and following the norms of pedagogical ethics. The main criterion for a school to receive its attestation is a positive summative assessment for no less than half its graduates during the three-year period before attestation. During and after the process of attestation, a school may receive help in different areas if needed.

School attestation is conducted by the regional education authorities or the special regional attestation service. All schools have to pass through the attestation procedure every five years. To conduct attestation at a school, a special attestation committee is organised for every school under attestation.

According to the established rules, any school under attestation in the country has to submit the following documents to the committee: an application form for attestation, all official school documents (the school charter, licence for educational activities, etc.), the school curriculum, the results of students' attestation (the results of the summative assessment of its graduates) for the last three years, and supplementary material about the school's activities in different areas (on a voluntary basis). Sometimes the attestation committee conducts some tests to assess the level of students' achievement in different subjects at the end of primary, basic and secondary school. Tests are administered anonymously because individual students' results are not analysed.

Any region in the country can, on the basis of the federal regulations on school attestation, develop its own model, content, instruments and procedure of attestation. These regional attestation models may include only the compulsory part of the federal documents or add to it evaluation of the upbringing process and the context of school life.

As an example, let us consider the content and the procedure of school attestation as used in one region in Russia, Rostov *oblast*, which has rich experience in school evaluation (Sbornik, 2005).

Its school attestation process includes five main steps:
- preparation for attestation. Studying school materials and documents describing school work for three to five years;
- analysis and evaluation of the main areas of school work at school;
- summarising of all attestation activities and preparation of the report;
- discussion of the report at school;
- dissemination of the report to other schools.

Before the attestation committee comes to a school, the school administration must complete a special information card and submit it to the attestation committee. The committee will analyse this information before visiting the school. The information card contains the following:

Information card of school

1. General information about the school (school charter, address, license, etc.);

2. Conditions of school functioning:

2.1. Structure of school (stages of the school including primary, basic or secondary);

2.2. Contingent of students (number of classes and students, profiles of classes, etc.);

2.3. Organisation of the educational process (duration of the school year, school week, lessons, intervals, etc.);

3. Content of the educational process:

3.1. School curriculum (the proportion of federal, regional and school components, student/teacher load, etc.);

3.2. Syllabus used at the school (typical, adaptive, experimental, etc.);

3.3. Forms and methods of learning (in classes, by correspondence, at home, etc.);

3.4. Profiles of learning (humanitarian, technical, natural sciences, economics, juridical, physics/mathematics, etc.);

3.5. Realisation of innovative programmes and technologies (names of programmes, names of classes and duration of implementation, etc.);

3.6. System of additional educational services (relationship with the community, types of additional educational services, number of students involved, etc.);

3.7. System for the upbringing of students (conditions/number of clubs and students' involvement, Olympiads, competitions, festivals, etc.; work with parents, number of cases of legal violations, etc.);

4. Conditions of provision of the educational process:

4.1. Scientific, methodological and instructional materials used at school (materials developed by teachers, teachers' participation in in-service training, experimental work, etc.);

4.2. Staff (educational level, qualifications, participation in in-service training, etc.);

4.3. School management (state-community forms of management, student self-government, etc.);

4.4. IT and technological provision (number of computers and their use, computer software, scanners, printers, fax machines, copy machines, TV sets, video recorders, library facilities, etc.);

4.5. Materials and technical facilities (school buildings, school yard, space, learning equipment, cars/vans, buses, etc.);

4.6. Medical and social conditions of the school (illness statistics, injury statistics, information about involvement in different physical education groups, etc.);

4.7. Legislative provision (a list of all official documents at different levels);

5. Data about graduate results for the last three years:

5.1. Results of the summative attestation of graduates of grades 9 and 11 (12) (data for each year, which includes the number of students attested and number of students at advanced level);

5.2. Results of participation in Olympiads (number of students participating in Olympiads and awards, list of subjects and level of Olympiads (school, city, region, federal and international);

5.3. Information about the number of school graduates accepted by universities, colleges or professional schools.

When an attestation committee comes to a school, it analyses the following areas:

1. School management and administration: the school council (members, planning of work, role of the council for developing democratisation among teachers and student collectives, school assembly, etc.); school planning and internal analysis of school work; work of the principal and other school management staff; the content of work with teachers; studying and implementation of educational research results and experience of other schools; work with young teachers; attestation of teachers' work, necessary help and retraining, etc.

2. The state of the learning-upbringing process, the use of innovative practices and technology: the level of intensification of the learning process (methods of learning), stimulation of cognitive activities, development of creativity and self-learning strategies, effective use of instructional time, homework, etc.; the democratisation of the learning-upbringing process, co-operative education, development of students' personality, the relationship between teachers and students, etc.; the humanisation of the learning-upbringing process, creating conditions for realising the students' abilities and interests, motivation to learn, development of cognitive activities and interests, personal development on the basis of common human values, etc.; the use of ICT in learning within classes and out-of-class activities; assessment of students (quality of achievements), coverage of the curriculum and programmes of study; development of creative activities, strategies for self-learning, learning skills; conducting practical work, laboratory work and investigations, level of equipment, etc.; and the professional orientation of students.

3. Extra-curricular activities: students' self-government activities; clubs, school museums, student magazines, etc.; scientific research with students; various out-of-school activities in the community, sports activities (clubs, competitions, Olympiads, tourism, etc.); music, arts, dancing, school theatre, etc.; technologically creative activities (exhibitions, technical centres, etc.); co-ordination of extra-curricular activities; analysis of library facilities (state of resources, use of these resources, clubs, conferences, etc.).

4. School financing, materials and technical provision.

5. Pedagogical staff and school leadership.

To prepare the attestation report, the committee may ask for any documents and material that a school should possess according to the official requirements.

So, as shown, school evaluation may cover almost all spheres of school life. In the context of the new educational policy, which places more emphasis on output data, particularly on the use of national examination data, many regions have started to consider the unified state examination data (school-leaver results) as one important indicator for school evaluation. School evaluation therefore comprises a very important part in quality assurance (QA) in the country.

Monitoring the quality of education relies very much on recording input data including teachers' qualifications, identifying outstanding results and paying less attention to monitoring averages and correlating these relevant background variables (OECD, 1998). Indicators of excellence may include the number of gold and silver medals awarded, Olympiad results per school subject and the number of students being admitted to prestigious higher education institutions (Bakker, 1998).

Standardised national examinations, known as unified state examinations, have recently been introduced, combining the general secondary education graduate examinations with higher education entrance examinations. Unified state examinations will be compulsory for all secondary school graduates from 2009.

Between 2001 and 2005 students' achievements were monitored nationally in about 2 000 schools from 76 regions as part of the experiment to modernise the structure and content of general education.

Since 1991 the Russian Federation has taken part in various international monitoring studies such as TIMSS (1995, 1999, 2003, 2007), CIVED (1999), PIRLS (2001, 2006), PISA (2000, 2003, 2006) and SITES (1999, 2006).

Every school participating in any study (national or international) receives a school report comparing its results with averages across the country.

In 2005, the Act on the Federal Programme on Education Development in 2006-10 was passed. This programme says that one strategic task is to develop a Russian-wide system of evaluating the quality of education at all levels and stages of education with the goal of providing QA and ensuring equal access to education.

1.2. Evaluation as an issue in teacher training

The curriculum of each higher education institution providing teacher training is developed on the basis of the state education standards for higher professional education, and includes the study plan, programmes of study for all subjects and courses, and programmes for teaching practice in school. The curriculum includes federal, regional or institutional and student components. The federal component, covering 70% of training time, ensures that all students across the country studying the same specialisation at higher education institutions will have 70% of the content of education in common. The amount of time spent on the institutional and student components is decided by the individual institutions.

The teacher-training curriculum includes four cycles of subjects and elective courses. Each cycle includes federal, regional or institutional and student components. The first cycle, consisting of general humanitarian and socioeconomic subjects, is almost the same for all higher education institutions regardless of their specialisation. This accounts for about 17% of their time and includes the following subjects: foreign language, physical education, history of the fatherland, philosophy, culture, politics, jurisprudence, Russian language and the culture of speech, sociology, philosophy and economics. Only four subjects from the first cycle are compulsory for all higher education institutions. The second cycle consists of general mathematics and general science subjects (5% of class time). The third cycle, general professional subjects (18% of class time), includes psychology, pedagogy, anatomy, physiology and hygiene, and the basics of medicine. Finally, the professional cycle accounts for the largest block of time (55% of class time), and includes the subjects of teacher specialisation, methodology and instruction in teaching the subject. Elective courses represent the smallest proportion in the curriculum (5% of class time). Evaluation and assessment are part of the pedagogy and didactics of the subject.

As a rule, school evaluation issues are considered in the system of in-service teacher training, not in teacher preparation. Teachers discuss different models of attestation, the model used in their region, and the content and analysis procedure. They become familiar with the objectives of student assessment, test specifications, examples of items, etc.

As a rule, teachers take part in in-service training every five years. In-service teacher training is no longer compulsory and is changing its orientation to come into line with the new goals of education, with a switch in emphasis from subject content to student development, so that teachers have more training in active learning strategies and child development.

According to the state education policy, teachers' work will be evaluated not on the basis of their knowledge level but according to the main developmental indicators of their students. Accordingly, during in-service training, teachers are taught new ways of assessing student achievement and development.

1.3. The use of evaluation results in schools and the educational system

After any school evaluation the school report is as a rule discussed at the school pedagogical conference, the school council, and the regional authorities meeting. The report as a rule includes recommendations for improvements.

In the case of school attestation, the results of attestation are confirmed by special order and disseminated among the schools in the region.

If a school is considered to have passed its attestation, it receives special documents and is awarded the new attestation for five years. If a school does not pass its attestation, however, the special commission will work in the school, looking at the reasons and developing recommendations for improving the situation. In a year this school will receive an additional attestation.

Attestation results are usually analysed at the internal (school) and external (regional authorities) levels. This provides a complex approach that can help schools to change their situation and to raise the level of qualification of teachers.

All teachers are now familiar with the results of school evaluation. They receive test result statistics and a comparison with other schools.

2. "The Tool for Quality Assurance of Education for Democratic Citizenship in Schools"

2.1. Comprehensiveness and coherence

The book as a whole is very informative and useful for Russian educators from several different perspectives.

Chapter 1 provides general information about the development of the tool and its place in the system of international agreements and actions. The chapter also gives an overview of possible uses of the tool; however, there is no special part that emphasises either the importance of this tool or clear evidence of how to use it.

The chapter shows that the problem of the existing gap between the declared goals and what has happened in schools in relation to EDC exists across Europe, not only in some countries (there are also similar conclusions across Europe).

The chapter also discusses the possibility of adaptation to the countries' individual circumstances. However, at no point does it describe the special situation of the countries in which this tool was initially developed. This suggests that there are no convincing examples that would motivate using the tool elsewhere. The specific historical situation in these countries and the events of the last decade are clear. It would be good if the chapter could include materials that show the common features that are shared by European and other countries around the world with these particular countries.

Reading this chapter the reader wants – but does not receive – answers to the following questions:
- Do we need this tool or not?

- Why do we need this tool in Russia?
- Do we need this tool in Russia at the federal, regional or local level?

The document does make a very important contribution – namely to show the whole process from formulating democratic values, developing them, showing their role and place in the general concept of quality of education, to describing the technology for QA in EDC. However, all of these factors do not create the whole picture of QA in general. Every country builds its own QA system. And the tool does not force one to use this or that QA model, but rather to consider the technology of QA through the way in which the self-development process is organised.

It is also good that the chapter emphasises the fact that EDC is valuable for schools not only as an area of learning, but as a powerful precondition for QA in schools, establishing a better school climate, stronger partnership relations between teachers and students and among teachers or among students, etc.

Chapter 2 makes a profound presentation of EDC at school as a set of practices and activities aimed at better equipping young people and adults to participate actively in democratic life by assuming and exercising their social rights and responsibilities. It describes the details of EDC as being at the heart of educational reform with a democratic nature.

It is very important that EDC is shown as a lifelong learning experience inside and outside formal institutions, with schools playing a key role in ensuring systematic learning of content and skills, and emphasising that the whole school life is a context for acquiring EDC literacy in a variety of learning situations.

The most valuable part of this chapter is the EDC capacity-building process, whereby different aspects of participation, rights and responsibilities are shown. Diversity is also seen to be valued, especially for countries that formerly had totalitarian systems. It becomes very clear, especially to policy makers, how important EDC is in teacher training, in preparing them to work in multicultural classrooms, in the context of ethnic conflicts and against the threat of international terrorism as the result of globalisation.

Chapter 3 is very important for Russia due to the goals established by the government in developing a Russian-wide system of evaluating the quality of education. For any country developing a new system of evaluating the quality of education, two aspects are of great importance:
- empowerment and accountability;
- quality control and QA.

In the Soviet era, schools were mainly oriented to the demands of the state authorities. Many teachers still cannot think about their work as being within the sphere of providing an educational service for individuals (children and parents with their own needs and interests), society (the needs of different groups and communities, etc.) and the state. In the past, schools were primarily accountable to federal, regional and local educational authorities. This chapter contains several ways of making schools accountable to parents and the general public (to citizens) that previously never existed in the Russian school system (for example, giving school reports to parents).

The idea of QA (creating and controlling the proper conditions for learning in order to achieve objectives) is one of the main methodological bases of the new Russian educational standards for general secondary education, which are currently being developed.

There is one more aspect that is also very important for the Russian educational system, namely the interrelation and mutual influence of elements, and the use of external and internal evaluation.

The idea of school development planning, which is presented in Chapter 4, is analogous to the theoretical research work that was conducted in the Soviet Union's Academy of Pedagogical Sciences in the 1970s and in the current work of so-called schools of developing learning. For this reason, this chapter is of great interest in comparing different approaches to school development planning.

The material in Chapter 5 is very useful from a theoretical and practical point of view. This chapter presents a framework to evaluate EDC. It first explains the main characteristics of the indicators, and then sets out the quality indicators of EDC that have been newly developed for this tool, based on the EDC principles presented in Chapter 2.

In relation to Chapter 6 on "School development planning of EDC", which explains how to carry out self-evaluation and development planning of EDC in schools, it would be useful to take a further step in evaluating progress in EDC-QA. For this, the questionnaire "Is this true for your class?" should have a second version or an additional amendment in order to measure progress, for example if it is used twice in one year.

Chapter 7, entitled "Towards a quality assurance system of EDC", looks at the key elements of QA of EDC at the system level. It examines in parallel the needs and implications of QA of EDC at the level of the education system, by (a) reviewing the system of QA and its components from an EDC perspective; and (b) examining the requirements for a specific QA system of EDC. It also provides a checklist of policy measures that are necessary for setting up a QA of EDC system. In the European context, educational systems, EDC and QA vary from country to country. Depending on the country's situation – or whether the starting point is EDC or QA or both – this tool can therefore be used in different ways: for awareness-raising on EDC and QA, as a starting point for setting up a QA system, or for integrating EDC into existing QA systems. In all cases and whatever the purpose, the EDC-QA tool needs to be adapted to each country's specific context.

It is very important to pay attention to the issue of working with students of different ages and experience with the same methods. It is not clear how the tool will take into consideration students of different ages and experience, how it will manage to stimulate interest in EDC-QA and not lose this interest later, or how it will ensure progress and developments in EDC-QA. It is clear that it is easier to start a progressive developmental system than to create one from scratch.

2.2. Corresponding material in Russia

There are some points of correspondence between the material presented in the tool and school practice in Russia. The main areas of correspondence are the following:

- knowledge, understanding and skills in EDC. If we consider knowledge, understanding and skills (Bîrzea et al., 2005: 18), similarities can be found with the elements of the school subject "social studies", related to democratic and citizenship culture. These elements are provided in the educational standards (at the federal level) in the form of knowledge, skills and social experience of democratic relations and decision making in real life;
- school self-government has existed in Russia at the level of theoretical and practical development for some time now.

  The ideas of self-government, self-management, self-organisation and self-analysis formed the basis of work developed in the 1970s (see Korotov and Likhatchov, 1967; Novikova, 1978). They developed not only a theoretical basis, but also the practical aspects of school self-government. There is now a special education magazine in Russia called *School Planning*.

  In analysing the Soviet era developments in self-government now from the new perspective of democratic development in the country, it is possible to say that the goals were not very democratic. The problematic character of the school-based management idea for teachers and school staff was never seriously considered. Why was this so? Probably because the idea of self-management for the pupils was regarded only as a useful strategy in the upbringing of young people. Thus, it presented no danger to the totalitarian state. But the self-management of teachers would be destructive to education as a part of the totalitarian system (Gazman, 1995).

  Only with the Provisional Act on State General Secondary Schools in the 1990s did the teacher councils become more democratic by transforming themselves into a school-based management structure. The chairpersons of the teachers' councils can be elected by teachers, and any teacher can chair a council. This form of school management in schools provides more experience of real democratic relations among students, teachers and parents;

- forms of evaluating the quality of education in terms of evaluating the relations between self-management (this includes self-evaluation, development planning, evaluation of plan fulfilment, and the development of new perspectives);
- teacher training programmes based on ideas of EDC-QA (for example, the Network Educational Programme for Innovative Centres of Improving the Qualification of Educational Staff).

3. The tool as an instrument of school evaluation in Russia

As Froumin (1995) states: "In modern Russian society, democracy is viewed as an exceptionally positive phenomenon. However, when striving to realise democratic values in all aspects of the educational system, considerable problems have emerged. No doubt, in every particular reform one can find errors and shortcomings, but in Russia it could be argued that reform leaders were not fully cognisant of democratic ideas and values, or were not quite committed to them. The danger in Russia today is that reforms, if poorly implemented, might lead to disillusionment with democratic values, and a rejection of democratic reforms in education may result. Indeed, a comparative analysis of educational reforms both in the West and in the East reveals a cyclic recurrence of 'democratic enthusiasm' and bitter disappointment in its results, as observed by Kirsty (1984)".

3.1. Conditions in schools for using the tool

As already noted, since 2000 the Russian Government has begun to develop a new educational reform programme with the main goals of modernising the structure and content of general education, raising the quality of education, providing equal access to education, developing effective mechanisms for transmitting social requests to the educational system, and broadening public participation in managing education.

The new educational standards with a competency-based approach were introduced in 2004. The objectives for every subject were formulated in such a way that every student should know and be able to achieve them in order to continue lifelong education, to solve problems from everyday life and to perform practical tasks.

Major changes have taken place in the social studies curriculum. In basic school the number of hours devoted to social studies has been doubled starting from grade 6 (before 2004 students only began to learn about social studies as a rule in grade 9). In upper secondary school, the number of hours for the basic course, which is compulsory for all students (except those that select advanced social studies courses), has been increased by about 30%.

The goals of social studies are concentrated on the personal development and upbringing of students, their acquisition of knowledge and skills, and the development of skills and competences to apply given knowledge and skills in real-life situations.

The content of the social studies curriculum was changed in order to increase the role of the course in the civil and spiritual development of students' personalities and in strengthening the practical orientation of the subject. The course aims at developing humanistic and democratic values based on the main ideas embodied in the Constitution of the Russian Federation. The materials reflect the current development of the country, and the regions are widely used in the course.

The content of social studies has thus become closer to that of EDC. For example, before the 2004 standards, democracy was considered mainly on the formal logical level (at the level of understanding the concept, characteristics and procedures). In the new curriculum priorities have shifted to the application of knowledge about democracy in the situation of cognitive and practical tasks, related to participation in society (community) activities and to the realisation of different kinds of rights.

For example, the federal component of state education standards for social studies with regard to "Experience of cognitive and practical activities" at the basic level includes:

- working with sources of social information using modern means of communication, including the Internet;
- analysing critically current social information taken from different sources, making personal judgments and reflections on the basis of this analysis;
- solving cognitive and practical tasks that reflect typical social situations;
- acquiring typical social roles through participation in role-plays and training courses in which real-life situations are modelled;
- applying knowledge to define what constitutes economically rational, lawful and socially accepted behaviour in particular situations;
- defending one's personal position with arguments, and learning to oppose different points of view through participation in discussions and debates;
- writing creatively on social issues.

Independent of the profile of learning, all school graduates have to achieve a basic level of competency needed for everyday life, labour and social activities, to deal with multicultural and multi-confessional reality, etc. All these are considered to be part of developing a civic culture at school.

The new content of the social studies course has resulted in the use of active forms of learning through participation in role-playing, situational games, training courses, discussions, debates, projects and community activities. The teacher becomes the organiser and moderator of students' creative activities.

Analysis of the results of the Russian students in international studies such as CIVED and PISA has shown that the content of student assessment mirrors the shortcomings of the educational system, namely, its orientation towards merely reproducing knowledge. The new system of national examinations (unified state examination) has confirmed the results of the international studies and has become the first attempt at introducing a new standardised assessment based on the new educational standards.

3.1.1. Circumstances that might promote the use of the tool

At the level of normative documents

There is a normative basis defining the development of democratic processes in education (the Constitution of the Russian Federation, various international conventions and pacts concerning the rights of the child and persons, the laws of the Russian Federation in the sphere of education and, finally, the charter of the school and its regulations about school self-management).

Article 2 of the Federal Law on Education determines the principles of "democratic, public governance of education" and "autonomy of educational institutions" as being among the political principles of the Russian state in the sphere of education. According to this law, school governing is provided by the founder (the institutions of local government) and a school (Articles 11, 13 and 32). Article 35 determines the principles of the governing of a municipal educational institution: "Governing of the state and municipal educational institution is based on principles of undivided authority and self-management. The forms of self-management are the Committee of Educational Institution, the Council of Trustees, the General Assembly, Teacher Council and other forms. The procedure of election of the institutions of self-governing and its competences are determined in the charter of the educational institution."

As already mentioned, Russian researchers working in the field of education and psychology developed theoretical as well as practical approaches to school management by students – self-government, self-management, self-organisation, self-analysis and planning. Self-government of students was considered in the process of self-initiatives, making decisions for the benefit of the whole collective or organisation. Self-government was realised through self-analysis, self-evaluation, self-criticism and self-beliefs, made by students in relation to their activities and to their school collective.

The experience of existing self-governing school collectives (bodies) confirms the idea that self-government represents the self-organisation of a community. The variety of self-organisational forms promotes establishing social relations in school. Given the lack of social relations in school, the starting point is the organisation of the simple forms of students' activities on the basis of their interests and the task of defending their rights.

The isolation of Russian pedagogical science, which during the Soviet era was mostly only based on research carried out by representatives of Soviet science and education, has now been overcome, and global community experience in education science has become accessible. Russian educators now have the opportunity to participate in international projects, to share their experience and to work together in solving shared educational issues.

Nowadays many regions of Russia, cities and schools have established strong relations with their foreign partners.

At the level of educational system

The reform of the Russian educational system shares the following features with other countries in the world:
- the transition to competence-based standards;
- creation of a national independent system of school examination;
- use of school self-evaluation and the growth in understanding of its importance;
- public involvement in school management at different levels (municipal, regional and national);
- changes in the evaluation of school work – from quality control to QA.

All these promise that a common platform of collaboration among countries may emerge with the use of the tool.

At the socio-political level

In the last decade many regions of Russia have initiated activities directed at creating regional programmes of civic education. These programmes involved different organisations such as educational authorities, teacher training and in-service training institutions, non-governmental organisations (NGOs), schools and others. These programmes include different kinds of activities conducted for different target groups.

For example, the Republic of Tatarstan has developed a special regional model for citizenship education, and it is now a very active contributor to the State Programme for Citizenship Education in 2006-10.

A second example is the regional programme Development of Civic Education in Perm Krai (a Russian region), which included the following areas of activities in 2005 and 2006:
- civic education of students in the classroom;
- civic education of students in out-of-school activities;
- civic education of students in the universities;
- civic education of teachers;
- a Forum on Civic Education in Perm Krai: Problems and Perspectives.[1]

---

1. www.perm36.ru/upload/1144006710.doc.

To discuss civic education issues, some regions organised conferences for teachers, school principals, representatives of the local educational authorities, the mass media and NGOs. The annual conferences on civic education organised by the Tomsk educational authorities may be considered a good example. It is very important to mention that Tomsk *oblast* has organised many activities in this area, including those of the Association of Democratic Schools and the Association for Civic Education. A special newspaper on civic education is published regularly in the region. The last conference on the topic related to civic education (The Modern Models of Development of Civic Education) took place on 5 December 2006, with the participation of more than 200 educators.[2]

At the local level

New approaches to school education based on liberal values (principles of democracy, principles of a collective nature, the efficiency of the school, situational leadership, the mutual interest of pupils and teachers) have appeared in schools. More and more schools have started to encourage self-management of students, including self-analysis and self-evaluation in daily activity planning, the organisation of activity; analysis and summarising of work; and the decision-making process.

The structure and forms of student self-management depend on local conditions and the interest of pupils, on the school's experience with democratic activities and culture, and at the level of social-pedagogical experience of the teachers at that particular school. Through their experience, schools prove that real improvement in the quality of education including EDC occurs not only when the qualitative parameters of the teaching-learning process and school activities are evaluated, but also when a comfortable environment for participants in the educational process (school climate) is established at school. This allows the long-term efficiency of the QA system developed at the school to be guaranteed.

It is important to mention in this context the constantly increasing provision of ICT facilities at Russian schools. This creates a good basis for exchanging information and school collaborations through online conferences at the national as well as at the international level.

3.1.2. Prospective difficulties and obstacles

To discuss the difficulties and obstacles that must be faced before the tool can be introduced into Russian schools, it is worth starting with special issues related to the country's historical and cultural traditions. Tubelsky (1995) explains some of these problems in connection to EDC in his article "The Acquisition of the Democratic Experience by Children and Teachers". He writes (Tubelsky, 1995: 204):

---

2. http://edu.tomsk.gov.ru/rcro/rez_konf_05-12-06.doc.

The assimilation of democratic values by Russian students is complicated by at least two circumstances. The first impediment is the lack of deeply rooted democratic traditions in the Russian family and society as a whole. Moreover, in the past, the communal consciousness of people gave rise to judicial nihilism and the conviction that individual self-realisation is possible without the observance of democratic norms. The second impediment, which is linked with the above, is the previous tendency to accept non-democratic behaviour among teachers. In their relations with students the majority of Russian teachers neglect the democratic norms and tend to be authoritarian. When conflict emerges, teachers solve it by relying on their previously formed 'common sense'. In Russia today politicians use certain words and clichés to convey democratic ideas, yet the mechanisms for the implementation of these ideas are yet to be developed. Therefore the majority of the population has yet to be convinced that the solution to social issues is closely linked to the level of democracy. It is common knowledge that, at the moment, Russia is making its first attempts to create a law-governed state. With this in mind, it follows that the social situation of Russian students differs considerably from that of their western counterparts, who have experienced and internalised the essentials of democracy in their families and environment, and through their relations with national institutions. ...

While the task of the Western school is simply to guide its students toward conceptualising the experience of democratic behaviour and linking it with historical and cultural tradition, the Russian school at this point in our history must become the major institution where such experience is generated. Within the framework of our conception of how to help children develop ability of self-determination, our institutions are searching for pedagogical conditions under which both children and teachers can acquire and reflect on the experience of democratic behaviour.

In addition, it is important to add some other circumstances that should be taken into account when introducing the tool in schools:

- conceptual understanding of EDC-QA. In evaluating the quality of education, Russian educators used to think more about students' achievement in knowledge and skills acquisition rather than about evaluating quality indicators of EDC in the curriculum or evidence of effective school leadership based on EDC principles. It is important to develop a positive view regarding the EDC-QA approach;
- role of tradition in education. The role of tradition in the Russian education system is strong. This means that the tool may be rejected as an "implanted" element. To overcome this prejudice, it is important to look for the interrelations between Russian traditions or works by famous Russian authors and the tool. This needs special activities, staff and financial support;

- teachers' readiness to accept EDC-QA. In Russia there is no compulsory programme of training and in-service training for any teacher. The requirements for teachers and other pedagogical staff to be qualified do not include any objectives related to EDC-QA;
- teachers' motivation to move to the new EDC-QA system. Experience with the introduction of self-management in schools allows us to predict a spectrum of negative positions from teachers who are not ready to move to the new system. Most common are references to previous negative experiences that may well have taken place ("It does not fit our needs", "It is too extreme for our school", "We managed perfectly in the past without that", "We already tried something similar earlier"), displaying only a very rudimentary understanding of existing words/terminologies, although they now have new meanings and were never realised before. Then there is the fear of something new ("We never did it before"); the desire to avoid any change in the settled style of school life ("We are not ready for it yet"), and the argument that "We have no time for it" (supporters of this argument usually underline the fact that teachers have additional duties, workloads, etc.), or simply one of money: "We are not being paid for that!";
- special issues concerning the tool. The book is well developed, but the level of the tool is rather theoretical and conceptual. For everyday use in school, more practical details and explanations to teachers are needed. A special "bridge" is thus needed between the tool and schools and teachers;
- the tool has a static nature. It is not sufficiently developed for multiple use for measuring progress. In order to disseminate the tool to all Russian schools, the book should be translated into Russian;
- financial difficulties. There is no special financial support for the implementation of the tool.

3.1.3. Parts of the tool with particular applicability

Most of the document could in principle be used in Russian schools, taking into account the recommendations for improvement formulated above. This especially concerns the planning, quality indicators and self-evaluation parts.

The tool should be adapted to the conditions of Russian schools in general and of the country's particular regions with different cultures and religious beliefs and practices.

3.1.4. Target groups of the tool

At the federal level, the target group in Russia may involve policy makers and decision makers in developing a national system of evaluating the quality of education.

At the level of the subjects of the federation (local level), it is possible to allocate as separate target groups institutions where school planning and self-evaluation have been developed, institutions where only some elements of self-evaluation are in place, and institutions where any EDC ideas do not work. Special programmes designed to maintain development of quality of education in each of these groups of institutions will be necessary at the level of educational administrators in the regional ministries and local authorities, and school inspectors.

At the school level, it is possible to identify the following as separate target groups:

- teachers of various school subjects;
- teachers of subjects in the social-humanities cycle (for example, programmes that include democratic values, and concepts of democratic and civil culture);
- classroom teachers;
- school principals and representatives of school administrations.

At the same level, it is probably possible to assign separate groups to the following:

- all students;
- representatives of school self-management bodies;
- all parents;
- representatives of parents in school self-management bodies.

3.2. Systemic conditions for using the tool

3.2.1. Correspondence of the tool and the system of quality assurance and evaluation

It is impossible to speak about the existence of a similar system of evaluation of quality of education in Russia. There are only separate elements and similar themes to the ones in the tool.

As mentioned above, there is the special magazine *School Planning* in Russia, which provides among its publications materials similar to those given in the tool.

As another example below, we provide a short description of the Network Educational Programme for Innovative Centres for Improving Qualifications of Educational Staff.

In this programme self-evaluation is considered as an innovative way of evaluating the general results of school work. For schools deciding to work on improving the quality of educational services as a priority, the most effective tool has proven to be a periodic carrying out of self-evaluations. For this purpose, special groups of employees are formed. All members of these groups are trained in order to become acquainted with the bases of standardisation, criteria of quality management models, algorithms and self-evaluation techniques. During the self-evaluation interview, information about the school's activities can be gathered from employees via questions or other methods. It is possible to receive answers that confirm with examples the working conditions of a school, answers that gather concrete facts instead of subjective opinions. The results have to be discussed, generalised and reflected in the report, which has to be presented to all school employees. In a cycle of self-evaluation results, two or three areas for improvements at school will be identified. Work in these areas for improvement will be organised by special working groups under the direction of employees appointed by the administration and given the necessary powers. Self-evaluation is usually repeated once a year. Changes in the areas previously highlighted as requiring improvement are especially closely studied; based on the results of each self-evaluation cycle, new areas for improvement are defined and work is organised.

The results of a school's self-evaluation can be used to draw up annual work plans, to prepare students for passing the state certification of accreditation, and to nominate students for competitions and programmes in the field of quality. Self-evaluation results also can be used to support the image of this educational establishment in society or to strengthen its position in the educational services market.

3.2.2. Preparation of teachers to work with the tool

Preparation for working with the tool implies that at least four target groups of school staff will require training: teachers of various school subjects, teachers of subjects containing elements of the social sciences/humanities (with curricula that include democratic values, and concepts of democratic and civil culture), classroom teachers, school principals and representatives of the school administration.

With reference to their various functional levels, the development of special training on EDC and QA programmes is both possible and reasonable.

To implement the tool it is necessary to define the theoretical basis of the new system for evaluating quality and learning authoritative domestic pedagogical theories.

It is important to emphasise the concrete needs, ways, models, ways of democratising school life and evaluating quality of education in connection with the interests of teachers. The development of special techniques designed to reveal the interests of participants in the educational process, their grouping, analysis and, finally, the development of programmes that could satisfy these interests to some extent should be planned.

4. *Ideas for the implementation process*

To start the implementation process it is necessary to consult at the ministry level. A special structure should be found that takes responsibility for implementing the tool in Russia. This special structure may be responsible for translating and adapting the tool into Russian, for preparing special recommendations to different target groups on how to start implementing the tool and how to evaluate the effectiveness of tool implementation, for organising seminars and conferences to exchange school experience, and for developing subsequent steps.

The following ideas may help in implementing the tool in Russia:

- socio-political scenario. All key people, namely the policy makers who determine the modernisation of education, the groups developing the new educational standards and specialists working on developing the new country-wide system for evaluating the quality of education, should be aware of the tool and be involved in planning its implementation. Their support of the tool will be of great help in official presentations, speeches and articles;
- ministry-level scenario. To implement the tool in Russia it is very important to have the support of the Ministry of Education and Science in order to define some regulations. For this reason, the tool should be presented by UNESCO or the Council of Europe at the governmental level;
- motivation scenario. Schools have suggested a great variety of innovations. Principals and teachers should therefore be motivated to select the tool. This requires special work in terms of organisation and financing starting from the ministry to teachers;
- school laboratories scenario. To develop the recommendations for schools, including the technology of tool implementation, it is necessary to have some schools working in these areas. These school laboratories should be located in regional centres. The leaders of these laboratories should be familiar with the tool, and should have access to the authors of the tool for consultations, and to other schools' laboratories for sharing experience;
- pilot schools scenario. Special pilot schools could be selected with different initial conditions for implementing the tool, such as:
  - schools with good experience of teaching social sciences/humanities and with developed school management;
  - schools without any experience in this area; and
  - schools with some experience in implementing EDC ideas.

  Different groups of schools make it possible to study the special conditions needed to implement the tool and to establish the most effective implementation methods;
- seminars and conferences scenario. The next step in implementing the tool may be seminars and conferences among school laboratories and pilot schools, inviting representatives from other organisations and countries (Ukraine, Belarus, the Baltic countries, etc.) with the goal of widening tool implementation as well as discussing educational problems that could be

solved by using the tool (for example, mass migration and intercultural interaction). One more topic for discussion is defining the groups of educators who need training in tool implementation, analysing their interests and developing special topics for training courses;

- collaboration and co-operation scenario. Schools need different ways of sharing and enriching experience. This could be ensured through direct contacts, for example, via the Internet. The initiative should be taken by a European country (potentially Germany) that has close access to the authors and to the original methodology.

References

Bakker, S. (1998). "Educational Assessment in the Russian Federation", in Voogt, J. and Plomp, T. (eds.), *Education Standards and Assessment in the Russian Federation*. Leuven: Acco, 113-124.

Bîrzea, C.; Cecchini, M.; Harrison, C.; Krek, J.; Spajic-Vrkas, V. (2005). "Tool for Quality Assurance of Education for Democratic Citizenship in Schools", Paris: UNESCO, Council of Europe, Centre for Educational Policy Studies.

Froumin, I.D. (1995). "The Child's Road to Democracy", in Chapman, J.D.; Froumin, I.D.; Aspin, D.N. (eds.), *Creating and Managing the Democratic School*, London: Falmer Press, 202-213.

Froumin, I.D. (2005). "Democratizing the Russian School: Achievements and Setbacks", in Eklof, B.; Holmes, L.E.; Kaplan, V. (eds.), *Educational Reform in Post-Soviet Russia*, London: Frank Cass, 129-152.

Gazman, O. (1995). "The Development of the Management and Self-government of Russian Schools and Pupils", in Chapman, J.D.; Froumin, I.D.; Aspin, D.N. (eds.), *Creating and Managing the Democratic School*, London: Falmer Press, 202-213.

Korotov, V.M. and Likhatchov, B.T. (1967). *Shkolnoe samoupravlenie* (School Self-government), Moscow: Pedagogika.

Network Educational Programme for Innovative Centres for Improving Qualifications of Educational Staff (2005). "Management of Quality of Education on the Basis of the Analysis of External Assessment of Educational Results", Saint Petersburg.

Novikova, L.I. (1978). *Pedagogika detskogo kollectiva. Sotsialno-pedagogitcheskie osnovy shkolnogo samoupravlenija* (Pedagogy of Children Collective. Social-pedagogical Basis of School Self-management). Moscow: Pedagogika.

OECD (1998). *Reviews of National Policies for Education: Russian Federation*, Paris: OECD.

Polodzenie o porjadke attestatsii I gosudarstvennoi akkreditasii obrazovatelnych uchretzeny (prikaz Ministerstva obtsevo I professionalnogo obrazovania Rossijskoi Federatsii ot 22 maja 1998 No. 13276 izvlechenia) (1998) (document about the procedure of attestation and accreditation of educational establishments).

Sbornik normativno-pravovych dokumento po attestatsii obrazovatelnych uchretzeny obtsevo obrazovania Rostovskoi oblasti (2005) (official documents for attestation of the educational establishments of general education in Rostov *oblast*). Rostov-na-Dony.

Strategy of Modernisation of Content of General Education: Materials for Developing Documents for Renewal of General Education (in Russian) (2001). Moscow: Mir Knigi.

State Law of the Russian Federation on Education (1992). Moscow.

Tubelsky, A. (1995). "The Acquisition of the Democratic Experience by Children and Teachers", in Chapman, J.D.; Froumin, I.D.; Aspin, D.N. (eds.), *Creating and Managing the Democratic School*, London: Falmer Press, 202-213.

Ukraine
Olena Pometun

1. School evaluation in Ukraine

The education system in Ukraine

Ukraine has inherited an education system that was tailored to support a planned economy. The education sector in Ukraine is predominantly public. The main features of the Ukrainian educational system are as follows.

There are three levels of education (general education was extended recently from ten to twelve years):
- primary education is provided in general primary schools;
- lower secondary education is provided in general basic schools;
- upper secondary education is provided in general senior schools, gymnasia, collegia, lyceums and vocational schools.

There are more than 22 000 secondary schools in Ukraine, providing education for more than 6 million pupils; out of these, an estimated 600 000 study in upper secondary schools.

Completing secondary education (primary, lower and upper secondary) is compulsory in Ukraine. Gymnasia, collegia and lyceums provide in-depth education in specific subject areas depending on their profile. Pupils take exams and are awarded a school-leaving certificate after completing a lower secondary education (Basic School Certificate) and an upper secondary education (Completed Secondary School Certificate). People with special needs are trained in special schools, which are by and large boarding schools.

Vocational and education training schools and lyceums offer a secondary education with professional training. Pupils take exams and are awarded a Completed Secondary School Certificate and occupational qualifications.

Educational institutes can be instructional (all types of schools) and also non-instructional (the Ministry of Education and Science (MES) of Ukraine, regional and local authorities, and the Academy of Pedagogical Science (APSU)).

Since independence, Ukraine has been able to sustain some of its comparative advantages in terms of excellence in education. The current phase of educational reform has recently seen the initiation of a process that includes redefined underlying principles and priorities for the entire sector. Relevance and improved service delivery from preschool through to tertiary education are key elements of the National Doctrine of Development of Education in Ukraine, which is guiding the educational reform process. The priority issues for the sector may be summarised as the introduction of an individual-centred approach, lifelong learning, securing equal access to quality education, and integration into the European education system. Modernising the curriculum is one of the main objectives of the overall process of educational reform.

In Ukraine the MES formulates the national curriculum guidelines and core curriculum together with the APSU, and acts as a quality assurance agent for the school-based curriculum, textbooks and teaching aids.

Consequently, there are three documents that form the contextual basis for the curriculum:
- national standards for junior and upper secondary education;
- the concept of profiling of upper secondary education;
- guidelines for the official recognition of textbooks and teaching materials.

The national standards define subject areas, describe their content, their provisional general level of mastering and in terms of compulsory core subjects and instructional workload.

At each level of education there is a block of core subjects that the government defines as instruction leading to citizenship or civic education, in particular: "Me and Ukraine" in primary education; ethics (grades 5 and 6) and civic education instruction, which are covered as cross-curricular themes in history and literature (grades 7 to 9), in lower secondary education; and law (grade 10), economics (grade 11), and "People and Society" or civic education (grade 12) in upper secondary education. Schools may choose to opt for compulsory subjects. "People and Society" is more focused on philosophical concepts, while civic education is an integrated course addressing core concepts of participatory democracy, market economy, human rights, real citizenship, etc.

This instruction takes place not only via the curriculum but also through extra-curricular activities along with important cross-curricular themes such as "Learning to Learn", health education, environmental education, etc.

In 2000 the European Commission (EC) supported a €900 000 pilot project entitled "Education for Democracy in Ukraine" (under the Civic Education Support initiative), funded by the EU-US Transatlantic Civil Society programme, as a result of which civic education became an optional subject in a limited number of upper secondary schools. Via the Ukraine Civic Education project Civic Education – Ukraine (2005-08), the EC is seeking to "institutionalise" civic education as a fixed part of educational provision within the new twelve-year programme. The EC also would like the project to focus on formulating relevant European action plans for Ukraine and on reforming the education system based on EU experience and on the Education and Training 2010 initiative (the Lisbon Strategy, which aims at promoting lifelong learning and the acquisition of skills as part of a knowledge-based economy).

The overall objective of the Ukraine Civic Education project is defined in its terms of reference as "to introduce civic education as a 'mandatory training' (sic) in secondary schools in Ukraine", with the specific objectives of developing a national curriculum for civic education and related (re)training programmes at universities and teacher-training institutes.

Specific focus is placed on the delivery of civic education through a group of related subjects in the social sciences/humanities (history, economy, law and philosophy), rather than solely through the compulsory grade 11 (12) programme, The Individual and the World. However, it is clear that the MES in particular also supports the institutionalisation of civic education in all schools by raising the awareness of all subject teachers and by providing training and guidance in how they can contribute to the development of civic education competences, including appropriate skills, attitudes and values.

The project also intends to ensure that there is an inclusive approach to civic education, with equality of access for all students, including those with special educational needs and those in vocational education, with the active involvement and participation of school heads and school communities (student councils, parents, local stakeholders, non-governmental organisations (NGOs), employers, etc.). This approach will also be reflected in the teaching and learning materials that will be produced by the project.

The main project objectives will be implemented though the Curriculum Development Working Group and its sub-groups (including one on material development) in close collaboration with the Teacher Training Working Group and other working groups as appropriate.

The MES is undertaking a widespread educational reform of basic and upper secondary education, supported by the four-year US$86.5 million World Bank Equal Access to Quality Education (EAQE) project (2005/06-2008/09 – Phase 1 of a three-phase US$300 million ten-year education sector reform programme). The World Bank project ("Appraisal Document", April 2005, Annex 4, section 2.1) supports "reviewing and improving the new curricula for Grades 5-12, piloting them in schools, implementing, monitoring and evaluating them as necessary". During the EAQE phase, the intention is to develop "a coherent national curriculum framework" and, *inter alia*, to "review, improve, debate and complete" the syllabi for grades 6 to 9, which have been selected under the current MES competition process.

The main area identified for enhanced activities in discussions with the EC, the World Bank and the MES is therefore curriculum development. Other project objectives remain unaffected by this proposal, such as the training and retraining of teachers to teach civic education and cross-curricular themes, the publication of a new students' book (based on improved existing materials) for The Individual and the World programme (grade 12), the organisation of extra-curricular activities through mini-projects, and support for teachers' associations and for children with special educational needs and their teachers.

The implementation of the new twelve-year education system began with grade 5 in September 2005; curricula for the new grade 10 will therefore be in use from September 2010.

Activities under the curriculum development component will take into account the key national policy documents, European approaches to citizenship education (*Citizenship Education at School in Europe*, Eurydice, June 2005; the *All-European Study on Policies for Education for Democratic Citizenship*, the Council of Europe), Education and Training 2010 (the Lisbon Strategy), the concept papers developed by the Education for Democracy in Ukraine project (on civic education) and the APSU (on civic upbringing), and the United Nations Development Programme (UNDP) and International Renaissance Foundation (IRF)-supported Reform Strategy for Education in Ukraine publication (Strategija reformuvannia osviti v Ukraini : recomendatsii osvitnioi politiki, 2003). They should also pay attention to ensuring continuity between the different stages of education.

1.1. School evaluation in Ukraine

Models of school evaluation

The quality of education is proclaimed to be a national priority, a prerequisite for the safety of the state, and a guarantee of adherence to international regulations and requirements on the implementation of citizens' rights with regard to education (the National Doctrine on Education Development in Ukraine in the 21st Century, 2002).

The quality of education is measured by monitoring procedures – a system of means of collection, processing, analysis and extending of information aimed at tracing and anticipating the development of educational subjects. The enhancement of the evaluation system of educational institutions on the whole and pupils' educational achievements in particular is one of the major means of applying quality assurance in education. Given certain positive changes that have recently occurred in this sphere – namely the introduction of a 12-mark evaluation system, the gradual implementation of external testing of educational achievements of secondary school graduates, and the introduction of a state certification procedure for educational institutions – the effective model of diagnostics of school-producing results has not been given a complete workout so far.

The adoption of state standards for basic and complete secondary education in 2004 brought to light the inefficiency of the state control system regarding educational institutions' activities. There is a discrepancy between out-of-date evaluation methods and new educational targets and results determined by the new needs of society.

The main form of state evaluation of (control over) educational institutions' activities is a certification procedure, which is generally conducted at least once every decade in full accordance with the relevant state document (the Order of State Certification of General Educational, Preschool, and Extra-curricular Educational Institutions, 2004).

The certification procedure has three main goals: checking educational institutions' execution of the legislative basis and normative documents on education and upbringing; determining the real potential of the establishment and efficiency of the financial and material use of resources allocated to educational development; and ensuring that the level of educational training conforms with state demands and standards. A tool kit for certification expertise has been developed to enable the state to evaluate educational institutions' activities in the following areas.

Organisation of the educational process:
- staff policy;
- material/technical and educational/methodological basis;
- financial provision of educational institutions' activities;
- efficiency of the educational process;
- the level of pupils' educational achievements;
- the results of the educational process;
- the management of the educational institution;
- the quality of planning and control;
- the public ranking of the educational institution;
- social protection, preservation and consolidation of pupils' and educational institution employees' health;
- creation of conditions for the provision of rights and freedoms of participants in the educational process;
- provision of social support for orphaned children, children from poor families and pupils in other vulnerable social categories;
- provision of medical support for pupils and educational specialists;
- provision of nutrition for pupils;
- state of traumatism among children;
- provision of conditions to preserve pupils' health;
- the state of physical education (health strengthening measures, mass sport activities, etc.);

- organisation of rest and health improving activities for pupils and teachers;
- additional directions and indicators of the characteristic educational activities of the institution in question.

According to the above-mentioned directions of certification examination, protocols for self-evaluation of an educational institution and its evaluation by experts have been developed.

The overall conclusion on the level of educational activity of a general education establishment is based on the total marks awarded:
- organisation of the educational process (a maximum of 14 marks);
- efficiency of the educational process (a maximum of 15 marks);
- management of the educational institution (a maximum of 18 marks);
- social protection, preservation and consolidation of pupils' and educational institution employees' health (a maximum of 15 marks).

A high level is reflected in a total score in the range of 52-62; sufficient, 35-51; medium, 20-34; and low, 19 and less.

Taking into account the significance of all sectors of indicators, the level of educational activity of an institution cannot be acknowledged as being high if the efficiency of the educational process is evaluated as being below the level of sufficient. An educational institution cannot be certified (even "conventionally") if the efficiency of the educational process is low.

Based on the outcome of the certification procedure (certification examination), the level of educational institution activity is determined as being "high", "sufficient", "medium" or "low". This then lays the foundations for the decision to recognise it as being "certified with honour", "certified", "conventionally certified", or "uncertified".

Summarised results of the certification of educational institutions are presented to the Regional Expert Committee, which makes the ultimate decisions on school activities. Information on all regional educational institutions is gathered by the statistical departments of the relevant regional educational administration, summarised by specialists and presented to the regional educational authorities and local self-governing institutions.

Simultaneously with the certification of general educational establishments, their managers are also certified. The manager of an educational institution is certified if the educational establishment is certified, and is uncertified if the level of educational institution activity is low.

Education management authorities in charge of the certification of general educational institutions can introduce substantial changes and supplements to the main evaluation criteria, taking into consideration their types, social and economic peculiarities of the region, and the possibilities of particular educational institutions.

It is worth mentioning that certification in terms of its contents, form and methods applied is a new form of state control, exercised through certification examinations conducted by expert committees of regional (city) education management administrations. An educational institution is evaluated in accordance with the educational activity indicators contained in the Preliminary Evaluation Criteria of General Educational Institutions (2003, 2006). However, the main complication that educational officials face these days is the practical procedure of evaluating school activities. There is basically no single approach to the certification procedure. It is often seen as being merely a form of control, which is considered to be a substitute for a front-end check of an educational institution, which was common practice in recent years. This procedure, though, does not take into account the fact that the evaluation of school efficiency should be based on educational monitoring and determination of educational quality, given that control is one of many other functions of educational management.

Expert committees make use of various methodologies to evaluate examination results. They are based on a qualimetric approach, which enables quantitative measurements to be carried out, but fails to provide an integrated approach to the evaluation procedure. Similar evaluations of educational institutions' activities are not only held during educational institutions' certification procedure, but also while researching particular indicators of their activities.

In full accordance with state documents (the Order of State Certification of General Educational, Preschool, and Extra-curricular Educational Institutions, 2004), an important constituent of certification is internal school evaluation, so-called self-analysis of an institution's educational activity over a period of no less than three years. This evaluation involves information on material, staffing and educational/methodological provision, organisation and implementation of the educational process. There is, however, no single procedure on how this internal self-evaluation should be performed. Educational institutions in different regions choose their own ways to evaluate the efficiency of their own educational activity. A descriptive characteristic of institutional activity is predominantly used, supplemented with charts, schemes, and diagrams. However, such a monitoring model does not have a defined set of standard procedures. This makes it difficult to compare data obtained outside school in order to carry out, for example, external analysis and to determine the efficiency of one's own activities compared to other schools.

In performing an internal evaluation not predetermined by any certification examination (namely, external control requirements), educational institutions are obliged to choose for themselves the direction for monitoring research, developing criteria and indicators, processing and analysing information obtained, and making management decisions. It is worth mentioning, though, that it is not within the abilities of every teacher or even the whole educational institution to cope with this task on their own.

Consequently, the modern system of external and internal school evaluation is imperfect owing to the following factors:

- the use of different terminology that determines the indicators used for evaluating school activity;
- ignorance of some essential indicators during evaluation;
- incompleteness of the evaluation procedure and results management;
- different views on the significance of some indicators by members of expert committees and educational institution administrations;
- the absence of a unified approach to obtaining certification results, and hence the impossibility of comparing results with those of similar institutions, or of tracing the dynamics of school work efficiency over a period of time.

In general, neither expert committees nor school administrations have specialised software to conduct evaluations.

Currently, the programme and procedure provision of educational institutions is insufficient, which results in certification being turned into administrative and control checks. School managers and regional education administration employees need to develop specific certification and monitoring procedures and methods that can be implemented based on thoroughly tested technology, technical support and software.

Taking the above points into account, Ukraine needs to introduce new mechanisms and procedures for such an evaluation in order to improve educational institutions. Scientists and practising teachers are actively seeking to move in this direction.

1.2. Evaluation as an issue in teacher training

The issue of school evaluation is not a new one for Ukraine, but the proposed approach or system of evaluation is, as well as its coverage in teacher-training programmes. The state in-service training system is therefore currently introducing innovative specialised courses that embrace theoretical knowledge on monitoring research and conduct training on the development of a monitoring research tool kit that could be used to evaluate educational institutions' activities. Classes will consider the notions and characteristics of external evaluation, its varieties, measurement as a formalised evaluation process, pedagogical measurement and its functions, the choice of a pedagogical diagnostics method, and the main categories of the measurement process. As a rule, such classes are at present only held for school heads and their deputies, and are unavailable to the vast majority of subject teachers.

Within the state system, teachers attend in-service training courses only once every five years. Therefore, only an insignificant number of teachers have been able to master such knowledge and skills since the contents were introduced into retraining in 2004-05. Furthermore, the contents have been developed by different teachers in different regions of Ukraine, and consequently the volume of material and approaches to crucial definitions vary considerably. Moreover, several institutions have no similar training courses at all.

Regional educational administrations try to make up for insufficient training of school administrations by holding workshops on practical evaluation issues. Such seminars, however, are not conducted on a systemic basis, and also vary in terms of volume and contents in different regions of Ukraine.

Being new and not included in the state curriculum, issues concerning quality evaluation of education are not taught in pedagogical universities. Classes devoted to this issue are solely conducted in a few universities by teaching specialists.

1.3. The use of evaluation results in schools and the educational system

The results of educational institutions' activities are discussed at school administration board meetings, which are designed to take better administrative decisions, as well as to organise correction work with pupils (to increase their educational achievement level) and teachers (to foster their motivation and pedagogical mastery). The full results of self-checks and state certification are similarly discussed during teaching staff meetings. In the process of discussion the school head is informed of certification outcomes and he or she discusses various aspects of these outcomes with teachers and school employees. Such meetings result in a decision that determines the achievements of an educational institution, the drawbacks of its activities, a deadline for the elimination of drawbacks, and the appointment of people in charge. Occasionally, such meetings can come up with a decision to penalise particular employees (for example, dismissal or a reprimand) if their activity indicators are low. In the latter case, the decision is reinforced by the school head issuing the respective order.

Particular aspects of certification outcomes are discussed at parents' meetings and school board meetings, namely pupils' educational achievements, social aid, pupils' health, issues of material/technical provision of the school, use of resources, etc.

Evaluation aspects connected with particular subjects are as a rule discussed during meetings of the School Methodological Union (a union of teachers of the same or similar subjects who carry out a common plan to improve the teaching of their subject throughout the year, usually consisting of four to five people). Here the discussion takes the form of a round table.

A general drawback of the current evaluation system is its concentration on processing the obtained information and its failure to achieve its dominant managerial function: anticipation of results and determination of an educational institution development strategy. It is next to impossible to introduce new approaches to school work planning and to involve all school employees, pupils, parents and community representatives given the fact that state certification takes place once every ten years, with no permanent monitoring (self-evaluation).

The yearly plan of an educational institution's activities, which is drawn up at the beginning of the year, sometimes omits self-evaluation data and fails to involve all participants in the educational process. The yearly plan is thus a rather descriptive and impractical document that does not clearly show the level the school is currently at, nor forecast further substantiated steps in its development.

Certification results are processed by expert committee members and school administration representatives. City expert committee members are responsible for summarising examination results, comparing them with different educational institutions of the given territory, and notifying school administrations of certification outcomes.

2. The "Tool for Quality Assurance of Education for Democratic Citizenship in Schools"

2.1. Comprehensiveness and coherence

On the whole, the tool is comprehensive and coherent. The main ideas of the text are introduced gradually and consistently, despite being fairly new. This is essential, since the meanings and definitions of these ideas may vary in different countries. It is very helpful that ideas are consecutively unfolded, always drawing the reader's attention to previous chapters and points. Thereafter, only thoroughly elucidated and clarified ideas are used. It is of great importance that the text makes a clear-cut distinction between its concepts: civic education, political education and education for democratic citizenship (EDC), quality control and quality assurance (QC, QA), etc.

The text is well structured. It is extremely helpful that the titles of chapters and points are formulated as questions, which stimulates the reader to think and provides guidance throughout the text. The text is divided into short segments, which significantly facilitates working with it. It is not purely informative and referential, but also empowering in terms of approaches stated, and the emphasis on the necessity of EDC development, as well as the importance and timeliness of using the tool.

The language of the text is fairly simple and specific. It can be used by education officials, parents and representatives of other interested groups.

The provision of tables, schemes and other visual devices facilitates presentation of the material and its practical application.

Chapter 1, "What is the tool about and how can it be used?", dwells upon the history of the issue and places emphasis on correlating different parts of the text and on how they are interconnected, which proves to be very helpful in further working with the text. This chapter initially establishes a connection between the notions of QA and EDC-QA, which is entirely new for Ukrainian readers, yet is core for understanding the basic theses of the text.

In Chapter 2, "What is EDC and what does it mean in schools?", the definition of EDC as a priority of national educational policy is crucial for Ukraine, since the traditional Ukrainian understanding of EDC reduces it to the sphere of education, one of multiple directions that an educational institution's activities can take, or even a separate subject of "civic education". An accurate definition of EDC helps to identify different phenomena in civic education and school life as being the ones relating to the given idea.

Sub-section 2.3, "Where and how does EDC happen in schools", lists reasons why school plays such an important role in EDC. These reasons convince the reader of the possibility and necessity of school development in this direction. The outline of the role of a civic education teacher that is given in the text is crucial for Ukraine. The reason for this is that the training system for teachers of this speciality is still absent in our country. Even civic education is often taught by general subject teachers after a short, one-off training course. What they deliver is merely the contents of the course, but sometimes without paying great attention to the characteristic principles and strategies of EDC.

The definition of EDC as a whole-school approach is significant for Ukraine, as the processes of democratisation and decentralisation in school management and the implementation of collective decision-making processes in some schools are not linked to EDC in our country. These ideas are not only differentiated in the minds of teachers and administrators; the approach is predominant in initial and in-service teacher-training establishments.

Each of the principles requires detailed description and adaptation to the Ukrainian context so that it can be easily understood by pedagogical staff, parents and pupils.

Chapter 3, "What is quality assurance and why is it important?", makes an important distinction between the notions of "control" and "quality evaluation", whereas the conventional notion of "school activity control" presupposes control being exercised by state educational administrations. The results of this control are not discussed by school staff, and are only reflected in educational management and in the school head's orders to impose penalties on teachers and school heads who produce poor results.

The characteristics of qualitative evaluation enable us to assess the problem in Ukraine. The basic system of educational quality evaluation is hardly dependent on the involvement of teachers, pupils, parents and local community representatives in the process. Pupils' progress in studies in separate subjects often serves as a main indicator of quality evaluation. Furthermore, the basic system does not motivate regional and local educational administrations to delegate and decentralise management, or to implement collective decision-making processes involving teachers, pupils, parents and local community representatives.

An analysis of Figure 2, "Components of the quality assurance system" (page 41), shows that only separate components of a quality system are present in Ukraine, such as external data collection, national educational targets and programmes, a system of in-service teacher training, and external control tools. The most crucial components of the system, namely school self-evaluation as a basis for planning school development, evaluative instruments and policies for school empowerment, are lacking.

Chapter 4, "What is school development planning?", dwells upon school development planning, and leads to the conclusion that a similar system for educational establishment development planning is absent in Ukraine. Analysis of the planning procedure that is in operation in the country shows that Stage 1 (who we are) is neglected in the majority of educational establishments, and therefore the whole planning process starts with either analysis of the previous year, or aims solely at external tasks set for regional or state educational managers. Such a system obviously fails to provide the possibility for a stable development of education quality. Moreover, planning is carried out by representatives of the administration, excluding other participants in the educational process and community representatives from the process.

It seems vital to us to use the school planning stages named in Figures 3 and 4 (page 53), because this very approach can consider multiple factors, determining either success or failure, and identifying the required changes.

Chapter 5, "Framework to evaluate EDC", essentially presents an accurate system of EDC indicators, subdividing them into groups and subgroups: areas, quality indicators and sub-themes. The approach, which treats EDC not merely as part of a pedagogical process, as it is commonly presented in Ukraine, but as a fundamental principle of school policy and organisation, is of especial interest for us.

Indicators are introduced in the book as an accurate and coherent system that can be comprehensible to school administrations, parents, etc. and not only to civic education specialists. Each of the indicators suggested can simultaneously represent a separate standard and a guideline for schools to orient themselves towards. The system of indicators is sufficiently flexible to be adapted to a specific country's situation in respect of EDC quality evaluation. The text itself is successfully structured as per Table 1 (page 58), which gives a general outlook of the system of indicators and consequently facilitates their further perception. The majority of indicators are clear and can serve as a powerful tool for detecting similar phenomena in school activities. However, in our view, several indicators call for more detailed specialisation with regard to education, traditions and the cultural peculiarities of Ukraine, in particular those related to school climate.

Chapter 6, "School development planning of EDC", reveals specific gradual steps for implementing this approach at school. The model described is clear and coherent; however, it calls for very extensive implementation work in each particular country and school, first and foremost in the relevant training of teachers and administrators. Without the motivation and training of participants, this multiphase, multifaceted planning approach seems over complicated, which could impede its implementation. The practical execution of the suggested procedure obviously requires significant adaptation to country-specific conditions, specifying and elucidating each step to participants in the process, and training a group of special national experts who would be able to take part in the activities of individual schools and consult them.

Chapter 7, "Towards a quality assurance system of EDC", revolves around the possibilities and conditions of EDC-QA implementation. The information presented enables us to see the milestones of EDC-QA development, plus the obstacles to be overcome within this work.

2.2. Corresponding material in Ukraine

Some experience with implementing school self-evaluation exists in Ukraine. Following the 2001 educational administration initiative of the Lviv authorities and the Political Technologies Institute (a Lviv local public organisation), the corresponding project was initiated. At that time, the educational administration was seeking a tool kit for evaluating the quality of school work, in order to trace the changes taking place in education in Lviv with regard to the execution of a strategic document, the "Main Principles of the Educational Policy of Lviv".

The project was based on evaluation procedures used in the Great Britain, which had been in operation in neighbouring Poland since 1997 within the framework of the TERM programme. Supported by the LARGIS project of the UK Department for International Development, over the period December 2001 to April 2002, 17 schools conducted self-evaluations, and reports on this were processed and presented to each school community to be further used in school development planning.

Self-evaluation procedures were enhanced in the Lviv region during the period 2002-03 within the framework of the Ukrainian-Polish educational project Monitoring of School Work Quality, executed by the Political Technologies Institute in Lviv, in co-operation with the Society of Teachers-Coaches in Warsaw, supported by the IRF and the RITA programme Changes in the Region. Some 30 schools participated in the project: 10 from the Sykhiv district of Lviv and 20 from different areas of the Lviv region. Within the framework of the project, school heads received relevant training, plus full sets of questionnaires for school self-evaluation, as well as the methodological assistance of the Political Technologies Institute regarding the processing of self-evaluation results.

The *Self-evaluation of School Work Quality* manual was prepared in the framework of the project and contained the following self-evaluation tools:
- a diagnostic school letter;
- a questionnaire for pupils ("My school");
- a questionnaire for parents ("The school my child studies in");
- a questionnaire ("The tasks of the school") (filled in by parents and teachers);
- a questionnaire for teachers ("The school I teach in");
- a questionnaire for teachers ("Motivation to work at school");
- a questionnaire for teachers ("Professional improvement");
- a questionnaire ("Contacts with the mass media") (to be filled in by the headmaster);
- an observational leaflet on the school evaluation process.

The manual also included a questionnaire processing programme. It was published with a print run of 2 000 copies, and attracted enormous interest among school heads of numerous regions of Ukraine. Taking into account this interest, a new project was organised embracing 144 general educational secondary schools from the Rivne, Volyn, Kirovograd, Poltava, Dnipropetrivsk and Mykolayiv regions of Ukraine.

In 2005 the methodology was extended to secondary schools in the Autonomous Republic of Crimea. Representatives of 100 Crimean schools took part in the project.

EDC-QA elements were present in the self-evaluation methodology proposed to schools: teachers, pupils, parents and school administrations were all closely involved in the project. The criteria for school development included "atmosphere at school", "co-operation with parents", "openness of the school", "availability of a school development planning tradition at school", etc.

Nowadays, some Ukrainian schools involved in the project are carrying on this work, but their number only amounts to 100-120 schools, according to our data. Unfortunately, this experience was not supported by the state; however, some elements of the school self-evaluation methodology were used by the MES in the preparation of the "Preliminary Criteria for the Evaluation of General Educational Establishments' Activities" document and the Dnipropetrivsk regional educational administration in developing a tool kit for school certification. As an example, these documents included the following evaluation indicators: efficiency and feasibility of plans and events aimed at developing an establishment; interaction between different school departments and pupils' and parents' self-government bodies; the public rankings of an educational institution (determined by the opinions of parents, pupils, graduates, the community, managers of local companies); and the level of collaboration and mutual respect of participants in the educational process.

It is worth mentioning that the above-mentioned state documents disregarded numerous EDC-QA aspects that had been explored in the "Preliminary Criteria for Evaluation of General Educational Establishments' Activities". Furthermore, the notion of "evaluation of educational institutions' activities" is interpreted in state policies as a form of "control" procedure. To illustrate the point, the introduction to the new 2006 edition of "Preliminary Criteria for Evaluation of General Educational Establishments' Activities" states that "State control is exercised with the aim to objectively evaluate implementation of state educational policy by educational institutions. Certification as a form of state control aims at determining the efficiency of an educational institution's activity with regard to state standards, the results of the educational process, analysis of potential possibilities of an educational establishment and the extent of their fulfilment."

Elements of school development planning were included in the activities of 70 schools during the implementation of the project Educating School Heads on Change Management, executed by the Teachers for Democracy and Partnership organisation in 2004-05. The idea of education quality monitoring was finally widely disseminated in 2003-04 while implementing a large-scale project for the UN Development Programme, Educational Policy and Equal-to-Equal Education, which was supported at state level.

In 2006 the Kiev-based NGO All-Ukrainian Association of Teachers of Social Sciences and Civic Education, supported by the EU, translated the "Tool for Quality Assurance of Education for Democratic Citizenship in Schools" from English into Ukrainian. There are now about 100 Ukrainian language copies of this book, marking the start of the beginning of the implementation process. Working with the Ukrainian version of the tool will help Ukrainian teachers and officials to develop new project ideas in relation to the work already completed.

3. *The tool as an instrument of school evaluation in Ukraine*

3.1. Conditions for using the tool in schools

3.1.1. Circumstances that might promote the use of the tool

About ten years ago civic education became an element in the national curriculum. So this self-evaluation tool, tested by teachers, is a practical way of assessing how developed citizenship education is in a school and what steps can be taken to improve its provision.

Sharing experience and good practice in citizenship education is extremely valuable. This tool draws on a range of expertise in the teaching of and learning about citizenship education. It is designed to be helpful to secondary and special schools, and will contribute to improving schools and raising standards. The messages with regard to teaching and learning are challenging in any subject. Moreover, the advice and help on developing self-evaluation will provide invaluable support to schools as they develop this approach in preparation for inspection by the educational authorities.

One of the most significant factors that could favour the promotion of the tool is the change of policy by the MES regarding civic education – in case it is transformed from one of many tasks facing the school these days into a fundamental principle of school policy and the main direction of school development. The issue of influencing the senior management authorities remains a primary one for our country, since the educational system of Ukraine is still centralised. For this reason, recognition of the tool's value is directly tied up with the objectives and priorities of educational policy. Therefore, preliminary work on the implementation of EDC-QA should be conducted at the level of managers of education – officials of the MES, local education administrations, and effective lobbyists for EDC-QA ideas.

On the other hand, promotion of the tool would largely benefit from familiarising the pedagogical community, the APSU, teachers and school administrators with the main ideas of the tool and the experiences of other countries with similar work. This could be carried out via publications in the specialised pedagogical press, and by training a group of QA approach experts in Ukraine. It could prove essential for the APSU to set up a counselling research centre in order to foster these ideas and to provide assistance to schools in EDC-QA implementation.

Within the educational and in-service training processes, it is necessary to convince teachers and school managers of the utility of the tool, the necessity of school development and change planning and of shaping policies at the level of their own educational institutions, and the advantages of a democratic management programme based on EDC principles. If all these strategies are combined, we can count on long-term success.

The most practical way of implementing EDC-QA is undoubtedly through special projects enabling Ukrainian schools to accumulate relevant experience. Such projects could be centred in one or two regions of Ukraine, in which the pilot schools would carry out this work over a period of three to five years in full consultation with the MES. The course of such projects presupposes special training for teachers and school administrators, relevant experience accumulation, its generalisation and its further up-scaling by the MES. The work in such schools should be conducted together with specially trained experts/counsellors, familiar with practice in other countries with the tool. It is similarly important to ensure that other schools' staff are aware of the tool, the importance of this work, its benefits for a developing school, etc.

Publication of the tool for mass discussion and use could become an important factor in promoting the tool.

3.1.2. Possible difficulties and obstacles

Implementation of the document in Ukraine appears to be a complicated task. In my view, the most difficult task is to overcome certain stereotypes, for example:

- civic education is seen as one of numerous school tasks aimed at shaping civic competence among pupils (knowledge, skills, attitudes characteristic of conscious and responsible citizens). This task is being solved through the introduction of special subjects (civic education), an emphasis on civic education elements in teaching other subjects (inter-subject approach), the organisation of extra-curricular work for pupils (social projects, service learning, etc.), the implementation of active strategies and methods in the educational process, and the development of pupils' self-government. Understanding EDC as a priority of education policies and practices is much broader and calls for more profound transformations in the understanding of this concept by both national system officials, and by pupils, parents and teachers;
- from the above-mentioned perspective, measuring education quality is understood as the supreme educational management bodies' control of the quality of knowledge and school activities.

A significant obstacle is the absence of sustainable democracy traditions, or an organisational culture that would be relevant to QA approach procedures in the educational management system as a whole. The conservatism of some educational managers, insufficient comprehension of the role of EDC, and a lack of desire to change authoritarian managerial approaches could also constitute difficulties in the promotion of the tool. With regard to this, the threat of substituting empowerment for administrative pressure on the part of regional educational managers also seems probable.

EDC-QA implementation is not possible without thorough and profound preparation of educational staff, and consequently without the gradual introduction of this element into teachers' and administrators' training as part of in-service and pre-service training at the state level, which will undoubtedly call for significant human and financial resources.

There are not enough publications and research data that could foster increased awareness of the tool among teachers and other interested parties, and promotion of the tool among of the rank and file could encounter difficulties as a result.

Ukraine does not have a sufficient number of experts and educational specialists who could implement, popularise and research the QA approach, and motivate schools to implement it in daily practice.

Implementation of the tool could face financial difficulties. Given the low salaries of school teachers and administrators, they are very unlikely to be willing to take on any supplementary work, especially a time-consuming one on a voluntary basis.

Moreover, the gradual development of this work calls for significant financial, material and human resources, especially at the introductory stage.

As teachers' salaries have lost their value, the profession cannot attract or retain well-trained young teachers; besides, teaching and learning resources are either lacking or outdated. In such a context it would be exceptionally beneficial if the implementation process could build on existing self-governance in the sector. In this respect, teachers' associations could play a vital role. Several of the most visible associations are the Ukrainian School Heads Association, Teachers for Democracy and Partnership, the Nova Doba Association of Teachers of History, Civic Education and Social Studies, and the Ukrainian Step-by-Step Foundation.

3.1.3. Parts of the tool with particular applicability

Different parts of the tool can nowadays be utilised in different ways. Chapter 2, dedicated to the definition and importance of the tool, should be used in Ukraine as soon as possible. Its main theses and notions should be proposed for discussion among educational employees and parents. Ukraine is ready for gradual acceptance and adaptation of key aspects of capacity-building for EDC-QA in schools.

Adaptation of QA-related material in Chapter 3 is also timely for Ukraine. The schools that already have experience using QA and are convinced of its effectiveness can become pilot schools for generating similar experience, customising the tool for Ukrainian conditions and further disseminating it through the country's educational system.

Chapter 4 of the tool could be implemented in school practice today via separate projects, presupposing training workshops for educational employees, counselling and organisational assistance. The structure of the text is comprehensible and practical; it meets Ukrainian conditions and can be individually adapted by school staff and used thereafter in school planning and development. School staff are only partially familiar with methods suggested for planning (Appendix 2), which shows a clear need for training workshops and recommendations on how to apply these methods in daily school practice.

As far as Chapters 5 and 6 are concerned (dwelling on EDC-QA), their integral implementation is only possible after the work mentioned in Chapters 2 to 4 of the tool has been completed. After public opinion of EDC changes and it becomes a priority in the national system of education, the transition to school development planning of EDC will be possible.

On the other hand, QA implementation in school work, and regional and national educational administrations will significantly facilitate the transition to school development planning of EDC. In this case, individual transition from school development planning to EDC planning will be possible, in that planning teams could operate at schools, all school staff will be motivated and prepared to take part in the planning process, and the school administration will be empowered for the participation of teachers, pupils, parents and local community representatives in the planning process. Schools will have accumulated a set of tools and methods for carrying out planning and subsequent development planning.

3.1.4. Target groups of the tool

The tool addresses all the key areas in successful implementation of citizenship education, including the most challenging such as teacher assessment. I am confident, therefore, that all senior managers and teachers of citizenship education will find it useful in judging the overall progress of their school. I am grateful to all those who, by sharing their experiences and expertise, have contributed to the development of this valuable document.

The target groups of the tool are school heads, school administration representatives, regional educational administration representatives, officials of the MES and teachers. Each of these groups, however, needs a special strategy to be developed on mastering and applying the tool.

The primary target group includes school heads and their deputies, since they determine school policy, the main directions of its development, and the organisation of school activities. School administration representatives are interested in school improvement, its constant development, the perfection of all school management tools, and the possibilities of reinforcing the school's position. As experience of previous projects shows, this group can be truly motivated to use the tool, initially as part of the project, and later on an ongoing basis.

Furthermore, the majority of these target groups have already been involved in the project and possess all the required knowledge and skills. The existing Ukrainian in-service training system can ensure fast training of school heads and their deputies on QA and then EDC-QA implementation, provided customised elements of the tool have been incorporated into the system. This target group must be addressed in the first place, if we are genuinely interested in the tool's promotion.

The second target group is teachers because they are the direct executors of school objectives. Teachers have the most intensive contact with pupils and their parents, and, consequently, have the greatest influence on them. QA, similar to school development planning, is only possible if all teachers participate in the process. Therefore, teachers need to be familiar with the tool, and motivated and empowered to participate in this activity. They also require training on the use of methods and necessary tools for participation in EDC-QA. Mastery of the tool can become an important part of their professional growth and development.

Regional administration officials constitute the next target group. This group is responsible for organising, controlling and encouraging school work. They carry out evaluations and inspections, and create possibilities for the professional and organisational development of schools. On a regional basis, the educational administration is autonomous to some extent, and is therefore in a good position to promote the tool in the various regions of Ukraine. Regional educational administration officials can act as counsellors and external experts in the process of promoting the tool. Besides, their tasks include the facilitation of exchange of best practices among the schools of the region. Consequently, tool mastery by this target group will boost more successful and efficient school work in this direction.

Officials of the MES responsible for developing the national educational policy should be regarded as a separate target group. They should be informed of the tool's existence, its essential characteristics, and its advantages compared to the traditional control and evaluation system. It is worth singling out those representatives of this group who are authorised to make decisions at the national educational policy level, and those who are able to lobby for such decisions.

Lecturers at pedagogical universities and postgraduate institutions constitute a specific target group. This group is to be specially trained to educate teachers and school administrators, and can later serve as agents for extending EDC-QA and reinforcing it in the Ukrainian system of national education.

Finally, pupils and their parents are a separate secondary target group. It is of great importance that this group should be informed of the main ideas and principles of EDC, motivated to participate in school self-evaluation and school development planning, and familiarised with the relevant evaluation and participation methods.

3.2. Systemic conditions for using the tool

3.2.1. Correspondence of the tool and the system of quality assurance and evaluation

On the whole, the tool corresponds to the tasks and ideas of education quality assurance and trends concerning EDC development in Ukraine, as particularly innovative projects in the field of EDC demonstrate. Discussion of the main notions with regard to educational quality is actively ongoing in educational circles. Familiarisation of educational officials with this coherently built quality evaluation system is likely to foster significant progress in these educational institutions and in national educational policy. The tool is of special importance for those schools and regions where QA elements are already in operation (namely, Kharkiv, Donetsk, Cherhigiv and Mykolayiv regions) and where tool implementation can contribute to the coherence and efficiency of this work.

The development of educational management policy over the last five to six years by the MES shows that there is an interest in quality evaluation of education and educational institutions' activities and a readiness to implement progressive innovations in this direction. In 2005/06, the MES and the APSU created special education quality evaluation and monitoring departments. These departments could benefit significantly from tool promotion and provide solid organisational and financial support.

A significant number of monitoring and quality evaluation-related publications in the pedagogical press signifies the importance of current tool implementation. Specialised editions for school heads put special emphasis on similar projects and approaches.

In my view, the tool does not include any aspects, issues or procedures that could appear problematic for its advancement in Ukraine. The main difficulty is promoting the idea of EDC as a priority for national educational policy and practice. Consequently, the combination of EDC and QA in a single approach to educational institution activity seems complicated. However, promotion of the tool will be successful and efficient provided implementation is gradual and well thought-out, and is carried out in parallel with its adaptation to the Ukrainian conditions, cultural context and specificity in the field of education.

3.2.2. Preparation of teachers to work with the tool

The initial and in-service training system that exists in Ukraine can prepare teachers for the individual application of the tool provided it is available in Ukrainian and Russian translations. These translations are essential, since some teaching processes in the eastern and southern regions of Ukraine are conducted in Russian. Using the original English version would be impossible under existing conditions, as the tool would be only available to an insignificant number of teachers (approximately 10%).

It would be desirable that the promotion of the tool should be accomplished through the state system of teacher training. It would be possible to create a national EDC-QA implementation centre via the National Skill Level-raising Institute. State support would lay solid foundations for the wider dissemination of the tool in future.

In this event it would be essential to provide special training for teachers via regional in-service training institutes, and to assist them in preparing special classes on the tool (its design, procedures, etc.). This programme should contain around forty or fifty hours, including lectures, workshops and training courses. Such classes could last two weeks for different target groups. Therefore, full-scale preparation of teachers requires:

– development of a study course that would reflect all aspects of the tool over a period of forty or fifty hours, including practical assignments on the individual application of evaluation methods and tools;
– the development of a teachers' guide that would instruct teachers on the tool;
– the development of computer presentations and CD materials that could be later on used by teachers in class;
– technological maps and computer programs for particular evaluation methods and tools;
– the elaboration of a system for testing the knowledge acquired;

- the development of criteria to assess the readiness of teachers to use the tool individually;
- the drawing up of a plan to educate regional teachers that could assure consistent promotion of the tool.

It could prove useful to provide more examples of the tool's application in countries where it is widely implemented. This would be especially useful with regard to examples of school self-assessment, educational institutions' development plans, description of schools' step-by-step development, etc. Data collection methods, being new for Ukraine, could be explained in more detail.

3.2.3. Other possible facilitators

The tool could benefit significantly from preliminary presentation, discussion at several national educational conferences, publication of the whole text or its annotation in the pedagogical press, and a pilot project in some Ukrainian educational institutions. For schools that have already participated in self-evaluation projects, education quality monitoring could be of great value. A good resource could also be provided by teachers of informal education and NGO representatives that participated in these projects. These NGOs could serve as agents for tool promotion at primary stages of its implementation. Many teachers and coaches of such organisations have extensive experience in customising international educational innovations for the requirements and possibilities of the Ukrainian educational system, developing training classes and building a teachers' educational system. Moreover, during the period 1995-2002, NGOs promoted EDC ideas, and therefore for this category of educational official, the combination of EDC and QA will be entirely natural and coherent.

Active involvement of NGOs can help to execute the tasks of tool implementation that have been set by the MES. Of all the NGOs actively working in this area, the organisation with the most experience in realising projects on the adaptation and implementation of the tool is the Teachers for Democracy and Partnership (which has existed since 2002 and has conducted more than 15 projects in the field of EDC). This organisation has wide experience in training school administrators and teachers in civic education, in adapting innovative experience in civic education in Ukraine, and in developing an EDC curriculum, textbooks and manuals. The organisation works in permanent partnership with the APSU and the MES. It has a team of well-trained young trainers and authors of textbooks and manuals for students and teachers in the field of civic education, and co-operates with all *oblasts*' ITTIs and local education authorities.

Some other organisations also possess relevant expertise in this field. The Ukrainian Step-by-Step Foundation has experience in organising co-operation between school and local communities. The Ukrainian School Heads Association has many ways of informing schools about the tool, introducing them to this activity and disseminating experience. Finally, the Nova Doba Association of Teachers of History,

Civic Education and Social Studies has experience in adapting foreign experiences of extra-curricular student activities in this field.

The state system of in-service training organised in co-operation with NGOs could reduce expenses in terms of the preparation of teachers, the basis for classes, necessary equipment, training of teaching staff, etc.

Engaging schools and NGOs in tool promotion activities could become a good impetus for them to regard this work as the next stage of their organisational and professional development.

Some schools have worked out teachers' evaluation criteria based on certain EDC-QA indicators and a system of encouragement for such teachers within the school framework. The participation of some Ukrainian scientists and experts in tool promotion would be very important, since they are closely involved in researching education quality and evaluation problems.

Regional administrations could be interested in using the tool with the aim of ensuring an objective and transparent procedure of evaluating educational institutions in their territory.

The tool undoubtedly requires adaptation to the national context. This adaptation should start by defining the main notions of the text in the terms used by the pedagogical community in Ukraine. It is very important to correlate the theses of the document with legislative educational documents. The formulation of questions and theses needs adaptation, too, considering the specific tasks and objectives of schools in Ukraine. Furthermore, the tool needs to be customised for the mode of operation and structure of Ukrainian educational institutions, and for the main procedures and requirements of school management and organisation of the educational process.

I do not think that the tool contains any theses that cannot be adapted to the national context of Ukraine and would thus need to be deleted.

It is obvious that different schools have different possibilities of applying the tool. The classification presented below is conventional, since there are many successful educational institutions even among those without significant financial opportunities. At the same time, we are convinced that all schools can be divided into several groups based on tool implementation conditions and the readiness of the school for such work.

I believe that high schools (referred to as "new-type schools" in Ukraine) have the best conditions for full-scale tool implementation. These schools include gymnasiums, lyceums and collegia. This group comprises pupils aged 14-17. As a rule, such schools have specialised types of education (so-called profiles), that is, particular focus is placed on teaching certain groups of subjects such as the mathematical branch, languages, history and law or natural sciences. The majority of such schools were established during the educational reform of 1992-93 after Ukraine gained independence. New educational technologies underlie the study process in such schools. These schools are well equipped, have good premises and means of study, and highly skilled teachers who receive better salaries compared to other schools. Mainly, the school climate is far more democratic in schools of this type than in other schools. The interrelations of administrators and teachers, teachers and pupils, teachers and parents are equal and fruitful partnerships that fully meet major EDC criteria. Teachers, pupils and parents are actively involved in decision making and school life in such schools. School administrators try to manage schools in a new way, and develop strategic plans of school development. These schools participate in a variety of innovative educational projects. All staff at such schools are perfectly aware of the need to improve education quality and to accomplish self-evaluation and external evaluation of their own activities, and actively search for relevant tools. Such schools could apply the tool in full and are sometimes ready to provide partial financial backing for their own employees and for training.

The second category comprises ordinary city, town and large village schools. These schools could initiate the application of separate QA elements, but full-scale tool implementation would appear complicated for the following reasons (which vary in their extent from one school to the other):

– the large number of pupils in such schools (in some Ukrainian schools between 1 000 and 2 000), which significantly complicates the realisation of any events involving significant numbers of teachers, pupils and parents;
– inadequate qualifications of teachers and administrators as a result of low salaries;
– lack of young teachers aspiring to change school life for the better;
– authoritarian methods and tensions among teachers and pupils;
– "closeness" of schools, that is, the lack of involvement in school life on the part of parents and local community representatives;
– absence of democratic procedures and traditions.

As a rule, EDC elements are not very well developed in such schools, and teachers and administrators lack understanding of its importance. To involve these schools in EDC-QA implementation, the tool would have to be fully adapted for the Ukrainian context and approved by the MES (or regional educational administrations) as a guideline for school activities.

The last category consists of small village schools with serious development problems. Such schools usually lack financial resources and the necessary equipment, and often have poor quality facilities. The lack of skilled teachers and the impossibility of attracting other teachers (owing to the remoteness of the village, for example) are all problematic. There are few pupils in such schools, which have limited teaching and administration staff. These schools seldom initiate innovative projects, introduce new subjects or approaches. The efforts of teachers and the administration are entirely focused on survival. Therefore, this category of school can only be persuaded to promote the tool if they receive substantial financial and counselling support.

4. Ideas for the implementation process

4.1. How to make working with the tool valuable for schools

There are several possible scenarios regarding tool implementation in Ukrainian schools. The optimal solution seems to be to set up a specialised project lasting several years performed by one NGO or a partnership of NGOs in collaboration with state bodies such as the MES or regional educational administrations. Such a project could comprise the following three-year plan.

First year:
- submission of the tool to the MES, a couple of regional educational administrations and the APSU with the aim of signing an agreement on intention;
- representation of the tool in the Ukrainian pedagogical press;
- selection of seven to 10 schools from two or three Ukrainian regions to participate in the adaptation of the tool;
- organisation of training seminars for adaptation teams with the participation of international experts from countries where EDC-QA is already in operation, the preparation of the necessary explanations, instructions and recommendations for Ukrainian teachers;
- carrying out of EDC-QA implementation work in educational institutions by adaptation teams simultaneously with the adaptation of the tool, in co-operation with the project organisers and international experts;
- preparation of the adapted version of the tool, supplementary materials and recommendations for its application in large-scale practice.

Second year:
- continuation of EDC-QA work in participating schools in order to accumulate experience with the tool in Ukraine and to build on it;
- widening to include a greater number of schools, with the involvement of new regions;
- development of an instruction model for large-scale practice for the state system of postgraduate education;
- testing of this model to train teachers and administrators of new school participants;
- preparation and editing of materials on tool application by teachers and administrators, inclusion of the tool as a separate programme in state in-service training courses for teachers and administrators.

Third year:
- organisation of an all-Ukrainian workshop for postgraduate education teachers to provide a transition for the application of the tool in large-scale practice;
- organisation of an all-Ukrainian forum of educational officials in order to present the tool as a national EDC-QA model.

It is essential to simultaneously organise systemic tool promotion via the press (*School Deputy*, *Open Lesson* magazines, etc.), pedagogical sites, presentational workshops, etc.

This scenario will undoubtedly require significant project support, but will succeed in providing a truly sustainable and reliable tool implementation model in the Ukrainian education system.

The second scenario for tool implementation presupposes the organisation of an independent centre for EDC-QA implementation and evaluation. Such a centre would be able to carry out tool-related instruction work for school heads, teachers, multilevel educational administrators and pedagogical staff from separate schools. The centre would also be able to adjust the tool to the national context and to prepare the necessary materials and recommendations. At the first stage of activity, dealing with QA, the centre would serve as an EDC booster. Following the evaluation procedure, the centre would be able to communicate recommendations to schools for their further development in keeping with EDC standards.

The provision of counselling services for schools would support the centre's activities. Ukrainian schools do not have any experience of preparing development plans. The planning of school activities is currently oriented towards preserving the status quo (in case it functions successfully) and eliminating the particular drawbacks of the previous year, when detected. With regard to this, tool promotion will be able to contribute to a new direction in the management of educational institutions and the renovation of schools.

The pedagogical press should broadly cover the evaluation results, the performance of the centre, and different aspects of tool application. Over time, EDC-QA implementation should become a prestigious and solid constituent of the ranking of any educational institution.

Within two years of operations of the centre, the tool should have become widely known throughout Ukraine. Later on, the centre would serve as an information resource on EDC-QA, gathering best practices regarding its application in Ukraine and the spread of similar experience.

The weakness of such a scenario is its primary dependence on external financial resources, and its need to be financed later at the expense of those to be trained. Therefore, while creating this structure, it is essential to draw up a business plan right from the start. Given the payment rate and the school financing system, the possibility of raising the skill level at a school's own expense does not always seem feasible.

Another important problem with such a centre is establishing a legitimate relationship with the MES and the search for state support in tool implementation. As Ukrainian schools are state institutions and are financed from the state budget, the sustainability of any educational project is directly tied to the support of state educational authorities.

NGOs operating in the educational sphere can become local tool promotion agents, for example, the Teachers for Democracy and Partnership (Kiev), the Centre of Educational Policy (Lviv), the Association of Crimean-Tatar Educational Officials (Crimea), etc. Depending on the form of tool promotion, local or national organisations may perform this role. In my view, their participation is needed, since they possess valuable potential in terms of qualified staff who have been fostering democracy and EDC in Ukraine and are, therefore, experienced in lobbying similar ideas. Such organisations have flexible and democratic structures that are able to respond in timely fashion to changes in external conditions, and have experience in project preparation and fulfilment, fund-raising and international partnerships.

The APSU can serve as another agent in tool promotion, as it has a department for quality evaluation of education monitoring. This department is responsible for research and the implementation of evaluation tools.

Any regional educational administration can be such an agent, too, as examination departments and quality monitoring of education also exist.

From my perspective, the best result would be achieved by the combined efforts of all the above-mentioned educational agents, as they are often tightly restricted by a rigorous framework of accountability and structured activities, making it difficult to adjust for any changes in habitual contents and modes of work.

In 2007, the charity organisation Teachers for Democracy and Partnership (Kiev), supported by the Council of Europe, began to realise a small test project entitled Implementation of the "Tool for Quality Assurance of Education for Democratic Citizenship in Schools" in Ukraine. The overall objective of this project is to promote the implementation of the EDC quality assurance methodology in general secondary schools in Ukraine by piloting the tool. The tasks of the project are:

- to train five pilot school teams to use the EDC-QA methodology;
- to pilot the EDC-QA methodology in the pilot schools;
- to develop recommendations on how to adapt and implement the methodology in Ukraine;
- to disseminate information about the methodology and the project results among Ukrainian educators.

The duration of the project is eight months (April-December 2007). Its main outcomes are expected to be:
- 25 representatives of the five pilot schools in the Cherkassy region will be trained to use the EDC-QA methodology;
- 150 teachers and 2 500 students will be able to work with the EDC-QA methodology;
- five schools will implement the EDC-QA methodology in their daily practice;
- representatives of more than 100 schools will be exposed to experience with EDC-QA methodology implementation;
- educators and managers in the field will be familiarised with the EDC-QA methodology through the pedagogical press and the Internet;
- a booklet will be developed providing project outcomes for the target group;
- the MES will receive recommendations on the approaches to adaptation and implementation of the EDC-QA methodology in the country.

All of the above represents a very important first step, although it is not sufficient for ensuring the sustainability of the tool in Ukraine.

4.2. How to integrate the tool into international partnerships

The tool can undoubtedly become a way of establishing international contacts between educational institutions of different countries. The tool implementation process can benefit significantly from international workshops, meetings of experts and exchange study trips for both teachers and pupils aimed at familiarising themselves with EDC-QA best practices.

International EDC quality certificates could be established and issued by different organisations in the country that are entitled to disseminate ideas regarding the tool and have experts and specialists who can provide instruction in EDC-QA. Upon concluding a specific agreement with the MES, this document would be recognised as an important constituent of educational institution certification. The aspiration of an educational institution to obtain such a document would provide a good impetus for EDC-QA implementation in one's own school and for bringing it into compliance with international guidelines.

In addition, participation in any educational project always encourages partnership among its participants, which positively influences the promotion of EDC principles and contributes to the success of the project.

4.3. Alternative scenarios for working with the tool

An alternative, even if less effective, option for implementation of the tool is the separate application of specific parts, for example the QA part for school self-evaluation. In this scenario, for example, a tool would be translated and customised for the Ukrainian educational situation and proposed to managers for familiarisation. Existing in-service training institutes would include information on the tool in their programmes. School heads and teachers, if they were interested, could carry out their own school self-evaluation individually. Such a situation presupposes that school heads are held fully accountable for the correct interpretation and application of the tool.

Another possible scenario would be to introduce the tool via the official state education management authorities in order to instruct in-service training system staff to train administrators and teachers. Such a scenario requires preliminary work on adjusting the tool to the national context, organising training workshops for regional institutes for pedagogical employees, and the official inclusion of the tool in retraining course contents. The conclusion of an agreement between the organisation that is to promote the tool in Ukraine and the Postgraduate Institute of Management on the conditions of such training (timing, staffing, necessary equipment for training, etc.) appears to be a positive and beneficial step.

The methodological departments of local educational administrations can also be involved in tool implementation. The training process for officials of these authorities should be properly organised. For them, the application of the tool in co-operation with teachers and school heads can lay a foundation for educational policy formation on a local basis, since such people are authorised to implement EDC-QA in their own territory. It is of prime importance that the tool should be extended to rural areas.

However, in my view, all these alternative scenarios are far less effective than the major one suggested above. The fulfilment of any of them implies, first and foremost, adaptation of the tool to the national context (with its testing in several schools in Ukraine) and, secondly, the development of a pool of materials for teachers (counsellors) who will train school administrators, teachers and all interested people on the practical application of the tool.

References

About Secondary Education. Approved by Presidential Decree No. 651-XIV, 13 May 1999.

Competency-based Approach in Modern Education: World Experience and Ukrainian Prospects (2005). Educational Policy Series, Kiev: KIS.

Concept of State Secondary Education (twelve-year school). Approved by the Government of Ukraine, 2001 (www.mon.gov.ua).

Derzhavni standarti bazovoi i povnoi serednioi osviti (2003). Director shkoli 6-7 (246-247).

Monitoring System of Quality of Education in Ukraine. Approved by Decree No. 1095 of the Cabinet of the Ministry of Education and Science, 25 August 2004 (www.mon.gov.ua).

Mi – gromadiani Ukraini (2002). Pidruchnik dlia uchniv 9-10 klasiv zagalnoosvitnioi shkoli. Lviv: NFV "Ukrainski tekhnologii".

National Doctrine of Development of Education in Ukraine in the 21st Century. Approved by Presidential Decree No. 347/2002 on 17 April 2002 (www.stat.gov.ua).

Order of State Certification of General Educational, Preschool, and Extracurricular Educational Institutions (2004) (www.mon.gov.ua/education/average).

State Committee of Statistics of Ukraine (2005). *Annual Report of the State Committee of Statistics of Ukraine* (www.stat.gov.ua).

Statement of Oriented Criteria of School Activity Evaluation. Order of the Ministry of Education and Science No. 99, 14 February 2005 (www.mon.gov.ua/education/average).

Strategija reformuvannia osviti v Ukraini : recomendatsii osvitnioi politiki (2003), Kyiv: K.I.C.

Ti i tvoi prava (2006). Posibnik z prav liudini dlia uchniv 10 klasiv zagalnoosvitnioi shkoli. Kyiv: A.S.K.

Zakon Ukraini pro zagalnu seredniu osvitu vid 7 grudnia 2000 r N° 2120-III, zatverzhdeno postanovoju Kabinetu Ministriv Ukraini, from www.mon.gov.ua.

Additional countries

Belarus
Galina Shaton

1. School evaluation in Belarus

1.1. Modes of school evaluation

Belarus has a highly centralised system of secondary education. The Ministry of Education conducts state policy in education and has total responsibility for maintaining and developing the country's educational establishments. At local level, the system is managed by the regional, district and town boards of education. Belarus has 4 006 secondary education establishments: gymnasiums, lyceums and general schools. Educational establishments vary in their size, location and the types of curriculum they are working with. All types of curricula are approved by the Ministry of Education. The system of secondary education is regulated by the Law on General and Secondary Education, which was approved by parliament in 2006.

Belarus performs school evaluations. Belarus has a system of external evaluation and also an internal system of quality assessment conducted by schools themselves. School evaluation is supposed to be the most important part of the state regulation of schools. It is connected with the highly centralised system of control of schools by the Ministry of Education. The most important peculiarity of the system of school evaluation is connected with the centralised and comprehensive character of all the evaluation rules and mechanisms. On the one hand, it can be said that Belarus has a well-organised system of school evaluation, since it is comprehensive and obligatory for all the country's educational establishments. On the other hand, this system is more connected with quality control than with quality assurance (QA).

In the Belarusian educational system, the most frequently used term is "state control of the quality of education". This is not accidental. All the work in the field of evaluation in education is organised within the state control of education. The term "quality assurance" is understood as quality control. The procedure for such control is regulated by normative documents that are mandatory for all educational system stakeholders, including not only the state educational establishments, but private ones as well. If a private educational establishment wants to operate in Belarus, it is required to comply with all the state norms of quality control.

The benefit of this system is also connected with its intention to conduct quality evaluations on a permanent basis: the structure of this system is divided into definite steps that are taken at different stages of the existence of the educational institution. Control starts with the first step – obtaining a licence – after which the next steps – accreditation, attestation and all other types of evaluation – follow.

According to the state policy on education, the main subject of the system of evaluation is the Department for the Control of Quality of Education, which was set up within the Ministry of Education. Within this structure there is a department that is responsible for control of secondary schools. The other important stakeholder in school evaluation is the Republican Institute for Knowledge Control (founded in 2000), which is responsible for designing final school examinations.

The most important type of institutional evaluation is accreditation, which is performed when a new educational institution is established. This accreditation is conducted by the quality control department of the Ministry of Education. This department also has the right to perform an attestation every five years that is obligatory for every educational establishment.

Within the framework of external evaluation conducted by state representatives, quality assessment also needs to be made of the students' achievements. This assessment takes the form of quality control. All such control mechanisms are prescribed by the Ministry of Education. Students have to take exams in schools in grade 9 to enter high school and in grade 11 to get a school diploma and obtain the right to apply to institutions of higher education. Grade 11 exams fulfil the role of final and matriculation exams. During these exams, students have to choose a definite number of different subjects to be awarded with the school diploma. The content of exams is determined by the school curriculum, and approved by the Ministry of Education. Teachers are not free to choose evaluation criteria, since these are determined by the state regulations. Sometimes students have the choice of the exam subjects to be taken, but the interpretation of the exam results and their content cannot be discussed or changed.

In grade 11, in addition to the final exams, students who want to enter university need to pass matriculation tests. These exams are organised like the national tests. A national test system is new for Belarus; it was only introduced three years ago, and has generated some degree of controversy, with many criticisms voiced by students, teachers, parents and educational specialists. Public criticism is directed towards the content and mechanisms of tests and the fact that there is no connection between the tests and the school curriculum. The situation is somewhat peculiar: in a highly centralised education system, as Belarus used to have, tests sometimes consist of content that is not taught in secondary schools. The national tests are designed by the Republican Institute for Knowledge Control, which is part of the state governance of education. The pedagogical community and students also criticise these tests on the grounds that they are too complicated and overloaded with secondary information. A very serious problem is also related to the fact that students are not accustomed to taking such kinds of test, and thus endure considerable psychological pressure in passing them.

Students have the right to choose the national matriculation tests they will take in accordance with the entrance examinations of the university they want to enter. In general they need to choose between tests on mathematics, Russian and Belarusian languages, foreign languages, and socio-historic subjects. In compliance with the admission politics of different universities, those who want to enter university need to pass oral or written exams, in addition to national tests. Students can pass national tests officially only once a year in special centres organised by the Ministry of Education, and they only have the right to apply with the results of these tests to one university.

The gap between the content of final school exams and the content of the matriculation tests creates numerous problems for students and forces them to have additional teaching in the final years of school, with special coaches, the majority of whom are teachers and professors at the universities. Students are thus restricted by this system in their choice, and must pass final exams and matriculation tests almost at the same time. Another major problem is also created by the fact that the matriculation rules are not stable: they change every year, and students typically are only notified about the new requirements in the second semester, leaving them with little time to prepare properly for the tests.

The results of these tests are published in special editions disseminated among schools for analysis. However, due to the gap in the content of the school evaluation system and the matriculation tests, real analysis is impossible. Very often schools are criticised because their pupils do not perform well at the tests. On the other hand, the schools are convinced that they have no chance to prepare their students adequately for these tests, since they need to fulfil the curriculum, which is extremely complex and overloaded with content.

The most general issues dealing with state control of the evaluation of education are regulated by the Law on General and Secondary Education, approved on 14 June 2006. In compliance with the law, one of the requirements of the state policy on secondary education is "providing the quality of the general basic, general secondary education" (Law on General and Secondary Education, 5, Article 3). However, in the main document regulating the educational system of Belarus, there is no other reference to such an important issue as the quality of education.

The concrete policies of the state are defined by a decree of the Ministry of Education. State control of the quality of education is conducted in compliance with state documents, and first of all with a decree of the Ministry of Education ("About Approval of the Decree on State Control of Assurance of Quality Assessment of Education in the Republic of Belarus", 2002). The decree states that the system of state control consists of self-control, inspection and attestation.

All these means can be used at all levels of the education process and conducted by the branches of the state system of the control of the quality of education. The main role of control belongs to the Department for the Control of Quality of Education of the Ministry of Education, which is also appointed as the main co-ordinator of efforts of different entities (ibid.).

This document also provides a detailed definition of self-control. This includes self-checking, self-analysis and self-evaluation, and is conducted like the procedure of internal evaluation of quality of education (ibid.).

All these levels of evaluation are interrelated. Self-control can be performed as part of the state control of education as the first step of inspection or attestation. Self-control can also be conducted by a school when it needs to prepare development plans or to implement some new experience or innovations. Criteria for self-control can be designed in accordance with state practice of evaluation whilst taking into consideration the concrete needs of the educational establishment. If self-control is conducted as part of state inspection, all criteria will be suggested by the officials in compliance with the goals of evaluation. All forms of self-control such as self-analysis, self-checking and self-evaluation are interconnected. They differ only in terms of the level of quality control and the goals set.

State inspection in education is more connected with analyses of the concrete field of school activities or with the quality control of teaching of definite subjects. State inspectors work at all levels of boards of education, and are used to performing routine control of the level of education on a permanent basis. The results of the state inspection are the subject of analysis in schools; there is a mandatory requirement to take decisions to improve the situation. All measures taken by schools in order to fulfil the conclusions and notes of state inspection must be submitted to the board that conducts the subsequent control. The criteria for inspection are taken from the state documents on quality control.

Attestation in accordance with legislation is performed every five years in all educational establishments. Self-evaluation can be the first stage of attestation, which is followed by state inspection. The results of attestation must also be the subject of discussions in schools, which have to be followed by the elaboration of special plans to improve work. All attestation criteria are prescribed in state documents.

The activities of the Department for the Control of Quality of Education are regulated by 22 state acts (the list of basic legal acts that regulate the department's control measures). It must be stressed that the majority of these acts are devoted to general issues of state regulation of the educational system, and especially to the system of higher education. Control of quality of education in secondary education is not regulated by special acts. This discrepancy is highly significant against the background of hundreds of state acts regulating the system of secondary education. Notwithstanding the state rhetoric about the significance of QA, in reality there is a lack of really well-designed documents on QA in the country.

The evaluation criteria in Belarus are designed to evaluate schools as a whole. QA alone, as a very important indicator of the functioning of the educational system, is not disseminated in educational practice. The approach to school evaluation via QA is thus effectively beyond the reach of educational administrations in the country. The criteria and indicators of quality of education that must be used during the quality control of school operations consist of purely quantitative indicators. These indicators include:

- the number of teachers at the highest level of qualifications;
- the number of students entering institutions of higher education;
- the number of students winning competitions and contests;
- the number of students participating in research projects.

Two out of 15 indicators deal with the number of teachers and students and two are connected with the number of books in school libraries and the number of computers the school possesses (ibid.). No indicator, however, can be called a quality indicator. This is understandable to a certain extent: quantitative indicators look more objective, as they can be counted and nobody will contest the result. In addition, all these indicators also demonstrate the level of education quality in both a direct and an indirect way. Indeed, how can we imagine a school with a good quality of education, if it does not have enough highly skilled professionals. However, on the other hand, the absence of quality indicators demonstrates that the system of evaluation is not complete and up to date.

There is one more type of evaluation in Belarus, which is called "monitoring of quality of education". The monitoring procedure is defined by a ministerial decree ("About Approval of the Criteria and Qualitative Characteristics of Teaching and Upbringing in the Educational Establishments of Secondary Education", 2003). Actually, this is one of the few documents that contains any qualitative characteristics which can be used for quality assessment.

In accordance with the document, the monitoring must be conducted on a continuing basis by regional bodies of education. It is very important that a special Department of Education Monitoring was set up in the National Institute of Education. It is impossible to overestimate the significance of this fact, since it is the only unit that can define scientifically grounded criteria for quality assessment, and not only conducting quality control as all the state organisations used to do. The criteria for upbringing are included in the document. It is said that a comprehensive system for upbringing exists in the country and is established in every region, taking into account the specific conditions.

The criteria of the quality of the educational system in accordance with the document are:

- pedagogical goals and principles for effective system functioning;
- educational relations in pedagogical interconnection;
- openness of the educational system.

In addition, several levels of the quality of education are set up and depicted. During the monitoring process the following tools can be used: questionnaires, observation, discussions, self-assessment, tests, etc.

1.2. Evaluation as an issue in teacher training

Belarus has several different types of teacher-training institutions. Pre-service teacher education is provided in state pedagogical institutions and universities. The number of students who are preparing to become teachers is fairly high due to the variety of educational establishments offering this type of education. At the same time, Belarus has a deficit of specialists, especially in the countryside. Besides universities (specialist diploma after five years of study), a teacher's degree can also be obtained from colleges providing training in the field of education in kindergarten and primary schools (after three years of study).

The main pedagogical teacher-training establishment is Minsk Pedagogical University. The content of teacher training consists of different subjects including pedagogy, methods of education, economics, political science and sociology. In the curriculum there is no such subject as civics or civic education, but some themes from this field could be included in political science and sociology, which are obligatory for students in all departments. Students preparing to teach history as a main discipline are educated more intensively in this area.

In the teacher-training curriculum, there are some disciplines connected with evaluation. In pedagogical institutions, students study methods of diagnosis and pedagogical analysis, but this is not sufficient preparation for the use of evaluation methods.

The subject of evaluation is not an important part of pedagogical education, and nor is the issue of pedagogical discourse.

Belarus has a well-organised system of in-service teacher training. In comparison with pre-service training, this system has a much more flexible and well-designed curriculum, which recognises contemporary trends in world education. The system of in-service teacher training consists of regional pedagogical training institutions, the Minsk City Training Institute and the Academy of Postgraduate Education. The latter works with school administrations and teachers from the most advanced lyceums and gymnasiums in the country. Special departments dealing with in-service teacher training also exist within the pedagogical universities.

In accordance with the decree on the criteria and qualitative characteristics of teaching, QA issues must be included in the content of teacher training in the system of postgraduate education (ibid.). The duration of teacher-training courses in Belarus is only two weeks, which is not enough to study all topics related to contemporary education. Topics dedicated to the problems of quality assessment are sometimes included in the content of teacher training. However, because of a lack of professionally prepared specialists in the field, such problems can only be based on the above-mentioned documents on quality assessment or on the personal experience of teachers. At the same time, there is obvious demand from students for modern profound knowledge in these fields. Sometimes when specialists from the Department for the Control of Quality of Education are invited to participate in such a course, they encounter substantial interest from trainees looking for relevant information in the field.

According to the author's survey conducted during her teaching practice in the Academy of Postgraduate Education, teachers participating in these training courses are mostly interested in:
- modern methods of quality assessment;
- understanding the difference between quality assessment and quality control;
- the contemporary meaning of quality of education;
- methods of self-evaluation;
- the use of evaluation results in educational practice.

1.3. The use of evaluation results in schools and the educational system

In accordance with state policy regarding evaluation, self-evaluation is the first stage of the process. The results of self-evaluation are discussed in the school after the procedures have been completed. The school administration is involved in the assessment of evaluation results, while external experts can insist on getting improvements done after the inspection.

2. The "Tool for Quality Assurance of Education for Democratic Citizenship in Schools"

2.1. Comprehensiveness and coherence

The tool is in general very comprehensive. All parts of the tool look very well organised and interconnected. It is very important that the content of the tool is designed in compliance with incentives for its use and development. This makes using the tool simple and productive in terms of outcomes. Among the advantages of using the tool, the following can be stressed:
- the possibility to apply contemporary methods of evaluation not only to the educational process, but also to the process of upbringing;
- clear and well-designed methods of evaluation appropriate for the assessment of those spheres of school education that can only be evaluated with great difficulty;
- a combination of quantitative and qualitative methods of EDC;
- a detailed depiction of methods of data collection and processing;
- a detailed definition of EDC in schools.

One of the advantages of the tool is a very clear and detailed definition of EDC. This is very important for countries that still do not have EDC as the main goal of education and do not have a well-organised QA system. The statement that EDC can be introduced in schools in different ways is also of interest. The idea that EDC can be "located within education policies, e.g. as a distinct EDC policy or as a component of overall education provision" can be used in developing the plan of EDC implementation in schools (Bîrzea et al., 2005: 23).

The situation of quality assurance and quality control in Belarus is very ambiguous. For many school education stakeholders, there is no clear difference between the two procedures. An excellent definition of quality control is given in Chapter 3: "Quality control represents an attempt to impose control on a system" (ibid.: 35). In many former Soviet Union countries, only a system of quality control exists in schools; QA is seldom provided, and is not in any case widespread.

The structure of the tool looks very logical and well prepared for use in daily school practice. At the same time, however, some articles of the tool could be clarified and improved. First of all, the document is called "the tool", but the text of the document and its structure looks more like a detailed analysis of the situation, theoretical justifications and concept verification. The document represents broad analyses, rather than concrete instruments applicable to school practices. The depiction of EDC looks quite complete and verified, but ways of establishing relations between EDC and QA are still not workable in daily practice. On the whole, the development of the idea of EDC in conjunction with QA looks very problematic given the current levels of qualitative and quantitative assessment in Belarus. The application of QA to the concrete subject field (EDC in this instance) is a challenge in that it provides entirely new types of cognitive styles and pedagogical methods of interpretation. To sum up, the tool comprises two parts (EDC and QA), and some related attempts to find out how these two parts are interconnected.

Taking into consideration that the chapters dedicated to the essence and content of EDC look most appropriate for immediate use in different socio-political surroundings, chapters dealing with concrete practical methods of concept implementation could be added, listing the specific means used in different regions of Europe.

The most interesting chapter from this point of view is Chapter 5, which is dedicated to the various methods of analysis. In order to stress the importance of school management in terms of QA for EDC methods and their implementation for local use, Table 1 could be added to the topic "Management and development" by posing the question "Is there evidence of the readiness of school administrations for effective management in EDC development and implementation?" (ibid.: 58). The point is that in highly centralised school systems, there is a great difference between formal management and informal leadership.

While stressing the positive characteristics of the tool, a clearer explanation of the difference between the methods could nevertheless be added to the definition of quantitative and qualitative methods. The point is that the use of quantitative methods in educational contexts is very difficult, since it demands special knowledge and skills. The majority of teachers and educational administrations in Belarus are not accustomed to using quantitative analysis and do not know how to apply mathematical statistics to the results of questionnaires. It would be useful at least to explain what factual analysis, a general sample, dependent and independent variables mean, etc.

More clarification is also needed to ensure better handling of data. Otherwise members of evaluation teams could experience difficulties such as data that cannot be structured and assembled in clusters for future reflection and analysis. It would also be useful to include, in the same part of the tool, an explanation of the possible ways of applying mathematical methods of data processing.

It should be noted that Appendix 2 contains a detailed definition of different methods of data collection. Methods such as rating scales and questionnaires are extremely important for the survey, regardless of how this part would look if it were enriched with additional data-processing methods. With more of an idea about future data-processing procedures, evaluation team members would make more deliberate choices regarding methods of evaluation.

Data collection methods (for example, questionnaires, interviews, peer interviews and focus groups) could look more complete if they were added to the general principles of data collection. It is very important to include in the tool some clear samples of questions that could be damaging and hostile, as well as at least a few sentences about the ethics of data collection. This will be very important in countries where the culture of the survey has not yet been formed. Team members must not forget that all their activities need to aim at improving the school's atmosphere and creating opportunities for the development of EDC.

The use of qualitative methods is connected with general inquiry in the humanities, which means that the investigator must not only depend on cognitive ways of thinking. The main instrument here is comprehension. It is necessary to clarify the application of a comprehensive way of thinking to make better use of qualitative methods. Methods such as interviews and observations must be considered.

Speaking about the qualitative indicators and evaluation means used in Table 6, it could be useful to include an array of tools such as the 360 questionnaire (ibid.: 68). Using such kinds of tool can be productive and sufficient, since it allows valid investigation results to be obtained. It is important to analyse the complex phenomenon of a teacher's activities from all possible dimensions, especially if objective knowledge is required. The results of students' attitudes towards teachers' efforts to teach them EDC could be dramatically influenced by their previous interrelations with that teacher or the fear that they could get into trouble by giving an honest answer. If a phenomenon (teacher's activities, for instance) is learned and evaluated from different points of view of various stakeholders (peers, managers, parents, etc.), it could be possible to obtain more objective results.

After conducting the survey, evaluation team members will have a large amount of data for processing. The quality of the outcome of this major task is contingent on the quality of the processing of the data collected. The idea of involving professional experts can only be realised if the school has sufficient money allocated for such activities (ibid.: 88). The majority of schools in Belarus have few additional funds available, so it might be useful to suggest some data-processing methods in the tool, and to introduce training courses for those team members who want to gain new knowledge to fulfil the task, rather than resorting to external experts. In any case, knowledge of this kind will be very important for teachers in terms of increasing their professional competence. In the event that a school needs to pay for external training on data processing, the costs will be reasonable since the school obtains in return a specialist for all future surveys and research work.

Chapter 6 consists of very important ideas and instruments concerning self-evaluation procedures. Taking into consideration that self-evaluation is a new topic for schools, it is also important to add to the chapter a main competences cluster that could be important for conducting performance evaluations. The majority of teachers and school managers have neither evaluation experience nor appropriate skills. It is important to mention such skills and competences and, if possible, to enrich the tool with guidance on training courses for teachers to acquire these new skills.

In this event, it will be valuable to suggest special internal training courses that could be informal in nature, and that continue through interaction and feedback among employees. In-service training can also be performed to prepare evaluation participants better.

Education and training of evaluation participants is key in all cases where there is no well-designed evaluation system in the country and where stakeholders have no way of developing their own methods and criteria or indicators relevant to the existing system. Under such conditions it could be fruitful to organise external training for evaluation participants and to include in the tool some samples of such training courses as well. Schools in post-Soviet countries lack good practice in monitoring and QA.

For local use of the tool, it is very important to include a more precise definition of the quality of education. At state level in Belarus there is no common concept of the quality of education. There is some research dealing with this issue, but results are not available for schools as the state has not approved their dissemination. While acknowledging the significance of the quality of education, it is necessary to realise that the concept of quality cannot be designed by the evaluation team participants. So it will be very important to include in the tool not only different definitions of these issues, but also to review the ways these models are constructed (ibid.: 100).

The real problem for QA in Belarus is connected not only with the lack of understanding of the essential characteristics of the quality of education, but also with difficulties on how to differentiate between the process of quality control (inspection) and QA done by the school itself. Taking into consideration that according to the tool "quality assurance is placed at both school level, through school self-evaluation and development planning, and at system level, particularly through accountability and support measures" (ibid.: 18), it is necessary to realise that in a highly centralised school education system (as in Belarus), the first level of evaluation is not considered to be connected with quality assessment. It is common to suppose that the priority of QA in Belarus belongs to state control and not to the other stakeholders of the process. However, at the level of state control there is neither a commonly accepted general QA concept, nor well-designed practice in applying practical assessment tools.

That is why in Chapter 7 it would be a good idea for the countries in a similar situation to present a more detailed definition of the theory and practice of quality assessment at different levels.

To make the process of quality assessment more comprehensive, it is important to provide the inspectors not only with guidance on the rules of QA, but also to introduce specific ways of applying the general principles of quality assessment to different fields (ibid.: 103). These principles can at least be enumerated in the tool: for experienced inspectors, it might be enough to conduct the QA procedure independently. In Belarus a trial QA training programme could be suggested in different fields (EDC included). In Belarus this training could be conducted by the Institute of Teacher Training.

While acknowledging the importance of EDC-QA measures, it is important to elaborate a specific e-learning programme that could be available for stakeholders of the process in different countries in Europe. A sample e-learning programme of EDC-QA activities could be added to the tool. It could be useful for countries where EDC-QA is still emerging. To bring that perspective closer, it might be sufficient to promote the concept and best practice of quality assessment in general, and quality assessment of EDC via independent sources of information. This means of dissemination would be extremely efficient for countries where the ideas of EDC are not yet widespread. Such a situation can result not only from a lack of definite theories and practices or a clear gap between the theoretical background and existing policies, but also from the political situation. In the latter, it will be difficult to rely on the activities of the Ministry of Education, which is not ready to develop EDC practice in the country.

For use in Belarus, Table 9 could be extended by including a special section dealing with education and training of educational administrations (ibid.: 106). The level of education of school management is extremely important, plus it differs in its content and methods from the education of teachers. This appears to be especially important for post-Soviet countries (Belarus included), where there is still no such kind of professional qualification as "school manager". Managers of educational establishments are appointed by state officials from the existing pool of experienced teachers. They have no special education for this, and lack experience in the main activities of successful management: strategic planning, decision making, corporate culture, designing and managing projects, etc.

In this case, introducing pre-service and in-service training for educational administrations in the field of organisation and management, concerning all steps of EDC-QA, in the recommendation on areas for action in Table 9 could be connected with the results and sustainability of the project (ibid.: 106).

2.2. Corresponding material in Belarus

Belarus does not have any such materials. QA is supported by official documents of state authorities at different levels. The topic of quality assessment is considered to be important, but nevertheless there have been only a few articles in popular professional journals that have been dedicated to it. Over the last few years, several state-financed studies have been conducted in different institutions, but their results have not been implemented in practice.

3. The tool as an instrument of school evaluation in Belarus

3.1. Conditions for using the tool

3.1.1. Circumstances that might promote use of the tool

There are some opportunities for using the tool in Belarus. These opportunities are connected with the existence of different organisations that are interested in civil society development and EDC implementation. First of all, Belarus has a non-governmental organisation (NGO) sector with many organisations participating in different projects dealing with civics and civic education. Due to current circumstances, EDC does not appear in school programmes as a comprehensive unit, but at the level of NGO activities many seminars, research projects and conferences on this topic have been conducted. During these seminars many participants acquired knowledge on basic aspects of civics, preparing them to continue their education and introduce new experiences in different fields.

State school programmes contain different topics on EDC in the framework of different subjects, but the main ideas and concepts on the topic have still not been included in the curriculum. Sometimes, it even appears that a definite misunderstanding exists in educational programmes regarding the basics of EDC, partially due to insufficient teaching competences, and partially due to state politics.

The most important factor that can promote use of the tool is the desire of the administration and staff to change the situation regarding assessment of education. The Ministry of Education is very interested in the QA system. The new Law on Secondary Education lists the maintenance of the quality of education among the most important directions of educational policy. One of the most powerful departments in the Ministry of Education is the Department for the Control of Quality of Education; its goal is to develop state policy on the quality of education. The Ministry of Education is conducting serious structural reforms of education, which concern changing periods of education, the instruments used in assessing the quality of education, and the content of education. A new system of knowledge control has been introduced recently. The country already has a developed system of quality control, and most stakeholders agree that the system needs to be improved to comply with future challenges for education.

Interest in improving the system of quality control is evident. However, the existing system was inherited from the Soviet era and is considerably influenced by the socio-political reality of the former system of education.

School principals and school administrations have shown interest in the ideas and instruments of QA. To clarify the situation on this matter, the author of the report conducted a focus group study. The group included 32 secondary school principals from different regions of Belarus. All the schools belonged to the mainstream educational system, providing general, non-elitist education. The main goal of this group research was to survey the situation concerning quality assessment in schools, as viewed by the main participants in the process – the school principals.

The problems under consideration were connected with the main context of this field in Belarus:

- Do you have a system of quality assessment in your school?
- Do you see any difference between quality assessment and quality control?
- Do you use qualitative methods in assessing the quality of education?
- Do you need new quality assessment methods?
- Do you use quality assessment as a key means for improving education?

During the discussion the principals came to a common conclusion: great attention is paid to quality control in their schools, but the existing perception of quality control was very limited. The control of quality is understood only as a function of external management, since it is prescribed by state officials. Furthermore, during the control examinations, the teachers expressed interest only in the results concerning the teaching of a definite subject, not in QA as the main tool for school development and reform.

Until now, schools have only possessed instruments of knowledge control, which are not sufficient to fulfil their mission. According to the focus group research, most principals mentioned their readiness to use modern means of quality assessment. They stressed that the means they have can only measure quantitative operational factors, but they also need qualitative tools for quality assessment to be ready to develop schools. Schools in Belarus are interested in using new and advanced instruments of quality assessment to develop education and fulfil their mission. The need for modern means of QA is evident since the schools in Belarus are involved in considerable educational reform. Among the measures of that reform, the system of quality of knowledge assessment is to be changed. Previously, schools used a grade scale from 1 to 5, and the difference between the best and the worst results was defined in a very rough and approximate way. Now a new scale of grades is in use, which ranks the results of education from 1 to 10. This looks more sophisticated and adequate. However, the logic for assessing the quality of knowledge is still very vague, and the teachers complained that they do not see the difference between various levels of knowledge.

The system of final school examinations has also been changed. As mentioned above, students are now required to pass uniform final tests instead of the exams they used to take previously. The quality of these tests, however, is still unsatisfactory; teachers, students and parents complain that the tests are overloaded with theoretical knowledge, they are too complicated, and that the criteria of quality assessment are not developed. In the present state of affairs, the use of the tool will be very important, since it has a very clear and developed system of criteria, which can be applied to different fields of QA.

Another important issue in respect of the need for the tool in Belarus is connected with changing the duration of school education, as Belarusian schools are switching to a twelve-year educational system. To organise high school education in an appropriate way there is a need to equip the QA system with contemporary tools. The implementation of the tool in schools could be an important step in the creation of a modern level of teaching and learning at the last stage of school education.

To summarise the circumstances that could help disseminate the ideas and mechanisms of the tool in Belarusian schools, the education system has various objective and subjective opportunities to accept the new QA model. Schools are now in a state of transition, and in order for them to meet new challenges and fulfil all their goals an advanced QA system needs to be introduced in the educational process. The system of quality control is not compatible with the new remit of school education. Subjective factors are also important, since teachers and principals are ready to acquire new knowledge and obtain new experience in QA, since they feel they lack the modern tools that are needed so dramatically.

3.1.2. Anticipated discrepancies and obstacles

One of the main problems regarding use of the tool in Belarus is the lack of education in democratic practices. As mentioned before, the idea of democracy education is still not present in the content of education. There are some subjects in the school curriculum that deal with the problems of political science, history and sociology, but democracy is not seen as being at the core of the humanities. In the current situation in Belarus, democracy is not considered as the main value of civilisation, and the idea of civic education is not accepted in schools.

A typical Belarusian school has no clear plan for EDC. The situation as regards democratic education and education for citizenship is also very ambiguous. Democratic values are not listed among the goals of education. Democratic education is seen as education for socialisation. However, socialisation is at the same time connected with the idea of citizenship. This idea is extremely important in educational discourse in contemporary Belarus. The most important evidence of this is the embedding of this idea in state ideology. The existence of a state ideology is the main peculiarity of the current state of the official spiritual life of Belarus.

The presidential decree on state ideology was published in summer 2004. In accordance with this decree, every state organisation was obliged to create a new position, Chief of Ideology (Decree of the President of the Republic of Belarus No. 111, 2004).

It can be hypothesised that one obstacle for the introduction of the tool in schools is connected with the gap between the idea of democracy and the idea of citizenship that exists in education. Objectively speaking, schools in Belarus pay considerable attention to social education and education dealing with citizenship, but the essence of this education is still very far from the education provided in other European countries.

At the same time, the existence of these problems does not mean that the introduction of the tool must be postponed. On the contrary, there is an urgent need to promote the tool, and to use its rich content and practical means to speed up change.

Parts of the tool with particular applicability in Belarusian schools

In the case of Belarus, the tool can be used as a starting point for the construction of a contemporary system of EDC. As in other European countries, use of the tool in Belarus is connected with its adaptation to the local situation. Although the Belarusian context looks difficult for the introduction and development of EDC, it is very important to open up new opportunities for the democratisation of society via the introduction of democracy and citizenship in school education.

The part that could be implemented as a first step is Chapter 3, "What is quality assurance and why is it important?" (Bîrzea et al., 2005). All points in this chapter are extremely important for Belarusian schools since, as already mentioned, the Belarusian system focuses more on the control of education than the assessment of the quality of education. So the main starting point must be a detailed look at general questions relating to QA in schools. It should also be stressed that it is very important to clarify each idea in the field, such as quality assurance, quality assessment and quality control, since the main stakeholders in the process have not mastered the modern terms of current educational discourse.

The idea in the tool that "the mission of the public education system is to offer the best possible education to all young people whom it serves" (ibid.: 33) is critical for the implementation of the tool. Introducing new effective means to improve education that have already been proven to work successfully in different countries will be of great interest to school staff.

Part 1 of Chapter 3 is very important in terms of implementation of the tool. The idea that new school improvement programmes are now available appears to be a substantial point (ibid.). The bond between school education improvement and QA is genuinely vital for Belarus, since the idea of QA is only partly understood, that is, only as a realisation of the control function that school managers exercise. It must be shown that today the only way to change the education system for the better is to establish a very close relationship between improving quality and developing schools. In turn, improving quality cannot be lasting without good QA. All educational managers use control functions, but pay no attention to what is needed in terms of quality improvement. Until participants in the process understand that improvements in the quality of education is connected with the efforts of all stakeholders in the education process, nothing will change.

The role of QA in the improvement of education could be a prerequisite to reconcile different participants in the process regarding school reformation and development. Part 3 of Chapter 3 contains a notion about the necessity of dialogue, involving schools and all stakeholders in discussing the problems of quality (ibid.: 35). The situation in such a tightly organised educational system as the Belarusian one is characterised by the absence of dialogue between those interested in the educational process. State officials try to prescribe all the activities of teachers and school administrations, with the intention of controlling everything, the quality of education included. The voices of parents are not heard at all: they have no chance to influence school operations. It is extremely important that such kinds of dialogue start with QA, which is one of the most significant topics for education.

The tool has some valuable instruments that deal with the concrete practice of how to underpin QA. These instruments can be of interest to schools and could be introduced into educational practice at the first stage. A QA scheme containing not only systematic issues but also a draft of the dynamic process is compatible with the needs of Belarusian schools participating in educational reform. The QA system represented in the tool could be very useful for schools in Belarus (ibid.: 41).

Chapter 4 is also apt for use in Belarusian schools. One of the points mentioned in the tool, that "school as a unit is the heart of the system" (ibid.: 44) is, theoretically speaking, acknowledged in Belarus. However, in practice it is the Ministry of Education that really provides the direction and defines development goals for schools. Some schools in Belarus design their own development plans, but they do not set goals for development, since these goals are still prescribed by state officials. Nor are these plans connected with QA.

The parts of Chapter 4 dedicated to the issue of self-evaluation as the core of the system of QA are suitable for introduction, since self-evaluation is familiar for the school administrations, even if its procedures are not effective in Belarusian schools. So if the schools are asked to come up with an effective self-evaluation strategy, they can use it as a suitable instrument for QA.

3.1.4. Target groups for the tool

There are several potential target groups in the Belarusian educational system for the tool:

- ministry officials. Officials of the Department for the Control of Quality of Education at the Ministry of Education comprise the most important target group. Professionals from this department feel that they lack methods to control education, and are always searching for opportunities to increase their skills and obtain new knowledge and instruments. It would also be fruitful to design different ways of presenting the tool to different groups;
- members of regional boards of education. Inspectors working on regional boards of education at different levels will be interested in obtaining new knowledge, since their daily work deals with quality control, and because they feel that they are not well equipped with new methods and instruments that they could apply while fulfilling their professional responsibilities;
- administrations and teachers at the teacher-training institutions. Belarus has teacher-training institutions in every region of the country as well as in the capital, Minsk. The main institution of this type is the Academy of Postgraduate Education. These institutions provide teacher training with the aim of increasing professional competence. Many highly qualified professionals work in these educational establishments and could immediately disseminate new topics for their courses and lectures among the teachers. The staff of institutions comprise highly experienced methodologists and professors who are eager to acquire new knowledge for their lessons. It must be mentioned that in Belarus, raising the level of one's skills is obligatory for teachers and for the school administration. Typically, once every five years all people working in education need to increase their professional skills. However, educational programmes in these teaching-training institutions lack any content dealing with QA. Sharing the tool with the administration and the professors of these teacher-retraining institutions would therefore represent an efficient way of promoting QA.

There is also a National Institute of Education, the main establishment of educational research in the country. This institute contains the Department of Monitoring of the Quality of Education. Since this department is in charge of not only monitoring, but also elaborating new methods, criteria and indicators for this monitoring, the department's specialists must also be ready to increase their knowledge and accept new skills from the tool;

- principals of schools and school administrations. School principals count among their professional duties certain activities such as quality control. This has the same logic as all the control functions of principals. School managers today realise that the content of QA is insufficient if it is not compatible with the complex challenges the school faces. If new quality assessment instruments were suggested, they could use them to elaborate a system of quality control. Although they need to follow all state regulations, they can improve the existing model to make it more flexible and up to date.

  Deputy principals, who are in charge of the educational process in schools, will be even more interested in the new methods, since they are the ones who conduct QA on an ongoing basis. They are responsible for upbringing and socialisation, and could also be interested in the tool, since they need to evaluate the results of the process of upbringing, but they are very limited in terms of diagnostics. They are equipped with the criteria and indicators to assess the quality of education in secondary schools that were published in 2003, but these can be applied more to assessment of the school as an organisation than to assessment of the quality of the educational process. If deputy principals are able to study new techniques of QA during the programmes in teacher-training institutions, they will not only perform their duties better, but will also enrich the practice of QA with new methods and approaches;

- teachers. School teachers are prepared to obtain new knowledge in QA since they use it every day, and they consider that all methods and instruments have to be perfect and up to date. They feel frustrated about the new tests elaborated by the Institute for Knowledge Control. Based on these tests, education results look very poor indeed. There is a strong belief among teachers of all subjects that the new system of controlling knowledge, as represented by the tests, does not work. Teachers are ready to participate in training courses and seminars, gaining new knowledge in the field, especially if these seminars are conducted in the framework of their education in teacher-retraining institutions.

3.2. Systemic conditions for using the tool

3.2.1. Correspondence of the tool and the system of quality assurance and evaluation in Belarus

Generally speaking, QA in every country is designed to improve education and to evaluate the results of education. The new Law on General and Secondary Education states that the "quality assurance of general secondary education" is under the direction of the state policy on education (Law on General and Secondary Education: G.3, A.1.6).

QA can thus be defined as the basis for the state policy on education. In any case, the state does not mention this important issue any further in the Law on General and Secondary Education. Practically speaking, none of the other official documents contains a clear definition of QA. The main document that regulates the practice of quality evaluation does not even contain the word "assurance"; instead, it only uses the word "control".

More difficulties in the introduction of the tool could be anticipated in terms of applying the tool in concrete terms to the field of EDC. As already mentioned, the idea of democracy is practically absent from any contemporary official document on education. The idea of civic education and citizenship is not included in the theory or practice of secondary education. As in many other former Soviet Union countries that have only recently begun their journey towards democracy and civil society, the context dealing with civics is connected with the idea of independence and sovereign democracy.

3.2.2. Preparing teachers to work with the tool

It is possible that there are already teachers who could work with the tool independently in Belarus, since there are teachers who are ready to acquire new knowledge and who are not satisfied with the existing QA system. In terms of being used independently, two main conditions must be followed to make this possibility real:
- the tool needs to be translated into Russian and Belarusian;
- the ways of delivering the tool to teachers have to be worked out. If the tool was recommended – at least partially – for teacher-training institutions or the National Institute of Education, this could open up an opportunity for teachers to grasp the ideas and scope of the tool. In the highly centralised Belarusian system of education, there are few opportunities for teachers to obtain information from independent sources.

On the topic of the independent use of the tool, it would be possible to suggest organising seminars on QA and diagnosis instruments at teacher-training institutes, and with their assistance in different schools. Since there is a real need for qualitative information on this issue, interest in conducting training courses and participation could be very strong.

To implement the tool, it will be very important to publish a book dealing with the contemporary methods of quality assessment and general questions about QA. Ideally, this book should contain ideas on how to adapt modern instruments to local education system conditions, and how to define the prospects of developments in this direction.

3.2.3. Other possible facilitators

Among other measures that can facilitate the implementation of the tool, one can also mention publishing articles in educational journals dealing with the ideas of the tool. It would seem particularly fruitful to prepare some serious articles on this topic, written in the context of different subjects of the school programme and especially in terms of the application of the tool in school management. To speed up this process, it will be important to provide information on other countries' experiences with this issue.

A special seminar could also be organised for countries with the same heritage and educational trends in order to exchange methods and ideas about implementing and using the tool. Different parts of the educational community could be invited to such seminars.

Various incentives for educators to implement the tool could be envisaged, such as participation in seminars and training courses and the possibility of publication. It is also very important to create new opportunities for obtaining information on this topic, such as a special website dedicated to questions of QA in education, accessible to teachers and school administrations.

Considering the possibility of adapting the tool to the local context, it looks sufficient to add some ideas on how to change the situation gradually, and how to implement the tool gradually. Additionally, it will also be important to show more vividly how school evaluation can improve quality assessment, since in Belarus, school evaluation is a traditional element of quality control, which is performed in a more formal way than development.

3.2.4. How the tool can be applied to different school types

The tool certainly looks particularly apt for gymnasiums and lyceums. These schools have the most advanced educational programmes and the most professional staff. It is very important that these schools have more freedom in their operations and that the principals are interested in development. The students' parents are also more involved in the educational process and the results of teaching: almost 100% of graduates in such kinds of schools become students at higher education institutions. Gymnasiums and lyceums have a special atmosphere of creativity, a spirit of unity and shared values that could be suitable for successful implementation of the tool.

4. Ideas for an implementation process

4.1. How to make working with the tool valuable for schools

The tool could be implemented in different ways. It could be done by suggesting new instruments for schools that can be applied to the existing system. In that case, schools will need new knowledge to use the tool. The tool could also be implemented with the assistance of NGOs interested in EDC development. In all these scenarios, the first steps in the project of implementing the tool might be connected with preparing the tool to be used in the local context. The tool has to be translated into Russian and adapted for use in local schools. Belarus has a highly centralised system of quality control, which is why teachers often have no experience of working with QA manuals.

The first stages of tool implementation could be carried out by pedagogical specialists, members of NGOs, prominent schools principals and teachers. It is important to invite specialists from different fields to assist in finding the best way of implementing the tool. All the next steps will rely on the results of the initial team work.

After the first steps of tool implementation, it will be important to conduct meetings with the directors and the administration of teacher-training institutions in Minsk and the regions, the Academy of Postgraduate Education and the National Institute of Education. The contents of the tool can be introduced in lectures and seminars conducted for teachers during their retraining programmes. The main argument for the introduction of tool elements in educational programmes is the need to integrate the modern scheme of QA within educational reform conducted in the country. It is also important to note that there is currently a lack of up-to-date information on this field in educational programmes, while at the same time there is demand from teachers for knowledge and skills dealing with the problems of QA.

To make the tool better known to teachers, it would be fruitful to conduct a course dealing with tool content directly in schools in response to their desire to improve the system of QA. In this case, it would be possible to organise work during the course programme dealing with self-assessment as preparatory work for elaborating a development plan as well. This strategy will provide an opportunity to enrich the programme by maximising the use of the wide range of possibilities of the tool. This represents a chance to use EDC knowledge and to apply it in the most practical way.

To implement the tool quicker, special courses could also be conducted on this topic for educational specialists. This is the most functional and productive way to disseminate the ideas of the tool, since the whole course could be dedicated to studying the tool. At the same time, this could also be very complicated; the course must be included in the coursebook of the institution, approved by the Ministry of Education, and ready for dissemination among the regional boards of education and schools. It will be a so-called "authors' course", taught by very skilled and well-known professors. Course participants will learn about the rich content of the tool and new ways of applying it to local conditions.

After conducting different kinds of seminars dealing with the content of the tool in institutes and schools, a conference could be organised on QA questions in the different fields of education. International specialists could be invited to participate in the conference. The conference materials would then be published and disseminated. After that, competitions could be announced for publishing books on the problems associated with the tool, and articles published in international journals. International Dialogue, a local agency, could participate in tool implementation and establish all the necessary contacts with the institutions, NGOs and professionals.

4.2. How to integrate the tool into international partnerships

The tool could be integrated into international schools via international conferences and projects, conducted as part of the implementation strategy.

4.3. Alternative scenarios for working with the tool

Other scenarios could be suggested in case the first one does not work. These scenarios would be connected with the use of the NGO network.

References

"About Approval of the Decree on State Control of Assurance of Quality Assessment of Education in the Republic of Belarus", *Nastavnizkay gazeta*, 30 September 2002.

"About Approval of the Criteria and Qualitative Characteristics of Teaching and Upbringing in the Educational Establishments of Secondary Education", *Nastavnizkay gazeta*, 28 April 2003.

Bîrzea, C.; Cecchini, M.; Harrison, C.; Krek, J.; Spajic-Vrkas, V. (2005). "Tool for Quality Assurance of Education for Democratic Citizenship in Schools", Paris: UNESCO, Council of Europe, Centre for Educational Policy Studies.

"Criteria and Indicators of the Quality of Education in the Institutions of General Secondary Education", instructive/methodological letter of the Ministry of Education, *Nastavnizkay gazeta*, 11 April 2003.

"Decree of the President of the Republic of Belarus on Perfection of the Personal Provision of Ideological Work in the Republic of Belarus", No. 111, *Sovetskay Belarussya*, 20 February 2004.

Law on General and Secondary Education.

Israel
Yael Ofarim

Introduction

Types of schools

The diverse nature of Israel's society is accommodated within the framework of the education system. Different sectors of the population attend different schools. Schools are divided into five major groups:[1]
- state schools (*mamlachti*), attended by the majority of the pupils;
- state religious schools (*mamlachti dati*), which emphasise Jewish studies, tradition and observance;
- state Arab schools, with instruction in Arabic, which follow the same pattern as Jewish education, with students learning about Jewish history, heroes, and the like, with a minor focus on Arab history, religions and culture;[2]
- independent religious schools (*hinuch atzmai*), which focus almost entirely on Talmud Torah and offer very little in terms of secular subjects;
- recognised unofficial schools that reflect the philosophies of specific groups of parents such as democratic schools. These are "magnet" schools for the upper-middle class, which are funded by the state and parents.

Despite adherence to a basic state curriculum, there are great differences among schools. All schools receive funding regardless of their adherence to the curriculum, although to a slightly different extent. The present research will refer in the main to the three streams of state schools.

Curriculum

The majority of school hours are devoted to the basic curriculum, which includes mathematics, English, mother tongue language skills (Hebrew or Arabic), science, history, Jewish studies or Arabic studies, art and physical education.[3] In the state

---
1. In all state categories there are vocational schools and academic schools although all schools aim for at least a partial matriculation certificate. There is also a major divergence in the quality of the schools between the periphery and the centre of Israel – in the centre there are many schools that charge high school fees, contrary to the directives of the ministry.
2. Arab education in East Jerusalem and the West Bank followed the Jordanian curriculum and students sat Jordanian examinations; the textbooks used, however, had to be approved by the Israeli authorities.
3. Although the Arabic state school system follows the Islamic holidays and includes Arabic studies, the curriculum of all other subjects including literature and history focuses on Jewish history and literature as taught in Jewish state schools.

schools, Jewish studies are given a national cultural interpretation without adherence to religious observance or belief, whereas in the state religious schools, the supplementary studies emphasise accelerated Jewish and religious studies, an atmosphere of Torah observance, daily prayers and religious norms. In 2004 the Dovrat Commission suggests a core curriculum including as a necessary minimum language, science and civics, and calls on the Ministry of Education to design the curriculum.[4] Whether this reform will be carried out, however, is questionable. The idea of a mandatory core programme is under public debate, and the issue of national funding only for schools which follow the core curriculum is perceived extremely negatively by the religious community.

Finance

The financing of the education system is complex. Most junior highs and all high schools are under the proprietorship of the municipalities and as such are financed by the municipalities, that is teachers' salaries, extra-curricular activities and maintenance are paid by the municipality and not the Ministry of Education. The Ministry of Education is responsible only for the curriculum. In addition, although school fees are unlawful in financially established areas, a legal entity called a "parent association" can be set up and parental contributions collected through the parent association and funnelled to the school.[5]

1. *School evaluation in Israel*

1.1. Modes of school evaluation

Evaluation of students in Israel is in the main evaluation of achievement, where achievement is defined in terms of output (as opposed to improvement or learning gains from one grade to another) and is evaluated through matriculation exams set by the Ministry of Education. The Israeli education system is geared towards, and in a sense determined by, the universities and their admission policy.[6] To go to university, one must have a matriculation certificate with a high score (and a good score in a psychometric examination). The goal of the education system (again in

---

4. For more information on the work of the Dovrat Commission see: cms.education.gov.il/ EducationCMS/Units/Ntfe/HdochHsofi/ p. 85 (sec 1.7.3).
5. For information regarding the citizenship orientation of both teachers and students in the three central streams of schools, see: http://cms.education.gov.il/NR/rdonlyres/14134502-F726-4962-804F-52F09DBE087A/10993/Finalreport0.rtf.
For a good review of peace programmes operating in Israel and their effectiveness, see: Nevo, B. and Brem, I. (2002), "Peace Education Programs and the Evaluation of Their Effectiveness", in Salomon, G. and Nevo, B. (eds.), Peace Education: The Concept, Principles, and Practices around the World, Mahwah, NJ: Lawrence Erlbaum Associates.
6. Universities give bonus points to certain subjects (such as sciences) and in this way influence the centrality of school subjects both with regard to the quality and quantity of students studying the subjects and the funding of the subjects by the ministry.

the main) is matriculation – students are evaluated and have possibilities according to their achievements in the matriculation exams, while schools are evaluated and assessed according to the percentage of those graduating with matriculation certificates and the quality of these certificates. The curriculum at high school is determined almost completely by the matriculation exams, and to a large extent in junior high.

Student evaluation

Students routinely take exams within school which are internal exams. In junior high there are more projects than in high school, but still grades are mainly determined by exams and only partly by "seriousness", that is, participation in the class and homework. Most of the "ideological magnet schools" try to emphasise educational values but, as a good matriculation certificate is one's entry card into society, they also largely prepare students for matriculation through exams.[7] Criteria and forms of evaluation (other than matriculation) are a matter of school policy. In some schools this is a topic of study and dialogue among staff. Guidelines are defined, but each teacher applies the criteria according to his or her interpretation. Evaluation for matriculation has accurate criteria, though these vary to some extent among schools. In most schools evaluation is based on exams (mainly simulated matriculation exams) and the issue of evaluation is determined by the school administration.

In subjects for which there are no official ministry exams (such as philosophy, anthropology, dance, etc.) there is a procedure through which schools can attain permission from the ministry to award internal grades for the subject.[8] Evaluation in this case is based on, firstly, an examination prepared by the teacher heading the subject in the school and, secondly, a paper or project prepared by the student with the guidance of the teacher. These subjects are matriculation subjects, that is, their grade is integrated into the matriculation average, but they do not receive a bonus from the universities. The existence of this track in schools varies greatly and is dependent on school initiative.[9]

As an alternative to an examination a student may choose to write a research paper or an artwork/composition either for credit in a subject in which he or she is not taking a matriculation exam or instead of a matriculation examination. This requires the permission of the school principal, and the student's work should be guided by a school teacher and an academic adviser from a university or college. This alternative is, however, very rarely taken up, and generally only by capable students in strong schools.

---

7. In democratic schools, matriculation is a choice for the students; most choose not to take it up.
8. The procedure consists of writing a study programme for the subject, which must be approved by the ministry. Thus, in certain subjects there is no official programme but different programmes in different schools.
9. Clearly this track is not common in "weak" schools.

School evaluation

As suggested above, schools are basically evaluated by the percentage of matriculating students in the school and the quality of their matriculation grades. In addition to this, the following procedures exist.[10]

1. Until 2006 every second year all students in grades 5 and 8 had to take the Meitzav Exam, which is a national evaluation test in the subjects of mother tongue language skills (Hebrew or Arabic), English, maths, science, technology and school climate. In grade 9 there is an additional evaluation test in the subject of "Heritage Zionism and Democracy". Questionnaires in this subject are closed multiple-choice questions, but in language skills, maths, technology and English, both open and closed questions are used. The questions are developed by evaluation experts external to the ministry in co-operation with ministry inspectors of the subjects being evaluated. The school climate evaluation tool was developed by the Evaluation Department of the ministry in collaboration with its Psychological Counselling Services Unit.

The results of the tests are outsourced for analysis, and the results are provided to both the schools and the Evaluation Department of the ministry. The treatment of the results varies among the schools and is affected by three variables:
– the capacity of the school management to understand the results and translate them into school policy;
– the support furnished by the municipality and ministry inspectors in interpreting the results and in building a work plan to address them;
– the school culture with regard to evaluation and work programmes. Schools with an evaluation and work programme culture formed work development plans based on the results.

Depending on the municipality inspector and subject inspector, schools were given aid in planning and extra hours for subjects with poor results in the Meitzav. There was no (and still is no) action plan issued by the ministry with regard to the results; reacting to the results is still a matter for the initiative of the school principal and management team. Until now the schools have tended to oppose the Meitzav as they are top down, too frequent and are understood as a means of control – that is, of checking up on schools and grading them (as opposed to ensuring an opportunity for learning and improvement). Public criticism to the effect that the Meitzav interferes with school work as schools direct their energies to studying for the Meitzav exams instead of education has been voiced loudly.

This year the Evaluation and Measurement Authority was established, taking the place and role of the Evaluation Department in the ministry. Professor Michelle

---

10. In the lower grades the criteria of evaluation are grades and the percentage of students moving to the next tier of education, namely junior high or high school.

Beller, head of the authority, is leading reform aimed at evaluation at the service of learning and improvement. In the main, the policy issued by Professor Beller is directed towards reducing the culture of over-evaluation in Israel and enhancing internal evaluation (in addition to external evaluation). The authority has declared that the Meitzav evaluation tests will be conducted once every four years (instead of every two years) and on a sample basis as opposed to on a national basis. Schools not chosen to take part in the sample will receive questionnaires for optional internal use and, if they choose to conduct the evaluation, will receive assistance and guidance from the authority in conducting the tests and analysing the results. The results of evaluations of schools not in the sample will be for internal use only and the schools will not be required to report the results to the ministry or the municipality. These are the first trust-building steps in the cultural reform of evaluation (which I believe will succeed).

2. Israel also participates in international evaluation tests such as PISA and TIMSS.

3. School evaluations on topics that are not related to the curriculum (such as violence in schools, drug use, etc.) are conducted in the following manner. The Minister for Education calls for an evaluation of a topic which is on his or her agenda or is a burning public issue (as was the case with violence in schools). He or she sets up a team within the relevant department of the ministry, which includes ministry experts and evaluation experts (but no school representatives). The team develops an evaluation tool, which is then distributed among all schools that must conduct the evaluation. The results are outsourced for analysis. The analysis is delivered to the ministry and, depending on the case, is sometimes (but not always) delivered to the schools. Based on this analysis, the ministry develops a work plan (again without the participation of school representatives), which is then distributed to the schools. Most often a workshop around the subject is organised by the ministry (if for example the action plan is to be headed by school councillors, then district councillors will conduct a workshop for school councillors on the subject according to the ministry, and the school councillors will in turn present the action plan to teachers and will lead the process in school). Depending on the school principal and the person within the school leading the implementation of the action plan, a school plan may be designed and applied.

4. High schools (and most junior highs) are financed by the municipalities. Municipality education departments are therefore real stakeholders in the quality of education and are keen to evaluate school performance. In the past it was common that evaluations were conducted by the municipality – the municipality education department would determine the subject for evaluation (grades, certain values, relations in school) and would outsource the process to institutions specialising in evaluation.[11] Although the Ministry of Education has ordained that such

---

11. The leading institute for such research is the Henrietta Szold Institute, see www.szold.org.il.

evaluations should not be conducted, some municipalities still continue with the practice, although to a lesser extent.

An interesting characteristic of the Israeli education system that is worth noting in this context is the role of school inspectors – they do not conduct evaluations, nor are they an authority that regulates internal school evaluation. Structure-wise, the Israeli Ministry of Education is divided into seven regional districts each with its own general inspector who in effect is the Deputy District Director. Next in line are the general inspectors, each of whom is in charge of 20 to 25 schools. Their role is counselling, and in the main they serve as a rubber stamp for authorising the continuation of school activity.[12] In addition, there are subject inspectors who are responsible for the implementation of the curriculum, for matriculation exams in their subject matter and for the further training and guidance of teachers in their field. Inspectors have the least influence in high schools (and some junior highs) as these schools (as suggested above) are financed by the municipalities and not the Ministry of Education.[13]

1.2. Evaluation as an issue in teacher training

Pre-service teacher training

Four major types of teacher education institutions exist in Israel:
- state teacher colleges;
- religious state teacher colleges;
- Arab state teacher colleges;
- universities with teacher education programmes.

Israel is saturated with teacher education colleges. Nevertheless, a shortage of teachers is forecast for the near future as many graduates do not enter the field of education but rather enter the programmes to obtain a degree. One of the Dovrat Commission's (2004) central recommendations in this field is to reduce the number of colleges while at the same time upgrading them academically.[14] This reform is already on its way with the merger of colleges and the academic upgrading of teaching staff.[15]

Teacher colleges train and certify teachers from kindergarten to grade 10. Within the colleges there are different tracks – kindergarten, primary school, junior high, special education, arts education, democratic education, etc. Students completing

---

12. This is true for most high school inspectors. In elementary schools their role is almost as "top" school head.
13. Also in most cases high school inspectors are not principals before they become inspectors, hence they have no professional authority over the principals.
14. See the Dovrat Commission report, available at www.nrg.co.il/online/1/ART/850/588.html.
15. The move is towards the academisation of teacher colleges so that they will eventually offer BA degrees in education similar to the universities (as opposed to B.Ed. degrees).

a teacher-training course receive a Bachelor of Education (B.Ed.) diploma in the track of their choice, for example a B.Ed. in Primary School Education.[16] Primary school programmes require students to study at least four subjects such as Hebrew, Bible studies, science and maths. Junior high training tracks require in-depth study of two subjects. Teacher students choose from a section of subjects. The standard subjects in humanities are history, literature and English; and in science, maths and biology.[17] A new teacher is certified as a junior high teacher in two subjects, for example maths and history.

In 1981 the Commission for Academic Tracks for Teacher Education, on behalf of the Higher Education Council, determined the academic model for teacher training in colleges. The model is obligatory for all training programmes, though each track requires a different emphasis depending on the age-group the teacher is training for. This model comprises five elements:

- sciences of education, namely psychology of education, philosophy of education and sociology of education;
- general pedagogy, namely theory of instruction, class organisation and management, and teacher curriculum planning;
- methodology of the instruction of specific school subjects, namely constructing a class in maths;
- a practicum, namely first-hand teaching in schools under the pedagogical guidance of the college;
- an academic subject matter of specialisation.

All colleges follow this core model, although programmes vary in accordance with the climate and vision of the different colleges. Evaluation is not part of the mandated model nor of the educational culture in Israel, and hence appears as mandatory only in one college. Most other colleges have a course on evaluation that is optional. In both cases the course focuses on student evaluation and not school evaluation. Civics is also not part of a teacher's education. In two colleges, Oranim Teacher College and the Kibbutzim Teachers College, there are education for democracy tracks. The Oranim programme focuses on the content of democracy and citizenship education, leading up to a B.Ed. in the field of citizenship and democratic studies. The Kibutzim College programme is an experimental programme in co-operation with the Institute for Democratic Education in Israel, and focuses on democratic education in the broader pedagogical sense (as well as on the content of democratic values and citizenship). The programme works on the tension between individuation and social activism, and seeks to understand the effects/relation of democratic education (pedagogy) and democratic and civic values and dispositions. Graduates of the programme receive a B.Ed. in Democratic Education in the Field of Humanities or Environmental Studies.

---

16. There are also M.Ed. programmes but these are rare.
17. Different colleges offer different subjects, but these are the most common.

Universities provide diplomas for teaching grades 11 and 12.[18] Teacher training programmes are a "track" within the schools of education and have a low standing within both the universities and the schools of education. The studies have a similar structure to those in the colleges: sciences of education, pedagogy, methodology, practicum and academic discipline. They differ with regard to:
- the practicum – there is very little practicum or pedagogical guidance;
- depth and intensiveness – the two-year programme is not very demanding;
- the disciplines that are studied in the university departments.

All teacher-training programmes have a compulsory course in student evaluation. Graduates of the teacher education programme in the universities receive a teaching certificate in the subject of their bachelor major but not a degree in the field of education. In the main, graduates of the teaching programmes at the universities have a deeper knowledge of the subject matter they teach, and less in pedagogy, unlike the college graduates who often teach very well erroneous subject matter.

With regard to civics, political science students can qualify for a teacher-training programme specialising in civics.[19] In addition to teacher training in civics, there are two MA programmes in civic education for practising teachers.[20] These are focused on the content of civics and democracy and provide very little on pedagogy, or school organisation and climate. None of the programmes addresses the issue of evaluation.

In-service teacher training

One of the problems of the Israeli education system is that teaching is not considered a profession. Accordingly, there is no track for professional development. In-service training is mostly optional and down to the school climate, school principal and the personal ambition of the teacher. The Ministry of Education runs workshops and qualification courses for teachers, for which credit and monetary betterment are received. Each teacher is free to choose which workshops and courses he or she wishes to participate in: teachers are not required to take courses in their subject specialisation, nor can the ministry or school principal compel teachers to participate in workshops or qualification courses if the teacher does not wish to do so. Evaluation (school and student) is one of many subjects offered for qualification. Only if evaluation is on the agenda of the school principal or specific teacher will in-service teacher training be directed towards it.

---

18. Teaching grades 11 and 12 requires by legislation a master's degree in the chosen subject, but this is very rarely enforced. Many students with BA degrees teach grades 11 and 12, college graduates teach all grades in high schools, and university graduates also teach lower grades.
19. Most civics teachers in schools are history teachers who were assigned civics in addition to their major. At the moment, as civics education is one of the four key aims of the Minister for Education, all universities will shortly be offering qualifications in civics.
20. The programmes are to be found at Bar Ilan University (www.biu.ac.il, political science, MA in Democracy and Citizenship), and the Gilo Center for Citizenship Education and Democracy at the Hebrew University (www.gilocenter.huji.ac.il, MA in Citizenship Education and Democracy).

2. The "Tool for Quality Assurance of Education for Democratic Citizenship in Schools"

2.1. Comprehensiveness and coherence

In general the tool is very coherent and proceeds in a logical form. The English and the style of writing are plain and clear, and the introduction to every chapter is effective in summarising the main ideas. The following themes I believe require further consideration.

Firstly, the word "tool" throughout the document seems misleading. As I read the document I asked myself what is the "tool" exactly? Much of the document presents an introduction to quality assurance (QA) in general, and I believe it is confusing to address the general framework of QA as the "tool". This is also the case for education for democratic citizenship (EDC).

As the system level and the school level are different reference points requiring different implementations of the tool, it might be helpful to divide the tool into two distinctive "sub-tools".

As regards section 4, "Capacity building processes for EDC in schools", of Chapter 2, "What is EDC and what does it mean in schools" (Bîrzea et al., 2005: 28). While I understand and agree with the claim that "teaching and learning and the learning environment must be coherent" (Bîrzea et al., 2005: 28), I believe the claim "this requires a capacity-building process which …" is not the direct consequence of the first statement and hence needs further explanation. Specifically, I would say that this capacity-building process is part of the process of implementation of EDC in schools (where the capacities are seen as objectives of EDC). Placing this section where it is makes the capacity-building process appear like a precondition for EDC as opposed to part of the process.

In addition, I did not understand the connection between this section and its subsections and the text, especially its location within the text. What is the purpose of this section? What does it add? Is it an illustration of EDC principles as defined from the perspective of the teachers and principals with regard to school practices? This was unclear to me.

In stage 3, "Implementation", of section 3, "What does SDP look like?", in Chapter 4, "What is school development planning?" (Bîrzea et al., 2005: 50), the tool determines two priorities: good teaching and learning, and a supportive school climate. Although these are obvious priorities, presenting them as "must-have priorities" contradicts the idea of stakeholders deliberating and choosing their priorities. As opposed to claiming that good school development planning (SDP) always works within the framework of these priorities (that they are the core tasks of school) and thus SDP must work with them, and presenting the danger of "competitive" SDP only in brief, it might be better to discuss the dangers of QA and SDP if they are wrongly interpreted and implemented, as they present a danger if not employed properly.

As regards Chapter 5, "Framework to evaluate EDC", I suggest, firstly, that indicator 3, "Is the design and practice of assessment within the school consonant with EDC", be addressed not only in Area 1 of "Curriculum, teaching and learning", but also as a sub-theme in Area 2 ("School ethos and climate"), as the way assessment is practised is a crucial element in determining school climate. Secondly, the concept of "Fairness" in this sub-theme – this interprets the idea of equality in terms of the "standard student", namely equal marks for equal knowledge and skills regardless of race, colour, gender, language, interest in subject, background, etc. Although this is advanced in order to battle discrimination, such a definition of equality in practice can be discriminatory. Unless diversity of students (in learning styles, culture, gender, etc.) is taken into account pedagogically (something that is usually not achieved), the difference between students is nullified and those unsuited to the system are discriminated against. This is very important if recognition of diversity is one of the principles of democratic citizenship.

As regards examples, I strongly suggest that at least one area of EDC should be fully developed, that is all the way down to complete and coherent questionnaires. The examples presented in the tool are good but not sufficient to fine-tune what form the tool will have in practice. I would add this "example" in the appendix.

2.2. Corresponding material in Israel

In answering this question I will address two aspects of possible similarity: the method of self-evaluation, and the content of the tool, namely civic education indicators.

Method

In Israel, as presented above, the official state (ministry) evaluation is top-down and external: (a) the evaluation tool is developed in the ministry with no school representatives, (b) it is compulsory, while (c) the results are not always made available to the schools. Professor Beller is leading reform aimed at internal evaluation, but this does not entail self-evaluation in the sense that school teams will write up their own evaluation tools. She has described the policy as one in which the Evaluation and Measurement Authority will prepare evaluation tools and the schools will conduct them.[21] By internal evaluation, she proposes a procedure in which schools (principal and managing team) will analyse their results, and learn and improve through this process of analysis.

---

21. See the authority's policy letter: http://cms.education.gov.il/educationcms/units/rama/odotrama/odot.htm.

In Israel there are, in addition to the Ministry of Education, many non-governmental organisations (NGOs) working in the field of civic education. These conduct external evaluations of their projects, that is they write the evaluation tool, and use the information to assess their own projects, especially to raise future funding.[22]

The Israel Venture Network (IVN), together with the Israel Foundation, the Ministry of Education and the municipality of Shderot, have instigated a pilot programme for participative democracy in Shderot, which focuses on the study of citizenship and is integrated with participation in the community. One of the objectives of the programme is self-evaluation – that is, the results are analysed by the civics team and incorporated into the work programme of the school. Although the initial objective entailed that the evaluation tool would be developed by members of the schools and municipalities participating in the programme, this was not achieved. The evaluation tool was developed by the NGO civic councillor, an evaluation expert from the municipality and the school civic co-ordinator.[23,24] For the content of the evaluation tool developed, see below.

Content

Here again a distinction is to be made between knowledge, dispositions, civic skills and civic school climate (in which I include management).[25]

Content knowledge

The Meitzav tests in "Heritage Zionism and Democracy" address knowledge content and present closed multiple-choice questions. The questions focus on basic concepts of democracy. Only a third of the test pertains to democracy.

School climate

The Meitzav test in grades 5 and 8 addresses very briefly the subject of school climate, and work environment. With regard to school climate, questions focus on the level of violence, discipline problems, relations between teachers and students – for example, are teachers offensive – and on student satisfaction with their school. Regarding the work environment for teachers, the focus is on teamwork, namely, whether it contributes to career development and to improving results, the degree to which teachers participate in decision making, and the professional level and motivation of the teachers.

---

22. In order to conduct an evaluation in school, permission from the ministry is required (which is not an easy task).
23. The civics co-ordinator is responsible for both citizenship studies and civic education in the school. The co-ordinator has weekly meetings with the NGO guide/councillor, who is an expert in civics.
24. This follows Joel Westheimer's distinction between three models of citizenship education in: Westheimer, J. and Kahne, J. (2004). "What Kind of Citizen? Political Choices and Educational Goals", *Political Science and Politics*, 37 (2), 1-15.
25. Most state evaluation tools can be found on the Ministry of Education website in Hebrew: http://cms.education.gov.il/EducationCMS/UNITS/Owl/Hebrew.

The Psychological Counselling Services Unit of the Ministry of Education has developed standards for the creation, management and monitoring of school culture and climate.[26] The standards address the following categories:
- the sense of security within the school,
- interpersonal communication and the relationships between school members: standard – the school develops and enhances a relationship of care and respect between the members of the school and fosters a feeling of belonging and participation;
- personal and social development – the school ensures emotional learning and social learning;
- cultural and value development: standard – the school advances the development of its students in moral, cultural, Jewish, Christian, Muslim, Druze Cherkesi aspects and regarding civic aspects;
- the relationship between parents and the school and its orientation towards the community: standard – the school furnishes parents with full information regarding the school and their children and collaborates with parents in decision making;
- differential treatment in the school regarding students with special needs;
- the quality and aesthetics of the physical environment.

The Department of Primary School Education is administering a programme on the subject of interpersonal communication focusing on: (a) the culture of discussion, (b) conflict management, (c) teamwork, and (d) decision making. The Evaluation Department monitors this programme and has developed a tool for evaluating its effect on interpersonal communication in school.

The Community and Adolescents Department has developed a tool for the evaluation of social education. The questionnaire is directed to teachers and addresses the following subjects:
- social and value education activities in the school;
- social education partners – teachers, students, councillors, parents and other stakeholders;
- the community of students – councils and forums of students in the school, expressions of participation and co-operation of the students;
- circles of parent involvement and partnership.

The questionnaires are only addressed to and answered by teachers.[27]

---

26. All categories have standards. The ones relevant to democratic civic education are presented in italics in the document.
27. The Ministry of Education has also developed many programmes that concern aspects of civics such as rights, identity and tolerance on a "touchy feely", theory-free or "soft" basis. Each school and each school teacher holding the position of what in Israel is termed a "class educator" can choose to implement whichever programme he or she wants, or indeed none at all. As the programmes are optional, there is no evaluation plan for them.

As noted above, many NGOs are working in the field of civic education. The following paragraphs provide details about NGOs with evaluation tools for their programmes.

As mentioned above, IVN, the Israel Foundation, the Ministry of Education and the municipality of Shderot are conducting a pilot programme for participative democracy and are concurrently evaluating the project. The evaluation tool applied addresses civic knowledge, civic dispositions and civic skills. Knowledge is being evaluated through regular content tests, dispositions are evaluated on the basis of the Israeli Democracy Index developed by the Israel Democracy Institute,[28] and partly on the basis of a translation of the IEA evaluation tool for civic knowledge and democratic values. Civic skills are evaluated through the civic activities of the school – are there councils, forums and workshops? Are the activities connected among themselves and to the curriculum? These activities are analysed over two dimensions: (a) organisationally – who initiates the activity, who takes responsibility for the activity, who determines the programme, on a scale from "top-down" to "full participation" – and (b) the nature of the activity – whether it is charity oriented, entrepreneurial in response to a community need, or change-oriented, namely ensuring a critical understanding of the problem and directing efforts towards change.[29]

The Israel Democracy Institute has developed a tool for measuring the effect of their Constitution by Agreement programme on students. This tool focuses on students' knowledge and disposition towards democratic values. The tool was partly developed in the institute and partly based on the IEA evaluation tool.

The Adam Institute for Democracy and Peace implements a wide variety of education programmes nationwide, adapting each programme to its community. The institute appoints an external evaluator to develop an evaluation tool and conduct an evaluation for each project. These usually focus on school climate and conflict resolution.

With regard to the parameters of the quality of management and school development, no such material exists except for the few questions in the Meitzav presented above.

In conclusion, I would contend that while there may be some standards and questionnaires in Israel that address similar issues to those addressed by the tool, there is no similar "tool" already in place. I base this claim on the absence of two central defining features of the tool in the Israeli evaluation tools:
- methodological – the concept of a school evaluating team developing and implementing a school evaluation has not been tried and hence no tool has been developed to this effect;

---

28. www.idi.org.il/english/departments, Israel Democracy Index
29. This follows Westheimer's distinction between three models of citizenship education (Westheimer and Kahne, op. cit.).

– civic education – no tool takes this concept as the organising concept of the school and works out standards for civics for the three parameters of the tool, namely curriculum teaching and learning, school ethos and climate, and school management and development.

The material in Israel addresses aspects of civic education in schools but does not evaluate civic education as such. The Division of Krimnizer Shenhar in the Ministry of Education, which is responsible for civic education in the widest sense (as opposed to civic studies), has recently requested help from the Evaluation and Measurement Authority in order to develop such a tool.

3. The tool as an instrument of school evaluation in Israel

3.1. Conditions in schools for using the tool

3.1.1. Circumstances that might promote use of the tool

At the national level, a window of opportunity has opened as three policy reforms have come together. First and most importantly, civic education is a central focal point in the work of Professor Yael Tamir, the present Minister for Education.[30] In her work plan, she has designated hours for civic education. She also intends to develop and put into effect a curriculum of civic education from grades 1 to 12, and stresses civic education (namely, skills, dispositions and participation in addition to a knowledge base). She has recently set up a team of experts from academia, the ministry and NGOs to develop the plan. Second, a reform that commenced four years ago but is presently being stepped up, namely the reform of "self-management". Specifically, the move is from centralised management of schools by the ministry controlling funding, expenditure, curriculum, etc. to school autonomy and self-management, namely the responsibility and accountability of principals in matters of funding, expenditure, curriculum, pedagogy and matriculation. Matriculation in this case is a standard for high schools. Third, there is the evaluation reform – Israel in general is undergoing a "cultural evaluation revolution", which has permeated the third sector and has now reached the public sector, particularly the Ministry of Education. The new Evaluation and Measurement Authority, which is directly responsible to the minister, illustrates this change. Given this window of opportunity (and the difficulties outlined below), I believe that the following circumstances might promote use of the tool.

Translation of the tool

First and foremost, translation of the tool into Hebrew and Arabic is required, as a necessary condition for its implementation is accessibility to all users. Even if

---

30. I stress "present" as it is not certain how long the current government will stay in power. Assuming new elections, it is hard to imagine that Professor Tamir would be reappointed Minister for Education.

in the first stages the tool will only be implemented in Hebrew-speaking schools, I believe the tool should also be translated into Arabic, affording Arabic-speaking educators both in schools and in the ministry the opportunity to get acquainted with it. While most Arabic educators could do this in Hebrew, I believe that in keeping with the values of the tool a translation into Arabic is required.

The right school

A key success factor in promoting effective implementation of the tool is finding the right schools for the pilot project. Here it is critical to find schools with principals devoted to the subject and who are looked upon as leaders by their staff. Without the support, enthusiasm and leadership of school principals, it will be very difficult to implement the tool, as implementation requires a large investment of school resources, especially time and teacher motivation. Taking the last point into account, this implies schools in which the success of the project is highly probable. This means that a second criterion for choosing schools would be at least the existence of a partly developed civic language.

Co-operation with an NGO already operating in school

Implementing the tool through an NGO already operating a civic programme within a school affords two advantages. First, the school would at least be partly civic-oriented, with at least some sort of civics language (satisfying the criteria suggested above) and would be committed to the subject matter. Second, the NGO would have organisational resources and civics experts working in the schools and sometimes also evaluation experts who can support and advise the evaluation team. The most important criterion in choosing an NGO pertains to its target group – only NGOs working with teachers as opposed to those working directly with children in the classroom should be sought out. This condition is important for two reasons. First, an NGO representative working in the classroom instead of a teacher or even with a teacher is damaging to the teacher's status and often impairs respect for the teacher. Second, and just as importantly, one of the major dangers of working with NGOs is that the knowledge they bring with them also leaves with them. The crucial question in this respect is how to maintain knowledge in the schools. Working with teachers in a long-term process and training them to lead the process is one way of ensuring that knowledge stays within the school.

Collaboration with the education department of a municipality

As presented above, municipalities are major stakeholders in the higher education system. Engaging the education department of a municipality in the implementation of the tool will serve as a top-down incentive for the schools. In addition, the municipality can offer substantial support in the form of financing additional civic education activities, especially teacher hours, guides and training hours. Ideally, the member of the evaluation division of the municipal education department would be part of the school development team or guide the team. In the long run, with this experience gained, the evaluation representative will be able to furnish workshops and offer some training for the implementation of the tool for other schools.

Resources

A school cannot implement the tool on its own and will require the guidance of civic experts and evaluation experts throughout the process. Thus, guidance for the school development team is not only conducive to implementation but, I believe, a necessary precondition. As the schools' financial resources are very limited, external funding for this process (at least for the experts) is required.

Proof and opportunity for success

Many schools (school teachers and management) in Israel are tired of "programmes", both from the state and from NGOs that come to operate within schools but leave too early without fulfilling the expectations they raised. Teachers are overworked and fed up with new ideas they must implement in addition to their already large workload. Engaging teachers in implementation of the tool can be facilitated by providing evidence of success cases, but most importantly by providing the required support and counselling for the full duration of the evaluation process (at least three years).

The official cachet and support of the ministry

At the system level, raising the status of civic studies is imperative if schools are to take on the project. As suggested, the Minister for Education is leading this agenda. With regard to the tool, this means having the ministry at least acknowledge the tool and encourage its implementation even if it does not support it financially. Giving the tool official status and backing from the ministry will motivate both schools and NGOs to take on its implementation. For this, the support of the Head of the Pedagogical Secretariat, Professor Anat Zohar, as well as the support of the Evaluation and Measurement Authority will be helpful. Alternatively, working under the umbrella of the Kremnizer Shenhar Division of the ministry, which is responsible for democratic education, could also achieve this.

Combining forces

The most effective scenario for promoting the implementation of the tool entails the combination of the above conditions. Specifically, bringing together the ministry, the municipalities' education departments and an NGO represents the most conducive and effective way to implement the tool. I will examine this possibility in further detail in Chapter 4 ("Ideas for an implementation process").

3.1.2. Prospective difficulties and obstacles

The question of implementation needs to be addressed on two levels: obstacles and opportunities for implementation in a school, and on a wider regional or national level.

Making the picture more complex is the diversity of schools in the Israeli education system and the degree to which they vary in quality. I will focus on the "average" state school and make distinctions where called for.

A. Obstacles for implementation at the school level

Lack of a knowledge base

As claimed above, in general, state school teachers have little knowledge of civics and evaluation. In addition, many schools do not have a civics teacher who is a political science major. In "strong" schools, knowledge of civics is common, but knowledge and understanding regarding evaluation is missing. As for the students, civics is optional in grade 3, optional in grade 9, and mandatory in high school for one year. Accordingly, many students first meet the subject only in the last stages of high school, and do not have the knowledge base to participate in an evaluation team before they are in grade 12.

Lack of evaluation culture

In Israel it is not common to plan ahead, follow a work plan, determine objectives or make evaluations. It is more of a "developing a solution or plan as we go along" culture. Although a cultural evaluation revolution is well on its way, it is still only budding in the public sector. Civil servants, in this context teachers, regard evaluation not as a source for improvement, but rather as a means of control and critique. Accordingly, there is not only a lack of expertise but also no motivation and even resistance to evaluation in many places within the system.

Over-evaluation in the system

In the past few years, the Meitzav exams have been conducted on a two-yearly basis, placing a major strain on schools. As they were external evaluations and their results were made public, they became a threat for schools, and schools devoted much time and energy to preparing for the exam. In addition, counter to the directives of the ministry that no evaluation in addition to that of the ministry should be held in schools, municipalities (which are the formal proprietors of many schools) conducted their own evaluations. Different NGO and ministry programmes are also administered. Given this and coupled with the fact that many of these evaluations were not valuable/useful for the teachers in any way, the problem of lack of motivation for evaluation has been intensified.

Teachers are overworked and underpaid

In order to implement the tool in an effective way, much work needs to be done by the teachers in the evaluation team and on the whole. Teachers in general will need to take a seminar and workshop in both civics education and evaluation and to administer the tool. Members of the evaluation team will need to meet regularly to construct workshops, develop the tool, work with the teachers, collect the results, analyse them as well as integrate the results into a work plan. Doing this seriously will place a very heavy load on teachers who are already overworked. In the last OECD report on education, Israeli teachers came third lowest in terms of pay, and fourth in terms of the crowdedness of classrooms. In Bagrut 2000 (a study on alternative evaluation conducted in 1995), 22 schools applied alternative evaluations that focused on process and included evaluations of portfolios, projects, etc.[31] The research showed an improvement in class atmosphere, teamwork, teaching methods and achievements in higher thinking functions and understanding. Although the conclusions pointed to an improvement in education, the research failed to produce a change in evaluation policy. One of its main conclusions is that this form of evaluation requires much more work from teachers, and that applying the alternative evaluation involved such a strain on teachers that it is not feasible under present conditions.

School management is beyond evaluation

School management will not endorse evaluation of its organisational and managerial values and effectiveness, especially by students and parents (but in some schools even by teachers).

Civics is in poor standing in the education system

As civics is not a central focus of the education system and since implementing the tool demands considerable time and energy from all participants, it will not be easy to persuade principals and teachers to engage in the evaluation project. In addition, the *raison d'être* of high schools and junior high schools is matriculation, and most energies and activities in high schools are directed towards this task. Civic education that addresses values and skills in addition to the matriculation curriculum will not be given high priority and hence not allocated resources in most schools.

In conclusion, I believe that the main obstacles lie in motivation and the knowledge base. Specifically:
- in recruiting and engaging school members (especially teachers) to participate and take it upon themselves to evaluate;
- getting them to focus on the project, which requires allocating the time and energy resources for the project;
- getting the school to the first basic level of speaking a common civic language in order to conduct the evaluation.

It is my contention that such an evaluation process in the school (even the first round) would require a project lasting three to five years. It will be very difficult to sustain such a project as the principal and teaching staff may change (and the

---

31. For Bagrut (2000) see: http://cms.education.gov.il/EducationCMS/Units/AlYesodi/Chalufiyut/AlYesodi_project22_t.htm

student body constantly does so). In order to implement the tool, at least in the pilot stage, principals who are educational leaders in the school and devoted to the subjects of civics and evaluation must be sought out. I dare add that the excellence of the tool – its depth and broad outlook – is also its Achilles' heel. In order to implement the tool seriously in a way that will bring about the hoped-for improvement, extensive resources are required in terms of time, energy, motivation and finance. The question is: Do schools have the resources, and if so, which ones?

B. Obstacles to implementation on a wider level: national or regional

Funding

In order to succeed, such a project requires funding, as most schools require training and counselling throughout the process. Although civics is high on the agenda of the present Minister for Education, the ministry has suffered from increasing cutbacks in the last five years and probably will not finance such a programme on a large scale.

The complexity of the education system

The Israeli education system is very complex, as it includes different strains of the state system, a geographical division into districts, overlapping with municipal education departments, many different disconnected divisions and departments, considerable personal politics and consequently little pooling of resources. In a word, it is rather chaotic and diffuse, and hence the possibility of effecting deep/ extensive reform is limited. As suggested above, the municipality might be the key point of entrance.

3.1.3. Parts of the tool with particular applicability

In this sub-section, I wish to address both the issues of methodology and of content.

Methodology

As self-evaluation is not customary in Israel, it can be argued that the tool is too "advanced" and in this sense not apt. As I will suggest in sub-section 3.2.4., the concept of self-evaluation is alien to both schools with a hierarchical culture and those with poor quality teachers and management. All the same, I believe that the idea of self-evaluation sits well with the spirit and disposition of the better half of Israeli teachers and principals, and that many schools would welcome a self-evaluation tool. I wish to explain this paradox by referring to the cultural disposition of proactiveness and "taking initiative" as opposed to top-down strategies. The idea of including students as equal participants in the evaluation team as well as ensuring transparency of results within the school (specifically for students and parents) will present a problem in all but a few schools, and the relevant stakeholders will require much convincing before agreement is attained. Nevertheless, I believe this can be accomplished.

Content

The areas of the curriculum, teaching and learning, and school ethos and climate seem suitable for use in the Israeli context. Indicators 2 ("Evidence of acquiring understanding of EDC and applying EDC principles") and 4 ("Does the school ethos reflect EDC principles") are particularly apt as they are already being considered and evaluated under different guises and hence there is awareness of them, although not through the civic lens.

Indicators regarding school design, development and assessment have not been developed as a consequence of the lack of a culture of development planning as well as the problem of evaluating management. This coincides with the problem of Area 3 of the evaluation of "Management and development". This area may present a problem on two accounts. From an organisational culture viewpoint, school development as defined in the tool is not part of school practice. Second and more importantly, the evaluation of management by schoolteachers and transparency of results will be unacceptable to many principals.

Finally, I wish to raise the dilemma of whether application of parts of the tool should be encouraged, or whether only implementation of the tool in its entirety can affect school practices, values and the way schools reflect upon themselves from the point of view of EDC.

3.1.4. Target groups of the tool

As explained above, for the tool to be most effective, all stakeholders should be involved in working with it – top-down and bottom-up. In this respect, three categories can be discerned – the national level, the local level and the school level.

1. At the national level, the support of the Minister for Education and the Head of the Pedagogical Secretariat would legitimise the project, give it weight and priority within the ministry and apply top-down pressure on the schools. Ideally, support might be translated into training hours. In the long run, with an eye on broad implementation and effectiveness, working hand in hand with the Evaluation and Measurement Authority is beneficial. The authority needs to be made interested in the project and to adopt it as a pilot project. For this, the blessing of the Pedagogical Secretariat is required.[32] The Kremnizer Shenhar Division, which is responsible for civic education in the Ministry of Education, is a sure ally and, as noted above, they are presently seeking an evaluation tool.

2. At the local level two target groups are relevant:

NGOs working in schools

As mentioned above, Israel has a large number of NGOs working on civic education. These "approach" schools with their own civic education programmes and

---

32. Realistically, the Evaluation and Measurement Authority is presently unable to adopt the tool as a pilot project. Co-operation with the authority is only feasible within a longer preparation.

agendas and are invited by the schools to work on them.³³ Engaging an NGO in the tool and implementing the tool as part of an NGO programme would be a clear win-win situation: the NGO has the civic experts in school who could be employed to guide the evaluation team. The NGOs would benefit from working with the tool and evaluating the effectiveness of their programme. Implementing the tool through an NGO programme would furthermore be beneficial to the school and teachers as they would not have to allocate resources to yet another project (namely, implementation of the tool), but rather implementation would be part of a working programme. However, there are dangers in working with NGOs, most specifically that the implementation knowledge will remain in their hands as opposed to in the school, and that NGOs working in the classroom as opposed to working with teachers damage the teachers' (already poor) standing with the children. Accordingly, only NGOs working with teachers and those involved for the long haul should be targeted.

Municipalities

In addition to the Ministry of Education, each municipality has a department of education. This department is responsible for the organisational aspects of schools – teacher salaries, school buildings, school registration zones, school transportation, as well as for monitoring the quality of education in the municipality with the aim of advancing the quality of education and promoting educational projects. Engaging a municipality education department for a pilot run would be effective in terms of raising financial support, obtaining evaluation expert support, providing training programmes, or in motivating principals to implement the tool or to implement it on a wider scale. I believe that for some municipalities this would also be of interest as they seek programmes in which they can influence content as in the formal curriculum they have no influence. In addition, if civics is interpreted as practice in the community this is beneficial for them.

3. At the school level, the principal targets are the principal and management team. Without the support, enthusiasm and leadership of the principal in implementing the tool effectively in a way that supports school improvement, its implementation will not succeed. In addition to the principal and management team, support must be rallied within the teaching staff. Getting the teachers to co-operate will be the hardest part, but I believe that they are the central target group, as successful implementation of the tool rests on their shoulders. In addition, I believe that from an educational viewpoint they should be a key target group, as the educational change they will undergo will affect their school activities in the long run. With regard to students, I believe that it is important for effective implementation that they should be a target group, even though their inclusion in school evaluation may present a problem.

---

33. Many NGOs operate quite differently. Some guide teachers on how to work in class, while others have their own teams who work with the children in the classrooms. In both cases the schools do not need the permission of the ministry to let NGOs operate within the school, although the ministry is trying as far as it can to regulate this.

3.2. Systemic conditions for using the tool

Correspondence of the tool and the system of quality assurance and evaluation

Evaluation is gaining standing in education and the ministry's policy regarding evaluation is currently shifting. The establishment of the Evaluation and Measurement Authority is of symbolic importance but also has practical implications. Professor Beller is leading a reform towards evaluation in the service of improvement and is advancing internal evaluation within the system. All the same, self-evaluation is not on the authority's agenda, even though Professor Beller is supportive of the idea. The mission of the authority is to compile evaluation tests on request from the minister or heads of office in the ministry, to administer the tests to a representative sample model and to furnish schools not in the sample with the opportunity to conduct an internal evaluation. The authority's vision entails that school evaluation experts in co-operation with the relevant school team will analyse the results.[34] It is important to stress that this is not opposed to the objectives and ideas of the tool, but rather that self-evaluation is not part of the vision.

In addition, the authority is not responsible (as of now) for matriculation examinations, which still hold centre stage in the education system. Although evaluation reform is set to take place, the education system is still in the main determined by the matriculation standard. It follows that although alternative evaluations (and in this means of self-evaluation) have been proven to be effective and are valued, the structure of the system is such that alternative evaluations cannot be implemented as a policy on a broad scale. Whether the matriculation standard will open up to alternative evaluations and whether internal school evaluations will be accepted for matriculation is a question for the newly appointed head of the Pedagogical Secretariat, Professor Zohar, who has not yet declared a new policy regarding this. In this respect, while the design and procedure of the tool match the objectives and ideas of QA and evaluation in the sense that they aim at bringing about improvement, they do not sit well with the hidden (patent) evaluation agenda of sorting and classifying as symbolised by the matriculation exams.

In conclusion, while the evaluative design and procedure of the eight stages of QA sit well with the evaluation reform taking place in Israel, the concept of self-evaluation by an evaluation team composed of students, parents and teachers is not in line with the objectives and ideas of evaluation. At the system level, internal evaluation is seen as complementary to external evaluation, not as substituting for it. At the school level, the idea that students may partake in school evaluation is contrary to the practice of evaluation.

---

34. The structural reform entails that in the near future each school will have an evaluation expert. For this purpose, the authority is establishing an evaluation training department.

3.2.2. Preparation of teachers to work with the tool

In addressing this question two perspectives must be taken into account: teachers' competence in evaluation, and their competence in civics. Given the background of teacher training, the quality of teachers in Israel and the nature of the tool, I believe that 30% to 40% of schools could work with the tool, but that most of these would still need much counselling in terms of writing up the tool for their context as well as guidance in its application, that is, in analysing the results and designing a development plan.

As presented above, teacher training does not see evaluation as an essential element in education and accordingly does not promote evaluation. Teacher education also does not mandate any course on civics and democracy and thus within the state system, teachers go by personal knowledge of the subject matter. "Weak" schools mostly on the periphery (this includes many Arab state schools) face the problem of staff with poor knowledge of civics and democracy. In addition, civics is not particularly held in high esteem as a subject and is not regarded as important in high school. Hence many civics teachers are history teachers who are not experts in the field of democracy and citizenship.[35] Teachers in state religious schools are found wanting with regard to civics and democracy both knowledge-wise and disposition-wise. In addition, the culture in many religious state schools and Arab state schools is very hierarchical and does not sit well with the idea and values of student participation and influence within the school (also with regard to teacher participation, although to a lesser extent).

Where knowledge is the problem, this can be overcome by study and workshops that might be part of the process the school is going through in applying self-evaluation. If the contestation of values and culture is the crux of the problem, independent work will not be achieved by the teachers. Neither teachers nor principals will aspire to implementing the tool.

Having said this, I believe that in many middle-of-the-road state schools, the tool could be used by teachers. Although the quality of a large portion of the Israeli teaching force is mediocre (and lower) with regard to their subject matter, with little knowledge of civics and almost none at all of evaluation, I still believe that most can work independently and advance the values of democratic citizenship. Still, disposition by itself is not enough, and there is a large knowledge of content problem in both civics and evaluation (as well as a motivational problem regarding evaluation).

Concerning training, this means that the process of both building the tool and implementing it must be accompanied by experts, and that a seminar or workshop will not be enough. What is called for is counselling with regard to civics and

---

35. If there are no history teachers available, either Bible teachers, sociology teachers or anyone needing the extra hours could teach civics.

evaluation throughout the process. A seminar and workshop on democracy and evaluation is the first step in getting the whole school, both teachers and students, to gain a minimum understanding of the subjects and a common language. This would be a good kick-off for the project. Then, in writing the tool itself, expert guidance for the evaluation team both in evaluation and in civics is required. In this, it will be necessary to work on the "case" of the school (as opposed to theory), and examples of questionnaires and interviews would be very helpful. Finally, the team would need guidance in analysing the results and transforming them into a work development plan.[36] If this process is accompanied by councillors for a sufficient period (I suggest three to five years with decreasing dependency), and a framework for the development of in-school experts on the process is developed, then schools will retain the knowledge and will be able to work independently with the tool.

Lastly, returning to the Achilles' heel of the tool, if we take into account competence in both evaluation and civics, it is patently obvious that those schools that need civic education most badly are the ones least able to work independently with the tool.

3.2.3. Other measures facilitating use of the tool

A key factor in implementing the tool is funding. The Israeli education system is so complex that almost anything can be done within it on a small scale and, if successful, adapted to a larger scale. A principal may advance any agenda so long as it does not impair matriculation results; in this sense, Israel is a "wild west" of educational entrepreneurship. Thus, for most leading principals, the problem of advancing an agenda is getting the funding to follow through on the project, since funding of schools either by the ministry or by the municipality is mainly directed to school hours and training hours.

Given the need for experts in both training and the guiding of the evaluation team (as outlined above), a school would need financial aid to implement the tool.[37]

Guidance of evaluation and civic experts throughout the process is imperative. This is called for not only from the knowledge-base perspective as outlined above, but also in terms of motivation. Taking into consideration the level of school expertise in civics and evaluation, it is clear that implementation will be a long process.

---

36. Here I wish to raise a doubt regarding the evaluation process as a whole. I contend that adapting the work plan for pedagogical purposes is the most difficult step, which is usually not given sufficient attention. Getting the evaluation development plan into the classroom, and specifically into the classroom practices of teachers, is the most difficult challenge and is left aside once the work development plan is in place. If the pedagogical challenge is not met, then the improvement of the school might turn out to be superficial, even though the school will be able to show an improvement in indicators.

37. If considering implementation of the tool at a wider level, namely in a number of schools and involving a municipality, an NGO and a ministry unit, a co-ordinator or project manager is also required.

Accordingly, it is imperative to suggest a long-term relationship and to build trust with regard to this, that is, by ensuring that the process and the guidance will not be "hit and run".

An important incentive would be the promise and high probability of success – especially if success is related to improving the school climate, communication within the school and to reducing violence. From this perspective, evidence of success of the tool in other places could be extremely valuable.

A "return on investment" for the teachers involved in the project is important. Sadly, most teacher efforts today yield no significant "return". In this project a "return" can be brought about through a development programme with overseas teachers, a significant (status) post such as head of the project, or stipends based on participation.[38]

3.2.4. How can the tool be applied to different school types?

As outlined in the introduction, the Israeli education system is divided into five major groups: state schools, state religious schools, Arab state schools, independent religious schools, and recognised non-official schools. For the independent religious schools, this sort of material is irrelevant as civics, in common with other "secular" subjects, is not part of the curriculum. While the agenda of many recognised unofficial schools is very close to the values of civic education (many of these are democratic schools) and such schools have the luxury of implementing alternative programmes and projects (as they have more resources through fees and are not wholly committed to the state curriculum), making them apparently particularly apt for the application of the tool – I would nevertheless not consider them a target group for implementation of the tool. Specifically, these schools do not represent the education system as they are relatively few and do not operate under the same constraints as the state schools. Thus, what works for them does not necessarily work for others, and as such they have little effect on the system. Accordingly, successful implementation of the tool would not be instrumental in adapting it to the national school context.

This narrows the field to the three main types of schools in the state system – state schools, religious state schools and Arab state schools. These three systems have a three-tier structure: primary schools for grades 1 to 6, junior high schools for grades 7 to 9, and high schools for grades 10 to 12. It is my contention that the tool is most apt for junior high schools, as at the primary level there is not enough of a common civic language for pupils to participate in the project, while in high schools most energies are directed towards matriculation. Having said this, there are primary schools that attend to civic education and have the capacity to imple-

---

38. The Ministry of Education does not have any mechanism for remuneration such as credit for participation, pay or designated extra work hours.

ment evaluation.[39] High schools with a social agenda, or those that cultivate leadership and regard themselves as rearing the leadership of the future, would also find the tool valuable and would direct resources towards its implementation.

In considering which school types the tool is most apt for, one must define what exactly is meant by "apt". If apt means schools that could successfully implement the tool, then schools that are apt are those that satisfy the following conditions:
– schools that are concerned with civic education;
– schools that have a knowledge base in civics and evaluation;
– schools whose ethos is coherent with EDC principles, especially those of transparency and pupil participation.

Viewed from this perspective, the most apt schools for using the tool are "strong" schools in the "regular" state system.[40] Strong Arab state schools, especially ones concerned with civics, would be a good target group; unfortunately, they are rare if not non-existent.[41] An additional target group that satisfies these conditions is schools already involved in civic education through NGO programmes. In this group, it is irrelevant which stream of the state education system the school belongs to. If success is a key factor, then the schools recommended by an NGO implementing a serious programme in them are most apt.

In conclusion, strong junior high schools with an existing civic education agenda and civic language in the state school system are those schools that would most easily implement the tool with a high chance of success. These are the schools in which the tool would raise the least resistance and which are most likely to value and maximise the benefits of the tool.

What problems occur for the other school types?

The tool is potentially problematic on three grounds: methodologically – the practice of self-evaluation, especially the principles of student participation and transparency; the content of EDC; and the content knowledge of both civics and evaluation. While the last aspect is common to all "weak" schools regardless of the stream of the state system they belong to (and this can hopefully be resolved by training and guidance), the first two are related to the culture of the Arab and the religious Jewish communities. Generally speaking, the culture in both communi-

---

39. The Adam Institute for Democracy and Peace is working at the municipal level in the city of Herzeliya, furnishing a civic education programme from grades 1 to 6. Schools partaking in this programme can work with the tool.
40. If what is meant by apt is most in need, then obviously "weak" schools with little civic knowledge and civic climate are the most apt for using the tool.
41. The elite Arab schools are private church schools accommodating both the Muslim and Catholic Arab upper-middle class. The Arab state school system is very poor as for many years it has been underdeveloped by the state, which has not invested in it to say the least. In addition, the Arab education system has many challenges to meet such as language skills.

ties, even more so in the Arab community, is hierarchical and this is reflected in school culture. In such a climate, the very idea of engaging students in school evaluation is problematic.[42] Concurrently, in such schools, the problem of the content of EDC also arises as some of the ideals and values of EDC, specifically a critical understanding of reality including a critique of one's way of life, plurality, active participation and accountability and transparency, are contrary to the schools' value system. An additional problem that arises in the context of the state religious schools is the relationship between civics and religion, particularly the question of contradicting duties between state and faith. Consequently, most religious state schools try to avoid the subject of civic education and focus instead on Jewish religious values and community values.

4. *Ideas for the implementation process*

4.1 How to make working with the tool valuable for schools

Introducing the tool as something helpful and relevant as opposed to another burden on teachers requires aligning the tool with existing school activities. This can be achieved either by:

– proposing the tool as an additional stage in already functioning civic education practices in school; or by
– enhancing an evaluation programme already being conducted in the school.

I believe the first path is better, especially as it can help in organising apparently eclectic school activities and bringing them together so that they have an impact. Adding the tool to an active NGO programme (or ministry programme) would facilitate the programme as well as help avoid overburdening teachers. Introduction of the tool as a means for improving the school climate, especially reducing violence, will make schools experience the tool as relevant and helpful.

The implementation process

In implementing the tool, one is faced with a dilemma regarding its effectiveness: if implementing the tool top-down, most probably the tool will reach many schools but will not "reach" any children, as most reforms and programmes stop at the classroom door in that they do not really affect school pedagogy and structure, but instead remain on the surface. On the other hand, if implementing bottom-up, the tool will have a great impact on the school when the "right" school is chosen, but one is then faced with the problem of how to make it effective at the system level, namely, how to move from the tool as a "boutique project" for the "right" schools to its implementation on a wider scale such that it will affect the system.

---

42. This I would say is also true of many "weak" schools in the "regular" school system.

Facing this dilemma, I believe that the entry point should be at a "mid-point" and I would suggest three scenarios: the municipality level, the NGO level and a joint venture.

In all three cases, the Ministry of Education must be an engaged partner.

Scenario A – The municipality

This scenario entails taking the long road that I believe is the shortest road to effectiveness at the system level. In the first stage, a municipality that is interested in civic education needs to be sought out and enrolled. Its participation entails three things: obligating schools in the municipality to take part in the project; obtaining an agreement to the effect that the municipality will keep the programme running (financially) after the exit point of the foundation; and ensuring the municipality can provide schools with evaluation experts and other educational guidance (specifically, the education trainers/guides of the municipality will join the training workshop preparing for the use of the tool and will follow the implementation process in the schools, becoming experts in implementation). The next group that needs to be enrolled is the district officials of the Ministry of Education. They will not only legitimate the project but also supply the support and guidance of the district civic education guides.[43] This is the long road, as I suggest that, after engaging the partners, a steering committee should be set up composed of education and evaluation representatives from the municipality; the school principals taking part in the project; leading teachers from the participating schools; a representative of the Ministry of Education; representatives from academia in the fields of education and evaluation (optimally a representative from the evaluation authority); and a representative from the foundation. This committee will take it upon itself to work out the implementation process of the tool in at least the following four areas:

– the themes from the tool to be focused on during implementation;
– the support of the implementation process in the areas of content guidance;
– support in training hours and in school hours to be furnished by both the municipality and the ministry;
– "pure" financial support.

This will be a long process but I believe a worthwhile one in two respects. First, it will get the municipality, the Ministry of Education and schools to work in relative co-operation, leaving aggressive politics at the doorstep. Second, the process will present an opportunity to build a common language regarding democratic citizenship between all partners, which is especially important in this context within the municipality. Having such a language will not only allow for better communication but will also make knowledge-sharing possible between schools and lead towards

---

43. As noted above, while the municipality is financially responsible for education, the ministry is responsible for content. In this capacity, it furnishes schools with training in the form of content guides.

the development of a learning community. I suggest that even when working at the municipal level, a pilot project should be launched that does not include all schools in the first stage (unless working in a small municipality).

After the steering committee has completed this first stage and principals and civic head teachers are already engaged, work on the preparation of the school level should begin. As this process is similar for all three scenarios, I will outline it at the end of scenario C.

Scenario B – NGOs

This scenario has the advantage that it is faster and probably cheaper to implement, that the participating schools can be "cherry picked", and hence the probability of success is high and a deeper impact at the school level is more likely to be achieved. In moving to the system level, it can be duplicated through all schools working with the NGO and, if implementation is successful on this larger scale, it can be "promoted" to the Ministry of Education and the Evaluation and Measurement Authority as a working model. This process is closest to the starting point of the implementation process in the schools as it involves choosing the "right" NGO (given the criteria above), and engaging the NGO, which is relatively easy (since it is a win-win situation for the NGO, as explained above). The NGO will be the one to choose the schools it believes are most appropriate for the implementation of the tool, and then preparation for implementation can begin. An important partner over the long term (though not a necessary partner for implementation, especially from the point of view of the NGO) is the Ministry of Education. Viewing the implementation process over the long term with an eye on its impact at the system level, I would suggest conditioning the involvement of the NGO with the co-operation of the ministry.

Scenario C – Joint venture

This scenario could arise if an NGO is already working in the municipality chosen for the project. In such a case, a representative from the NGO should join the steering committee. This will additionally complicate the work of the committee, as a range of different interests and perhaps values will enter the forum, but it does offer two advantages. First, it will furnish an additional perspective on the capabilities and possibilities of the schools. Second, when the time comes for implementation, the schools will already have some sort of civic language and civic experts in place, and experts in a position to guide the evaluation team. This scenario is a win-win situation for the NGO as it gives them full reach in the municipality.

Working with the schools

First and foremost, the right school or schools must be chosen for a pilot. In this I mean schools that are enthusiastic regarding civic education and evaluation – most importantly, a keen principal, plus support from teachers. In scenario A these should be chosen by the committee for the pilot project, and in scenario B by the NGO.

After choosing the schools and obtaining the support of management and the head civics teacher for the implementation of the tool, staff and students need to be engaged. If the tool is to be effective and result in changes in the school, it is important (albeit difficult) to get most staff involved and supportive. The problem in most schools is that the teachers typically divide into "education activists" (20%) and those who focus on their subject matter alone (80%). In addition, the need for civics and civic education is not clear to most teachers, and much work will be needed within the schools to gain their support. As noted above, this work has partly been done in schools where civic education NGOs already operate.

Next, a project head must be appointed to head the evaluation team. Following this, the evaluation team needs to be established. The team should be open to teachers who wish to participate, but must include the school director of pedagogy and the school civics head teacher. The team must also include a civics expert (who could be the school civics teacher, a trainee from the Ministry of Education, or the NGO staff member working at the school) and an evaluation expert (for this position a trainee from what is left of the ministry's Evaluation Department, from the Evaluation and Measurement Authority, or from the district/municipality evaluation department may be found). Students willing to participate should also be on the team. I would also suggest a person from the maintenance team of the school (especially the janitor), which is both in keeping with the values of the tool but also, just as importantly, because these members of the school community have a good insight into what is going on at school.

An introduction to the project, which would entail a seminar and a workshop in both civics and evaluation, needs to be held in school. The responsibility for the development/organisation and co-ordination of these should be with the evaluation team headed by the team director. The target group of the seminar and workshops are the teachers plus the representatives from the municipality and ministry, and students interested in the project. Holding such a seminar and workshop will also serve to put civics centre stage as the focus of the school agenda. In addition, I would suggest one day of workshops for the students in EDC (in place of regular curricula) in order to establish a minimum common civic language and to emphasise the importance that EDC has for the school.

With a knowledge base and a common language in place, the work of the evaluation team on implementation of the tool in school may begin. I suggest that the EDC evaluation team should meet regularly on a twice-weekly/bi-weekly basis throughout the process of writing up the evaluation, administering it, analysis and the preparation of the development plan, for three consecutive years. Such "hand holding" is crucial as one of the major problems with the involvement of external projects and bodies in the schools is how to keep the knowledge in the schools (as opposed to the knowledge staying with the NGOs or any other intervening body/project as stated above). I suggest that this long-term "hand holding" will give time and opportunity to develop the expertise of quality assurance of EDC in the school. In order to keep the knowledge in the school, to promote knowledge-sharing between schools as well to furnish an incentive for the teachers to develop the tool, I suggest that the leading teachers in the evaluation team should be the ones who train teachers in other schools and guide similar processes, so that a network of school teachers who are professionals in QA of EDC can be developed. This will keep the knowledge with the teachers as well as offer teachers a career development track.

Evaluation of the project is required throughout the process. I would suggest a researcher from either a university or a research institute to accompany the process.

Who might comprise the local contact persons or agency?
- the Evaluation and Measurement Authority: the chances are that the authority will not embrace the tool at the moment as it is under construction and is focusing on evaluating ministry programmes and reconstructing the Meitzav;
- the Head of the Pedagogical Secretariat, Professor Zohar: getting support in terms of legitimacy, funding and pressure from the Pedagogical Secretariat would be very helpful in moving from the pilot stage to broader implementation;
- the Kremnizer Shenhar Division at the Ministry of Education, which is responsible for the implementation of the Kremnizer Shenhar report on civic education: the head of the division has already informally expressed her support for the tool and the help of her division in implementation. She is also a good source for understanding the internal politics and agendas of the different municipalities in the field of education, and is a well-informed partner for choosing and enrolling a municipality;
- heads of departments of education in the municipalities: here personal acquaintance with the heads of such departments and their agendas is required. As pointed out above, enlisting a municipality education system and implementing the tool under its umbrella would be a major step in the direction of implementing the tool at the system level;
- civic education NGOs: in Israel there are close to 15 NGOs operating in the field of civic education. As argued above, only those working with teachers (as opposed to children) should be approached.

4.2. How to integrate the tool into international partnerships

Teacher and student exchanges are a good avenue to pursue as they will add prestige to the project and offer an incentive to those teachers investing time in it.

If a professional track in QA of EDC is developed for teachers including continuing training and development of the tool, and a network of such local expert teachers working in their own schools and leading evaluative teams of other schools is developed, then this model can be developed to form an international professional network.

4.3. Alternative scenarios for working with the tool

Two additional scenarios present themselves as interesting alternatives for the application of the tool:
- teacher education programmes that focus on democracy and civic education. They would gain from implementation of the tool, both in evaluating their programme from this perspective and from introducing the tool to their students;
- education programmes for principals. Certification for principals entails a two-year study programme, which includes over one hundred hours of practical studies in which the trainees must initiate and carry out a project within the school. The tool could be recommended as such a project.

Chapter 3 – The tool from the point of view of evaluation theory

Harm Kuper

1. Introduction

The "Tool for Quality Assurance of Education for Democratic Citizenship in Schools" (Bîrzea et al., 2005) is designed to reduce the discrepancies between intentions and reality concerning education for democratic citizenship (EDC) in European countries. In seeking to evaluate clear steps as a way of reducing these discrepancies, the user of the tool is confronted with a task that is easily definable in formal terms, but in practice difficult to achieve: What are the criteria for successful education for democracy?

This contribution makes several suggestions on how the possibilities for evaluation projects could be made more concrete, and how to conceptualise evaluation studies. To do so, this paper considers the country-specific starting conditions for education for democracy. It also establishes connections between expectations regarding education for democracy, and these countries' own experience with the development of democracy. Furthermore, this paper looks at how the formal constitution of the school system influences expectations of how education for democracy can be put into practice.

2. The conceptual elements of the tool

Education for a democratic citizenship

To reduce the possible range of questions regarding evaluation studies, it is necessary to start with a definition of EDC. As described in the tool, EDC is:

> a set of practices and activities aimed at making young people and adults better equipped to participate actively in democratic life by assuming and exercising their rights and responsibilities in society.

The tool aims to define what individuals require in terms of the complex forms of organisation of political decisions and the structuring of societal communication. These requirements can be conceived in two dimensions: firstly, in the cognitive dimension of knowledge about democracy; and, secondly, in the normative dimension of attitudes to democracy.

Knowledge about democracy contains historic, judicial, social and political facts about democracy. Thanks to this knowledge, democracy can be understood as an abstract subject, which is normally (especially for students) not accessible through everyday experience. An example of this dimension is knowledge about the history of democratic political systems (elections, parliamentarism, parties, government, etc.). This knowledge can be structured in curricula for teaching purposes.

Attitudes to democracy are much more difficult to grasp and apply in practice in schools. However, they form an important basis for the building of capacity with regard to communication and action in democratic societies, thus complementing cognitive knowledge. Attitudes favouring democratic action, which are part of the preconditions of democratic societies, cannot simply be produced via a clearly defined bundle of measures or fixed as aims in curricula. Rather, these attitudes need to be acquired via practical experience. For this reason, the social environment is crucially important.

Both dimensions – democratic knowledge and democratic attitudes – are mentioned in the tool but little explicated. The tool requires school to be understood not just as a place where knowledge is imparted, but also as a place where social practice can be experienced at first hand. EDC is therefore characterised as a "whole school approach". This approach is broadly explained by Dürr (2005), Himmelmann (2001) and Sliwka (2006). Even though this integrated perspective has to be endorsed, for the purposes of evaluation a distinction has to be made between the different goals of EDC. Therefore, each country's specific requirements have to be considered. The tool does not suggest that an overarching EDC concept should be achieved, as this is improbable in view of the diverse conditions in the various countries. However, the requirements of EDC for schools as an institution can be stated in a general way. Country-specific preconditions have to be considered when making claims. These preconditions are based on a distinction between the school as a place for providing knowledge, and as a place for social experience. They offer different opportunities to consider the theme of democracy in the curricula or in a school programme. This way, both dimensions offer the basis for completing and systematically implementing the quality indicators that are discussed in Chapter 5 of the tool ("Framework to evaluate EDC").

Table 1: Framework for quality indicators for EDC in schools

Aim of EDC	School as a place for knowledge transfer	School as a place for social experience
Subject-oriented teaching	Democracy as a historic and social scientific theme	Controversy (interaction)
Subject-independent teaching	Interdisciplinary approaches to the theme of democracy	Controversy Specification according to subjects
The "democratic school" as a social leitmotif		Participation of students in decision making Defining procedures Substitution Articulating interests
School as an institution of a democratic society		Functional specialisation Integration of active citizens and social networks "Political democracy"

Teaching democratic knowledge

When providing instruction in specific subjects, emphasis is put on knowledge transfer coupled with systematic and abstract approaches to the theme of democracy. The aim is to foster the students' abilities to reflect, evaluate and argue with regard to questions of politics or social life by means of strengthening their knowledge of the subject. This goes hand in hand with teaching goals that can be clearly operationalised and evaluated, such as knowledge about democratic institutions and their historic roots, and the identification and attribution of political positions.

The distinction made by EDC between aims according to school grades, which is often mentioned in the country reports concerning the tool, is fundamental for the concept of subject-specific teaching. The complexity of this issue will have to be addressed in the curricula developed for secondary school instruction by differentiating between a wide spectrum of subjects in a historical and social science context. Apart from the systematic approaches to the subjects, the way the subjects are taught can also provide an opportunity for social learning in line with the goals of EDC.

The variety of methods (student-centred instruction, discussion) provides practice in terms of dealing with controversial issues and discussing at the interactive level of instruction without the pressure of decision making. The teacher's expertise allows him or her to teach students to weigh the importance of facts and opinions regarding controversial issues. This is accompanied by experience of different social roles (student/teacher) and professional competence in terms of knowledge.

Approaches to democracy that are introduced from the perspective of individual subjects can be presented and linked to each other through subject-independent teaching. This enables the spectrum of subjects taught in a school to introduce a basic fact of democratic existence: that there are many different approaches to the world. Related to this is an overall aim, namely to characterise the various approaches to the world – the natural scientific-mathematical, linguistic, artistic-expressive and normative-evaluative approaches – as facets of one social practice. At the same time, the importance of different subject-specific expertise can be stressed in terms of solving practical problems.

Social experience in subject-independent teaching can be supported, for instance, by organising project weeks, during which students can, accompanied by their teachers, develop aims in a responsible and self-organised way, based on a clear division of labour.

Social experience and democratic attitudes

The school organisation offers opportunities for social experience in terms of EDC. The patterns of social interrelations that form the basis for democratic societies are represented in the organisation of school: vertical relations between individuals and the authorities; horizontal interrelations between formally equal persons. Moreover, there are commitments to imposed school rules and autonomously decided (school programme) rules of behaviour. For EDC to succeed, it is important that all the students or individual groups of students succeed in bundling their interests, articulating these and making them effective for the arrangement of the school.

In the tool, the aims of EDC are addressed at the school level with regard to school atmosphere and school ethics. These informal aspects are very important for the development of a democratic way of life (Diedrich, 2006). Nevertheless, this can be criticised, as it only partly describes the context of EDC in schools. In addition, these informal aspects offer little leverage for training activities with a particular aim in mind, and are moreover difficult to access in terms of making an evaluation. In a complex institution like a school, democracy cannot be fully described by the rules of community, such as fairness, tolerance, co-operation and social responsibility. Moreover, school offers the possibility to formalise the democratic participation of students. This is related to the experience that participation in a democratic sphere is strongly connected to rules, and that these rules themselves are only in a limited way subject to democratic decisions.

The formal side of the students' participation in decision making regulates the limits of the decision-making process and the methods of students' participation in this process. Their participation in decision making at school is structurally restricted by the bureaucratic organisation and the professionalism of the body of teachers. Against this background, two interconnected criteria become clear if EDC is to be successful at the school level: firstly, the range or competence of students' participation in decision making; and, secondly, the ability to apply successfully the students' role and competences in decision making.

The ways in which students participate in this decision making ensure that they take part in decisions relevant to the school. In addition, they ensure that students' representative bodies are legitimised and that their interests are articulated. Again, some criteria for successful student participation in decision making can be identified, including their participation in student bodies or in the electoral process for such bodies, the distribution of information among themselves, and the efficacy of decisions made by student bodies. The formalisation of students' participation in decision making also takes into account that the various cohorts of students only belong to the organisation for a limited period of time. The formalisation of student representation also ensures that every time a new cohort of students enters school, it does not have to work hard to participate in decision making. In this regard, one criterion for successful democratisation is continuity concerning students' participation in decision making across several cohorts as well as the integration of new students in this process.

The extent to which the idea of a democratic school can be realised depends on the social environment of the school in question. A relevant issue here is the degree to which individual schools are dependent on surrounding conditions of the educational system. This dependency is indirectly important with regard to the degree of experience that schools offer their students, and is governed by the decisions of school principals and teachers. As a space for experience as envisaged by EDC, the teachers' ability to manage conflicts in school is important. This applies, for example, when students' possibilities of participation in decision making reach their limits. In this case, their interests should be weighed against the functional requirements of the school. This way, school organisation offers an opportunity to experience the very abstract mechanisms of functional differentiation in democratic societies.

The various political and social controversies experienced in a democratic society are only indirectly accessible to schools via teaching. Students can experience present controversies by inviting speakers to explain their positions and interests or discuss with their political opponents in front of the students. To serve as a sphere of experience regarding general political or societal issues, school has to open up to its social environment. This allows the plurality of interests in society and the controversies of a political democracy to be illustrated.

Against this background, the activities in EDC should be distinguished according to their levels, and the evaluation should inquire into the separate preconditions and criteria for success according to these levels.

At the teaching level, the activities concentrate on curricular considerations concerning the theme of democracy and appropriate forms of instruction; at the school level, the participation of students is central; and at the level of the social environment of schools, activities aim at illustrating important controversies affecting society.

Quality assurance and school development

The tool distinguishes between quality assurance (QA) and quality control. Both procedures have in common the idea of gaining empirical information via the evaluation of EDC. This information can be used for practical decisions regarding the arrangement of EDC. Quality control occurs in a hierarchical relation in which the work of individual systems (schools) is controlled by a central authority, whereas QA emphasises the self-regulation of the system's single entities and therefore their (relative) independence from a centralised control system (see page 35).

Quality control and QA are introduced by the tool as mutually exclusive methods; however, considering the specific national characteristics of school systems, it could be wise to ascertain in which way these two criteria could actually complement each other. Quality control must not necessarily require a controlling authority to determine the actions of the system's entities (as described in the tool). Basically, control can be used as a strategic steering instrument. This way, responsibility for the exercise of actions lies in the hands of the individual entities. This consideration introduces, in addition to the distinction between quality control and QA, a distinction between strategic and functional aims. This allows general strategic aims for an educational system to be formulated (for example, educational standards, graduate quotas, the political participation of adolescents, etc.). In addition, responsibility for the implementation of these aims can then be transferred to a local context, as can the responsibility for achieving these aims, which can be transferred to the schools as decentralised entities of the educational system. Centralisation and decentralisation, quality control and QA are therefore not contradictory elements, but rather two sides of the same coin in complex educational systems (Böttcher, 2002). It is therefore the task of the educational policies and the development of individual schools to decide on the relationship between both sides. The implementation of evaluation studies and the use of evaluation results for the development of schools are two important aspects when it comes to putting the arrangement into practice.

In this respect, the authors of the tool rightly draw attention to the fact that questions about the evaluation procedures and perceptions of responsibility for school development cannot be answered independently from questions on how to incorporate democracy into the educational system. Thus, a possible function of the evaluation is to inform the public about the publicly financed educational system, as well as the professionals who work in the system itself. Further functions can be the control, but also the increase of scientific findings about the educational system. To implement the tool in the various countries, the authors' advice for the EDC's stakeholders should be followed (page 38). Independently from the peculiarities of the single countries, several stakeholder groups should in general be identified. For each of these groups, the evaluation has particular functions, from which particular perspectives for the development of schools can be developed.

With regard to the public, the most important function of evaluation is to assess the performance of the educational system and its institutions. Since the public is not represented by a single actor and therefore cannot act in a uniform way, it is impossible to initiate specific school development projects at the public level via the evaluation process. At the same time, public discussion about school and its tasks is remarkably important for the social atmosphere in which schools can develop. Other questions that are publicly addressed in a democratic society regard how schools can take over responsibility for EDC, and with which other societal institutions (families, associations, political parties, enterprises) they can share this responsibility. This way, an informed public is essential for a successful harmonising of the development of schools with societal needs. However, attention also has to be paid when publishing the results of the evaluation, insofar as these could unwittingly damage the image of individual institutions.

For the administration, the evaluation can have – depending on the judicial constitution of the educational system and the actual application of formal power – the function of controlling and/or promoting development. A central, external evaluation by the administration can make comparative data available for the various educational institutions and contribute to favourable conditions that enable individual schools to develop; the risks of a central evaluation lie in judgments of the capacity of individual institutions that are based exclusively on data from the evaluation without considering actual conditions on the ground. Whether external evaluation is used together with the schools, in the sense of promoting school development, or whether it is used to assess the school in the sense of controlling it remains a question to be determined by educational policy, and at least partly requires democratic legitimation.

If evaluation results are used to enable schools to develop, school principals are the main target group. Part of their task is also combining societal demands on the schools with internal planning and with initiating reform processes. School principals therefore occupy a key position with regard to the dissemination of information drawn from the evaluation studies and the conclusions reached by these studies.

Experience from subject-oriented evaluation studies indicates that the use of evaluation results is most productive when school principals take into consideration external evaluation data. These data help to assess the performance of their school in comparison to the performance of other schools, and encourage staff to scrutinise the school's results. Both approaches require a responsible and autonomous use of the results at the school level.

Teachers need the evaluation results within the framework of their own professional practice. The aspect of (professional self-) control is here just as useful as the quality development dimension, as only teachers can reasonably interpret the results that are reported in the evaluation against the background of the practical concepts of action and the conditions for action. The use of evaluation results needs professional interpretation, which in turn requires a high degree of expertise. However, this expertise refers less to carrying out the evaluation itself than to interpreting its results and justifying the conclusions that are drawn from these results.

For parents and students, evaluations are important because they can help them articulate their expectations concerning education. Evaluation therefore provides a necessary information basis for the reaching of democratic decisions in the educational system. But this aspect of evaluation can easily clash with using the evaluation results professionally (for example, by teachers), whereas parents and students perceive evaluation results mostly as laymen and relate them to their individual situation. In conclusion, professionals must be able to draw systematic and case-specific conclusions from the evaluation results to justify further actions.

Given these multiple evaluation functions for different stakeholders, the components of a QA system need to be considered in terms of their respective systems of information and evaluation (as summarised on page 41 of the tool). The way they are presented gives the impression that the components could be activated and combined in complete independence of each other. However, in reality it is necessary to assume various complex interdependencies. Depending on the respective institutional conditions of an educational system, evaluation results can be used in very different ways and can serve the separate interests of individual stakeholders. This way, comparing data about schools can be used, for instance, by the public or the administration to put pressure on poorly performing schools. This can lead to damaging consequences for particular schools; however, the data can also be used to initiate co-operation between schools – co-operation that enables best-practice models to be exchanged, thereby fostering further development. A school inspection can be a form of control, but it can also provide useful advice for development. In similar fashion, the publication of evaluation results can stimulate a discourse about the educational system, which is imperative for democracies, but could also damage the image of the system's institutions.

Evaluation and QA are carried out in a social environment in which they are exposed to the ambivalence of different interpretations, and can be exploited for different interests. Every responsible evaluation should be conducted keeping in mind its social embedded nature, in order to anticipate and control its possible use for specific target groups. Against this background, it is recommended to fix the targets of the EDC in a given context in as detailed a manner as possible, to identify the possible actors and to conceptualise the instruments of the evaluation and the QA according to the needs for information of these relevant actors. Given the often very diffuse expectations concerning the aims of EDC, a limitation of the claims could prove very helpful, as it encourages a gradual introduction of EDC at the different levels of the educational system. Furthermore, it prevents unrealistic expectations from arising that cannot be met in reality.

The prerequisites for EDC and QA in the countries

The country reports about the applicability of the tool contain information about the institutional constellations that have to be taken into account when promoting EDC and implementing the corresponding QA systems. Two aspects in particular are discussed below: the expectations regarding the tool that are articulated in the country reports, and the assessment regarding the compatibility of the tool with the given measures for realising the EDC and its QA.

The broad approval that the tool has received from the individual countries is remarkable, given that these countries have very different political traditions, their educational systems are organised differently, and they are in different phases of construction, consolidation and preservation of a democratic community. This result confirms that the tool has successfully been designed to be generally applicable. However, this broad applicability does require some degree of interpretation; hence in almost all country reports, one can find remarks on how the tool needs to be adapted to specific circumstances.

The criticism that has occasionally been expressed in this regard, namely that concrete measures are insufficiently detailed, hints at the strength of the tool. EDC and programmes like QA are supposed to promote school autonomy. The question regarding the extent to which an issue like the EDC and programmes like QA should actually define action steps seems worthwhile discussing. The reactions expressed in the country reports on the existing ambiguities of the tool therefore also indicate the readiness and capability of these countries to manage these insecurities, which are after all connected with the "risk of democracy".

The following paragraphs summarise the country reports, emphasising any similarities between starting conditions and expectations regarding EDC and QA. This typology can then be used to indicate how the tool could be developed further given certain starting conditions. This procedure does, however, entail some restrictions when it comes to presenting the individual country profiles. Moreover, assessing these profiles is also methodologically problematic because it is often impossible to distinguish in what way the country reports are influenced by the author's personal judgment, or whether they actually open up any objective possibilities of comparison between countries.

The primary criterion for distinguishing the types is the degree of centralisation of the respective school system as represented in the country reports. This criterion is meaningful for two reasons. Firstly, the degree of freedom that schools have to organise their pedagogical work depends on the degree to which the decisions taken in the educational system are centralised. Schools can only implement measures in the EDC and take responsibility for accomplishing and evaluating them if they also fulfil the organisational requirements for professional work. The availability of criteria for assessing the success of pedagogical work forms part of these requirements, as well as the possibility to decide on whether to implement the operative work on the ground.

Secondly, even the success of democratic decisions is connected to the degree to which a system's decision-making structures are centralised. The more a system is structured in a decentralised manner, the wider the requirements for assuming responsibility in this system have to be distributed. This interrelation is also valid for democracies. Democracies have to renounce – just like decentralised systems – the control of single processes in the system and therefore make room for unplanned developments. Nevertheless, centralising decision making and democracy do not exclude one another: they can be combined, for instance, in the form of a representative democracy, although this may well require complex methods of legitimising decisions.

Altogether, the country reports can be grouped into three categories with regard to the way that they deal with the requirements of EDC and QA instruments.

EDC in the authoritarian structure of centralised school systems

This group comprises some countries belonging to the former Soviet Union and other countries from the former Eastern Bloc, namely Poland, the Russian Federation, Belarus and Ukraine. The reports describe clearly the persistence of very centralised educational systems, which are not purely the legacy of many years of state-sponsored socialism, but still supported by other post-socialist institutions. In general, structurally conservative forces predominate in the educational systems of these countries.

The authors of the reports, who are very open to the ideas of EDC and QA and link them to hopes for reforms, are ambivalent concerning the importance of the central administrations for education. On one hand, the administrations are regarded as necessary for introducing innovations in the educational system (for example, in the Russian Federation). On the other hand, they are also criticised for hindering innovations (for example, in Belarus). The authors describe a situation in which schools are for the most part unable to introduce EDC autonomously. Some report that the interests of the schools and educational administrations are contradictory – for instance in Poland, where support for school autonomy comes up against tendencies to restore a central educational policy. Other reports express the hope that school administrations could take over the implementation of EDC. Belarus, for example, has been advised to improve the schools' resources setting and to integrate the school inspectors into the process of promoting EDC. However, in both cases it is clear that in these countries the institutional structure of the educational system and/or the system of values regarding the educational system, which is based on the social context, are the limiting factors for the introduction of EDC and QA in schools.

Accordingly, for a country-specific revision of the tool, the question arises to what extent schools can in principle be convinced of the aims of EDC and how far they can assume responsibility for implementing it, based on the assumption that they are autonomous. Presumably, to achieve this to the greatest possible extent in the sense of a democratisation of the whole school, certain requirements (for example, a liberal climate, a permissive institutional structure) have to be fulfilled that are apparently not taken for granted in these countries. While this does not necessarily exclude promoting the EDC initiatives at individual schools, these are nevertheless exposed to the risk of placing themselves in opposition to the administration's set policy, which could lead to conflicts and an actual expansion of central control (instead of QA).

The reports contain a number of suggestions and warnings regarding the best way of dealing with such situations. The aims of EDC must be kept realistic, particularly to avoid causing reforms to fail and therefore resulting in a "disappointment in democracy" (Russian Federation) due to unreachable aims. Given this starting position, it seems most appropriate to discuss separately the aims of specific schools regarding this tool and the aims of educational systems. For this reason, different circles of addressees are made accessible, starting with the educational policy across the administration and covering all practical experience. For these addressees and against this background, the above-mentioned differences in the way in which evaluation instruments function for different actors in the educational system have to be taken into account.

Democracy, as a core teaching subject, represents the starting point for all EDC projects. This seems to be universally valid for all countries. The reports regard overcoming a too-detailed focus on subject-specific teaching as a main aim. Thus, the whole school approach is appreciated. This perspective also implies taking the first steps towards elaborating the tool in more detail in terms of subject-specific teaching. Starting from there, they could develop participation-oriented and discursive forms of teaching.

It is therefore advisable to implement the tool for these countries, starting on the one hand with the issues that are fixed in the curricula and with the respective forms of teaching, and on the other, making schools more autonomous concerning the need for educational policy reform. Regarding this, the report from Ukraine wisely suggests launching the discussion on EDC by raising awareness with the help of educational science. In this spirit, public discussion about EDC can be promoted by the tool as an aim of the school and via its official adoption into the school's regulations.

The last point also includes the question of how to specify the instruments of the QA. The proposals made in some of the reports to complement the tool with statistical information should be critically analysed in two main directions. Firstly, the necessary differentiation can hardly be achieved within the framework of a tool; secondly, a technocratic application of empirically based QA instruments by the presentation of statistical algorithms should not be favoured. However, professional competences at schools, which are connected with this aspect, should be promoted, and this seems to be very important for the possibility of conducting an internal evaluation in principle.

The countries under consideration have evaluation experience largely only with external data on subject-oriented performance, and are primarily used for controlling. The introduction of EDC and QA therefore represents two separate demands for the educational systems of these countries. Against this background, the close interlinking of EDC and QA in the tool appears to be problematic. Provided that their aims are realistic, it seems to make sense to differentiate between these countries. Appropriate aims for the teaching should be defined. Furthermore, the differentiation should allow for experience to be obtained with a school-internal, development-oriented evaluation, initially for the conceptionally less complex area of subject-oriented teaching.

EDC as an aspect of modernisation, but one that is aware of traditions

According to the country reports, the Baltic countries (Estonia, Latvia and Lithuania) and the Czech Republic are all following the pattern of modernisation that simultaneously is aware of traditions. The reports from these countries give the impression of a societal climate that can reach broad consensus on the aims of an all-embracing EDC. In addition, all these countries refer to reforms that have effectively changed their political institutions and moved them in the direction of democratisation. Last but not least, the positive effects of EU membership on these countries have to be considered (however, this is not true of fellow new EU member state Poland at the historical moment when the respective report had been written).

The expression aware of traditions marks the orientation towards reform of these post-socialist societies. This orientation is partly connected with the cultural and political identity resulting from the first half of the 20th century. Whereas Type 1 countries typically are said to lack democratic traditions on which EDC could be built up, the representatives of Type 2 countries look for the value basis of EDC in a pre-socialist past.

Yet these countries suffer from hardly any constraints that could hinder the introduction of EDC and QA at the school level. Rather, it is reported that the efforts to decentralise the educational system could strengthen the schools' autonomy. QA that is school based is therefore compatible with educational policy premises and already partly an element of the practised steering of school. Furthermore, EDC is in accordance with the official aims of the educational policy, or can be related to its basic political ideas. Thus, the fundamental structural conditions of these countries can be described as being favourable.

Criticism first and foremost relates to requirements at the operative level of the educational system. The impression is given that the initial experiences with the themes of EDC and QA have already led to the acknowledgement that the limiting factors lie in the schools' own requirements for action. In this context, the competences of teachers in particular are a matter for discussion, as well as their attitudes.

Against this background, the proposals of these countries to revise the tool should be considered. These proposals request:
- a clearer specification of the aims and courses of action of EDC and QA. This allows the need for action-orientation and methods for school practitioners to be taken into account. The instrument must be practicable for the "ordinary teacher";
- the tool to be elaborated for different forms of schools and different age cohorts;
- a more distinct borderline to be established between EDC and QA (Estonia). The aims of EDC should be implemented more effectively in order to have instruments for a QA whose functions and addressees have to be determined;
- access to information about EDC activities at schools via the Internet;
- the definition of responsibilities (and division of labour) of EDC and QA at schools.

The Type 2 countries have only very restricted expectations from the tool regarding an initiative to introduce projects concerning the theme of learning democracy or increasing attention to EDC. These diffuse desires do, however, give way to much more specific expectations concerning functions with regard to concrete measures in EDC. It seems that it makes sense to meet these expectations by providing additional material for the tool – material that can basically be used in the in-service training of teachers.

EDC as a differentiation between the forms of academic learning

For the countries that belong to Type 3 (Germany and Israel), there are no easily identifiable formal criteria (for example, post-socialist state). Yet the commonality that can be derived from the reports is that the embedding of the educational system in the firm structures of a democratic community is not put into question. EDC is consequently relieved from the pressure of expectations, namely to establish the requirements for a democratic commonwealth by promoting individual competences; rather this community in turn can be assumed as a precondition. This aspect is expressed in the reports by clues regarding the various activities with which the schools, regarding questions of education for democracy, establish a bridge to their societal environment. For example, Germany had programmes for learning democracy based on political initiatives. In Israel, connections to NGOs exist that help initiate pilot projects for education for democracy. In these countries, the systems for evidence-based controlling of schools are also very advanced. There are reform efforts geared at interlinking central evaluation with school-internal

QA measures. The reports clearly show how very differentiated conceptualisations of EDC can be produced on the basis of these favourable starting conditions. These integrate aspects of democracy into everyday school life (for instance, via the question of the fairness of appraisals).

With the advanced development of democratic traditions and their connection to school, expectations regarding a specific function of the tool have increased. This becomes very clear, for instance, in the critique from the Israeli country report, in which the general introduction of EDC and QA by the tool is appreciated, but the shortage of manageable proposals is criticised. The differentiated specification of the tool for demand at different levels in an educational system (educational policy, administration, schools, teachers) is exposed. The tool should thereby serve actors at the operative level as preparation for the practice of education for democracy. In addition, it should serve the administration as an instrument that identifies activities that are worthwhile promoting, and defines an autonomous area of responsibility for schools.

3. Concluding remarks

The country reports provide a valuable insight into the complexity of the task of EDC. Its realisation depends strongly on the according conditions of the countries and school systems which, in turn, rely to different degrees on democratic traditions. A uniform sequence of steps to promote and evaluate EDC therefore hardly appears reasonable. In particular, anchoring EDC in a system of values that cannot be established (only supported) through EDC turns out to be an encompassing difficulty that has to be mastered, especially by those countries with weak democratic traditions.

Something similar applies to the evaluation, too: technical instruments (operationalisation of survey instruments, collection of data, evaluation of data) that call for a high level of expertise are required for the evaluation process. Last but not least, the reasonable level of use of evaluation depends on attitudes, at least some of which partly show a surprising closeness to "democratic virtues". Evaluation can only be practical if:

- agreement has been reached on the question of the evaluation;
- fair agreements have been concluded on the use of the information;
- the interpretation and conclusions drawn from the information involve actors from the field of praxis;
- all parties concerned can appropriately appreciate the importance of empirically proved, fact-oriented arguments.

Just as democracy cannot be established purely through the implementation of democratic codes of practice, so too a practically important evaluation cannot result from the mere use of survey instruments, as the required attitudes or value systems on which the democratic action and evaluation rest cannot be produced by goal-oriented measures. Instead, these value-based attitudes can only develop gradually during the practical realisation of democracy and evaluation. This requires the applied procedural methods and techniques not to overburden the actors. They must be linked to the actors' models of action. This idea underlies the tool – especially in the chapter about school development planning. Nevertheless, the suggestions made by the tool in terms of a stepwise approach to school development (see page 71) tend to trivialise the view of the complex arrangement of instruments for evaluation and the evaluation culture. This must reflect two issues.

Firstly, how to transfer the high methodical requirements of the evaluation into the practice of schools. Since evaluation requires very varied methodological expertise, the models of school-internal division of labour and using external advice appear reasonable. By contrast, making broadly accessible methodical knowledge by minimising expectations appears to be mistaken.

Secondly, how to ensure the readiness to participate in the evaluation. A prior development of an evaluation culture – as suggested in the tool – appears to be difficult because it is not a matter of a target that can be made operational, while the required methods cannot be named. Instead, from the beginning participation in the concrete development of evaluation projects has to be secured, for instance by discussing the questions and information needs. Thus, a gradual enlargement of the claims and themes of evaluation projects is advisable. The development of an evaluation culture can be expected if the gradual consolidation of the practical application of evaluation succeeds.

References

Bîrzea, C.; Cecchini, M.; Harrison, C.; Krek, J.; Spajic-Vrkas, V. (2005). "Tool for Quality Assurance of Education for Democratic Citizenship in Schools", Paris: UNESCO, Council of Europe, Centre for Educational Policy Studies.

Böttcher, W. (2002). *Kann eine ökonomische Schule auch eine pädagogische sein?* Weinheim: Juventa.

Diedrich, M. (2006). "Connections between Quality of School Life and Democracy in German Schools", in Sliwka, A. et al. (ed.), *Citizenship Education*, Münster: Waxmann, 121-134.

Dürr, K. (2005). *The School. A Democratic Learning Community. The All-European Study on Pupils' Participation in School*, Strasbourg: Council of Europe Publishing.

Himmelmann, G. (2001). *Demokratie Lernen*, Schwalbach: Wochenschau-Verlag.

Sliwka, A. (2006). "Citizenship Education as the Responsibility of a Whole School: Structural and Cultural Implication", in Sliwka, A. et al. (ed.), *Citizenship Education*, Münster: Waxmann, 7-18.

Chapter 4 – Preconditions for tool implementation

Sarah Werth

Introduction

This chapter aims at providing an overview of the crucial preconditions in the countries addressed in the study that will need to be faced should the tool be implemented. It identifies three main preconditions for the implementation of the tool: coherence of regulations, status of the teaching profession, and the capacity of teachers. The first part of this chapter accordingly examines legal regulations concerning the status of schools, general evaluation, EDC and EDC-QA within the educational system. The second part assesses the attitude of educational staff and administrative bodies towards general evaluation, and EDC-QA, looking in particular at the encouraging and discouraging factors named in the reports. Finally, the third part describes the capacity for tool implementation by examining initial and in-service teacher training, available expertise, support systems, and additional programmes, each topic related to general evaluation, EDC and EDC-QA. It should be noted, however, that while these categories are described separately, they are not independent, but rather closely interconnected. Each part will therefore in some cases point to the potential interrelations between categories, either based on data from the reports or on educational theory. In the last part of the chapter, finally, some effects on ideas for tool implementation mentioned in the reports are described.

Owing to the diversity of the 10 countries comprised in the study, the presentation of common features typically runs the risk of making generalisations without paying sufficient attention to country-specific idiosyncrasies. To provide deeper insight, countries will be grouped into smaller units of three or four countries, whenever this seems to fit the data.

The outline for the country reports actually did not explicitly ask for EDC. However, information on EDC was provided by all reports. The establishment of EDC can be regarded as closely related to EDC-QA, and information given in the reports will thus also be presented in this chapter. The information on EDC presented in this chapter can be augmented by further consulting Bîrzea (2004), another study by the Council of Europe, whose findings are similar.

1. Preconditions with respect to legal regulations concerning the status of schools, general evaluation, EDC and EDC-QA within the educational system

When exploring preconditions for tool implementation, it is necessary to examine the existing regulations that are related to the core content of the tool, namely QA, EDC and EDC-QA. Whether there are regulations of a kind that could support tool implementation, whether these regulations are coherent or maybe in competition with other regulations and, finally, how these regulations are implemented in practice, are criteria that shape the context for tool implementation. The coherence of regulation, or gaps and competition between regulations, are, however, not only important as forming the legal basis to support tool implementation, but also as the coherence or inconsistency of regulations affect other crucial factors for tool implementation, such as the motivation and capacity of educational staff. Decentralisation and output control, for example, create the need for a different kind of evaluation system than an input-oriented educational system, and thus not only affect the kind of evaluation methods and instruments, but also the kind of expertise needed to run an evaluation. On this basis, the following three sections of Part 1 will deal with regulations related to the educational system, QA, EDC and EDC-QA before addressing the issues of motivation and capacity in Parts 2 and 3 respectively.

Preconditions with respect to legal regulations of the educational system

The degree of centralisation and where the steering of the educational system is located can be seen as key criteria when describing the features of an educational system.

In general, it can be stated that most of the 10 countries studied had introduced – partly still ongoing – reforms proceeding in the direction of decentralisation, raising school autonomy and public involvement in education management, also including new financial mechanisms in the educational system (see Froumin, 2004: 103).

Examining the countries in the study more closely, it can be concluded that Belarus, Ukraine, Russia and Germany are all rather centralised, but differ in terms of where power is located. In Germany and Russia, for instance, steering is located at the federal level, whereas in Belarus and Ukraine it is located at the national level. There are also key differences with regard to school autonomy. Although all four of these countries are said to use national educational standards or tests, only the Ukrainian report mentions that despite centralisation, school heads in Ukraine retain a high degree of autonomy.

The Czech Republic, Estonia, Lithuania, Latvia, Poland and Israel, in contrast, can be regarded as having rather decentralised educational systems. As they are obliged to meet national standards, the municipalities are in charge of the schools and deliver, in turn, much responsibility to the school heads.

1.2. Preconditions of evaluation with respect to legal regulations of the educational system

One more point of interest is the respective evaluation systems of the 10 countries. Criteria of differentiation are the frequency and type of evaluation, namely, accreditation, assessment, inspection and monitoring, internal versus external evaluation, the purpose (for example, control of compliance, development of the individual school) that they serve, and the coherence of elements within the evaluation systems.

The majority of reports, for instance, mention that most countries have announced a shift from quality control to quality assurance, and that the indicators used for external and internal evaluation are more or less only quantitative if developed at all. Furthermore, guidelines for evaluation are often too detailed, and thus schools rarely have the chance to choose topics of interest to themselves. In addition, in the majority of countries, national assessment or matriculation exams and additional means of evaluation are in competition with each other, which seems to be supported by school rankings published in the media. As shown in detail in Chapter 4, besides these common features, the complexity and consistency of most procedures differ widely between the countries.

In Ukraine, Russia, and Belarus, for instance, evaluation mostly consists of a combination of accreditation/certification and attestation, which is conducted once every three, five or ten years. In addition to this kind of evaluation, there are also annual national assessment tests and national standards or, in the case of Ukraine, internal evaluation as a constituent part of the certification procedure. Regarding fines for non-compliance with regulations and standards, treatment of development reports, and the kind of acquainted data, the evaluation systems in these countries can be characterised as rather aiming at checking compliance with national standards and regulations. Although areas of evaluation are clearly defined, the reports mention a lack of a unified approach, a shortcoming that can partly be related to the recent implementation of the respective reforms.

In the Czech Republic, Estonia, Lithuania, and Latvia, which are all rather decentralised, evaluations are conducted more frequently, namely, on an annual basis, or once every two years or three years. Besides serving to check compliance with binding regulations, their evaluation systems comprise many elements that aim at the individual development of schools, including the choice of their own topics of evaluation and a developed feedback culture where inspection has the function of "soft supervision". This is especially true of Estonia, Lithuania and Latvia, all of which have an interrelated system of external and internal evaluation or even self-evaluation, guided by detailed descriptions of the evaluation process and the areas that are to be evaluated.

By contrast, for Poland, Germany and Israel, which have either just initiated or are about to initiate major reforms concerning evaluation, it is not yet possible to comment with any degree of certainty about the future development of the evaluation system. Germany, for instance, has begun to initiate a reform of its evaluation system after the publication of the first PISA results in 2001 and is still in the process of developing an evaluation system that comprises external and internal evaluation. Poland, on the other hand, has a long-standing evaluation system consisting of external and internal evaluation, which was – among other changes – restricted to external evaluation in 2006. Israel's evaluation system – which formerly mainly consisted of national annual or biannual assessment tests and thematic evaluations – has also been undergoing reform since 2006, and is likely to be upgraded by including internal evaluation and reducing student assessment.

In conclusion, assessment and inspection procedures and the establishment of internal evaluation are increasingly applied in all countries, though the complexity and consistency of these procedures differ widely (see also Bîrzea, 2004).

1.3. Preconditions of EDC and EDC-QA with respect to legal regulations of the educational system

Regarding EDC, two issues are of major interest in the case of tool implementation: whether there are any binding regulations related to EDC, and whether approaches to EDC-QA are already in place. As Bîrzea (2004) has extensively explored the issue of whether EDC is represented in education policies, this section first summarises the most important facts about legal regulations related to EDC before examining existing approaches of EDC-QA.

Though a wide variety of terms are used for EDC with an extremely diverse interpretation of what they actually denote, it can still be concluded that there is a core content of EDC policy statements in nearly all countries covered by the study. Whether they are included in the respective national constitution or educational law – either as an overall educational aim or restricted to a specific school subject – almost all countries have normative documents that guarantee a favourable basis for EDC-related issues. In the majority of countries, however, there is a gap between these documents and practice, such as the prevalent voluntary character of the subject for pupils in most grades and the weak position (for example, in terms of time allocation in the weekly timetable) of EDC-related subjects in relation to more traditional subjects. Another common feature is the mostly knowledge-based approach (what Mikkelsen (2004: 85) calls the "about" approach to EDC).[1] Despite that, at least in those countries covered by the study

---

1. Mikkelsen mentions three approaches to citizenship education, namely the "about", "for" and "through" approaches. While the "about" approach comprises the knowledge perspective of citizenship education, the "for" approach "is broader and more focused on values, understanding, skills and the development of tolerance" (Mikkelsen, 2004: 85). The "through" approach, finally, comprises "experiences of formal and informal participation and of democratic teaching and learning approaches in school" (ibid.).

that have a decentralised educational system, some common tendencies of school development that can be regarded as favourable preconditions for EDC do exist, such as increasing school autonomy and participation of pupils and parents, partly based on organisational theories, partly in order to establish democratic structures. These tendencies are additionally supported by the introduction of activating learning methods, though in many countries the importance of active citizens and learners is less appreciated than good results in assessment tests, especially if the national teaching style has been of a rather authoritarian type for a long time. Altogether, it can be stated that the efforts made to implement EDC are partial strategies rather than a comprehensive approach to EDC implementation and differ greatly between countries. In some countries, for instance, attempts to reduce the relevance of EDC can even be identified, whereas others are developing curricula for civics.

As Bîrzea (2004: 50) also mentions, monitoring and quality assurance related to EDC are essential if EDC policy implementation is to be successful. Given that most of the countries in the study rather follow the "about" approach to democracy (Mikkelsen, 2004: 85), EDC can be regarded as a part of evaluation in the restricted form of final exams or national assessment tests in civics, and in some countries even in the form of questions about school climate. Except for Belarus and Ukraine, all countries additionally took part in CIVED 1999, and the majority of countries have initiated national or regional pilot programmes and conducted unconnected small-scale studies related to EDC. Based on these reports, we may conclude that though EDC is mentioned as being one of the prior goals of education policy, in practice more attention is paid to the outcomes of students, teachers and schools than to the implementation of EDC, even if EDC-related programmes offered by NGOs are appreciated in nearly all countries (see below).

2. Preconditions with respect to motivation for engagement in general evaluation and EDC-QA

This part switches from a macro to a micro perspective, and examines the motivation of several stakeholders with regard to general evaluation and EDC-QA. To do so, it looks at certain key questions, such as to what extent are teachers in the respective countries motivated to take part in additional evaluation in general? Do the reports name factors that encourage or discourage teachers and other stakeholders? Especially if we regard the tool as an additional form of evaluation besides mandatory evaluation, the findings presented in this part can be regarded as crucial preconditions for its implementation. Motivation regarding general evaluation and EDC-QA, however, depends on a combination of regulations and capacity, and for this reason the following part also points to some interrelations that were named in the reports.

2.1. Motivation regarding general evaluation

With respect to motivation of educational staff regarding evaluation, the reports name several constraining factors such as long experience with evaluation and knowledge about evaluation, binding regulations to conduct evaluation, penalties for bad results in evaluations, and pressure due to school rankings. Reasons for a lack of motivation regarding evaluation, in contrast, include the high workload of teachers, time pressure, national examination pressure, a lack of knowledge about evaluation, excessively detailed guidelines, or too much work created by evaluation reports, too many reform activities accompanied by frequently changing guidelines, disconnected forms of evaluation, and a lack of feedback.

Despite these similarities with regard to the factors that increase or decrease motivation regarding evaluation, the diversity of readiness for evaluation differs greatly among the countries covered by the study. In Russia, Belarus and Ukraine, for instance, the recently established obligation to conduct evaluation without having sufficient knowledge about methods of evaluation accounts for much of the motivation regarding obtaining more information about evaluation. This motivation is additionally raised by fines for bad results in evaluations and assessment tests increase the motivation to improve, and thus in many cases school staff would like to learn how to identify areas that could be improved and how improvement could be managed. Existing student assessment tests, however, already put teachers under considerable pressure and are thus a discouraging factor.

In the Czech Republic, Estonia, Lithuania and Latvia there is awareness of the advantages of internal evaluation as a possibility of improving pupils' results in tests and thus gaining a better position in rankings. In the Czech Republic, fines linked to shortcomings might be an additional reason for wanting to take part in voluntary additional evaluation. As a discouraging factor, the lack of time and teaching workload are again mentioned.

Poland and Israel are in general familiar with regular evaluation, although in both national examinations create high pressure. The Polish report additionally mentions that – except for some school heads who still appreciate the advantages of internal evaluation – educational staff generally felt relieved when internal evaluation was abolished, thus making it no longer necessary to write reports. In Israel, teachers seem to be tired of programmes in general, though it is mentioned that the so-called "better-educated" teachers are still more motivated towards evaluation than staff who work in "weaker" schools. In Germany, resentment towards evaluation is probably strongest. In the ex-Soviet countries, conversely, the tradition of inspection had been interrupted for a long time and the issue of quality control/quality assurance is something quite new to the teachers; supervisory authorities, however, are highly interested in this possibility of control.

With respect to ministries and administrative bodies, in general, the situation is similar to the situation mentioned in the German report: the majority of reports mention interest in QA, especially on the part of those bodies that are in charge of financing schools; teachers, however, tend to be rather more sceptical.

2.2. Motivation towards EDC-QA

The reports suggest that it is appropriate not to be over-enthusiastic concerning the motivation of teachers to conduct additional EDC-related evaluations. In nearly all countries, the workload of teachers and the pressure due to assessment tests is already very high, thus making it difficult to motivate teachers to conduct additional evaluations. For example, even in Latvia, which has mastered general evaluation, it is not certain whether teachers would appreciate the advantages that EDC-QA offers; while in Poland, despite awareness of the importance of democratic structures, teachers were relieved when internal evaluation was abolished.

Nevertheless, despite this potential lack of capacity, there is, as mentioned in the German report for example, still the chance that teachers could become aware of the advantages of EDC-QA, either as part of individual school profiles, which are obligatory in some countries or as a possibility of improving the teacher-pupil relation, especially since pupils are said to be extremely interested in enhanced participation.

In addition to these general findings related to EDC-QA, there are some country-specific features that are worth mentioning. In Russia, Belarus and the Ukraine, for instance, educational staff generally seem interested in democracy, but have little experience with EDC and have additionally been disappointed several times by failed attempts to raise awareness of EDC in schools. Furthermore, health, literacy and IT-related issues in these countries seem to be an urgent topic on the agenda of schools, which could explain why EDC-QA is not of major interest for both ministries and schools, or could even be completely restricted to active learning methods.

In the Czech Republic, Estonia, Lithuania and Latvia, the attention of teachers towards EDC is mostly enhanced by obligatory final exams in civics; this, however, results in the opinion that civics is largely the responsibility of civics teachers. This assumption is further supported by lack of interest in broader participation on the part of parents, who seem more interested in school rankings than in democratic structures.

In Poland awareness of the importance of democracy seems to be quite strong, even if the current government's educational policy was broadly unsupportive at the time when the report was written. In any case the focus of teachers is, as in other countries, mostly on final examinations. Israel offers a similar situation: despite broad awareness of the importance of EDC, teachers do not seem to be motivated to take part in additional evaluation, either because of high existing workloads, or owing to current involvement in ongoing programmes. In addition, the report mentions that Israel explicitly aims at developing internal evaluation methods instead of self-evaluation. Finally, in Germany the importance of democracy is unanimously acknowledged, yet awareness of the importance to integrate this theme into the classroom is weak, even though the report emphasises that raising teachers' awareness of the advantages of EDC-QA (see above) would increase potential motivation towards EDC-QA.

3. Preconditions with respect to professional development and school support systems

This part examines further the preconditions for tool implementation concerning capacity in the form of preparing teachers, building expertise at universities and institutes, and making support systems available. The following sections will deal with the regular inclusion of general evaluation, EDC and EDC-QA in initial and in-service teacher training (3.1, 3.2), available expertise on these issues (3.3), and the establishment of support systems (3.4). Finally, section 3.5 evaluates temporary programmes dealing with evaluation either initiated by the respective government or by NGOs in this area. In common with the other parts in this chapter, capacity factors are similarly interconnected as well as related to both regulations and motivation. Not only does the expertise available at universities and research institutes influence the quality of teacher training courses that often takes place at universities, but so too does the establishment of binding regulations without giving the necessary support affect the motivation of educational staff towards an issue like QA. This chapter does not aim at detecting causalities in the strict sense, but does present information given in the reports that could be relevant in case of tool implementation, highlighting potential interrelations on the way.

3.1. Initial teacher training

General evaluation as an issue of initial teacher training

Although there is a long-standing tradition that school inspection is the responsibility of governmental school inspectorates, in all countries the performance of evaluation in the sense of internal evaluation can be regarded as a rather new topic in initial training, if included at all. Many country reports mentioned the fact that the issue of evaluation is restricted to methods of student assessment, and that QA is mainly included in some MA and Ph.D. programmes. However, it is important to note that these are mostly attended by principals who are in charge of internal evaluation, often including responsibility for the choice of methods, writing reports and for setting up development plans.

There are also differences between countries concerning the issue of evaluation as part of initial teacher training. In the Baltic countries, where well-developed guidelines for external and internal evaluation are provided and internal evaluation seems to be a valued part of mandatory evaluation, teacher trainees at least get in touch with evaluation when doing practical work at school, while universities offer MA programmes and diplomas in school management. Other countries that have recently initiated reforms of their evaluation systems, however, only offer optional courses dealing with evaluation.

EDC and EDC-QA as an issue of initial teacher training

EDC, as such, is not treated as an explicit issue in initial teacher training in any of the countries. Even student teachers who are studying politics or social sciences are not familiarised with approaches to EDC apart from the "about" approach. Thus, Bîrzea's (2004) finding that EDC is rarely represented in initial teacher-training schedules still seems valid.

On top of the apparent lack of comprehensive EDC-QA, the evaluation of EDC also does not seem to be part of initial teacher training in any of the countries in the study.

3.2. In-service training

General evaluation as issue of in-service training

Though still not included in the schedule of initial teacher training, the importance of teacher training on the issue of evaluation and especially student assessment seems to be acknowledged by most countries and is thus included in in-service training. In many cases, however, it is difficult to say how binding participation is, and whether there are differences in the availability of these programmes between urban and rural areas. Additionally the reports of some countries mention that teacher training institutes themselves lack expertise due to the somewhat recent establishment of evaluation in schools. Differences, however, between countries can be stated concerning the frequency of in-service training and the content of these training courses.

Like the conception of initial teacher training, evaluation as an issue in in-service training is mostly restricted to methods of student assessment, while special MA programmes on QA and educational management are only provided for principals (or are at least rarely attended by normal teachers). An exception in this context are the Baltic countries, where the establishment of an interrelated system of external and internal evaluation was accompanied by the provision of training on internal evaluation as part of in-service training.

EDC-QA as an issue of in-service training

Concerning the inclusion of issues related to EDC-QA in in-service training, only the Israeli report mentions the provision of two MA programmes on civic education, although these did not include EDC-QA or follow a whole-school approach to EDC.

(For further information concerning the inclusion of EDC, it must again be mentioned that the outline of the reports does not ask for EDC as part of in-service training; for further information, see Bîrzea, 2004.)

3.3. Knowledge about evaluation

Knowledge about general evaluation

Taking into account the many differences concerning the implementation of evaluation, namely the kind of evaluation system, binding regulations, the frequency of evaluation, the involvement of educational staff and how they are prepared by training courses, etc., it comes as no surprise that the QA-related knowledge of educational staff varies greatly between the countries in the study. Though all reports except for those of Lithuania and Latvia mention lack of knowledge about evaluation, some differences are worth mentioning. To start with, the stated lack of knowledge concerns mostly quantitative evaluation, namely statistical background knowledge, methods on how to conduct evaluation, which indicators to use, and how to process data. As already mentioned, indicators proclaimed by national guidelines, if already developed at all, are nearly all quantitative. In addition, in some countries it is up to the respective principal to choose methods and to make conclusions based on the findings as, with the exception of the obligation to conduct internal evaluation, neither guidelines nor indicators are mentioned. According to these reports, despite the provision of training on educational management, principals do not seem sufficiently prepared for this challenging task, even if they are said to be interested in further information related to QA.

The knowledge of teachers, who rarely attend such courses, seems to be restricted to conducting student assessments. Still, most teachers have already experienced other kinds of evaluation, for example, internal evaluation, although their lack of training on these kinds of evaluation means that they lack the knowledge to reflect critically on these experiences. The QA-related knowledge of educational staff remains mostly insufficient, with the quality of internal evaluation depending in many cases on the coherence and information content of the respective guidelines. Taking into regard the rather recent implementation of internal evaluation in many countries and the fact that guidelines are often still inconsistent and very general, awareness of the advantages of internal evaluation among principals and teachers seems, understandably, to be rather weak, and interest in further information can mostly be attributed to the obligation to conduct internal evaluation.

Lithuania and Latvia, on the other hand, do not seem to suffer from this lack of knowledge, and awareness of the advantages of internal evaluation seems widespread. Countries like Poland and the Czech Republic, where schools have come into contact with voluntary additional and partly commercial evaluation motivated by fines for low outcomes, this kind of evaluation seems to be appreciated as a means of improving schools' outcomes. These cases therefore suggest that despite a lack of theoretical knowledge about evaluation gained by initial teacher training or in-service training, some countries at least have some experience with internal evaluation.

On the part of administrative bodies, the level of expertise related to evaluation in a different form than that of inspection seems to be generally low. Theoretical knowledge in particular is rarely available, even if in some cases, for example Ukraine, representatives of the administration have been involved in projects and thus have at least some experience with external evaluation.

Knowledge about EDC and EDC-QA

As a consequence of insufficient representation of EDC in teacher training, there seems to be rather experience with EDC instead of knowledge about it. At many schools, for instance, despite the stated prevalent "about" approach to EDC (Mikkelsen, 2004: 85) student councils have been established, and experiences made in the context of programmes initiated by NGOs are mentioned. Knowledge related to EDC-QA, however, is rarely represented or at least restricted to the assessment of students' outcomes in civic-related subjects, and in the majority of countries there is little awareness of the importance of implementation and evaluation in the sense of a "whole school" approach to EDC.

Poland and Lithuania are an exception to these findings: Poland has a rather broad understanding of EDC, while Lithuania provided some materials related to EDC-QA.

3.4. Research institutes, inspectorates and agencies

As the reports mention, evaluation in a different form than that of inspection is a new and challenging task for all countries that the study covers, and the implementation of new methods of evaluation, the development of instruments and indicators is, *inter alia*, based on existing expertise. When analysing the preconditions for future tool implementation, it is thus also important to examine the kind and capacity of research institutes, inspectorates and agencies dealing with evaluation.

Institutes, inspectorates and agencies dealing with general evaluation

According to the long-standing tradition of inspection in the ex-Soviet countries, the Baltic countries, Poland and the Czech Republic, or due to regular national examinations in Israel, nearly all countries contain a wide range of inspectorates or agencies dealing with the controlling of schools. Due to recent reforms of their respective evaluation systems, however, new methods and thus a different kind of evaluation-related expertise has become necessary, and nearly all countries have established new institutes. These are in many cases affiliated to universities or ministries, and serve to develop methods of mostly quantitative evaluation, indicators and test instruments and to process data gained by student assessment, external and internal evaluation.

Countries differ first of all concerning the expertise available at these institutes. The Latvian report, for example, names research institutes as addressees in the case of tool implementation, since these are either involved in the development of instruments and indicators or at least have sufficient expertise to appreciate, support and, if necessary, modify the tool. The report additionally points out that they often work closely together with ministries and universities and could serve as a useful basis for making contacts. Many other reports, however, state a lack of expertise even at research institutes and, when asked to name target groups, rather name single experts who have already been involved in former surveys rather than referring to institutes, inspectorates and agencies.

Institutes, inspectorates and agencies dealing with EDC and EDC-QA

Regarding EDC, only the Israeli and the German reports explicitly mention state institutes that deal with the support of and research on EDC. This could be related to the fact that the outline for the reports did not explicitly ask about that kind of information. Moreover, while many national and international foundations and other non-profit organisations are active in this sector, their activities may well be of a temporary character (see the following part "Programmes dealing with evaluation"). Concerning EDC-QA, none of the country reports mentions institutes, inspectorates or agencies that are especially focused on EDC-QA or which are developing instruments similar to the tool.

3.5. Programmes dealing with evaluation

Programmes dealing with general QA

In general, it may be concluded that recent reforms of the respective evaluation system have resulted in the creation of many programmes. Participation in international studies, for instance, can be stated for all countries except Belarus, and all countries without exception are highly interested in international assessment studies. Concerning national programmes, many countries are about to develop their own instruments, to conduct pilot projects related to internal evaluation, to train experts to conduct evaluation, and to initiate national and international conferences on QA-related issues. Though these governmental programmes do not automatically lead to the establishment of country-wide changes, and moreover differ widely concerning feedback and follow-up programmes, they do serve to promote the development and implementation of QA in these countries.

Besides the state as a provider of QA-related programmes, in some countries NGOs play a crucial role as a provider of additional internal evaluation. This is especially noteworthy in the Czech Republic and Poland, where schools voluntarily participate in partly commercial evaluation in order to improve their results. The programme in Poland comprises up to 500 schools and, according to the reports, initial experience seems quite positive.

Programmes dealing with EDC and EDC-QA

Especially in the context of EDC and EDC-QA, programmes that are either initiated by the government or by NGOs are of great importance in terms of enhancing knowledge and awareness of these issues. Despite the rather low country-wide implementation of EDC, almost all countries covered by the study were conducting regional and/or temporary studies, programmes and conferences on EDC-related issues, such as the civic education study, conducted in 1999, which covered all countries in the study except for Belarus and Ukraine. Concerning these programmes, it is worth mentioning that many of the programmes named in the reports are sponsored by American and European funds.

Differences between the countries, however, exist concerning the intensity of governmental efforts to initiate such programmes and the degree to which NGOs are engaged in the provision of programmes, such as in-service training on (EDC-related) school development programmes and conferences. Especially NGOs in Poland and Israel seem to be very active and successful in the support of the implementation of EDC, sometimes even closely and successfully co-operating with state bodies. This is especially the case where there is no support by state bodies, when NGOs can be practically the only actor actively promoting EDC. Thus many reports refer to NGOs as being the relevant experts in this field, with often good contacts with schools and principals that could be useful in the case of tool implementation.

4. *Conclusions*

The highlighted features of the 10 educational systems, which were mostly chosen based on educational and sociological theories of change and implementation, reveal the difficulty of estimating findings and especially the interrelations between them. For instance, data from the reports cannot reveal whether teachers who are better trained on issues like QA or teachers who lack this knowledge but need it for mandatory evaluations are more interested in the tool. On one hand, this difficulty occurs since the importance of the features explored in this chapter is highly dependent on the respective culture. On the other hand, however, the reports are also highly influenced by the different backgrounds of the authors themselves. Being aware of these difficulties, the outline of the reports also asks for ideas on how to implement the tool, in order to get information by the respective expert for each country. This part therefore does not summarise the findings presented in the previous parts, but rather gives some brief examples of the extent to which these reports provide information on the means of tool implementation (this will be presented in detail in the next chapter).

Overall, the country reports propose either to integrate the tool into existing guidelines if these are already coherent, or to fill this gap using the tool where regulations are still inconsistent. For instance, reports that mention the combination of mandatory evaluations and insufficient preparation of educational staff on these issues predict interest in the tool as being an already developed instrument for internal evaluation, and additionally propose to upgrade the tool by providing more information on methods, as teachers will be interested in learning more about these issues.

It can also be concluded that ministry support for EDC and EDC-QA seems to have some influence on the way of implementation proposed by the reports. In countries that seem to favour the enhancement of general evaluation, EDC or EDC-QA, the reports emphasise how important it is to involve ministries and administrative bodies to build legitimacy regarding tool implementation. However, in countries where ministries do not seem to put much effort into enhancing EDC and EDC-QA, the reports mostly propose to work together with NGOs, since they are often experts in this field and have in most cases an existing network. Finally, in countries where principals are quite autonomous, the additional possibility is named of addressing the head directly, although this depends on the features of the respective educational system.

In general, the data presented in this chapter can be seen as preconditions that shape the context for tool implementation. However, it is impossible to answer precisely how much influence single features have, how suitable special features of an educational system are, or to what extent these features are interrelated – these are empirical questions.

References

Bîrzea, César (2004). "EDC Policies in Europe – A Synthesis", in Bîrzea, César (ed.), *All-European Study on Education for Democratic Citizenship Policies*, Strasbourg: Council of Europe Publishing, 13-61.

Froumin, Isak (2004). "Eastern Europe Regional Synthesis", in Bîrzea, César (ed.), *All-European Study on Education for Democratic Citizenship Policies*, Strasbourg: Council of Europe Publishing, 101-109.

Mikkelsen, Rolf (2004). "Northern Europe Regional Synthesis", in Bîrzea, César (ed.), *All-European Study on Education for Democratic Citizenship Policies*, Strasbourg: Council of Europe Publishing, 83-90.

Chapter 5 – Approaches to enhancing use of the tool

Hermann Josef Abs

The main objective of this study is to provide a basis for taking decisions on the promotion of pilot projects in and between different nations. For this purpose the respective systems of school evaluation and further preconditions in each country are described in individual country reports; these conditions have been analysed in the two previous chapters. This chapter presents a systematic overview of the different ideas that have been advanced to enhance the use of the tool.

Because different cultures vary with respect to how they understand quality and evaluation, they have also come up with different concepts to enhance the use of the tool. In the following subsections, these approaches are examined according to the degree of involvement needed from external partners into: (1) actions to make the material available for users in target countries; (2) ideas for raising awareness; (3) the production of supporting material; (4) possible support via training; and (5) ideas for projects. The objective here is not to repeat what can be found in more specific detail in the country reports, but rather to develop a more systematic matrix of what seems feasible in general, thereby functioning as a background for the suggestions made in the individual country reports. The chapter concludes with some (6) reflections, looking at how theory might affect our understanding of implementing the "Tool for Quality Assurance of Education for Democratic Citizenship in Schools".

1. Extending availability

Although the tool has been placed on the Council of Europe's website, it is not considered ready for universal use. The lack of translations from English means that it is not comprehensible to most teachers in the target countries. Although many teachers are able to understand some English, few work with English books that deal with quality assurance or are familiar with the professional terminology used. This is reflected in the requests made in most country reports for the tool to be translated. In the meantime translations into Polish and Ukrainian are available. The situation is further complicated by the fact that there is more than one language of schooling within certain countries, making it necessary to translate into more than one national language. In Estonia, for example, there are not only schools in which Estonian is used, but also schools where Russian is the working language; similarly Israel has both Hebrew and Arabic schools. In such countries, any decision to translate into one language and not the other(s) risks making a politically insensitive statement. Translating the tool into the languages of all relevant groups, while more burdensome, could on the other hand represent a valuable starting point for joint work on the topic between the language groups of a country.

Most country reports emphasise the need to adapt the tool to their specific context. Therefore, all translations should resemble work in progress, in that there is no use editing a book that would in any case quickly turn out to be incomplete or inadequate.

The country reports vary with regard to the recommended distribution of the translated tool. Translations may be distributed to all the schools in a country, combined with information on how they could become involved; or, alternatively, only to those schools that have already decided to become involved in a respective project. On the other hand, it would also be possible not to issue the material to schools directly, but rather to the administration, on the grounds that the latter is in charge of quality issues and has to integrate relevant concepts into existing plans. In any case, the material has to be provided to policy makers.

Classically, people tend to prefer to read printed information, but the importance and user acceptance of electronic formats is growing, and an increasing number of European schools are able to deal with such formats. In line with this observation, some country reports have requested Internet platforms that would be linked to national platforms. The reports differ, however, with regard to the ideal service provider: for example, the Czech report suggests that the Ministry of Education would be the ideal host, while the Polish report recommends that a non-governmental organisation would be optimal.

Interestingly, the reports emphasise that information should not purely be a one-way process. They also think that collecting material that is already available in the countries should be translated as it could be of use in other European countries.

2. Raising awareness

The reports indicate that the issue of education for democratic citizenship (EDC) is not as central to school-related discourse as other areas of performance. Therefore the whole area, and the tool in particular, needs greater awareness to be created, so that this issue is accepted as important and so that the tool can be used as an instrument for working in schools.

In general, applying thinking about quality to EDC may help, because currently issues of quality assurance have a higher profile than EDC as such. Reports differ, however, as to the best starting point within the system for awareness-raising activities. For example, while the Estonian report recommends starting at the school level and targeting school principals, teachers and self-governing student bodies, the Russian report suggests an international conference in Russia with the involvement of the ministry. Such different ideas may be attributed, on the one hand, to national traditions, and on the other to the size of the country concerned, its administrative structure and the function of each unit in that structure. Moreover, the readiness of each part of the school system to become involved with EDC-related questions may be subject to change according to country-specific political developments.

It is basically necessary in each case to make a careful assessment of political conditions to establish whether it could be useful to target those representatives who are authorised to make or lobby for decision making and provide them with privileged access to information, or whether it would be more useful to agree on an approach that makes information available to everyone right from the start.

Within a school system that has recently developed a framework for internal evaluation (for example, Lithuania), it seems plausible to target first those people who are responsible for that framework in order to discuss how far EDC aspects are represented in terms of methodology and criteria. This option is not possible for those countries that have abolished internal evaluation (for example, Poland at the time when reports have been written), where a broad awareness-raising campaign would appear to be the best approach. Finally, in those countries (for example, Belarus) in which the issue is completely new, it may be most helpful to publish best practice reports from other countries in national journals. Additional key players in the awareness-raising process could include teacher associations and universities.

3. Producing supporting material

The reports indicate that working with the tool demands a high level of commitment, time and competences – abilities to develop methods and more detailed criteria that not all authors believe that teachers in their country possess (cf. Chapter 4). Notwithstanding the fact that one of the central principles of self-evaluation is to develop as much as possible the criteria and procedures within each organisation (cf. Chapter 3), the country report authors see a need to provide schools with additional supporting material. They suggest a wide range of such material that could assist schools, such as the following:

– checklists (cf. Bîrzea et al., 2005: 59 ff.) could be made more explicit. There is the expectation that checklists could be used to govern the whole evaluation process and to provide more detailed means of analysing certain features of schooling;

– other reports would like to see the development of a model copybook, which would support teachers by providing them with master copies, worksheets and other hands-on material they could use in the implementation process;

– rather than be so prescriptive, support could consist of examples of how other schools have worked with the tool and what kind of regulations they

have developed. Examples should be analysed in terms of how far they constitute good practice;
- other reports suggest the need for supporting materials to be developed in terms of tests on knowledge, skills and attitudes. These tests should lead to comparable data that could help determine more precisely the developmental needs of students and teachers;
- other reports highlight the need to develop supporting material in terms of extending their national audit material, so that there is no difference as far as formal aspects are concerned;
- finally, from a different perspective, it could be useful to have specific material for each of the target groups within the school system (namely, teachers, students, parents and principals). This would prove particularly useful should the entire project be changed into a student enterprise.

The availability of all supporting material needs to be carefully determined. Several reports are very positive about the possibilities that an Internet platform could provide. This would allow not only papers to be distributed, but could also give schools the opportunity to present best practice projects and enhance their links with each other. The reports also mention that video/film documentaries could be a useful media supplement to the printed word.

4. *Providing training*

An additional means of enhancing use of the tool is via teacher professional development (see Villegas-Reimers, 2003; Huddleston and Garabagiu, 2005). The reports examine different stages of teacher training, focusing strongly on in-service training. In general the writers share the opinion that teachers will not be able to implement the tool without some kind of induction and/or expert monitoring. Strategies for training differ with respect to who needs to be trained, by whom and on which issues, and the way in which teacher training should be delivered.

The priority target groups for in-service training range from teacher-training experts (for example, Belarus) to principals (for example, Poland) or to teachers (for example, Latvia). Interestingly, some reports also think of students as an equal priority for training on the tool (for example, Lithuania). Other ideas expressed include establishing a unit on the tool in pre-service teacher-training programmes (for example, Ukraine) or in the obligatory training courses for principals (for example, Israel).

With respect to national culture, and on the basis of their own institutional connections, experts recommend different organisations to conduct training courses. Logically, universities are recommended where they are focused on teacher education and already play a significant role in in-service teacher training. In most countries, teacher-training agencies are seen as very important (or at least more practically oriented) in the area of in-service training. Additionally, non-governmental organisations (NGOs) could be involved, both as partners of governmental organisations or on their own. NGOs are seen not only as providers of funding but also as centres of expertise in the field of citizenship education. Only occasionally, scepticism is expressed against NGOs; much more common is the contrary wish to hand over more public duties to them.

Finally, the reports vary with regard to the relevant content of training courses. The reason for shifts in focus may again be found in the specific nature of many national contexts. In countries with a broader tradition in internal evaluation, it seems natural to focus more on democracy-related content. In such situations, indeed, this may even be a starting point to begin with parts of the whole tool rather than all of it. By contrast, in countries where internal evaluation is more or less alien, this seems to represent a good argument for starting with the part on quality assurance. The reports also differ with respect to whether training should provide more or less a complete framework on how to work in schools, or whether training should more support self-development.

Additionally, it is suggested to combine training with projects. For instance, training on democratic school development could work as a joint activity with projects run by the participants themselves in their schools. This aspect links neatly into the topic of the next section.

5. *Ideas for projects*

The basic distinction between a project and an organisation is that the former is more limited in scope. While the underlying objective of every organisation is to ensure its existence, projects are limited in time. When one has to start with a new idea, it is easer to agree on some projects than to build up an organisation; and in the end it is always easier to finish a project than to change an organisation. Organisations are built to continue, and provide permanent service on a broader scale, whereas projects are undertaken to make a more immediate contribution to change.

There are several approaches that can be taken in order to implement projects, and several levels to which projects can refer. Projects can be undertaken by one organisation and financed by another, or both can be ensured by a single organisation that possesses the necessary resources. A further option consists of collaboration between the funding body and a second organisation on the same project. The organisations involved in any given project may be governmental or non-governmental, while the projects may be implemented at school, region, country or even international level. All these parameters have to be taken into account when thinking about a project.

The most frequently encountered project structure within the country reports consists of a smaller project designed to develop or test strategies and material, followed by a larger, more standardised project. This whole developmental process may culminate in the creation of an organisation like an EDC centre. A variant of this structure uses units from the pilot project as a form of "lighthouse" that can form the basis for the development of new, more in-depth units.

Different reports suggest that work should commence with certain types of schools, either ones belonging to a certain language group, or to a particular track within the national system. Such decisions require much thought about the possible gains that obtaining easy access to the system might provide, as well as the risk of failing to establish a working relationship with those who need support most urgently.

While all these projects mostly work by developing material and competences, projects which include a network component aim at stabilising the work within one unit (for example, schools) by setting up networks between units. Within such networks, individual units may be more concentrated on each other, or alternatively focused on a common centre for counselling and support. The special challenge that this approach poses is making these new approaches sustainable after the network has disappeared.

There is moreover considerable variety with respect to the target groups that have been defined by the respective strategy as being central to the entire project. Of course, entering a school or any organisation without involving the leadership is a recipe for failure, but nevertheless there are huge differences in the way participation is organised. For example, the principal can be asked to share more tasks within the project and even to share contact with external partners with other members of the school; or he or she may remain the only representative in direct contact with external bodies. Some reports claim that power-sharing should be integrated into each project in order to ensure the participatory nature of EDC. Participation always means allocating a higher degree of responsibility to those who participate. This is also true for student organisations, which can receive relevant mandates, training and advice, as one report states.

A special type of project focuses on acknowledging the value of good practice. This could be done by issuing EDC quality certificates to schools that fulfil certain standards, or by conducting competitions whereby schools exhibiting best practice can compete for awards or prizes. Again, the challenge posed by competitions is that this instrument helps to show where the "lighthouses" (that is, best practice establishments) are. However, it is not helpful for schools that are in genuine need of development.

As a way of combining acknowledgement and the wish to stabilise work within schools, international exchange programmes represent an important and valuable approach. These programmes should help in recognising the different conditions, opportunities and difficulties that schools and EDC face in different countries. Further group exchange programmes bear the advantage of extreme transparency, because the focus of interest with regard to each exchange project has to be agreed and presented at an international level. Last but not least, exchange programmes help transfer good practice internationally from one country to another.

As a final point, some reports have asked for research projects to be set up. These projects would work as a conceptual foundation and/or as a means of evaluating ongoing projects. Research should either focus on the effects of such projects, or identify further developmental needs as well as the potential for optimising existing approaches. Undertaking such research may also provide a firm basis for taking decisions on new projects.

6. *Concluding reflections*

The word "tool", as it appears in the first word of the title "Tool for Quality Assurance of Education for Democratic Citizenship in Schools", is clearly intended as a metaphor. The notion of producing and using tools is derived from handicrafts, and is commonly used in different academic disciplines. This final section draws upon the work of two authors who have utilised this word as a metaphor within their theoretical work. We take this chance to apply their concepts to our study on the tool with the aim of broadening our understanding of difficulties as well as opportunities in the implementation process.

The first of our authors is Vygotsky (1978), who sees tools as symptomatic artefacts of culture as opposed to nature. They fit purposes that are estimated as meaningful in given cultural surroundings. Following on from this, tools remain useful as long as the purpose they have been designed for is accepted by the user as being more important than another purpose, and as long as they have not been superseded by a more efficient tool.

Tools are used for a pre-established purpose. Vygotsky differentiates between mental and generic tools. Mental tools allow common goals to be identified, and can be related to each other by interaction. In this sense, tools are a way to mediate culture and individual thinking. Generic tools (toolmakers' tools), on the other hand, are intended to support the production of specific tools which could not easily be produced without such aid, if at all. Generic tools envisage the development of more specific tools that are better adapted to the developer's needs, and are necessarily narrower in their functionality.

With these assumptions in mind, we can better assess the opportunities as well as the limitations of material like the tool. In terms of the purpose, all European countries are to some extent in favour of citizenship education, quality assurance and democracy. However, national traditions also predominate in terms of how they understand these terms. The tool requires a certain understanding of citizenship education and democracy, whereby it challenges national approaches. Therefore an important subtext of the country reports is the extent to which the implicit purposes of the tool are exactly in line with the dominant purposes of the educational systems within specific countries. In all countries the tool challenges the way citizenship education and quality assurance are conducted.

As a generic tool, the tool has the limitation that its procedures and indicators are not worked out to the degree of detail that is requested by most actors in the field. However, this is an opportunity as well as a limitation, as adaptability is a precondition for being useful in different cultural contexts.

Our second author who uses the metaphor of a tool in a sociocultural sense is Hood (1983). When analysing the ability of governments to make a difference, Hood distinguishes between four groups of tools. First, governments can make use of publicity tools. All governments have at least some control over the public distribution of information; moreover, governments are in a privileged position to gain and distribute information. The central recourse needed to use publicity tools is nodality. Second, governments can use tools of authority, which consist of exercising power, for example via a law. The central recourse here is legitimacy. The third group is called "treasure tools", a term that highlights the potential of governments to finance certain actions, and to withhold money from others. Mainly financial resources are needed to exercise this tool. Fourth, there are organisational tools that circumscribe the possibility of operating directly in a field. To use this type of tool, governments need not only a power base and financial resources, but also qualified personnel who are able to perform the job as intended.

Based on this systematic analysis of governmental tool kits, we can now analyse the different suggestions made in the country reports. Accordingly, the first three sections above can be seen as focusing on publicity tools, whereas the following two sections are focused on organisational tools. Authority tools and treasure tools are more seen as attendant or antecedent. For instance, reports hint at preconditions in the legal organisation of school evaluation in their countries as well as at financing that is needed, even if projects are based on the work of volunteers.

The whole governmental tool kit reflects the complex reality of a social system with its intervening conditions. The different groups of tools represent constituent fields in the process of social interaction within a society. Therefore, decision makers who want to contribute to change or to enhance the use of the tool must consider all different options and their interdependencies.

References

Bîrzea, César; Cecchini, Michaela; Harrison, Cameron; Krek, Janez; Spajic-Vrkas, Vedrana (2005). "Tool for Quality Assurance of Education for Democratic Citizenship in Schools", Paris: UNESCO, Council of Europe, Centre for Educational Policy Studies.

Hood, Christopher C. (1983). *The Tools of Government*, London: Macmillan Press.

Huddleston, Edward and Garabagiu, Angela (eds.) (2005). "Tool on Teacher Training for Education for Democratic Citizenship and Human Rights Education", Strasbourg: Council of Europe.

Villegas-Reimers, Eleonora (2003). *Teacher Professional Development. An International Review of Literature*, Paris: UNESCO International Institute of Educational Planning.

Vygotsky, Lev S. (1930). *Mind in Society: The Development of Higher Psychological Processes* (1978 edition), Cambridge, MA: Harvard University Press.

List of authors

Dr Hermann Josef Abs
German Institute for International Educational Research (DIPF),
Centre for Educational Quality and Evaluation, Frankfurt, Germany
E-mail: abs@dipf.de

Associate Professor Dr Elvyra Acienė
Department of Social Work, Klaipėda University, Lithuania
E-mail: sdk.svmf@ku.lt

Dr Rudīte Andersone
Faculty of Education and Psychology, University of Latvia, Riga
E-mail: rudite.andersone@lu.lv

Tobias Diemer
Faculty for Educational Science and Psychology,
Freie Universität Berlin, Germany
E-mail: tobias.diemer@fu-berlin.de

Dr Viola Horská
State Research Institute of Education, Prague, Czech Republic
E-mail: horska@vuppraha.cz

Dr Galina Kovalyova
Centre for Evaluating the Quality of Education, Russian Academy of Education,
Moscow, Russian Federation
E-mail: gkovalev@aha.ru

Professor Dr Harm Kuper
Faculty for Educational Science and Psychology,
Freie Universität Berlin, Germany
E-mail: harm.kuper@fu-berlin.de

Dr Yael Ofarim
Department of Education, Kibbutzim College of Education Arts and Technology,
Tel Aviv, Israel
E-mail: yael_ofa@smkb.ac.il

Alicja Pacewicz
Centre for Citizenship Education, Warsaw, Poland
E-mail: ceo@ceo.org.pl

Professor Dr Olena Pometun
Academy of Pedagogical Science of Ukraine and
NGO "Teachers for Democracy and Partnership", Kiev, Ukraine
E-mail: teachers@ukr.net or pometun@hotmail.com

Dr Elena Rutkovskaia
Centre for Evaluating the Quality of Education, Russian Academy of Education, Moscow, Russian Federation
E-mail: elena.rut@mail.ru

Dr Galina Shaton
Academy of Postgraduate Education, Minsk, Belarus
E-mail: gshaton@yahoo.com

Professor Dr Anu Toots
Institute of Politics and Government, Tallinn University, Estonia
E-mail: anu.toots@tlu.ee

Sarah Werth
Institute for Educational Research, University of Tübingen, Germany
E-mail: sarah_werth@gmx.net

Professor Dr Irēna Žogla
Faculty of Education and Psychology, University of Latvia, Riga, Latvia
E-mail: irena@latnet.lv or irena.zogla@lu.lv

Sales agents for publications of the Council of Europe
Agents de vente des publications du Conseil de l'Europe

AUSTRALIA/AUSTRALIE
Hunter Publications, 58A, Gipps Street
AUS-3066 COLLINGWOOD, Victoria
Tel.: (61) 3 9417 5361
Fax: (61) 3 9419 7154
E-mail: Sales@hunter-pubs.com.au
http://www.hunter-pubs.com.au

BELGIUM/BELGIQUE
La Librairie européenne SA
50, avenue A. Jonnart
B-1200 BRUXELLES 20
Tel.: (32) 2 734 0281
Fax: (32) 2 735 0860
E-mail: info@libeurop.be
http://www.libeurop.be

Jean de Lannoy
202, avenue du Roi
B-1190 BRUXELLES
Tel.: (32) 2 538 4308
Fax: (32) 2 538 0841
E-mail: jean.de.lannoy@euronet.be
http://www.jean-de-lannoy.be

CANADA
Renouf Publishing Company Limited
5369 Chemin Canotek Road
CDN-OTTAWA, Ontario, K1J 9J3
Tel.: (1) 613 745 2665
Fax: (1) 613 745 7660
E-mail: order.dept@renoufbooks.com
http://www.renoufbooks.com

**CZECH REPUBLIC/
RÉPUBLIQUE TCHÈQUE**
Suweco Cz Dovoz Tisku Praha
Ceskomoravska 21
CZ-18021 PRAHA 9
Tel.: (420) 2 660 35 364
Fax: (420) 2 683 30 42
E-mail: import@suweco.cz

DENMARK/DANEMARK
GAD Direct
Fiolstaede 31-33
DK-1171 COPENHAGEN K
Tel.: (45) 33 13 72 33
Fax: (45) 33 12 54 94
E-mail: info@gaddirect.dk

FINLAND/FINLANDE
Akateeminen Kirjakauppa
Keskuskatu 1, PO Box 218
FIN-00381 HELSINKI
Tel.: (358) 9 121 41
Fax: (358) 9 121 4450
E-mail: akatilaus@stockmann.fi
http://www.akatilaus.akateeminen.com

FRANCE
La Documentation française
(Diffusion/Vente France entière)
124, rue H. Barbusse
F-93308 AUBERVILLIERS Cedex
Tel.: (33) 01 40 15 70 00
Fax: (33) 01 40 15 68 00
E-mail: commandes.vel@ladocfrancaise.gouv.fr
http://www.ladocfrancaise.gouv.fr

Librairie Kléber (Vente Strasbourg)
Palais de l'Europe
F-67075 STRASBOURG Cedex
Fax: (33) 03 88 52 91 21
E-mail: librairie.kleber@coe.int

**GERMANY/ALLEMAGNE
AUSTRIA/AUTRICHE**
UNO Verlag
Am Hofgarten 10
D-53113 BONN
Tel.: (49) 2 28 94 90 20
Fax: (49) 2 28 94 90 222
E-mail: bestellung@uno-verlag.de
http://www.uno-verlag.de

GREECE/GRÈCE
Librairie Kauffmann
28, rue Stadiou
GR-ATHINAI 10564
Tel.: (30) 1 32 22 160
Fax: (30) 1 32 30 320
E-mail: ord@otenet.gr

HUNGARY/HONGRIE
Euro Info Service
Hungexpo Europa Kozpont ter 1
H-1101 BUDAPEST
Tel.: (361) 264 8270
Fax: (361) 264 8271
E-mail: euroinfo@euroinfo.hu
http://www.euroinfo.hu

ITALY/ITALIE
Libreria Commissionaria Sansoni
Via Duca di Calabria 1/1, CP 552
I-50125 FIRENZE
Tel.: (39) 556 4831
Fax: (39) 556 41257
E-mail: licosa@licosa.com
http://www.licosa.com

NETHERLANDS/PAYS-BAS
De Lindeboom Internationale Publikaties
PO Box 202, MA de Ruyterstraat 20 A
NL-7480 AE HAAKSBERGEN
Tel.: (31) 53 574 0004
Fax: (31) 53 572 9296
E-mail: books@delindeboom.com
http://home-1-worldonline.nl/~lindeboo/

NORWAY/NORVÈGE
Akademika, A/S Universitetsbokhandel
PO Box 84, Blindern
N-0314 OSLO
Tel.: (47) 22 85 30 30
Fax: (47) 23 12 24 20

POLAND/POLOGNE
Główna Księgarnia Naukowa
im. B. Prusa
Krakowskie Przedmiescie 7
PL-00-068 WARSZAWA
Tel.: (48) 29 22 66
Fax: (48) 22 26 64 49
E-mail: inter@internews.com.pl
http://www.internews.com.pl

PORTUGAL
Livraria Portugal
Rua do Carmo, 70
P-1200 LISBOA
Tel.: (351) 13 47 49 82
Fax: (351) 13 47 02 64
E-mail: liv.portugal@mail.telepac.pt

SPAIN/ESPAGNE
Mundi-Prensa Libros SA
Castelló 37
E-28001 MADRID
Tel.: (34) 914 36 37 00
Fax: (34) 915 75 39 98
E-mail: libreria@mundiprensa.es
http://www.mundiprensa.com

SWITZERLAND/SUISSE
BERSY
Route de Monteiller
CH-1965 SAVIESE
Tel.: (41) 27 395 53 33
Fax: (41) 27 395 53 34
E-mail: bersy@bluewin.ch

Adeco – Van Diermen
Chemin du Lacuez 41
CH-1807 BLONAY
Tel.: (41) 21 943 26 73
Fax: (41) 21 943 36 05
E-mail: info@adeco.org

UNITED KINGDOM/ROYAUME-UNI
TSO (formerly HMSO)
51 Nine Elms Lane
GB-LONDON SW8 5DR
Tel.: (44) 207 873 8372
Fax: (44) 207 873 8200
E-mail: customer.services@theso.co.uk
http://www.the-stationery-office.co.uk
http://www.itsofficial.net

**UNITED STATES and CANADA/
ÉTATS-UNIS et CANADA**
Manhattan Publishing Company
468 Albany Post Road, PO Box 850
CROTON-ON-HUDSON,
NY 10520, USA
Tel.: (1) 914 271 5194
Fax: (1) 914 271 5856
E-mail: Info@manhattanpublishing.com
http://www.manhattanpublishing.com

Council of Europe Publishing/Editions du Conseil de l'Europe
F-67075 Strasbourg Cedex
Tel.: (33) 03 88 41 25 81 – Fax: (33) 03 88 41 39 10 – E-mail: publishing@coe.int – Website: http://book.coe.int